Baltic Sea U.S.S.R.

Kaliningrad
(Konigsberg)

Gdansk
(Danzig)

E A S T   P R U S S I A

POMERANIA

Szczecin
(Stettin)

P O L A N D

Poznan
(Posen)

G

Wroclaw
(Breslau)

SILESIA

CHO-
SLOVAKIA

A U S T R I A

//////////	EASTERN LIMITS FEDERAL REP.
⊥⊥⊥⊥⊥⊥⊥⊥⊥	ODER – NEISSE LINE
———————	GERMAN LIMITS OF 1937
- - - - -	LAND BOUNDARIES IN FED. REP.
⊂	AIR CORRIDORS TO BERLIN
▤	THE EASTERN TERRITORIES

BERLIN

FRENCH
SECTOR

Pankow

5 miles

Spandau

BRITISH
SECTOR

Gatow
x

SOVIET
SECTOR

Tempelhof
x

U.S. SECTOR

Potsdam

100 miles

▤ Lakes   ⧄⧄⧄ The Wall

✠ ✠

THE QUEST FOR A UNITED GERMANY

THE QUEST FOR A UNITED GERMANY

by Ferenc A. Váli

The Johns Hopkins Press, Baltimore

✼ ✼

PREFACE

Hitler's Germany was defeated more than two decades ago, but the problem of Germany has not yet ceased to worry the world. Whether a dynamic, robust force, as she was before 1914, or a menace to mankind, as she was under Hitler; whether a decaying corpse, as in the immediate postwar world, or a nation divided, as at present, Germany continues to be an international problem. There is no dissent between East and West that Germany poses a problem; only the source of the problem is moot.

In November, 1965, a public discussion was held in Hamburg with the participation of a French professor, a correspondent of *Pravda*, and a Czech historian; the panelists were called to answer the question: "Is your country afraid of the Federal Republic of Germany?" The discussion revealed that all three participants were worried about the "German unrest." Only the reasons for their worry differed. The Soviet and Czech panelists were concerned because West Germany refuses to recognize the "realities" of the postwar situation; the French professor considered the situation poisoned because the Soviet side refuses to show understanding toward the German view which must find it hard to accept the "realities of 1945."[1] No German, representing his country's public opinion, took part in the discussion; had one participated, his thesis would have been that the Germans, too, were worried, because for them the division of their land is both unnatural and intolerable.

With regard to Germany's unsolved problem, two inconsistent assumptions oppose each other in world politics: (1) the existing division of Germany is the main source of tension between West

[1] See *Die Welt*, November 22, 1965.

and East in Europe; and (2) the German desire to reunite their country is the principal cause of this tension. If the first assumption is correct and Germany's division is a potential danger to peace, the unification of Germany should be promoted by all means, short of war; in that case, even the Soviets must consider the merger, with all possible safeguards, of East and West Germany to be in their ultimate interest. If the second assumption should prove correct, general interest would demand the rejection of the German quest for unification. This reasoning is based on yet another assumption; namely, that the maintenance of world peace is a postulate which precedes in importance the political aspirations of all peoples, including the Germans themselves.

That the division of Germany into a Federal Republic and a German Democratic Republic may "objectively" be a danger to peace is supported by historical experience; no great and self-conscious nation can be expected to tolerate for long its own involuntary partition. If the Germans were told that their reunification policy, however justified, endangers peace, they could reply that opposition to their desire to unite is the source of the conflict. In such a way, one subjective contention opposes the other.

The problem of the existing "realities" invoked by both sides, realities which are called upon to prove or disprove the right to German unity, is ultimately a problem of values, for these realities are but symbols of the deeper division which cuts the problem. The most outward manifestations of this division are the sets of invoked realities which are intended to oppose one another in the discussion of the problem. Thus, the reality of Germany's single nationhood, now divided, opposes the reality of the East German political entity; the reality of the German desire for reunification can be opposed only by that of a border studded with minefields, barbed wire, and the repugnant vision of the Berlin Wall; the reality of a popularly elected West German government must be weighed against that of the East German regime protected by twenty Soviet divisions.

Whatever value we would accord to those many "realities," the attitude of the Germans should not be omitted from this evaluation. There appears to be a tendency, not for the first time in recent history, to ignore German views and motivations. Failure to assess the reactions and intentions of German leaders and of various segments of the German people has in the past proved to be a tragic mistake which has brought disaster to the entire world.

The awareness that Germany—because of her geographical location, the number and quality of her people, and her economic-military strength or potential—is an indispensable element of political equilibrium in Europe has twice, after two world wars, belatedly been recognized. Stability within her nevralgic area is also a requirement for the stability and security of Europe.

Just as the Germans, alone, are incapable of solving their present problem, so the German problem cannot be solved without or in opposition to the Germans: Herbert Wehner, the German Social Democratic leader, was right in saying that *when* German unity is to be achieved depends on other powers, *whether* it will be achieved depends on the Germans themselves.[2]

That the German question demands to be settled is also strongly supported by the argument that every broader European problem is inevitably intertwined with the solution of the German issue. Since the end of the last war, East-West negotiations have moved in a vicious circle: without the solution of the German question, none of the wider European issues could be settled or even brought nearer to settlement; on the other hand, it has been cogently demonstrated that the German problem may be solved satisfactorily only within the frame of a larger European settlement.

There are a host of questions closely linked with the German problem. They include: the future of NATO and of the Warsaw Treaty Organization; the status of East European countries, especially that of Poland and of Czechoslovakia; questions of arms control and disarmament; disengagement in Europe (withdrawal of foreign troops); prevention of nuclear proliferation; European economic and political co-operation; and Atlantic partnership. Without West German participation, any agreement of this type would remain nugatory. On the other hand, no such participation can be expected in arrangements which would solidify the present division of Germany. In fact, the Federal Republic, for lack of other inducements at its disposal, is eager to collect trump cards to be used for the promotion of German unity.

Amputation of a nation always raises both international and internal issues. Division of what used to be united is viewed by the leaders and the people of the truncated nation as an internal question. In West Germany, refugees from East Germany and the former German Eastern Territories significantly contributed to the

[2] Speech of June 19, 1966, before the West Prussian refugee organization as reported by the SPD *Auslandsbrief*, dated June 24, 1966.

forming of public opinion and, with their votes, to electoral results. In this and many other ways, the quest for German unity has directly affected the domestic political process, elicited disputes as to priorities, determined the scale of political values, and influenced the position of political parties. The juridical-constitutional aspects of Germany's status gave rise to doctrinal opinions which guided political decision-making. Without the comprehension of the generally accepted doctrinal standpoint on reunification, the West German *Deutschlandpolitik* cannot properly be appreciated.

The present situation of Germany is also the result of a complex historical process; contemporary phenomena can be understood only within the context of this development. The first chapter is accordingly devoted to a discussion of the evolution of the German problem. The other six chapters, essentially functional in character, discuss the impact of the reunification issue on West German politics, the reactions of the people of West Germany, the East German state's response to the question of German unity, Berlin as a capsule replica of the German issue, and the reunification question in international politics; and the last chapter adds some concluding observations.

The ramifications of the German problem and its intricate nature make its comprehensive presentation within the limits of a manageable volume a matter of painful selection and difficult apportionment. A review of the topic from its many angles as well as the necessity of organization lead unavoidably to arbitrary arrangements in the placing of individual issues and also to some inevitable duplication. To avoid a surfeit of material, the discussion of concrete cases in the grand debate on reunification had to be reduced, and the cases treated had to be sifted according to their precedent value. I wished to refrain from the temptation to offer detailed plans or blueprints for the solution of the German problem. I preferred, rather, to limit myself to an objective presentation and analysis of events, views, trends, and forces, and to venture only a few suggestions on basic issues and principles.

By caprice of chance, I have been fortunate enough to have had direct insights into the German scene at various turning points in Germany's recent history. As a boy, I happened to be in Berlin during the first days of August, 1914; I traveled widely in Germany as a student in 1921 at the time of the occupation of the Ruhr and the catastrophic inflation; before World War II, including the weeks of Hitler's advance to power, I was a frequent visitor to the

Reich. By another happenstance, I stayed in Berlin at the beginning of the blockade and the airlift in 1948. Eight years later I saw West Germany, phoenix-like, risen from her ashes.

However, the present study originated from the research conducted under a grant awarded to me by the Rockefeller Foundation. Under this grant, I spent several months in Germany in 1963, returning there again in 1965. During my sojourns, I greatly profited from interviews and discussions with members of the Bundestag from all the three parties, officials of the German Foreign Office, economic leaders, leading intellectuals, and many others. I am very grateful to all of them for having given me so liberally their valuable time.

For advice and help in preparing my research and interviews in Germany, I should like to express thanks to Professors Robert R. Bowie, Harold J. Gordon, William E. Griffith, Henry A. Kissinger and Philip E. Mosely. For similar assistance given to me by German scholars, I wish to thank the late Professor Arnold Bergstraesser, Professors Karl Dietrich Bracher and Richard Löwenthal. I am particularly grateful to Professors Wilhelm Cornides and William E. Griffith and to Mr. Albert D. Kappel for having carefully read and copiously commented on my manuscript.

I feel deeply indebted to Mr. George A. Kelly for his invaluable assistance in reading, revising, and improving the first draft of this book. My sincere thanks are due to Professor Terence Burke for having designed the map of Germany.

Without the generous aid provided by the Rockefeller Foundation, this book could not have been written. Thanks are also owed my own institution, the University of Massachusetts, for having assisted me during various stages of this work with financial aid for travel, the purchase of books, and other services. I am grateful to the staff of the Goodell Library at the University of Massachusetts, the Harvard Center for International Affairs, the Library of the Bundestag, and the librarians of the Deutsche Gesellschaft für Auswärtige Politik in Bonn for their efficient help and advice.

Finally, I should like to thank Mrs. Beverly Penny whose editing eliminated flaws of expression and inconsistencies, and Mrs. Doris Holden who bore the burden of typing the manuscript in its final form.

Ferenc A. Váli

Amherst, Massachusetts
January, 1967

TABLE OF CONTENTS

✳✳✳✳✳✳✳✳✳✳✳✳✳✳✳✳✳✳✳✳✳✳✳✳✳✳✳✳✳✳✳✳✳✳✳

THE QUEST FOR A UNITED GERMANY

CHAPTER I

✱ ✱

GERMANY: ONE OR MANY

The Germanys

The rivalry for control in and over Germany has been a recurrent spectacle over the ages. Germany has been, for most of her history, a divided people or nation. It has even been suggested that, because of their geographical position in the middle of the European continent and because of their peculiar history, the Germans have been, or are still, prone to succumb to temptations or pressures of separatism.[1]

Although, in the opinion of the present writer, other causes have also contributed to the division of Germany—among them blunders of leadership and vagaries of history—we should understand today's situation in historical perspective as another occurrence of a repetitive phenomenon in the life of the German people. The compulsion of external forces and international treaties is not an entirely new feature of German history. The problem of German unity and disunity has been for centuries much more portentous than similar problems of other nations.[2] Centrifugal tendencies have been particularly strong in peripheral regions and have resulted in the permanent separation of parts of Greater Germany, like the

[1] Fritz R. Allemann, *Zwischen Stabilität und Krise* (Munich, 1963), p. 293.
[2] See Carl Hinrichs and Wilhelm Berges (eds.), *Die Deutsche Einheit als Problem der Europäischen Geschichte* (Stuttgart, 1959), a series of lectures given in 1958–59 before the Historical Society in Berlin.

Netherlands, Switzerland, and Austria. In the past, "Germany" had different territorial meanings and passed through many meta-morphoses: there has been a German Kingdom, the Holy Empire, and the German Bund; there were long periods when Germany was more a geographical than a political concept, and from 1806 to 1815 Germany was even formally nonexistent.

From the tenth to the early nineteenth century the Holy Roman Empire, the Reich, was the universal empire of west-central Europe; it was the putative successor to the Imperium Romanum as well as to the empire of Charlemagne, who himself had derived his title from Rome. The Holy Roman Empire was at no time a German national state; its characterization as Römisches Reich deutscher Nation (Roman Empire of the German Nation), as it was sometimes yearningly called, was a misnomer. Indeed, the Holy Roman Empire was a typical universal state in the Toynbean sense: in theory it was to include all Christendom (at least the Christendom of the West; the East had its own empire, the Byzantine, and later the Russian) and was to represent universal Christian unity.

During the centuries when other European nations were achieving their ethnic identity within the frame of a single political unit, the German ethnic body was undergoing the painful process of fragmentation into several territorial states ranging in size from minuscule to significantly large. The fragmentation of the Empire was brought about by many circumstances: the Emperor's reliance on the support of feudal lords in his struggle for authority and the imperial crown; the religious split following the Reformation; the tendency of different imperial dynasties to strengthen their own princely territories.

During the seventeenth and eighteenth centuries the Empire dissolved into its component units; as imperial authority weakened, the component territories of the Empire grew into centralized political entities. Finally, the Empire became not much more than a frame devoid of substance while the partite units had become sovereign states, though not nation-states. They were then popularly known as "the Germanys." However, the concept of the quondam medieval world empire still lingered in German minds; despite its unreality German thinkers and statesmen frequently surrendered their vision to the fascinating ghost of the past.[3]

[3] "While in the West the universal tradition vanished, while in the East it began to emerge into a politically ephemeral though metaphysically more last-

4

Since the end of the Middle Ages, history of each century has produced problems engendered by the *Zerrissenheit* (dismembered status) of the German people, problems peculiar to Germany but, at the same time, impinging on other states and nations. The "German problem" of the sixteenth century, also a European problem, was the religious split which separated Germans from Germans more deeply and more evenly than it did any other big European nation. In the seventeenth century the religious cleavage produced the devastating Thirty Years War, both a European and an internal German struggle. The "German problem" of the eighteenth century was characterized by the rivalries between the two German superpowers, Austria and Prussia.

The end of the eighteenth and the beginning of the nineteenth centuries witnessed a French invasion of Germany which led to her amputation, the dissolution of the Reich, defeats of Austria and Prussia, and the creation of the Confederation of the Rhine—which was an aggregation of Napoleonic satellite states. After the downfall of the first French Empire, the Congress of Vienna maintained the reduction of German states from 365 to 39 and set up, in lieu of the defunct Holy Empire, an equally frail scaffolding of Germany, the Bund (German Confederation). Dismemberment of Germany thus continued; economic factors and the increasing quest for unity led, however, to the creation of the Zollverein which, to some extent, paved the way for a political union.[4]

The attempt to establish unity through popular parliamentary methods (today we would say: self-determination) by the Frankfort Diet in 1848 had failed. After the frustrating events of 1848–50, most of the German intellectual and political leaders, including liberals, became convinced that German unity could not be achieved by democratic methods. Priority was given to unification over demands for political democratization.[5]

From 1866 to 1871 Prussia, under the leadership of Bismarck, contrived to achieve the so-called *kleindeutsch* (little-German), in-

---

ing existence, Germany in the center of the continent seemed to hesitate between West and East, between consolidation into a national state and the still powerful tradition of world empire. The tradition's survival in Germany was supported by the complexity and irrationality of the Empire's constitution, by the vagueness of its frontiers and the ambiguity of its ambitions. . . . " Hans Kohn, *The Idea of Nationalism* (New York, 1944), p. 332.

[4] See Golo Mann, *Deutsche Geschichte des Neunzehnten und Zwanzigsten Jahrhunderts* (Frankfurt/M., 1961), pp. 136–38.

[5] Karl Jaspers, *Freiheit und Wiedervereinigung* (Munich, 1960), p. 16; Koppel S. Pinson, *Modern Germany* (New York, 1954), pp. 114–19.

stead of the *grossdeutsch* (great-German) solution by creating the Second Reich with the exclusion of Austria.

The decades following the creation of the Hohenzollern Empire saw the grand-scale development of German military and economic power. By its mere existence and nature it had upset the traditional European balance of power. While Bismarck anxiously endeavored to present the Reich as a territorially satisfied state, under the ambitious William II new Germany embarked on an aggressive nationalistic course.

The "Belated" German Nation

The German national feeling, so powerfully aroused and stimulated by Napoleonic domination, had no territorial message to convey. At the turn of the eighteenth century, and even later, nation and state had become divergent if not antagonistic concepts for the Germans, unlike those held by such nations as the French or English. Because of her weakness, portions of Germany's ethnic body had broken off in the course of centuries, some of them forming separate nations. She lost the Dutch and the Flemings in the northwest, the Alsatians in the west, the Swiss in the south, and, finally, the Austrians. She compensated herself, however, by pushing far into the east, mixing with and absorbing Slav populations but without reaching anywhere natural and clear ethnic frontiers.

Generally speaking, the basic nonstatist concept of German nationalism, based on Herder's nonpolitical notion of a nation, meant that all persons of German tongue and culture were considered members of the German folk-nation, a concept later successfully exploited by the adherents of pan-Germanism and abused by Hitler.

The Bismarckian Reich, when created, possessed no nationalist-ideological basis;[6] it was intended by its founders to be a greater Prussia, that is, the Prussian military and bureaucratic machine enlarged by permanent confederates. Thus, Prussian power hunger and nationalistic aspirations to German unity could be satisfied at a stroke and for the benefit of all.

With the establishment of a Prussia-led unified Germany, the center of German national life shifted to the east. For centuries

---

[6] Bismarck himself was a power-minded political realist, "the least ideological of modern politicians." Golo Mann, "Bismarck in Our Times," *International Affairs* (London), January, 1962, p. 12.

the weight of Germanism had essentially been situated between the Rhine and the Elbe; the directing centers of high-level politics, Vienna and Berlin, seemed more or less outside the limits of Germany proper, as was Paris, which exercised no small influence in German affairs.

Germany proper, prior to 1871, had no single political or cultural center. After the foundation of the Second Reich, political, cultural, and economic activities became concentrated in Berlin, a city a hundred miles east of the Elbe River and overshadowing in splendor and importance the various regional capitals of the Empire.[7]

The intermingling of different parts and regional elements of the Reich between the East-Elbian subjects of the Prussian state and the more Western-minded Germans of the Rhineland and South Germany, though not complete, gradually brought the Germans into political and economic coalescence. This evolution, though mitigating cultural and social incongruities, inspired a number of fateful problems and reactions. The unfulfilled dream of complete German unity and the lack of ideological values to support the new state[8] as well as "the sense of inadequacy of this power-state unification under Bismarck kept alive other nationalist ideological expressions, especially among intellectuals."[9]

The yearning for a spiritual content in the power-state, the search for a tradition which some thought to find in the mystical concept of the medieval Empire, the cultural condemnation of Western liberalism combined with radical nationalism, the plunge into irrational racialism or pathological individualism—all beamed low like a hidden fire during the lifetime of the Second Reich. This fire would flame up in the interwar period. While expressions

[7] The Elbe River, as a historic and cultural divide, has played a role equal to if not more important than the Rhine: in the early Middle Ages the Elbe was the border of Germanism and of Christianity; the area beyond was subsequently colonized by Germans. By and large, the social and cultural, and also the economical, structure of East-Elbian territories (characterized by what was genuinely Prussian) differed from those west of the river. The Elbe was approximately the border of Napoleonic domination, and it was along this river that American and Soviet forces met at the end of World War II. See Friedrich Kracke, "Die Elbe—Europa's Schicksalsstrom," *Politische Studien*, May–June, 1963, pp. 324–29.

[8] It has been pointed out, for instance, that the Bismarckian *Reich* lacked a leading constitutional theory: the theoretical justification of the Constitution was merely that "it worked." Fritz Stern, *The Politics of Cultural Despair. A Study in the Rise of the Germanic Ideology* (Berkeley, Calif., 1961), p. xxv.

[9] William J. Bossenbrook, *The German Mind* (Detroit, 1961), pp. 4–5.

7

of revolutionary conservatism and extreme nationalism also occurred in other countries, nowhere did these revolts of the mind acquire such political significance as in the Germany of the Kaiser and, even more so, during the Weimar interlude.[10]

Until the Bismarckian unification the Germans had been an "inchoate nation"; after 1871, however, Germany definitely became a nation-state, though a belated nation-state.[11] The symbiosis of Germans within the confines of the Second Reich shaped them into a self-conscious national community. While, on the one hand, those who had so far lived outside Prussia experienced the regimentation into Prussian discipline and orderliness, Prussia, on the other hand, became more exposed to German idealism and romanticism, for better or worse.

The coherence and resilience of the new German nation-state, badly tested after the defeat suffered in World War I, withstood the trial. It is reasonable to believe that, even after the much greater catastrophe of 1945, the German state would not have fallen apart if zonal occupation had not forced upon it a political division. Here, as already mentioned, we have to consider the significance of Germany's geographical location which has invariably had an impact on German destinies.

Germany is located in the very center of Europe; she is surrounded by small but also by two big nations: the French in the west and the Russians in the east (Poland lies between the Germans and the Russians, and has four times been partitioned by them). A centrally situated country without conspicuous natural boundaries, such as Germany, is more likely to suffer amputation and dismemberment than nations of peripheral location. The Hapsburg Empire was, in its time, supranational and held the periphery of Germany only, extending far into the east and south. Prussia, also peripheral in her original location, was able to expand toward

---

[10] See, in particular, Armin Mohler, *Die konservative Revolution in Deutschland, 1918–1932* (Stuttgart, 1950); Hermann Rauschning, *The Revolution of Nihilism. Warning to the West* (New York, 1939); same author, *The Conservative Revolution* (New York, 1941); Peter Viereck, *From the Romantics to Hitler* (New York, 1941); same author, *Conservatism* (New York, 1956); Klemens von Klemperer, *Germany's New Conservatism. Its History and Dilemma in the Twentieth Century* (Princeton, N.J., 1957); Klaus Epstein, *The Genesis of German Conservatism* (Princeton, N.J., 1966); Stern, *The Politics of Cultural Despair;* Bossenbrook, *The German Mind;* Pinson, *Modern Germany.*

[11] See the German view on Germany's "belatedness" as a nation in Helmuth Plessner, *Die verspätete Nation* (Stuttgart, 1959), *passim.*

8

the east and into the heart of Germany because of her Spartan-like military and political organization. Before 1871, without these two powers or whenever they faltered, divided Germany was nothing more than an agglomeration of buffer states.

When lacking power, as in Napoleon's time, the German area became a route of march and a battleground for foreign armies and easy prey for the victors. When powerful after her unification, despite her fright from a two-front war, Germany soon became a threat to all her neighbors. In two world wars she tried to establish a continental hegemony but failed. Hitlerite *hubris* not only dislocated the entire world and caused unspeakable human miseries, but also wrought havoc on the German nation itself. The gruesome chaos of Nazi Germanism fell into the hands of the Allies, called to dispose of the lifeless body of the defeated giant, Hitler's Third Reich.

The problem of how to deal with the defeated Germany had become a concern of the Allies as soon as the dawn of victory appeared on their horizon. The wartime proposals for Germany's future, including the question of occupation zones, are not only of interest to the historian. These considerations reflect political thinking and planning which has not lost its momentum and significance in the present. The partition of Germany, though not a direct result of these ideas and plans, grew nevertheless out of those wartime and postwar deliberations, plans, and arrangements. Unintentionally, they contributed to the creation of the present bipartite (or, with West Berlin, tripartite) Germany.

Planning Germany's Dismemberment

The question of how to handle defeated Germany was a subject of considerable discussion and controversy in both official and unofficial circles in the United States and Britain.[12] It was on the agenda of the wartime summit conferences of Teheran and Yalta; the Potsdam Conference was almost entirely devoted to this issue. Overwhelming public opinion in the western democracies demanded that Germany be penalized for having provoked the war and, thereby, having caused death and suffering for tens of mil-

[12] See John L. Snell, *Wartime Origin of the East-West Dilemma Over Germany* (New Orleans, 1959), pp. 1–39; *Survey of International Affairs, 1939–1946: Four Power Control in Germany and Austria* (London, 1956), pp. 34–37; Philip E. Mosely, "Dismemberment of Germany," *Foreign Affairs,* April, 1950, pp. 488–98; Donald F. Lach, "What They Would Do About Germany," *Journal of Modern History,* XVII (September 1945), pp. 227–43.

lions. By identifying Nazism with the German people, many wished to make the German nation as a whole responsible for Nazi atrocities.[13] Others, wishing simply to render postwar Germany incapable of any future aggression, proposed political, military, and economic measures stern enough to achieve the desired result. Among the various preventive means against renewed aggression, partition of Germany was presented as the most appropriate.

The story of planning for a dismembered Germany reflected a line of inconsistencies. President Franklin D. Roosevelt and Prime Minister Winston Churchill wished to promote a "voluntary" separation of German states; they were, however, opposed by their experts who warned them against the harmful precedents of post-World War I and the vain French efforts to support German separatism. The wartime conferences revealed the incongruity and even contradiction in what the Allied leaders envisioned for Germany; they found no solution to how these Germanys could be prevented from reuniting except by the constant use of force. Stalin, sensing the inconsistencies of these projects, stressed at Teheran the necessity of keeping the portions of a future Germany divided "by various economic measures, and in the long run by force if necessary."[14]

Similar ambivalence prevailed with regard to the territorial configuration of partitioned Germany. One cannot reasonably support dismemberment in the abstract: one must have in mind certain sound guiding ideas of how the new map of Germany is to be shaped. But the proponents of such plans failed to agree on any

---

[13] A plan submitted by Henry Morgenthau, Jr., Secretary of the Treasury, foresaw not only the dismemberment of Germany but the complete removal or destruction of her key industries and the "agrarization" or "pastoralization" of that country with a permanently unemployed multitude of at least ten million destitutes and a mere subsistence level for the rest of her population. Morgenthau also published a book explaining his plan: *Germany Is Our Problem* (New York, 1945).

[14] Winston S. Churchill, *The Second World War—Closing the Ring* (Boston, 1951), p. 402. For the discussions at Teheran and Yalta on Germany's future status, see further: Herbert Feis, *Churchill, Roosevelt, Stalin—The War They Waged and the Peace They Sought* (Princeton, N.J., 1957); Winston S. Churchill, *The Second World War—Triumph and Tragedy* (Boston, 1953); William D. Leahy, *I Was There* (New York, 1950); Sumner Welles, *The Time for Decision* (New York, 1944); Robert E. Sherwood, *Roosevelt and Hopkins* (New York, 1948); Cordell Hull, *Memoirs* (New York, 1948); Richard Thilenius, *Die Teilung Deutschlands* (Hamburg, 1957); Wolfgang Wagner, *The Genesis of the Oder-Neisse Line* (Stuttgart, 1957).

common denominator except perhaps that Prussia must be broken up. It was held that this would benefit the Germans by restoring certain of their benign national characteristics effaced through the Bismarckian unification.

Churchill shared the view of many experts that by pulverizing Germany a vacuum would be created between "the white snows of Russia and the white cliffs of Dover." His imaginative mind envisioned, for a moment, the creation of a Danubian confederation bolstered by the Catholic states of southern Germany, separated from the Protestant North and Prussia. But when the Yalta Conference opened, he showed marked reluctance to commit his country to the principle of Germany's dismemberment. The attitude of the British Premier and also of President Roosevelt can be explained by the evident change in the military situation. A fragmentation of the German area into miniature states would have played even more into Soviet hands than did the penetration of the Red Army into Central Europe. For them, delay was the diplomatic answer to Soviet entreaties to make a final decision on the question of dismemberment.

The dismemberment still lingered over international parleys of the Allies until it was finally exploded by Stalin himself on May 9, 1945, when in his victory proclamation he announced: "Germany has been smashed to pieces. The German troops are surrendering. The Soviet Union is celebrating victory, although it does not intend either *to dismember* or to destroy Germany."[15]

The disharmony and lack of enthusiasm on Germany's political partition died, chiefly because it could not be fitted into the post-World War II foreign policy concepts of any of the "Big Powers." For the Western powers, a fragmented Germany would hardly have been a bulwark and an ally against the threats of the East. For Moscow, at that moment, the coveted price was: Germany undivided. A congeries of smaller German states, under French or British protection, might have frustrated this most ambitious plan. None of the powers, at that time, envisaged that occupation zones might develop into spheres of influence or that the United States would be prepared to station forces in Germany many years after the end of the war.

[15] *New York Times,* May 10, 1945; Feis, *Churchill, Roosevelt and Stalin,* p. 620; Snell, *Wartime Origin of the East-West Dilemma,* p. 183. Italics have been added.

11

The question of Germany's future border was closely linked with that of the postwar extension of Poland's frontiers. The three big powers were in agreement that Poland's eastern borders were to correspond to the "Curzon Line," which meant the surrendering of about one half of Poland's 1939 area to the Soviet Union. Poland was to be compensated for her losses in the east "by moving her westward," that is, by giving her a share of prewar German territory.[16]

At the Yalta Conference the Soviet leaders proposed the extension of Poland to the Oder and Neisse rivers, thus enlarging her with most of East Prussia, with Silesia and eastern Pomerania; the Soviet Union sought the annexation of the northeastern portion of East Prussia with the city of Königsberg. Although the latter demand was not opposed by the Anglo-Saxon powers, they refused to approve the Oder-Neisse frontier.

A three-member European Advisory Commission worked out recommendations for all European questions and drew up plans for the military occupation of Germany. The eastern portion of Germany (about 40 per cent of the territory of the Reich) was assigned to occupation by Soviet forces. Northwest Germany was to become the British and Southwest Germany, the American zone of occupation. After initial objections by the United States, the above distribution of the zones was accepted. This approval also included accepting Greater Berlin as an area of joint occupation by the three powers (city sectors were later agreed upon) without, however, making provisions to secure access routes for the Western powers across the Soviet zone surrounding Berlin. Subsequently, a French zone was carved out of the American and British zones, and France was also to share in the joint occupation of Berlin.

The European Advisory Commission also reached agreement on the governmental structure of occupied Germany. Each commander-in-chief was to be the supreme authority in his respective zone, and joint control over all Germany was to be exercised by a Control Council of Germany composed by the three (after France's participation, four) commanders-in-chief. Berlin was to be governed by the so-called Kommandatura.[17]

[16] At the Teheran Conference, Churchill graphically demonstrated the moving of Polish borders westward with the help of three matches: like soldiers taking two steps "left close."

[17] The Kommandatura (the Russified version of the German Kommandantur, a city military commandant's office) was the council of the four Berlin military governors, under the authority of the Control Council of Germany.

The Potsdam Conference

At the time of the German surrender, the American and British front line, facing the Russians across Germany, did not coincide with the borders of occupation zones as agreed earlier. The withdrawal of American and British forces had to be traded in return for their entry into their respective sectors of Berlin. No written agreement was signed concerning the rail and road routes to be used by the Western powers to reach Berlin.[18]

The concluding summit meeting of the wartime leaders was held in Potsdam in late July and early August, 1945. Here the political and economic principles which were to govern the treatment of Germany had to be decided. It was agreed that "for the time being no central German government shall be established," but it was expressly provided that certain essential German administrative departments shall be set up, particularly in the fields of finance, transport, communications, foreign trade, and industry. In the economic field, the Potsdam Protocol most emphatically decreed that "during the period of occupation Germany shall be treated as a single economic unit." This principle was, however, initially infringed by allowing both the Soviet Union and the United States and Britain to satisfy their reparation claims by removals from their zone of occupation. The Soviet Union was also to receive additional machinery from the Western zones in exchange for food and raw materials from its own zone.

The question of Poland's western border almost brought the conference to a dead end. The Russians, after their conquest of the German Eastern Territories, had transferred all the area lying east of the Oder and Neisse rivers to Polish administration. Most of the German inhabitants (which formed the majority of the population), about six to seven million people, had fled or had been expelled. President Truman accused the Russians in Potsdam of having created a "Fifth, Polish Zone of occupation."

No final agreement was reached, however, on the Polish boundary question. The compromise agreed upon provided that "the final delimitation of the western frontier of Poland should await

---

[18] The reason for not insisting on written agreements stipulating selected access routes was the belief that a right to free access was established by the fact of occupation by Western forces of Berlin. See Philip E. Mosely, "The Occupation of Germany: New Light on How the Zones Were Drawn," *Foreign Affairs*, July, 1950, pp. 603–4; Lucius D. Clay, *Decision in Germany* (Garden City, N.Y., 1950), pp. 25–27; Herbert Feis, *Between War and Peace— The Potsdam Conference* (Princeton, N.J., 1960), pp. 147–49.

the peace settlement." Pending the final determination of this border, the German territories east of the Oder and Neisse rivers (which we shall call Eastern Territories) "shall be *under the administration* of the Polish State and for such purposes should not be considered as part of the Soviet Zone of occupation in Germany."[19] The Conference gave its approval that the remaining Germans of these areas should be transferred "in an orderly and humane manner."

Most of the Potsdam arrangements for governing occupied Germany remained or soon became dead letters. Even at the time of their conclusion, they had scarcely concealed the deep disagreements between the signatories. Whatever the merits or demerits of the Potsdam Agreement, this instrument was, at least theoretically, to govern allied action in Germany. In some respects, its impact is felt even to this day. Its alleged violation—an accusation leveled mutually by East and West—triggered the developments which have since taken place in the western and eastern zones of occupation.

From Quadripartite to Bipartite Germany

In the months following the German surrender, wartime agreements of the Allies and the Potsdam Protocol became operative. In view of the ambiguities relating to the powers of the Control Council and the divergent policy objectives of the individual Allied powers, it was uncertain whether the locus of principal authority to rule Germany was to rest with the Control Council or whether it would be fragmented between the four zonal military governments. It was questionable whether the Control Council, through the willingness of its members, would be ready to assume the role of an effective central government for Germany, bound as it were by the unanimity rule.

The Council of Foreign Ministers, set up by the Potsdam Conference, was designated, *inter alia*, to prepare the peace settlement for Germany, a document which was to be accepted by "the Government of Germany" when such government was established. Plans began to crystallize for the eventual establishment of a central

---

[19] U.S. Senate, Committee on Foreign Relations, *Documents on Germany, 1944–1961* (Washington, 1961), pp. 37–38; Beate Ruhm von Oppen (ed.), *Documents on Germany Under Occupation, 1945–1954* (London, 1955), p. 49. Italics have been added.

German government to operate under the supervision of the Allied Control Council.

Of the three Potsdam Conference powers, the Soviet government was the most eager to proceed with the creation of a German central authority. It is hardly possible to conjecture what the consequences would have been if central German executive departments and later a central German government could have been set up. Was it the existence of an Austrian government which secured unity for Austria despite the four-power occupation? The analogy, though possibly pertinent, is little convincing because the magnified size, geographical position, and power potential of Germany gave her a different place in the judgment of other states.

However, during the first year of the operation of the Control Council, all attempts to establish even German administrative departments were frustrated by the French veto. France had not been allowed to participate in the conferences of Yalta and Potsdam; therefore, the French government was not obligated by the decisions reached at those meetings. The French recognized only those measures relating to the administration of Germany which agreed with their policy. France opposed any German central administration before her territorial claims were met; i.e., the separation of the Rhineland and the Saar district from Germany and the internationalization of the Ruhr.[20]

Both the United States and Britain rejected French demands, while the Soviet Union so cast itself as the champion of German unification that it opposed attempts to federalize the German state structure. In order to break the stalemate, Secretary of State Byrnes proposed a twenty-five-year treaty for the disarmament and demilitarization of Germany in the spring of 1946. Soviet Foreign Minister Molotov rejected the proposal because, in his view, the proper sequence of actions was, first, to set up a German government, then to conclude with that government a treaty of peace which would provide for the demilitarization of Germany.

The entire German question appeared to be caught in a vicious circle: the French refused the establishment of a central German

---

[20] France's position was set out in a Memorandum of September, 1945; see Oppen (ed.), *Documents on Germany Under Occupation, 1945–1954*, pp. 66–68. See also James F. Byrnes, *Speaking Frankly* (New York, 1947), pp. 169–71; Clay, *Decision in Germany*, pp. 39–40, 109–12; Thilenius, *Die Teilung Deutschlands*, pp. 134–35; Ernst Deuerlein, *Die Einheit Deutschlands*, Vol. I (Frankfurt/M., 1961), pp. 123–32.

administration and government until their territorial demands had been met; the Russians refused preparations for a German peace treaty until a German government had first been set up. The British vetoed going ahead with the creation of a central German administration by ignoring French opposition. While the Soviet Union gave lip-service to German unity, it prevented the management of Germany's economy as that of a single unit, a principle solemnly laid down in the Potsdam Agreement.

While the struggle between German state unity and fragmentation, and between economic order and chaos was being fought in an unhappy merry-go-round at the conference tables of the Control Council and the Council of Foreign Ministers, the German people were submerged in a struggle for individual survival. The nightmare which had come over them because of the mistakes and crimes of their leaders obscured, for the time being, all but the concern of staying alive. National emotions were lost in the problem of satisfying one's primary needs.

During the winter of 1945–46, the economic situation in Germany, especially that of the Western zones, had become catastrophic. A level of 1,500 calories a day per capita could not be maintained, especially because of the influx of millions of refugees from the Polish-administered territories, from Czechoslovakia, and from the Soviet zone. Imports of many millions of tons of food were needed—imports paid for by the American and British zonal administrations and, ultimately, by the taxpayers of those two countries. In the meantime, reparations deliveries were flowing from the Western zones to the Soviet Union. Food and raw material deliveries from the Soviet zone failed to arrive, though Russia continued to import food from her own zone. All this clearly conflicted with the idea of treating Germany as one economic unit. In May, 1946, the American military government stopped all reparations deliveries, a step which the Soviet government considered "illegal."[21]

According to the Potsdam Agreement, administration in Germany was to be directed "towards the decentralization of the political structure," a measure which the Western powers interpreted to mean that their zones be divided into smaller states (*Länder*, in German), mostly in accordance with earlier historical state entities. The Russians were, however, the first to introduce a central

[21] Clay, *Decision in Germany*, pp. 120–22; Byrnes, *Speaking Frankly*, pp. 174–75.

zone administration. The Saar territory was first handled as a *Land* of the French zone; in December, 1946, despite the protests of the other occupation powers, a customs union between France and the Saar was announced and the latter area was withdrawn from the authority of the Control Council.

Thus far, the authority of the Control Council was hardly noticeable. The few laws and directives issued by it contained mostly noncontroversial generalities. In February, 1947, the Control Council abolished the State of Prussia when there was no longer any such state in either of the zones. As Byrnes expressed it: "So far as many vital questions are concerned, the Control Council is neither governing Germany nor allowing Germany to govern itself."[22] Indeed, the Control Council proved entirely nominal, immobilized by the veto power its members held and without any executive power of its own.

The initiative to end the impass of German economy and statehood came from Secretary of State Byrnes. In his speech in Stuttgart on September 6, 1946, Byrnes outlined the road for a complete economic rehabilitation of Germany, to be followed by political rehabilitation. He said that, if "complete unification [of Germany's economy] cannot be secured, we shall do everything in our power to secure the *maximum possible* unification."[23]

For the time being, the maximum possible unification was the economic merger of the American and British zones, known as Bizonia, in December, 1946. Although the invitation for a fusion of zonal economies was issued to all four occupation powers, the creation of Bizonia provoked strong Soviet protests.

Another important turning point along the road of German partition was the Moscow Conference of Foreign Ministers held in March and April, 1947. An American proposal to set up a German government composed of the heads of the governments of the *Länder* was strongly opposed by Molotov who wanted a strongly centralized government. The Western delegations gained the impression that the Soviets desired a centralized German government so as to facilitate a Communist take-over of the country. Only in one respect was the Moscow Conference a "successful failure."[24]

---

[22] U.S. Senate, *Documents on Germany, 1944–1961*, p. 58.
[23] Oppen (ed.), *Documents on Germany Under Occupation, 1945–1954*, p. 155. Italics have been added.
[24] Walter Bedell Smith, *My Three Years in Moscow* (Philadelphia, 1950), p. 211.

It contributed largely toward ending French obstructionism and paved the way for successful three-power co-operation in Germany.

The last, for the time being, conference of foreign ministers in London ended with another fiasco. The Western powers now decided to turn the bizonal economic area, increased by the French zone, into a self-governing German political federation. The Soviet government did not fail to recognize that such a plan would frustrate its projects. Under such circumstances, Stalin was ready to resort to coercive measures, which he had not yet employed in Germany against the Western Allies.

The Battle for Berlin—A Battle for Germany

In the spring of 1948 the Cold War was in full operation. Its epicenter was now Germany. After the London Conference, any reasonable agreement with the Soviets concerning the establishment of a German central authority and the preparation of a treaty of peace with Germany appeared hopeless. The Western powers now decided "to do it alone." A conference on Germany held in London during the first half of 1948, attended by the United States, Britain, France, Belgium, Holland, and Luxembourg, agreed to re-establish a German government. The minister-presidents of the Western zones were authorized to convene a constituent assembly in order to prepare a constitution for the approval of the participating German states. Hopes were expressed that, eventually, the re-establishment of German unity, "at present disrupted," would become possible.[25]

In order to meet the challenge of the impending political integration of the Western zones, the Soviet government prepared drastic reprisals. On March 20, 1948, stating that because of independent Allied action "the Control Council virtually no longer exists as the supreme body of authority in Germany," Marshal Sokolovsky, the Soviet Commander-in-Chief, left the meeting of the Council. Thus ended formally the quadripartite Allied government of Germany.[26] The Berlin Kommandatura continued to func-

[25] For the text of the communiqué issued by the London Six-Power Conference, see U.S. Senate, *Documents on Germany, 1944–1961*, pp. 87–88; Oppen (ed.), *Documents on Germany Under Occupation, 1945–1954*, pp. 286–90.
[26] Clay, *Decision in Germany*, pp. 355–57; for Sokolovsky's statement, see Oppen (ed.), *Documents on Germany Under Occupation, 1945–1954*, pp. 284–85.

tion for another three months but was not in a position to direct the German City Council because of the unanimity rule.

Soviet propaganda announced that, owing to the end of quadripartite rule in Germany, the Western garrisons no longer had any right to be stationed in their Berlin sectors because all Berlin was in the Soviet zone. Soviet military authorities began to hamper transport and communications between Berlin and West Germany. On June 16, 1948, the Allied split in Germany was followed by a similar split in the microcosm of Berlin; after a stormy meeting, the Soviet member of the Kommandatura walked out on the pretext of American "rudeness." In Berlin the struggle for Germany was joined head-on over the problem of national currency reform.

Since German economic recovery depended on the introduction of a stable monetary system, the three Western powers decided to exchange the former Reichsmark for the new Deutsche Mark. The right to mint or issue money had always been considered an essential attribute of sovereignty; under the mixed system of authority in Berlin, the issue of new money became the formal reason for the battle for Berlin. As soon as the Soviet command was informed of the impending currency reform, all train and road traffic to and from Berlin on the interzonal border was stopped. The Soviet authorities wished to introduce their own currency in the Soviet zone as well as in Berlin; however, the Western powers decided to circulate the Western Deutsche Mark in West Berlin, a move which had not been planned originally.[27]

The Western powers chose to defy the Soviet blockade by initiating the "air lift," thus keeping West Berlin supplied by air transportation with food, coal, and other articles needed for its sustenance. Fortunately, three air corridors were available for this purpose, under earlier decisions of the Control Council, and the Soviet command did not dare to interfere with the air traffic.

Not only the Allied four-power administration of Berlin but also the German city government was soon split because of the crisis. Elections, due in December, 1948, could not be held in the Soviet sector; a rump City Assembly deposed the lawful city government

[27] See the Law for Monetary Reform of June 20, 1948, Oppen (ed.), *Documents on Germany Under Occupation, 1945–1954*, pp. 292–94, which ordered only the conversion of currency for the three Western zones without mentioning Berlin. For all aspects of the monetary conflict and the Berlin crisis, see Manuel Gottlieb, *The German Peace Settlement and the Berlin Crisis* (New York, 1960), *passim*.

19

and set up a separate Berlin Magistrate for the Soviet sector only. Thus, the Berlin city administration, like all of Germany, was split from top to bottom.

The Berlin airlift was an outstanding success.[28] A counter-blockade, prohibiting all traffic, did considerable harm to the Soviet zone. Early in 1949 Stalin seemed to have realized that the Berlin blockade had failed to achieve its expected success. After various face-saving devices, the Soviet government was ready to end the siege of Berlin; and on May 9, 1949, a joint four-power communiqué announced the reciprocal lifting of the blockade and the convocation of the last foreign ministers' conference in Paris.

Since the last East-West exchange of views, the Western powers had moved ahead in creating a West German state. Their victory over the Russians in the battle for Berlin had greatly enhanced their determination, and they felt secure of having the overwhelming majority of German public opinion behind them. Soviet appeals to German nationalism in defense of German unity appeared insincere. Furthermore, the only thing the Soviet representative could offer in Paris was the restoration of the status quo before the breakdown of quadripartite Allied control. On the other hand, the Western powers were only ready to admit the Soviet zone into the system they had already created in the West. After frustrating and lengthy discussion, no agreement could be reached on the issue of German reunification. Another attempt to restore unity of the government of Berlin also failed. The currency problem—the original cause of the Berlin conflict—was hardly mentioned.

The Paris Conference of 1949 marked the last opportunity for the Soviet Union to participate in the control of all-German affairs. Their strength in the earlier phase of Allied control rested with their veto power in the military supervision of German affairs. Because of the deficiencies of Communist totalitarianism, as well as the historic antipathy of the Germans toward Russia, their possibilities for reaching out, through the Communist party and its affiliations, could not be exploited. The Russians slowly came to realize that they had lost all chance to gain ascendency in western Germany or in West Berlin. What remained for them was to strengthen their hold over their own zone and to try to prevent or slow down developments in western Germany, especially the in-

---

[28] The story of the Berlin blockade is told by Robert Murphy, chief political adviser to the U.S. government in Germany, in his *Diplomat Among Warriors* (Garden City, N.Y., 1964), pp. 312–23.

clusion of the West German state in the alliance system of the West.

German Governments in the West and East

The flare-up of the Cold War and the ensuing division between the Soviet zone and the Western zones were not willed by the Germans, nor could they have prevented them. Only when the Western occupation powers decided to go beyond the establishment of German administrative agencies and bring about a unification of the western *Länder* into a federated state were political-conscious German elements—political parties, pressure groups, and other elites—called on to collaborate in the vital matter of refashioning Germany. They had serious misgivings about whether the establishment of a West German government would not jeopardize chances of reunification, whether it would not rather strengthen and perpetuate Germany's partition. The Federal Republic of Germany could not have been created without the active makers were led by a healthy egoism. The East zone could not now participation of the *Länder*.

It appears that the majority of the West German decision- be helped by them; why should their inability to rescue one third of their co-nationals prevent them from emerging from a state of political impotency and economic debility into a status of self-government with good prospects of obtaining complete independence. It would be, however, incorrect to interpret this attitude of German leadership as indicating a lack of devotion to the cause of German unity. Most of the political actors may seriously have believed that the success of a German state in the West would attract the East and, in fact, serve unification.

In other words, the advantages of creating—for the time being, as it was believed—a German government in the area of the Western zones were felt to outweigh the dangers. It was, nevertheless, considered important that no definitive or permanent form should be given to the political unit to be established and that its provisional and territorially incomplete status should by all means be emphasized. The German leaders, therefore, objected to naming the assembly proposed by the London Conference (which was to draft the constitution) a "Constituent Assembly" and the document to be drawn a "Constitution." Instead, they suggested calling the meeting a "Parliamentary Council" and the constituent law of the new state the Grundgesetz (Basic Law). These semantic changes would conclusively point out that no definitive constitution was planned and would underline the temporary nature of the state organization to be created.

The delegates to the Parliamentary Council, which met in Bonn on September 1, 1948, had been elected by the legislatures of the *Länder*. Delegates from Berlin were denied the right to vote (under the instructions of the occupation powers) but were allowed to attend the assembly. Members of the principal parties were divided on the crucial issue: whether to give greater powers to the central government or to permit larger competences to the individual *Länder*. Another thorny issue of the deliberation was the status of Berlin. The Allied military governors vetoed the inclusion of Berlin as a regular member of the Federation. Accordingly, no voting membership in the Bundestag (the Federal Parliament) was accorded to the deputies from Berlin. The designation of the new capital city was another bone of contention: the Western powers opposed the move to make Berlin (West Berlin) the capital of the West German Federation, a move which was to be a demonstration for unity and a challenge to Soviet intransigence.[29]

Eventually, on May 8, 1949, the Parliamentary Council passed the Basic Law of the "Federal Republic of Germany." Bonn was chosen as its capital. The Basic Law was approved by the legislatures of all the *Länder*, except "states'-rights"-minded Bavaria. But even Bavaria accepted it subsequently.

Under the new regime the Federal Government was to exercise full legislative, executive, and judicial powers as provided by the Basic Law (and the *Land* governments, likewise), subject to the reservations contained in the Occupation Statute. In August, 1949, the first elections under the new constitution were held; a Federal president, elected; and the first Federal Chancellor, Konrad Adenauer, appointed.

Since the beginnings of integration in West Germany, the Soviet government had not evolved any constructive scheme to counter Western plans. All it could offer were actions aimed at delaying or obstructing progressive developments: violent measures (such as the Berlin blockade) alternated with propaganda exhibits, such as the "People's Congress" or the "People's Petition for German Unity." Only after the actual foundation of the government in the West did they step out of their lethargy and counter the Western

---

[29] For a complete story of the proceedings in the Parliamentary Council, its decisions, and the aftermath of its deliberations, see John F. Golay, *The Founding of the Federal Republic of Germany* (Chicago, 1958); Peter H. Merkl, *The Origin of the West German Republic* (New York, 1963).

constitutional evolution by similar actions in their zone. In October, 1949, the German People's Council reconstituted itself as the Provisional People's Chamber of the "German Democratic Republic." Earlier, the People's Council had voted a constitution which was now adopted as the legal basis of the new East German state.[30]

The establishment of a government in West Germany had provoked violent protests from the Soviet government. The sudden creation of an alleged "counterpart" government in the Soviet zone was equally denounced in the West. Secretary of State Dean Acheson declared:

The United States Government considers that the so-called German Democratic Republic established on October 7 in Berlin is without any legal validity or foundation in the popular will. This new government was created by Soviet and Communist fiat. It was created by a self-styled "People's Council" which itself had no basis in free popular elections. This long-expected Soviet creation thus stands in sharp contrast to the German Federal Republic at Bonn which has a thoroughly constitutional and popular basis. . . .[31]

Chancellor Adenauer denied any legitimate status to the "administrative whole" of the Soviet zone because it did not rest on the freely expressed will of the people. He declared before the Federal Parliament:

Thus the Federal Republic is—pending the achievement of German unity—the sole legitimate political organization of the German people. This has certain consequences for internal and foreign policy on which I cannot dwell in detail today.
The Federal Republic of Germany also feels a responsibility for the fate of the 18 million Germans who live in the Soviet Zone. It assures them of loyalty and care. The Federal Republic of Germany is alone entitled to speak for the German people. It does not recognize declarations of the Soviet Zone as binding on the German people.[32]

Similar claims to represent the entire German people were advanced by Otto Grotewohl, the East German Prime Minister:

The Government takes its origin from the first independent German people's movement and is thus the first independent German Government. . . .

[30] See the announcement for the impending establishment of the German Democratic Republic and the "Law on the Establishment of the Provisional People's Chamber," in Oppen (ed.), *Documents on Germany Under Occupation, 1946–1954*, pp. 420–22.
[31] *Ibid.*, p. 424.
[32] *Ibid.*, p. 432.

The Government will do everything to serve the unity of Germany.
. . . We are sure of our historic success in Western Germany, too, because
we are in complete accordance with the natural and simple laws of our
people's existence. . . .
Germany's political and economic unity will no more be given us as a
present than will the abolition of the Occupation Statute and the separate
West German state or the withdrawal of all occupation troops from
Germany. . . .[33]

As a result of political and administrative developments, Potsdam
Germany (the area originally subjected to the four-power control)
had, by 1949, become dissected into five parts: (1) the Federal Republic of Germany; (2) the Saar territory, integrated economically
and politically with France; (3) the German Democratic Republic;
(4) West Berlin, under three-power control; and (5) East Berlin,
under Soviet control.

While the separation of the Saar was resented in West Germany,
the establishment of what was believed to be a Soviet puppet-gov-
ernment in East Germany was considered a national affront and
disaster. On both sides of the Iron Curtain—and at that time the
zonal border was far from being as impenetrable as later—protests
were voiced. It was widely held that partition was intolerable and
could not last long.

European Integration, Rearmament, and Reunification

At the time of Germany's surrender in 1945, the "German Problem" meant for the Allies the prevention of renewed aggression by
the Germans and, to this end, the sharing of control in Germany
and the shaping of her future as a peaceful nation. But five years
later the German problem concerned the restoration of German
unity, the establishment of an all-German government, and the conclusion of a peace treaty. Within the following five years, the problem of Germany for the Western Allies would consist in the search
for integrating West Germany into a European and Atlantic system
and rearming her in order to strengthen Western defenses against
the Soviet Union.

While the East German regime, recognized only by the Communist confraternity of states, wished to behave and be treated as a
sovereign political unit, the popularly supported German state of
the West displayed certain hesitations before assuming the power
and responsibilities of statehood. West Germany's desire to be only

[33] *Ibid.*, pp. 430–31.

a temporary substitute for a future all-German state was severely tested when the dilemma of joining the Western alliance and of re-arming—and thereby strengthening the division of their country—was faced by her leaders.

The relative harmony which eventually had prevailed over West Germany's "first dilemma"—the question of whether and how to establish the "provisional" Federal Republic of Germany—came to a quick end as soon as the new state-structure began its operations. The project of German rearmament and the concomitant participation in a West European integration process and in the Atlantic alliance, when contrasted with the postulate of reunification, created a violent dispute between government and opposition.

With the disappearance of Germany as a power factor in the heart of Europe, the traditional balance of power shifted in favor of the Soviet Union. With France enormously weakened by the war, the unprecedented advance of Russian authority to the line from Lübeck to Trieste threatened to engulf all of Western Europe. By 1949 the West had the North Atlantic Treaty Organization and successfully set up a West German state in order to bolster the sagging defenses of Continental Europe. The West had slowly become aware of the fact that the power vacuum created by the destruction of German might would have to be replaced and that even an American commitment and presence was not entirely sufficient for a restoration of the balance of power in that part of the world.[34]

In June, 1950, the Korean War exploded, thus revealing the possibility of Soviet aggression in other portions of the world. The West's inferior strength in available military manpower along the European Iron Curtain had become glaringly manifest to Western leaders, especially in the United States.[35] German military power would have to be rebuilt for the sake of restoring the military and political balance of power in the center of Europe. NATO commitments to hold the Elbe-Rhine line appeared ludicrous without German participation.[36]

Nevertheless, weighty psychological and political reasons militated against such a project. The bogey of German military power was still calculated to frighten Germany's hereditary foes—the

[34] See the interesting article on the subject by Louis J. Halle, "Our War Aims Were Wrong," *New York Times Magazine,* August 22, 1965.

[35] See Harry S. Truman, *Memoirs,* Vol. II, *Years of Trial and Hope, 1946–1952* (Garden City, N.Y., 1956), pp. 419–22.

[36] See Hans J. Morgenthau (ed.), *Germany and the Future of Europe* (Chicago, 1951), pp. 148–50.

Russians, Poles, Czechs, and also the French. The attitudes of the Germans themselves were far from unanimous. They had been told, time and time again, that Germany would remain disarmed; now they were invited to rearm. They easily recognized their exposed position: early in the Korean War, when Communist forces threatened to push Americans into the sea, malicious voices from East Germany warned their Western co-nationals that they might have to share the fate of the Koreans who set their store in the Americans—that reunification might come from a contrary direction.[37] The German public in the West expected, in case of a Soviet attack, to be defended by the occupation powers and not to be liberated by them—subsequently. Convincing news about the remilitarization of the German Democratic Republic added to the uneasiness felt in Bonn.

The Western powers traveled a long way within a few years. From a dogmatic condemnation of German militarism, they turned to the advocacy of German rearmament, even against the wishes of large sections of the German people.[38] The disregard of power realities, so noticeable in the American approach to Soviet expansionism during World War II and shortly after, rebounded sharply on those policy-makers who had blithely ignored the strength and nature of the Soviet challenge while continuing to tilt against the windmills of German militarism.[39]

In December, 1950, the NATO Council unanimously agreed to invite the Federal Republic of Germany to participate in common defense measures and asked the three occupation powers to begin conversations with the Federal government. A lengthy and many-sided international discussion on German rearmament thus began. The debate created a heated struggle between the political parties of West Germany—a struggle essentially centered around the impact of rearmament on the future of reunification.

The admission of the Federal Republic into the Western system of alliances and its remilitarization was only acceptable with certain reservations: the French, for instance, first sternly opposed the establishment of an independent German army. After the experiences of the past hundred years, it has become axiomatic to say that European peace hinges on Franco-German understanding or hostility.

---

[37] *Survey of International Affairs, 1949–1950* (London, 1953), p. 78.

[38] This paradox is presented by Hans Habe, *Our Love Affair with Germany* (New York, 1953), pp. 23–24.

[39] See Morgenthau (ed.), *Germany and the Future of Europe*, pp. 76–80.

Following World War II, a European system of competing national sovereignties seemed outdated and anomalous in relation to the new power structure in which the giant continental states were paramount. An integrated Western Europe, with supranational institutions, would—it was thought—solve both the problem of Franco-German rivalries and those of a resurrected German power which would thus be prevented from seeking alignment with Russia and remain an orderly member of the Western European family.

In defeated Germany the combination of frustrated national sentiment and supranationalist idealism persuaded an unusual proportion of the leadership groups that European strength and peace could be insured by close integration of the nations. The first step in this direction was the establishment of an international authority for heavy industries—the European Coal and Steel Community—initiated by French Foreign Minister Schuman and followed later by the European Economic Community.

After considerable hesitation, the French government reluctantly agreed to the creation of a European Defense Community (Pleven Plan) for the establishment of an integrated European army to which Germany would contribute with strictly limited units. The conclusion of the European Defense Treaty, in the eyes of its draftsmen, would finally bind Germany militarily to Europe. There would be no room for the dreaded German *Schaukelpolitik* (the playing off of the West against the East and vice versa) or for independent German attempts to unify the nation by force.

The German opponents of the official policy of European integration and rearmament reflected different shades of opinion. There were those who opposed these policies on principle and those who considered partnership with the West inopportune before Germany had achieved unification or ascertained that unification was unattainable. The first group included neo-Nazis, conservatives, pacifists, Communists, and fellow travelers.[40] All these groups carried little

[40] Among prewar German leaders, former Minister Andreas Hermes, former Chancellors Heinrich Brüning and Josef Wirth advocated neutralism; former Ambassador in Moscow, Rudolf Nadolny, suggested a "Rapallo" approach to the Soviet Union; the Nauheim Circle under the leadership of Professor Ulrich Noack asked for withdrawal of all occupation forces; see Clay, *Decision in Germany*, pp. 389–90; Terence Prittie, *Germany Divided—The Legacy of the Nazi Era* (Boston, 1960), p. 315; Hubertus Prinz zu Löwenstein and Volkmar von Zühlsdorff, *Deutschlands Schicksal, 1945–1957* (Bonn, 1957), pp. 185–86; *Survey of International Affairs, 1949–1950*, pp. 74–75; Richard Hiscocks, *Democracy in Germany* (London, 1957), p. 113; T. H. Tetens, *Germany Plots with the Kremlin* (New York, 1953), p. 171.

weight in parliamentary politics. The antimilitarist campaign was conducted with the help of the *"Ohne mich"* ("without me," "don't count on me") slogan—a war cry employed by all shades of opposition to remilitarization. Protestant theologians rallied to this view, among them Pastor Martin Niemöller who had spent many years in Hitler's concentration camps.[41]

The most powerful opposition arose, however, within the Social Democratic Party (SPD), whose leader, Kurt Schumacher, had now become the foremost critic of the "Adenauer line," in its turn supported by the majority party, the Christian Democratic Union (CDU), and its Bavarian affiliate, the Christian Social Union (CSU). But there was opposition even within the government: Gustav Heinemann, the Federal Minister of the Interior, tendered his resignation in October, 1950, because, in his opinion, rearmament would be against "God's will" and would prevent reunification.[42]

Schumacher was not fundamentally opposed to Germany's remilitarization. But he wanted to use remilitarization or the threat of it for the promotion of German unity; and he believed that, by giving policy priority to reunification, it would prove feasible to obtain it despite Soviet opposition. The Social Democrats of Germany, partly to refute accusations against them of being "internationalists," partly to please their disgruntled electorate and to distinguish themselves from the Communists, championed the German national cause in a manner which set them apart from the more moderate and "European" Christian Democrats.

A powerful opposition against Adenauer's European policy was lined up by the SPD in the Bundestag. The signature of a defense agreement with the Western powers—a final commitment to the West—they maintained, would not only prejudice German unity but would also make it downright impossible. Schumacher and his followers, however, never made it clear what price they would be ready to pay for reunification; they possibly might have offered the neutrality of united Germany had such an opportunity arisen. Their attitude has thus to be differentiated from that of outright

[41] Pastor Niemöller had earlier (December, 1949) declared that the majority of the Germans would prefer to have their country reunited, even under a Communist government, than to leave it divided. He also claimed that the division of Germany was the greatest blow to Protestantism since the Reformation, calling the Federal Republic the result of a Popish plot "conceived in the Vatican and born in Washington." *Survey of International Affairs, 1949–1950*, p. 76.

[42] See Prittie, *Germany Divided*, p. 317; Löwenstein and Zühlsdorff, *Deutschlands Schicksal*, pp. 217–19.

"neutralists" or pacifists or adherents of the East-oriented *Schaukel-politik*.

The essential difference between Adenauer's view and that so tenaciously held by Schumacher was a matter of diplomatic timing: the Socialists and other nationalist groups wished to give first priority to the unification question and reproached Adenauer for sacrificing German unity to a policy of pleasing the Western powers. On the other hand, Adenauer and his Party considered the security and freedom of the Federal Republic to be the necessary prerequisite of achieving unification. Konrad Adenauer stated his position tersely in the following form: "As things stood it simply was a fact that if we did not align ourselves with the West, with Europe, we would not thereby approach by a single step the reunification of Germany in freedom."[43]

The conflict which arose in 1950 centered around questions of priority or emphasis in regard to how and when the reunification issue should be taken up and whether it should have absolute priority over all other policy goals. Would the choice in favor of West Germany's rearmament in alliance with the West and her integration into the Western alliance system affect chances and prospects of reunification? Or would an integration into the power system of the West be conducive to the unification "in peace and freedom" of the severed portions of the German people? The age-old German "East-West dilemma" had again emerged but in a new form, offering new alternatives though none of them was a clearcut solution; what proponents of opposing arguments could submit in respect to the prospects of reunification were just tentative, inchoate policy-plans or mere contingencies.[44]

The Free Democratic party did not follow the Socialists in their

[43] Konrad Adenauer, *Memoirs, 1945–1953* (Chicago, 1966), p. 431. The Chancellor's position is thus summarized by a leading German commentator: "The majority of people in West Germany realize by now that they cannot have both unity and freedom. For the time being we must choose either the one or the other. Faced with this alternative it seems more opportune to be content with freedom now, and to work for unity later rather than to begin by striving for unity which can be gained only under Russian domination and to renounce freedom forever." Marion Dönhoff, "Germany Puts Freedom Before Unity," *Foreign Affairs*, April, 1960, p. 400.

[44] Among German writers discussing their country's dilemma, see Ernst Majonica, *Deutsche Aussenpolitik* (Stuttgart, 1965), pp. 15–28; Paul Noack, *Deutschland von 1945 bis 1960* (Munich, 1960), pp. 53–83; Hans-Adolf Jacobsen and Otto Stenzl (eds.), *Deutschland und die Welt* (Bonn, 1964), esp. pp. 86–143. Among non-German appraisals, see James L. Richardson, *Germany and the Atlantic Alliance* (Cambridge, Mass., 1966), pp. 11–23.

all-out battle against the European Defense Treaty and rearmament. They included so many different shades of opinion that it was not easy for them to find a common platform. The Party continued to support the government in which it participated with several ministers.[45]

On May 26, 1952, the so-called Contractual Agreements were signed in Bonn, providing for the abolition of the Occupation Statute and granting full sovereignty (with certain reservations) to the Federal Republic. On May 27, the European Defense Treaty was signed in Paris. Nearly two years would pass before the Bundestag ratified these treaties; and in August, 1954, they would fail of ratification by the French Parliament. During all this time, East-West exchanges concerning reunification did not cease to attract attention and raise the hopes of the Germans.

East-West Exchanges on Germany's Unity

Having created their "Germany," the Russians continued to press for the restoration of German unity on their terms, passing the blame of Germany's division to the other side of the Iron Curtain wherever possible. The idea of German unity was to be kept alive; the Soviets and their East German satellite were to be posed as the real champions of unification, so as to prevent West Germany's rearmament and her joining the Western political and military alliances.[46]

The dictatorial methods of the "Pankow regime" (as the East German government was contemptuously called after the East Berlin District where it had its headquarters) and its dependence on Moscow made official contacts repulsive. Frequent high-level West and East German pronouncements, therefore, remained monologues. The Communist policy-makers of East Germany took special advantage of the leaders of "bourgeois" satellite parties in

[45] Karl-Georg Pfleiderer, FDP deputy and former diplomat, submitted to the government in 1952 a memorandum, known as the Pfleiderer Plan, which, while not suggesting Germany's neutralization, wished to guarantee her neutrality in the case of an East-West armed conflict. See Wilhelm G. Grewe, *Deutsche Aussenpolitik der Nachkriegszeit* (Stuttgart, 1960), pp. 174–80; Alistair Horne, *Return to Power* (New York, 1956), pp. 355–56. Pfleiderer's name again became prominent when, as Ambassador in Belgrade, he opposed the severance of diplomatic relations with Yugoslavia under the so-called Hallstein Doctrine, shortly before his death in 1957.

[46] For a good analysis of Soviet policy toward Germany in the years from 1946–55, see Werner Erfurt, *Die sowjetrussische Deutschlandpolitik* (Esslingen, 1956).

contacting West German political organizations and leading citizens.[47] The avalanche of Communist propaganda slogans and attacks was met by Western proposals for free elections in the whole of Germany. Early in 1951 the Volkskammer (East German parliament) called on the Bundestag for the formation of a constituent assembly "on a parity basis." Adenauer, supported this time by Schumacher, declared that, in view of the forthcoming four-power talks, this latter conference should agree on "free, general, equal, secret and direct elections for an all German Parliament."[48]

The Soviet government, in notes addressed to the three Western powers, proposed on November 3, 1950, to convene again the council of foreign ministers to examine the fulfillment of the Potsdam Agreement on the demilitarization of Germany. A preliminary conference to establish the agenda for the proposed meeting of foreign ministers was held in Paris in the *Palais Rose* from March 5, to June 21, 1951. After prolonged negotiations, no jointly accepted agenda could be drawn up so as to contain all the items of discussion in a sequence acceptable to both East and West. The conference at the *Palais Rose* can be furnished as a proof that the Russians, at least at this time, were insincere in their expressed desire to promote German unity. As the meeting in Paris progressed, the German question receded into the background and, finally, the foreign ministers' conference was never held because the Soviets insisted on including two non-German items in the agenda (NATO and the question of American bases). Had the Russians really been sincere, they would not have thwarted a conference which originally they had proposed.[49]

In the next three years, whenever an agreement or ratification of an agreement between West Germany and the NATO countries was pending, the Soviet government would show marked interest

[47] Otto Nuschke, chairman of the Soviet zone Christian Democrats, came several times to Bonn to discuss German unity with the leaders of the CDU/CSU. He was coldly received and, later, not received at all.

[48] *New York Times*, February 8, 1951. With regard to the proposed constituent assembly, composed of equal numbers of representatives from Eastern and Western Germany, Secretary of State Dean Acheson remarked: "Would the East German representatives be appointed by the Communist Party regime or would they perhaps have the added cover of a fake election of the type held in Eastern Germany on October 15? And why should the 18 million captive Germans of the East have equal representation with the 47 million free Germans of the West?" Oppen (ed.), *Documents on Germany Under Occupation, 1945–1954*, p. 534.

[49] The final communiqué of the *Palais Rose* Conference is published in *Documents on International Affairs, 1951* (London, 1954), p. 260.

in a discussion of German unity, holding out attractive concessions and even "free elections"; the interest and concessions would evaporate when the gambit was no longer timely. Offers originating in the German Democratic Republic showed a similar ebb and flow.

In the early spring of 1952, agreement on Germany's accession to the Western alliance system seemed assured; this elicited a series of notes from the Soviet Union designed to delay or prevent the signature and later ratification of the Contractual Agreements and of the European Defense Treaty.

The first Soviet note was delivered on March 10, 1952, to the three Western powers. It dropped the demand for German disarmament, up to then the prime Soviet condition, but substituted for it with a plan to secure Germany's nonaligned status, the withdrawal of all foreign troops, and the recognition of the Oder-Neisse Line as the eastern boundary of Germany.[50] The Western governments replied later in March; they objected to the independent German army which Moscow had offered and rejected the idea of a permanently neutralized Germany.[51]

On April 9, 1952, Moscow sent another note; it now recognized the necessity of all-German elections but again insisted that the Potsdam Agreement had finally resolved the eastern border question. The Western powers now asked the Soviet government to allow an inquiry into the conditions of East Germany, an inquiry to be followed by free elections. The Soviet rejoinder came on the eve of the signature of the Bonn and Paris treaties, containing this time propagandistic accusations. A Western note then emphasized that free elections had to precede any other action, including a peace treaty which could only be concluded with a central German government. The last Soviet note, in this exchange of notes, submitted a timetable which differed sharply from that of the West: first, preparation of a peace treaty; then, establishment of an all-German government (by a fusion of the East and West governments); and, last, the holding of elections. In September, 1952, the Western powers, on their part, insisted on their priority of action.[52]

The Soviet March note and the subsequent diplomatic exchange have occasionally been cited as one of the "missed opportunities"

[50] The Soviet note failed to explain how a united Germany was to be created; *Documents on Germany, 1944–1961*, pp. 116–17; *Documents on International Affairs, 1952* (London, 1955), pp. 85–88.

[51] *Documents on Germany, 1944–1961*, pp. 119–20; *Documents on International Affairs, 1952*, p. 89.

[52] *Documents on International Affairs, 1952*, pp. 94, 96, 100, 175, 186, 195.

for achieving German unity.[53] A close scrutiny of the Soviet diplomatic correspondence, however, does not warrant the belief that Moscow would have been willing to abandon its East German fief even for the neutralization of a reunited Germany. The Soviet notes, while suggesting an uncommitted all-German government, were never ready to allow for free elections as a first step toward setting up a central German government; again and again they insisted on the fusion of the East and West German regimes on a parity basis. This meant the equation of a democratically elected parliament with one emanating from undemocratic single-list elections. The Soviet demand for acceptance of the Oder-Neisse frontier prior to the signature of a peace treaty in itself precluded any chance of accommodation.

Stalin's death on March 5, 1953, raised hopes in the West that Soviet intransigence on German unification would be modified; there was a desire to see if Stalin's successors had changed their attitudes. The Berlin revolt of June 17, 1953, suppressed by Soviet tanks, demonstrated, on the one hand, the fragility of the East German regime; on the other, it showed Russian determination to use armed force to maintain puppet governments.

In September, 1953, general elections took place in the Federal Republic; they resulted in a resounding victory for the Chancellor's party. The dilemma which the Western electorate faced at the 1953 general elections was, in a sense, unique: it had to express an opinion on a highly speculative subject. The SPD told them that joining the West meant "forgetting" the other Germany; the CDU/CSU replied that joining the West would be an important step toward the reunification of their country. In other words, "if you go West, you really go East." Evidently, the voters, having witnessed Hitlerite adventurism, had no taste for risks or uncertainties; furthermore, they instinctively distrusted Soviet readiness to negotiate and wished to place their stake on the West. The impact of United States influence on West Germany's politics was also clearly reflected in this vote. German national feeling had become defensive and self-centered instead of expansive and romantic.

[53] For literature on the question of "missed opportunities," see Grewe, *Deutsche Aussenpolitik*, pp. 228–234; Claus Jacobi, "German Paradoxes," *Foreign Affairs*, April, 1957, pp. 432–40; G. A. Bürger, *Die Legende von 1952* (Celle, 1959); Rudolf Augstein, "Konrad Adenauer und seine Epoche," *Der Spiegel*, October 9, 1963, pp. 75–77, 79–82, 84–88; same author, *Konrad Adenauer* (London, 1964), esp. pp. 68–107; Richardson, *Germany and the Atlantic Alliance*, pp. 24–38.

The post-Stalin Foreign Ministers' Conference met in Berlin from January 25 to February 18, 1954. The East German government had made frantic efforts to participate. The Federal government sent only an adviser-representative (Professor Wilhelm G. Grewe) and did not wish to be officially represented in order to avoid equal rank with the representatives of East Germany.

The British Foreign Secretary, Anthony Eden, submitted a plan for the unification of Germany according to the following time-table: free elections under the supervision of the four powers; the assembly thus elected would draft a constitution and form a national executive; a government would then be formed according to the new constitution and would participate in the negotiation of a treaty of peace. Soviet Foreign Minister Molotov opposed the Eden Plan and held to the view that united Germany should not be allowed to enter into any political or military alliance. Secretary of State John Foster Dulles proposed that the all-German government should have authority "to assume or reject the international rights and obligations of the Federal Republic and those of the Soviet Zone."

Molotov had still other projects: that a provisional all-German government be formed by the parliaments of East and West Germany; that a General European Treaty on Collective Security in Europe be signed by all European governments, including the "two Germanys"; and that the United States and (Communist) China should participate as observers. These projects, if accepted, would have meant the dissolution of NATO and the exclusion of the United States from European politics.[54]

The Berlin Conference was absolutely unproductive as far as the German problem was concerned. Neither the Russians nor the Western positions had changed essentially. The Soviet proposals were aimed not only at preventing the possibility of Germany's alignment with the West but also at arranging, in advance, the character of the future all-German government. Nevertheless, in many circles of West Germany, especially among the Social Democrats, Western attitudes at the Conference were considered too inflexible. According to this view, a renunciation of Germany's participation in the European Defense Community in exchange for Soviet approval of free elections should have been made.

[54] *Documents on International Affairs, 1954* (London, 1957), pp. 116–27; Heinrich von Siegler (ed.), *Wiedervereinigung und Sicherheit Deutschlands* (Bonn, 1964), pp. 39–43.

West Germany Joins the Atlantic Alliance

French refusal to ratify the European Defense Treaty and its twin, the Contractual Agreement, thoroughly upset Western diplomatic strategy and deeply stirred German public opinion. After having co-operated with the Western powers—even, as many thought, to the detriment of national unity—the restitution of sovereignty was still in abeyance. The opposition, this time supported by a much greater number of Germans, was inclined to believe that the entire Adenauer policy had ended in bankruptcy.[55]

The situation was saved by a skillful British initiative. A Nine-Power (United States, Britain, Canada, France, the Federal Republic, Belgium, the Netherlands, Luxembourg, and Italy) Conference opened in London on September 28, 1954; it accomplished the "near-miracle" of successfully substituting for the defunct Defense Community a reshaped Western European Union to which the Federal Republic and Italy were now admitted. In pursuance of the agreements reached in London, the representatives of the interested powers met again in Paris and on October 23, 1954, signed a number of treaties, protocols, and declarations which raised the Federal Republic to the rank of a sovereign power, included it and Italy in a revised Western European Union, and admitted West Germany to the North Atlantic Treaty Organization. Bonn had, however, to accept certain restrictions on her right to rearm; she was required not to manufacture on her territory atomic, biological, or chemical weapons, long-range or guided missiles, large warships or bomber-aircraft.[56]

For West Germany, the most important result of the Paris Treaty was the ending of the occupation regime. It was, however, in harmony with the German national interest when Article 2 of the new Contractual Agreement provided that: "In view of the international situation, which has so far prevented the re-unification of Germany and the conclusion of a peace settlement, the Three Powers retain the rights and responsibilities, heretofore exercised or held by them, relating to Berlin and to Germany as a whole, including the re-unification of Germany and a peace settlement. . . ."

Concerning the status of the Federal Republic, it should be re-

---

[55] *Frankfurter Allgemeine Zeitung,* September 1, 1954.

[56] For the text of the Final Act of the Nine-Power Conference held in London from September 28 to October 3, 1954, see *Documents on Germany Under Occupation, 1945–1954,* pp. 600–9; for the Paris Treaties, Protocols, and Declarations, see *Documents on Germany, 1944–1961,* pp. 155–75.

membered that the London Declaration of October 3, 1954, contained the following statement by the eight governments: "They consider the Government of the Federal Republic as the only German Government freely and legitimately constituted and therefore *entitled to speak for Germany as the representative of the German people in international affairs.*"[57]

In return, the Federal Republic had declared ". . . never to have recourse to force to achieve the re-unification of Germany or the modification of the present boundaries of the Federal Republic of Germany, and to resolve by peaceful means any disputes which may arise between the Federal Republic and other States."

The Paris Treaty, further provided: "The Signatory States are agreed that an essential aim of their common policy is a peaceful settlement for the whole of Germany, freely negotiated between Germany and her former enemies, which should lay the foundation for a lasting peace. They further agree that the final determination of the boundaries of Germany must await such a settlement."

The Western powers, accordingly, committed themselves to the fundamental aim of West German foreign policy; namely, the furtherance of German unity. They recognized the Federal Republic as the only mouthpiece entitled to speak and act for the whole German people and agreed to withhold final recognition of the eastern border of Germany until a peace settlement.

A special declaration was devoted to the status of Berlin by the governments of the United States, Britain, and France in the London Protocol: "The security and welfare of Berlin and the maintenance of the position of the Three Powers there are regarded by the Three Powers as essential elements of the peace of the free world in the present international situation. Accordingly they will maintain armed forces within the territory of Berlin as long as their responsibilities require it. They therefore reaffirm that they will treat any attack against Berlin from any quarter as an attack upon their forces and themselves."

The Federal Republic, on its part, agreed to provide financial aid to Berlin which would remain in the Deutsche Mark West (West German mark) currency area. It would also "ensure the representation of Berlin and of the Berlin population outside Berlin, and facilitate the inclusion of Berlin in the international agreements concluded by the Federal government, provided that this is not precluded by the nature of the agreements concerned."

[57] Italics have been added.

The London-Paris agreements thus did not settle the question of whether West Berlin was or was not a part of the Federal Republic. Like many controversial points of principle recorded in international documents, this matter has been left open.[58]

The London-Paris agreements also included one between France and West Germany concerning the Saar. Under this agreement the Saar was to be given a "European statute within the framework of the Western European Union," a status which, however, had to be approved by a referendum of the people of the Saar. The referendum was held in October, 1955, and, despite the recommendation by Adenauer that this provisional arrangement be accepted, the great majority of the voters rejected the European statute, thus expressing their desire, once again, to rejoin Germany. The French proved realistic enough not to oppose the people's will any longer and, on October 27, 1956, concluded an agreement providing for the reunification of the Saar territory with the Federal Republic of Germany. Thus, German unity along the western borders of this country was re-established.[59]

The sudden understanding reached in London and Paris took the Soviets by surprise when they had already started to exploit the frustrating effect on the German mind of the European Defense Community's collapse. On the day when the Paris Treaty was signed, a new Soviet note suggested a four-power conference to consider German unity. The note assured the Western powers that the Soviet government was ready to re-examine the proposal for the holding of free elections in Germany in accordance with the Eden Plan submitted at the Berlin Conference. Again, the timing of the note suggested that the Soviet accommodation was just a maneuver to delay or prevent the final conclusion of an agreement between the Western powers and the Federal Republic. The governments of these countries were now resolved not to participate in any conference with the Soviets until the London-Paris treaties had received final approval.

The agreements of October, 1954, were subsequently approved

---

[58] See Chapter V.

[59] The question of the Saar in its post-World War II development received an exhaustive treatment in the three-volume work by Robert H. Schmidt, *Saarpolitik, 1945–1957* (Berlin, 1959, 1960, 1962); see also Jacques Freymond, *Die Saar, 1945–1955* (Munich, 1961). Some minor territorial changes, other than the Saar, were negotiated in the subsequent years and settled between the Federal Republic of Germany, on the one hand, and Belgium, the Netherlands, and Luxembourg, on the other.

by the parliaments of all the signatories. The ratification debates in the Bundestag demonstrated that for practically all Germans these treaties were not considered a realized goal but only a step toward the achievement of that final goal: the reunification of their country. The Social Democrats once again opposed approval of the agreements before all the possibilities of an understanding with the Soviet Union had been thoroughly explored and exploited. The official position of the Federal government was that reunification could be achieved if the West showed unflinching determination and unity. Adenauer also pointed to the weaknesses and instability existing in the Soviet Union (the rivalry between Stalin's successors); he dismissed Soviet notes and declarations as mere propaganda for the purpose of thwarting Western integration moves.[60]

Thus, German public opinion was conditioned to believe that alignment with the West and German contribution to the Western military preparedness would force the hand of the Soviets and bring about the long-expected Soviet concession of genuine free elections and, as their result, the unity of Germany. Moscow, on the other hand, seeing that its diplomacy had failed to prevent Western understanding, realized the necessity for changing its tactics. It would now have to adjust to the consequences of the independence attained by the Federal Republic and rely, even more strongly, on its "two-Germanys" policy.

The Spirit of Geneva and Reunification

In the spring of 1955 Moscow, after years of delaying tactics, suddenly declared its readiness to complete the Austrian State Treaty on the condition that Austria assume the permanent status of a neutral country.[61] Before the *volte-face* with regard to Austria, the Soviet official position that an agreement on Germany must precede the completion of the Austrian treaty had been strongly upheld. This precedent is often held to demonstrate that the Soviets are capable of sudden changes of view and concessions. The real reasons for the Russian change of mind can only be assumed. The new Kremlin policy might have been aimed at consolidation; consolidation in Germany meant the build-up of two Germanys; in

[60] See *Verhandlungen des Deutschen Bundestages* (Bonn, 1955), Vol. 22, pp. 3121–3250; Vol. 23, pp. 3512–72, 3859–74.
[61] The treaty recognizing Austria's independence and providing for the withdrawal of occupation forces was signed in Vienna on May 15, 1955.

Austria, it meant neutralization of that country and mutual withdrawal of forces. Moscow might have foreseen a slight possibility that Austria, frustrated by the Soviet delaying tactics, might throw in her lot—after the West German model—with the West and create an unpleasant situation for the Soviets with Vienna as a second Berlin. But it is less likely that the Kremlin wished to make neutralized Austria an example for Germany. The events of 1955 produce no evidence of any serious Soviet willingness to trade German unity for neutralization; neither was such an offer ever made by the Western powers or the Federal Republic.

Having brought their arrangements with West Germany to a successful conclusion, the Western powers offered two conferences to the Soviet government: one to be attended by the heads of government, followed by a second to work out the details of the decisions reached by the first. The Summit Conference of Geneva (July 18–23, 1955), having no fixed agenda, was preceded by polemics which were, on the Western side, designed to emphasize the priority of the German question and, on the part of the Soviets, intended to show that they considered disarmament the paramount topic.

Before the opening of the Summit Conference, on June 7 a note was handed to the West German Embassy in Paris by the Soviet Ambassador to France expressing a desire to normalize relations between the Soviet Union and the Federal Republic and inviting the Federal Chancellor to Moscow.[62] This Soviet move was part of a diplomatic reorientation, largely misunderstood in Bonn. Instead of trying to please German national feeling, the Russians were attempting with this move to familiarize the world with the existence of two Germanys. The Soviet demarche was an implicit invitation to the West to do likewise and to take up diplomatic relations with the "other" German state—the Democratic Republic.[63]

The Summit Conference resolved to discuss the question of Germany's division, European security, disarmament, and contacts between East and West. It was soon discovered that these questions were interdependent. It was the emphasis on or priority of these questions which divided the Soviet representatives from those of the West. President Eisenhower, Prime Minister Eden, and French

[62] *Documents on International Affairs, 1955* (London, 1958), pp. 245–48.
[63] For an appraisal of the Soviet move, see Grewe, *Deutsche Aussenpolitik,* pp. 214–20.

Premier Edgar Faure wished to connect German reunification with European security and consider disarmament later, while Soviet Premier Bulganin insisted on making progress on disarmament first. Eventually, this Conference produced only some empty generalities; the much praised but evanescent "Spirit of Geneva" showed that spirit alone is not a practical product of international gatherings.

In the interval between the two conferences, the Federal Chancellor journeyed to Moscow. Earlier, he had indicated that he wished to discuss reunification and the question of German prisoners still in the Soviet Union. In his opening address Adenauer declared that the resumption of diplomatic relations between the two countries was unthinkable unless these two questions were solved. Bulganin denied the Chancellor's right to speak on behalf of all Germans and insisted that there were only German war criminals in the Soviet Union. It was subsequently suggested that at this moment the Chancellor should have broken off negotiations and returned home.[64] That he did not was probably a result of his concern over the German prisoners. He decided to stay and retreat from his original position.

The outcome of the Moscow talks was not a compromise, as has been alleged, but a victory for the Soviets. The two countries agreed to exchange ambassadors without fulfillment of any conditions by Moscow. An exchange of letters between Bulganin and Adenauer only expressed hope that the resumption of diplomatic relations would contribute to the solution of "the principal national problem of the German people—restitution of the unity of a German democratic state."

Adenauer, before leaving Moscow, addressed another letter to the Soviet Premier in which he maintained "the Federal Government's legal position with regard to its right to represent the German people in international affairs and with regard to the political conditions in those German territories which, at present, are outside its effective sphere of authority."

In the Soviet reply the Federal Chancellor was told that "the question of Germany's frontiers was settled by the Potsdam Agreement and that the Federal Republic of Germany is exercising its jurisdiction over the area which is subject to its sovereignty."[65]

[64] Löwenstein and Zühlsdorff, *Deutschlands Schicksal,* p. 291.
[65] *Wiedervereinigung und Sicherheit Deutschlands,* p. 45; *Documents on International Affairs, 1955,* p. 254.

Thus, although neither of the two opposing legal and political positions was violated, the Soviet government achieved its objective. As if to compound the failure of the Chancellor, shortly after his departure a delegation of the German Democratic Republic, led by Prime Minister Grotewohl, was received with much fanfare. In a new agreement, signed on September 20, full exercise of sovereign rights, including the conduct of international affairs, also "in its relation to the Federal Republic of Germany," was conceded to East Germany.[66]

The "acid test" of the Summit Conference, as President Eisenhower stated, was the second Geneva meeting where foreign ministers were expected to transform vague formulas into concrete agreements. All that the heads of government conference had achieved with regard to the German problem was a short directive addressed to the foreign ministers which, temporarily, had raised optimistic expectations, later to be sadly frustrated by the attitude of Foreign Minister Molotov. The directive contained the following passage: "The Heads of Government, conscious of their common responsibility for the solution of the German problem and the re-unification of Germany, are in agreement that the German question and the questions of Germany's re-unification by free elections should be solved in harmony with the national interest of the German people and also for the sake of European security. . . ."

A new version of the Eden Plan, submitted jointly by the three foreign ministers of the West, failed to interest Molotov. He introduced a somewhat new element by claiming that reunification should not jeopardize the "political and socio-economic achievements" of the German Democratic Republic, which meant that there could be no German unity unless the Communist system were maintained (and, by implication, extended to the West). Molotov also insisted on the establishment of an "all-German Council" composed of equal numbers of representatives of the East and West German parliaments, instead of the "free elections" mentioned in the directive.

The positions taken on Germany by the two sides were irreconcilable: no progress could be made on European security as long as German reunification was considered "the indispensable premise" of any such agreement. Molotov advocated the view that European security would assure the security of the German people; the Western view was that without solving the German problem no security

[66] See Grewe, *Deutsche Aussenpolitik*, p. 221.

could be given to Europe. Thereafter, the only agreement which was reached was that of breaking up the Conference.[67]

It became clear as a result of the two Geneva Conferences (if it was not before) that the West had nothing to offer the Soviet Union in return for East Germany; treaties of guarantee, demilitarization, even neutralization of Germany (which was never offered), were commitments unequal in value to the tangible advantage of holding onto the eastern portion of Germany. The failure of the policy of the "positions of strength" was not immediately realized in Germany. But those who had already viewed the alliance with the West as harmful to German unity and had reluctantly followed the Chancellor's circuitous all-German policy—the Free Democrats—withdrew in February, 1956, from the cabinet and went into opposition. Their leaders, especially Thomas Dehler, now supported some form of neutrality which would make large-scale rearmament superfluous.[68]

While the "policy of strength" had failed to advance the cause of reunification, the policy of rapprochement with the Soviet Union failed equally to bring about a sustained easing of tensions and, in its wake, a measure of disarmament. The German stalemate and the continuing Cold War induced the Soviets to exert pressure outside Europe: the Middle East, Southeast Asia, Africa, and Latin America. Nevertheless, for reasons inherent in the East German situation, Khrushchev would again have to turn back to the most sensitive point of the German dilemma: Berlin.

Stalemate over Germany

With the Soviet Union's endorsement of the "two Germanys" concept and the Federal Republic's and its Allies' commitment to the "one German state" doctrine, the possibilities of diplomatic maneuvering were considerably narrowed down, if not altogether eliminated, after 1955. In the years following the Geneva deadlock, the diplomatic exchange on the German problem became monotonous and repetitive. The Soviet Union wished to leave negotiations on reunification, which it claimed to be an internal German matter, to the "two German states." On the other hand, the Federal Republic vainly tried to initiate meaningful discussions with the Soviet Union—the "occupation power" of East Germany.

---

[67] See *Survey of International Affairs, 1955–1956* (London, 1960), pp. 167–69; U.S. Department of State, *The Geneva Meeting of Foreign Ministers, October 27–November 16, 1955* (Washington, 1955).

[68] Löwenstein and Zühlsdorff, *Deutschlands Schicksal*, pp. 298–99.

The diplomatic relations established in 1955 enabled the West German and Soviet governments to exchange notes and memoranda. After the frustrating events of 1955, the Federal government undertook to keep the reunification issue alive by dispatching, in 1956 and 1957, several memoranda to Moscow explaining Bonn's point of view. Soviet replies reiterated their thesis and advocated direct contacts between the Federal government and the German Democratic Republic. Soviet Prime Minister Bulganin and Chancellor Adenauer exchanged letters. The plan of a "German Confederation" to bring the "two German states" under a common roof was rejected by the Federal government.[69]

The East German regime, following Moscow's opinion, exerted efforts, blandishments, and pressures to participate in an exchange of views with the Federal Republic and have itself recognized as a co-equal partner with its western neighbor. Walter Ulbricht, First Secretary of the Socialist Unity party (SED), submitted to the Central Committee of the Party on December 31, 1956, the plan for establishing a confederation of the two Germanys. Under this plan, the "two German states" should send equal numbers of delegates into an all-German council. The council should act as the government of the confederation and prepare the eventual unification of both parts of Germany. The government of Bonn, on the other hand, rejected any plan which would recognize democratic and undemocratic representations as equal and continued to insist on "reunification in freedom," which meant free elections for an all-German government and constitution.[70]

The ideal of German unity was already sharply contradicted by the hard facts of life: two state and governmental structures faced each other along a line which had acquired all the characteristics of an international frontier, not even one in the Western sense but a section of impenetrable Iron Curtain. "Germany" was again a geographical rather than a political notion. In the German Democratic Republic the word "Germany" was even banned from use on maps and books on geography, to be replaced by expressions denoting the existence of two German states.[71] In the Federal Republic, however, official terminology continued to name the East German area

---

[69] For texts, see *Wiedervereinigung und Sicherheit Deutschlands,* pp. 51–91.

[70] See *Wiedervereinigung und Sicherheit Deutschlands,* pp. 64, 84.

[71] Since December 16, 1957, the East-West zonal border was officially to be known in the German Democratic Republic as Western State Border (Staatsgrenze West). The East German Encyclopedia thus defines Germany: "a country in Central Europe, systematically split into two states with entirely different socio-political orders." (*Meyers Neues Lexikon,* Vol. I, p. 507).

as "Soviet Zone of Occupation" or "Central Germany," and the authorities and government of that area as "zonal" authorities or the "zonal" government.

Despite the evident failure of the Adenauer government to achieve reunification as a result of both Western integration and re-armament of the Federal Republic, the elections held on September 15, 1957, increased the majority of the ruling CDU/CSU parties and made it possible for them to dispense with support from other parties. How far this vote of confidence reflected approval for the government's policy concerning reunification, or whether it re-flected satisfaction with other domestic items of Adenauer's platform, is difficult to ascertain. Public opinion polls register an increased interest in the reunification issue after 1956.[72] We may only conclude that the public had not and has not yet abandoned its belief in the official thesis on reunification. There was no indication that the majority of voters shared the view strongly advanced by the SPD that past opportunities had been missed which, if properly exploited, could have led to German unity.

The situation of Berlin presented a sharp contrast to the frozen positions and hardened borders dividing East and West Germany; the access routes to West Berlin constituted a gap in the Iron Curtain and West Berlin itself, an open society surrounded by Communism. West Berlin, an isolated outpost, combined advantages and disadvantages for both sides: it was a dagger directed against the surrounding Soviet-controlled area, a propaganda window and also a haven of refuge; on the other hand, being an enclave with tenuous lines of access, it easily lent itself to dangers of complete isolation and conquest.

In this state of congealed fronts and diplomatic trench warfare, Khrushchev launched his attack in November-December, 1958, against the exposed stronghold of West Berlin, demanding its trans-formation into a neutralized free city, thus demonstrating the stra-tegic truth that points of strength may become points of extreme weakness. With his broadside against the Allied and free German position of West Berlin, the Soviet leader at least temporarily man-aged to separate the Berlin issue from its logical association with the question of German partition. After the end of 1958, the struggle for German reunification became secondary to the diplomatic bat-tle to defend West Berlin, in which the Soviets had gained the

[72] Karl W. Deutsch and Lewis J. Edinger, *Germany Rejoins the Powers* (Stanford, Calif., 1959), p. 178.

initiative. Now Western efforts had to be concentrated on preserving the Berlin status quo instead of changing the divided status of Germany.[73]

The Soviet government, while trying to ignore the connection between the reunification issue and the "abnormal" situation of Berlin, nevertheless demanded the conclusion of a peace treaty with the two Germanys and also with a German confederation, if it were set up before the peace treaty was concluded. It showed reluctance to discuss the unification of Germany at the suggested international meeting "because this question is outside the competence of the U.S.S.R., the United States, Britain, and France" and can be solved only "through rapprochement and agreement" between the two Germanys.[74] But the Western powers maintained that the "Berlin problem involves the question of re-unification of Germany" and also that of a European security treaty and a peace treaty with Germany.[75]

The Soviet counterstroke against Berlin in November and December, 1958, took Bonn by surprise. The Federal government, as in subsequent situations, preferred to leave the conduct of Berlin's defense to the Allied powers, primarily to the United States. On January 10, 1959, the Soviet government suggested the convocation of a peace conference on Germany with the participation of both German governments and transmitted a draft text of the treaty of peace. Heinrich von Brentano, the Federal Minister of Foreign Affairs, with the consent of the three major political parties, rejected both the idea of a peace conference and the text of the draft treaty.[76]

On March 26, 1959, the Federal government agreed, however, to send observers to the forthcoming Foreign Ministers' Conference, even though the German Democratic Republic was also to send observers. It should be remembered that in 1954 Bonn refused to allow its observers to sit at the Foreign Ministers' Conference table when observers from East Germany were also admitted. Even so, the Federal government was criticized by some of the more rigid adherents to the nonrecognition thesis for having consented to being seated at the "children's table" together with the representatives of

---

[73] Details of the second battle for Berlin will be discussed in Chapter V.

[74] Soviet note of January 10, 1959; *Documents on International Affairs, 1959* (London, 1963), pp. 1–9.

[75] Replies to the Soviet note of November 27, 1958, dated December 31, 1958; *Documents on International Affairs, 1958* (London, 1962), pp. 166–72.

[76] *Wiedervereinigung und Sicherheit Deutschlands,* pp. 131–32.

the "Pankow regime." If the Geneva Conference gave up none of the fundamental theses of the West, it nevertheless showed considerable accommodation toward certain Soviet concepts.

The Foreign Ministers' Conference, held in Geneva from May 11 to June 20 and again from July 13 to August 5, 1959, though mainly concerned with Berlin, devoted considerable time to the reunification issue as well. The Western "package plan," also known as the Herter Plan after Secretary of State Christian Herter, combined a temporary solution of the Berlin question with a final settlement of the reunification problem.[77] The immediate reason for the failure of the Conference was the lack of a common answer to the question: what should happen to Berlin if, within a stated time, no agreement could be reached on the reunification question?[78] The Conference failed to restore the pre-eminence of the problem of German unity over the isolated issue of Berlin. In the latter stages of the Conference, only the future of West Berlin was discussed instead of that of all of Greater Berlin.

The rigid application and interpretation of the "one German state" doctrine seemed a hurdle on the road of flexible approaches to the Berlin question endorsed by the State Department subsequent to the Geneva Conference. These avenues of approach, often containing formulations or proposals which appeared heretical to the dogmatists in Bonn, became a source of nervousness and anxieties in the Federal Republic after 1961. Thus, following the erection of the Berlin Wall on August 13, 1961, Adenauer had to agree that the Berlin issue be treated independently of the question of German unity. In April, 1962, an American "package offer" to the Soviet Union, which combined a nonaggression (in other words, a status quo) commitment with the Berlin question, was withheld because of West German opposition. A slightly modified plan concerning the internationalization of the access routes to Berlin which would have given a certain limited recognition to the German Democratic Republic almost caused the downfall of Foreign Minister Schröder.[79] This proposal, nevertheless, proved unacceptable to the Russians.

[77] For the Herter Plan submitted to the Geneva Conference on May 14, see *Documents on International Affairs, 1959*, pp. 34–39.

[78] The Western proposal was that in such case the Berlin status quo would be re-established, whereas the Soviets wished to have a free hand in dealing with Berlin; see *ibid.*, pp. 40–53.

[79] Flora Lewis, "More Germans Listen to a New Voice," *New York Times Magazine*, October 14, 1962.

The federal elections held in September of 1961 presented a reversed trend. The CDU/CSU obtained only 242 seats in the Bundestag (against 270 in 1957), while the SPD now received 190 seats (instead of 169 in 1957) and the FDP, 67 seats (41 in 1957).

The elections had been held shortly after the disaster of the Berlin Wall that divided East and West Berlin and closed the door to the thousands of refugees who had streamed from all parts of East Germany into this haven of refuge. It is most likely that the frustrating effect of this event turned part of the electorate against Adenauer; it is also possible that some of the voters had become weary of the old Chancellor. The SPD (the elections had taken place after its reversal on the reunification issue) no longer campaigned against the reunification policy of the government and, therefore, the conclusion cannot be discarded that this issue played only a secondary role in the elections. The electorate might have felt that it was not called to vote on this question; had reunification been a practical issue, it is unlikely that the voters would have shown indifference toward it.

Under Adenauer's successor, the policy on reunification did not essentially deviate from the course set by the first chancellor of the Federal Republic. But it was to become more "pragmatic"; that is, the doctrine was not applied for its own sake but with the end of facilitating German unity. Thus, it could be expected that the doctrinal rules would be "stretched" as far as possible without doing injustices to the underlying political principles.

Thus, Chancellor Ludwig Erhard, in his inaugural address to the Bundestag of October 18, 1963, opposed any agreement between the Western Allies and the Soviet Union "at the expense of Germany's vital interests," which, first of all, included the demand for German unity. Erhard referred to the often-heard reproach against the nonrecognition policy of Bonn when he stated: "We are told that the division of our country is a 'reality' that has to be accepted. Of course, it is a reality, but it is an unbearable one.

Injustice is also a reality, and yet we shall have to do all possible to remove it. Above all, if the division of our country is put forward as a reality, the will of the German people to restore its unity is a far stronger reality."[80]

Khrushchev's offensive against West Berlin proved hardly more successful than West German endeavors to promote reunification of Germany. While the erection of the Wall may have saved the East

[80] *New York Times,* October 19, 1963.

German state, the Soviet Premier's leapfrogging into Cuba ended with a crushing defeat and, apparently, cut short his hopes of changing the existing status quo in Germany.

The German deadlock led to a political war of attrition and placed the achievement of German unity in the remote future. While the voters and the masses may have recognized tardily the existing deadlock on the reunification issue, the stand-pat position of the diplomatic front did not fail to impress the policy-makers of the Federal Republic. It persuaded them to adapt their methods and their thinking to long-term effects. The perspective created by the developments of the German question resulted in the contemporary policies and opinions which we shall undertake to examine in the following chapters.

Important principles may and must be flexible.

—Abraham Lincoln
April 11, 1865

It is in the uncompromisingness with which dogma is held and not in the dogma or want of dogma that the danger lies.

—Samuel Butler
The Way of All Flesh
Chapter LXVIII

CHAPTER II

✳ ✳

THE REUNIFICATION QUESTION IN
WEST GERMAN POLITICS

The *Deutschlandpolitik* (policy of unification of Germany) of the Federal Republic—both the official policy and that of the major political parties—is anchored on constitutional-legal concepts whose principal source is the Basic Law, the Federal Republic's constitutional document. Thus, foreign policy is being steered by German constitutional-legal doctrines rather than by pragmatic ideas or considerations of expediency. But the West German state was not the first one known in history in which legal-constitutional theory served as guideline or yardstick for political behavior and action. Such theories were mostly the product of some unusual political-constitutional situation; they were used initially to explain some peculiar situation in constitutional-legal terms, and subsequently they became the basis of future policy. Such doctrines may shape political institutions and constitutional and international enactments, and they may direct public policy. The Constitution of the United

49

States and its interpretation formed the theoretical basis of Union politics before, during, and after the Civil War and tended to enhance legalism in politics.

The West German political leaders and the majority of the country's political elite, though realizing that the goal of reunification was to be achieved by means and methods of a foreign policy, could not help conceiving the question of German unity in terms of internal German politics. The ambivalence, inconsistencies, and misunderstandings created by this double approach were obvious; nonetheless, the doctrine, supported by motivations of righteousness and national sentiment and by the legal education of the policy-makers, continued to serve as the permanent basis of the reunification policy despite some of the practical difficulties and inconveniences of its implementation.

West Germany's desire to consider the "temporary" division of Germany as an internal German affair was given clear expression in its constitutional document. Under this organic statute, the Federal Republic was to be only a temporary substitute for a future all-German state. It was thought that the compromise formula of creating only a "provisional" state would not foreclose the chances of reunification. A comparison with Weimar Germany is not without irony: the Weimar Constitution of 1919, intended to be a definitive one, was considered by many Germans a *pis aller* (a temporary expedient). The constitutional document of the Federal Republic, planned by its authors to be provisional, has outlived the lifetime of the Constitution of Weimar. The Basic Law, which reflected the Federal Republic's foremost policy objective—reunification of Germany—proved to be a *provisoire qui dure.*[1]

The Basic Law and German Unity

The Basic Law of the Federal Republic of Germany is, by its own terms, a provisional constitutional document intended for a "transitional period" only. Though some national constitutions intended to be permanent have been replaced within a relatively short time, the provisional constitution of the Federal Republic has actually outlasted the thirteen-year lifespan of the definitive Weimar Constitution. By declaring itself temporary in character, the Basic Law constitutionally enacted the fundamental political goal and

[1] For an analysis of the theoretical considerations of Germany's present status, see Ferenc A. Váli, "Legal-Constitutional Doctrines on Germany's Post-World War II Status," *North Dakota Law Review*, Vol. XLII, No. 1 (November, 1965) pp. 20–45.

raison d'être of the Federal Republic: to preserve the "national and political unity" of the German people. Thus, with not negligible political effects on the German mind, the West German state considers itself a truncated unit of the nation and its government the only true representative of the German nation-state, no matter what future name the state will take.[2]

State names may acquire particular significance. It should be remembered that the West German state does not call itself *German Federal Republic* but rather Federal Republic *of Germany* (the East German state's name is German Democratic Republic). In German, the difference is even more expressive: West Germany is Bundesrepublik Deutschland instead of Deutsche Bundesrepublik.[3]

According to its peamble, the Basic Law was enacted by the German people in the *Länder* of the Western zones and "also . . . on behalf of those Germans to whom participation was denied." The preamble also called upon the entire German people "to achieve, by free self-determination, the unity and freedom of Germany." German politicians and publicists, therefore, do not fail to point out that the furtherance of Germany's reunification is, under the terms of the Basic Law, not only a political objective but also a duty prescribed by the provisions of this Law.[4]

The area of application of the Basic Law is not identical with the areas of the *Länder* which, according to the preamble, participated in its enactment. Article 23 mentions, in addition to the states of the Western zones, Greater Berlin as one of the territories in which the Law applies.[5] In other parts of Germany, "it shall be put into force

[2] The Basic Law differentiates between the Federal Republic of Germany and *Germany* (without more proximate designation) and the Reich. The Federal Republic, as distinguished from the constituent states (*Länder*) is also referred to as the *Bund* (federation or confederation).

[3] One is reminded of the objection raised by Bismarck in January, 1871, against King William of Prussia assuming the title of "Emperor of Germany" (which appeared to him inconsistent with the "sovereign" rights of the princes). King William, on the other hand, refused to be called "Emperor of the Germans" which smacked of democracy. His title, finally, was to be "German Emperor" with more of a connotation of national appurtenance and less of territorial authority.

[4] Grewe, *Deutsche Aussenpolitik*, p. 324; Rudolf Schuster, *Deutschlands staatliche Existenz im Widerstreit politischer und rechtlicher Gesichtspunkte, 1945–1963* (Munich, 1963), pp. 138–42. The preamble of a law is, under the German legal doctrine, not "normative," only programmatic (political); it is, however, advanced that above injunction (to promote reunification) should be considered "normative" by the support it received in various articles of the main body of the Basic Law.

[5] It may be noted that Article 23 expressly speaks of "Greater Berlin" and not of the Western sectors of that city.

on their accession."[6] The Basic Law may, thus, be extended to those parts of "Germany" where, because of the existing international situation, it cannot be made applicable; and it may become the constitution of reunited Germany. But the Basic Law also provided for its own replacement by a permanent constitution when it pronounced in Article 146 that it shall cease to be in force "on the day on which a Constitution adopted by a free decision of the German people comes into force."

Under the Basic Law there is only one kind of citizenship: German citizenship. There is no special citizenship reserved for the inhabitants of the Federal Republic.[7] "Germany," in the meaning of the Basic Law, is the area which was the German Reich on December 31, 1937, before Hitler embarked on his road of conquests. Citizens of the Reich, as it was at that date, their descendants, and also refugees or expellees of German stock are "Germans" within the meaning of the Basic Law. It follows that no citizenship of the German Democratic Republic would be recognized by any agency of West Germany.

German political and legal scholars have pointed out that the Basic Law as well as the official political philosophy held by the Federal government rest on three fundamental theses: (1) the continued legal existence of the German nation-state; (2) the territorial integrity of this Germany, as long as a treaty of peace, to be concluded with an all-German government, has not changed the territorial status quo; and (3) within the confines of this German state there exists only one legitimate state-structure and government: the Federal Republic of Germany and its government.[8]

The Federal Republic's basic policy goals are said to be inspired by these theses. There exists a general consensus among all major parties and policy decision-makers concerning these principles; however, they fail to explain fully the constitutional-legal and international-legal status of those political entities which exercise governmental functions in the area of Germany. The circumstances surrounding divided Germany have engendered constitutional and

[6] Article 23. This Article was applied when the Saar returned to become a *Land* of the Federal Republic in 1956.

[7] Therefore, Germans from West Germany hardly ever call themselves "Federal Republicans" (Bundesrepublikaner) but simply "Germans." Inhabitants of East Germany, wishing to differentiate themselves in third countries from those of the West, occasionally call themselves "Democratic Germans" which is giving rise to some misunderstandings.

[8] Grewe, *Deutsche Aussenpolitik*, p. 95; Schuster, *Deutschlands staatliche Existenz*, pp. 261–62.

legal theories concerning the survival of the German state and the legal position of the two German governments, as well as the controversial situation of Berlin.

The constitutional-legal theories generally undertake to explicate three specific controversial points in terms of known constitutional or international legal tenets: continuity or discontinuity of the former German Reich; legal relationship of the Federal Republic with the former German state; and the question of legitimacy of one, or more than one, German political entity. It is, of course, understood that the above-mentioned areas of controversy often overlap or are logically dependent on one another.[9]

The complete surrender of Germany, Allied assumption of integral control over the country, and the subsequent revival of a native governmental machinery gave rise to various doctrinal interpretations. Outside Germany some held that with Germany's unconditional surrender the German state had ceased to exist; these views were shared by Germans, too. As to the postsurrender status of the German area, opinion varied from asserting the existence of an inter-Allied *condominium*[10] to the denial of any state power over Germany.[11] Others, mostly West German scholars, developed the doctrine of German state survival: the German state as a legal entity had never ceased to exist; it had only lost its self-governing capacity to the inter-Allied government.[12] This view received official confirmation by the wording of the Four-Power Declaration of Berlin (June 5, 1945) and by that of the Potsdam Protocol.[13]

The theories of the continuity of discontinuity of the German state are now of less political significance, but they are associated with doctrines relating to the present-day status of the Germanys. Since the re-establishment of sovereignty in the Federal Republic and in East Germany, a maze of conflicting or complementary

[9] For details see Váli, "Legal-Constitutional Doctrines," pp. 27–30.
[10] The chief protagonist of the condominium doctrine is Hans Kelsen, "The Legal Status of Germany According to the Declaration of Berlin," *American Journal of International Law*, 1945, p. 519; *Principles of International Law* (New York, 1952), p. 263.
[11] According to Michel Virally, *Die internationale Verwaltung Deutschlands* (Baden-Baden, 1948), p. 29, Germany, after her surrender, had become a *terra nullius*—that is, a no man's land, under international law.
[12] See, among others, Erich Kaufman, *Deutschlands Rechtslage unter der Besatzung* (Stuttgart, 1948); Alfred Verdross, "Die völkerrechtliche Stellung Deutschlands von 1945 bis zur Bildung der westdeutschen Regiereung," *Archiv des Völkerrechts*, 1951/52, p. 129; M. E. Bathurst and J. L. Simpson, *Germany and the North Atlantic Community* (London, 1956), pp. 188–95, 196–98.
[13] See U.S. Senate, *Documents on Germany, 1944–61*, pp. 12–17, 29–39.

state theories has grown up. We are here primarily concerned with views held in West Germany; those propounded in the German Democratic Republic as well as those relating to the status of Berlin will be considered in their respective chapters.

The state theories stressing the continuity and singularity of the German state either explain the Federal Republic as a Germany reduced in size (contraction doctrine) or as conterminous with the German state of 1937 but prevented, *de facto*, from extending the authority of its constitutional order beyond its factual borders (kernal- or core-state doctrine).[14] The area of Germany beyond the constitutional authority of the Federal Republic is either considered as under foreign occupation or as international no-man's land.[15] Under these doctrines the Federal Republic is either identical with the former Reich or sole successor to the Reich.[16]

Some constitutional scholars in Germany argue that the Federal Republic of Germany is legally co-extensive with historic Germany (within its boundaries of December 31, 1937) even if the area of validity (implementation) of the Basic Law is restricted to the area presently known as the Federal Republic.[17] If this is correct, it would signify that the name Federal Republic of Germany might become, after the expected unification, the name of reunited Germany, unless replaced by some other appellation such as the Reich.

There exists a two-state doctrine whose practical conclusions are not basically dissimilar to those of the single-state doctrines. This "unreal" two-state theory differentiates between the dormant all-German state (which used to be called the German Reich) and the rump state which functions within part of its territory. The all-German state has so far failed to recover its capacity to function, while the Federal Republic possesses almost all the prerequisites of a sovereign state and is, because of its democratic legitimacy, entitled to represent, as a kind of trustee, the still inactive all-German state. The Federal government is, thus, one German government but not *the* German government, and at present there is no other German government. The "so-called" German Democratic Repub-

---

[14] Theodor Eschenburg, *Die deutsche Frage—Verfassungsprobleme der Wiedervereinigung* (Munich, 1959), pp. 25–26; Klaus Vocke, "Politische Gefahren der Theorien über Deutschland," *Europa-Archiv*, 1957, pp. 10199–10215.

[15] See Schuster, *Deutschlands staatliche Existenz*, pp. 84–90.

[16] See Fritz Münch, "Zur deutschen Frage," in German Foreign Office, *Gibt es zwei deutsche Staaten?* (Bonn, 1963), pp. 20–21.

[17] This appears to be the prevailing official position of the West German government; see Schuster, *Deutschlands staatliche Existenz*, pp. 152–64.

lic—also according to this view—fails to possess the characteristics of statehood because of its complete lack of popular democratic legitimacy. This doctrinal explanation appears to be the official view of the Social Democratic party on the constitutional-political status of Germany and of the Federal Republic.[18]

Another genuine two-state doctrine based on the continuity of Germany considers the German Democratic Republic as the secessionist part of Germany. Completed Germany is identified with the state presently known as the Federal Republic of Germany. A so-called roof-theory recognizes the existence of a nonreactivated Germany together with the partially limited and, therefore, not fully sovereign West and East Germanys: the first is considered to exercise its authority legitimately, while the second is only a *de facto* entity upheld by a foreign power. Finally, according to the theories which reject the continuity of Germany, the Federal Republic is regarded as a new state, successor to the Reich but not identical to it; only the German nation has remained, not the former German state. The German area east of the border of the Federal Republic is, by this view, considered "unredeemed" (*irredenta*) national territory under foreign domination.[19]

The Basic Law, by its reference to "Germany" (the reference to the Reich appears whenever the pre-1945 situation is meant), by its insistence on one German citizenship, and by its claim to valid extension over the whole of "Germany" is said to be in conformity with the core-state doctrine [20] or an interpretation of the roof-state doctrine which would recognize limited statehood for the Federal Republic but deny it to the German Democratic Republic.[21]

It should be emphasized that all these subtle doctrines, however divergent in their theoretical explanation of Germany's present

[18] The principal proponent of this theoretical view is Professor Adolf Arndt, *Der deutsche Staat als Rechtsproblem* (Berlin, 1960); see also his "Deutschland als Wahrheit und Wagnis," *Die Zeit*, March 4, 1954.

[19] These various doctrines are represented by Hans Reuther, *Bundesrepublik Deutschland und Deutsches Reich* (Erlangen, 1951), secessionist doctrine; Baron Friedrich August von der Heydte, "Deutschlands Rechtslage," *Friedenswarte*, 1950/51, p. 323 (roof-theory); Helmut Rumpf, "Aktuelle Rechtsfragen der Wiedervereinigung Deutschlands," *Europa-Archiv*, 1957, p. 9723.

[20] The practical conclusions drawn from this doctrine appear in the policy and statements of the Federal government; the nonrecognition of the East German state, the so-called Hallstein Doctrine, as well as the official views of Western governments are, more or less, in conformity with the theoretical frame of the core-state doctrine.

[21] Many of the official views expressed by the Social Democratic party appear to be based on the application of this theoretical view.

status, are convergent with regard to their concluding principles which determine West German policies: namely, the continued existence of the pre-1945 German state within its 1937 boundaries and the sole legitimacy, within these boundaries, of the Federal Republic. The constitutional interpretation of the Federal Republic, as a continuing form of the Bismarckian German state created between 1867 and 1871, makes the demand for reunification more than a policy objective: it is the justification of the very existence of today's free German state.

The Western powers and all the signatories of the revised Brussels Treaty have endorsed the thesis that the government of the Federal Republic is the only legitimate government *in* Germany. The relevant declarations always speak of the Federal Republic as the government "in" and not "of" Germany. This subtle differentiation may indicate that there might be one day another legitimate government *in* Germany. Or it may also indicate the support for the thesis that there is a theoretical, now dormant, all-Germany; and the Federal Republic, within the area of its own jurisdiction, is the ersatz government as long as the present provisional situation lasts.

Thus, the doctrine and practice of the singularity of the German state, as embodied in the Federal Republic, diametrically oppose the theory of two German states (or three German states if we include Berlin), the official thesis of the East German regime and its supporter, the Soviet Union.

Constitutional-legal theories spur the momentum of politics by mingling political expediency with juridical arguments, but they also may place hurdles before pragmatic political planning. In a country like West Germany, where not only the powerful bureaucracy, including the staff of their Foreign Office, but also a great many politicians and publicists received legal training, constitutional theories supporting the idea of German unity—even if they are not always understandable to the ordinary laymen—are of considerable political and practical importance. Statements made by the Federal government, diplomatic notes of the German Foreign Office, arguments advanced by German legal scholars, writers, and journalists are today under the influence of the prevailing doctrines relative to Germany's international and constitutional legal status.

A political-legal doctrine that purports to explain the inner inspirations of a nation is both a source of strength and a source of weakness. It is a comfortable guideline for decision-making, a lodestar for public opinion, and a standard by which actions or attitudes can be measured. Doctrines often simplify decision-making, but they may hinder the solution of problems which could be solved if greater flexibility were employed. Such doctrines incline policy-shapers toward inflexibility where suppleness would be expedient.

It can never be ignored that the theoretical foundations used for explaining the status of the Federal Republic of Germany, of Berlin, and of the problems of Germany's unity are inseparable from the understanding and appreciation of West German attitudes and foreign policy toward the fundamental issue of reunification.

The Federal Government and the Reunification Issue

Under Chancellor Adenauer's administration, West German policy of Germany's unification was far more programmatic and legalistic than pragmatic or political. Although the government in Bonn never ceased to pay lip-service to the goal of German unity, it appeared to be giving preference to European integration and participation in the Atlantic Alliance over the fundamental German problem. In the Weimar period the German government endeavored to maintain a politically productive balance between *Ostpolitik* and *Weltpolitik* (the name given to policies toward the great powers of the West); however, under Adenauer there was, practically, no *Ostpolitik*. That *Deutschlandpolitik* was essentially *Ostpolitik* was belatedly realized.

Until the last years of Adenauer's chancellorship, foreign policy remained the exclusive domain of the aged head of the Federal government. He, personally, was responsible for the foreign policy choices, although each time he obtained an endorsement of his policy by the West German voters. When his *Deutschlandpolitik* proved barren, he was blamed for its failure. The opposition always objected to the priority of his choice. The question of whether the Soviet Union had, in 1952, and again in 1954, meant business is moot. More moderate critics admit that the Chancellor may have been right in assuming that the Soviets used delaying and obstructing tactics without serious intentions of agreeing on reunification but for obtaining such evidence he should have promoted negotiations.[22] By others he was blamed for his failure to admit that Western political and military integration was incompatible with a realistic policy for German unity.[23] But his adherents were ready to

---

[22] Jacobi, "German Paradoxes," p. 437; Augstein, "Konrad Adenauer und seine Epoche," pp. 75–110.

[23] Klaus Bölling, *Republic in Suspense* (New York, 1964), p. 261.

absolve him by arguing that his policy was essentially correct, only the West "was not strong enough."[24] And many in West Germany, though they may be reticent to express views on this subject, believe that Adenauer's line was correct "anyhow."

It is fair to assume that at the time the choices were made (and many in the CDU/CSU thought that there were no "real choices") Adenauer genuinely believed that his policy of *detour*; namely, that pressure by the West would force Soviet hands and would "spontaneously" produce German unity. While the prolonged negotiations on the Federal Republic's rearmament and admission into NATO were pursued, Adenauer considered talks with the Soviet highly undesirable.[25] Later, after West Germany's integration into the West was achieved, he expected fruitful negotiations with the Soviet Union; but for this he waited in vain. Moscow simply refused to recognize that "it was beaten in Germany."

The conclusion that in Adenauer's scale of values entry into the Western political and military system and Franco-German reconciliation preceded the goal of reunification appears correct.[26] Adenauer's concept rested also on an exaggerated estimate of Western strength and on an underestimation of Soviet abilities and power. On the other hand, his opponents will never be able to prove (unless Soviet archives, if opened, would produce such evidence) that reunification would otherwise have been possible.[27]

The successful founder of the Federal Republic had played his card on the reunification issue and lost. His personal charisma (source of much of his success) also faded after 1958, both domestically and internationally. His Christian-oriented quondam partners, John Foster Dulles, Robert Schuman of France, Alcide de Gasperi of Italy, and others, were no longer there to support him. His pliable and Western-oriented Foreign Minister, Heinrich von Brentano, was replaced by the more self-willed and more nationalistic Gerhard Schröder. As one commentator pointed out, the leading personnel of the Federal Republic, Adenauer, Brentano, and Franz Josef Strauss—all Catholics and devotees of European integration—had, by 1963, been replaced by Ludwig Erhard, the new Federal Chancellor; Schröder, the Foreign Minister; and Kai-

---

[24] Hans-Georg von Studnitz, *Bismarck in Bonn* (Stuttgart, 1964), p. 214.

[25] Augstein, *Konrad Adenauer*, pp. 80–81.

[26] Robert d'Harcourt, *L'Allemagne d'Adenauer à Erhard* (Paris, 1964), p. 79; Werner Feld, *Reunification and West German-Soviet Relations* (The Hague, 1963), p. 23.

[27] See Klaus Epstein, *Germany After Adenauer* (New York, 1964), p. 7.

Uwe von Hassel, the Federal Minister of Defense—all Protestants.[28] This momentous change of the guard coincided by-and-large with the realization that the road to European political integration and to an Atlantic partnership was blocked. These developments, together with the deadlock of the reunification policy, did not fail to impress them.[29]

There can be no doubt that the reunification question was to be the *primum mobile* of West German foreign politics under Erhard and his successors, a reunification policy more realistically viewed and pursued than earlier. Though rhetoric could be dispensed with, emphasis was to rest on a pragmatic rather than a merely declarative policy. This did not mean that the government would devote less attention to its relations with the West; the "policy of movement" was still to be conducted under the aegis of "Four-Power responsibility for German unity." Erhard announced that "even if our German policy is only part of our foreign policy, it is nevertheless its deciding element." While the *Deutschlandpolitik* was to be reactivated and its methods changed, the basic principles were to remain unchanged: "the claim to represent all-Germany must remain inviolable."[30]

It is certain that the second chancellor of the Federal Republic did not share those inhibitions with regard to German unification which the first was often suspected of harboring. While Adenauer's outlook may rightly have been considered anti-Prussian and "Rhenish-provincial" and also much influenced by his Carolingian-Catholic Weltanschauung, Erhard's Bavarian-Franconian birth, his contacts during his career in various parts of Germany and his general world-outlook prevented him from being a regionally oriented German. The election results of 1965 were generally considered his personal and not his party's success. The CDU/CSU managed to increase the percentage of its votes from 45.3 per cent in 1961 to 47.6 per cent. The opposition SPD gained 39.3 per cent (as against 36.2 per cent in 1961); the losers were the FDP (a decrease from 12.8 per cent to 9.5 per cent) and splinter parties which received less than the statutory number of votes for obtaining seats in the

[28] Richard Lowenthal, "The Germans Feel Like Germans Again," *New York Times Magazine*, March, 1966, p. 42.

[29] The different religious allegiances of the members of the two teams are rather incidental, though religion has a marginal importance in the outlook toward reunification. See Chapter III, pp. 121–24.

[30] The quotations are from Chancellor Erhard's interview broadcast of April 23, 1966, as reported by the German News Service, May 2, 1966.

Bundestag. It seems fairly evident that the reunification issue had no impact whatsoever on the outcome of these elections.

Gerhard Schröder, the initiator of the "policy of movement," is another specimen of a deregionalized German. His father, originally from the Protestant North, was an employee of the Reich railways who happened to be stationed in Saarbrücken when his son was born. The Foreign Minister spent his youth in Southwest Germany, studied law in Köngisberg, East Prussia, in Berlin, and in Bonn. After World War II, he settled in Düsseldorf, in North Rhine-Westphalia. As Minister of the Interior for eight years, he proved to be a versatile tactician. His assumption of the post of foreign minister after the 1961 elections heralded a greater flexibility in handling a problem which heretofore had been dominated by the doctrinal cliches adopted in the Foreign Office under Walter Hallstein, State Secretary, and Wilhelm G. Grewe, head of the Political Section in the mid-fifties, with the approval of the Chancellor and the then-Foreign Minister Heinrich von Brentano. Schröder's greater "pragmatism" soon brought him into conflict with Adenauer and the punctilious legalists of the CDU/CSU. Under the post-Adenauer administration, Schröder, no doubt, has enjoyed greater freedom of action. Nevertheless, he has remained exposed to the often extremely sharp criticism of the members of his own Party and dependent on the influences of his own Foreign Office bureaucracy.

The domestic and diplomatic staff of the German Foreign Office is in a position to exercise independent authority in matters of policy detail and to have considerable influence on questions of principle in the decision-making process.[31] Foreign Office officials who handle current business in matters of the "Soviet Zone of Occupation," of Berlin, and Soviet and East European questions are engaged in a relentless, exacting struggle against encroachments or attempted encroachments on West German and Allied rights and positions. They generally have a realistic and down-to-earth view on these questions. They are aware how dangerous it is to give way on seemingly minute changes introduced by the adversary and how important it is to prevent precedents from being created over what appear to be harmless procedures. They are conscious of the fact that past weaknesses or oversights have later been

[31] For good information on the organization and decision-making process in the German Foreign Office, see Majonica, *Deutsche Aussenpolitik*, pp. 274-304; and Studnitz, *Bismarck in Bonn*, pp. 217-304.

formidably exploited. When in 1955 nonmilitary traffic to West Berlin was handed over by the Russians to the officials of the German Democratic Republic, there was only a lame protest by the Western powers. The incorporation of East Berlin into the German Democratic Republic hardly elicited formal protests by the West. By similar "salami tactics" is the East German regime intent to have itself recognized as the other German state.

The Foreign Office feels that it is its task to forestall any further erosion of Western positions or rights vis-à-vis the German Democratic Republic, both regarding the international status of the latter and the situation of Berlin. Its watchfulness is alerted to prevent any "upgrading" of the East German regime which would eventually lead to the recognition of Ulbricht's government. It knows that this struggle can be fought only in full agreement with the Western Allies, especially the United States, and that the Federal government is far from having freedom of action in the matter.

Foreign Office personnel often deplore having to ward off Communist encroachments passively with little opportunity to initiate offensive diplomatic actions against vulnerable positions of the adversary. At present, they consider the Soviet offensive against West Berlin to have failed. It is, however, admitted that the Wall has, for the time being, saved the East German regime from collapse; in this respect, the division of East and West Berlin has proved to be a political success. The practical advantages of the Wall are, it is asserted, largely counterbalanced by the propagandistic disadvantage it has evoked.

The German Foreign Office considers the Hallstein Doctrine (that no diplomatic relations can be maintained with states which have officially recognized the German Democratic Republic) [32] not only useful but absolutely indispensable for the purposes of West German policies. In the view of their leading officials, this doctrine has proved more resistant to erosions and exceptions than originally imagined. They are, however, conscious of the drawbacks in the application of this policy. Rigid advocates of the Doctrine point to the utter sterility of the diplomatic contacts with the Soviet Union (which was exempted from the application of the Hallstein Doctrine) and envisage no greater hopes from contacts with either Warsaw or Prague. Other officials who, sympathetic to the United States' view, favor greater flexibility, consider full diplomatic con-

[32] For a detailed examination of the Hallstein Doctrine, see Chapter IV below, pp. 148–56.

tacts with East European Communist powers (except of course, East Germany) as likely to produce fruitful results. But even these "progressives" view the setting up of diplomatic relations with these countries as maximum concessions within the frame of the Hallstein Doctrine.

The flexibility which the German Foreign Office and its minister, with the approval or tolerance of Chancellor Erhard, have been practicing in handling the East-West issues, including those of reunification and Berlin, was constantly subjected to the scrutiny and criticism of the three major political parties.[33] Any major deviation from the official legal position would create more than ministerial crisis; it would be considered a real *crise d'état*. Not only would the foreign minister's position be at stake, but also the belief would be held that Germany's future was being jeopardized.

While Adenauer with his foreign ministers was able to carry on his foreign policy with minimum interference by the coalition parties and with an undisguised disdain for criticism, Erhard and Schröder were not unmindful of the need to implement a foreign policy in agreement and accommodation with the opposition party. Consensus of all three major parties for the pursuit of vital national goals was certainly their wish. Such a course was made possible by the adoption of the government's position on reunification by the Social Democratic party. The quasi-unanimity of all three parties on this crucial issue has, however, allowed the creation of internal rifts in all major parties that make foreign policy somewhat less than bipartisan.

The CDU/CSU and Reunification

The leaders and parliamentarians of the Christian Democratic Union and of its Bavarian branch, the Christian Social Union, acted under Adenauer's leadership as guardians of the correct interpretation and application of the prevailing doctrine and policy concerning the quest for German unity. But even for the most faithful adherents of the "one state" doctrine, this concept, in its variations and subtleties, may have presented pitfalls. In fact, even the speakers of the CDU/CSU lacked the semantic adroitness to conform to the requirements of the official state doctrine. Thus, if (perhaps ironically) the "East Zonal Republic" is mentioned instead of the correct "Central German Soviet Zone," the speaker may expose himself to

[33] See Karl-Hermann Flach, *Erhards schwerer Weg* (Stuttgart-Degerloch, 1963), esp. pp. 68–83.

criticism. Even such a seemingly correct expression that the Federal Republic "represents All-Germany" may be taken as an endorsement of the "roof doctrine," assuming the existence of two entities: one which represents and the other which is represented; correctly stated, the Federal Republic is the "provisionally contracted form of All-Germany." Similarly, it is not without ambiguity to doubt the "legitimacy of the Soviet Zonal government" because thereby the speaker might have implicitly admitted the existence of a state which only fails to have, for lack of popular representation, a legitimate government.[34] These slight deviations, however, have mostly been overshadowed by more serious aberrations of the opposition parties that at times gave rise to violent and acrimonious debates.

The phenomenal success of Adenauer, except in the matter of reunification, silenced critics within the ruling party. This does not mean that there was no opposition to the priority which Adenauer, without openly admitting it, assigned to Western integration above German unity. Jakob Kaiser, Ernst Lemmer, and others— most of them either refugees from the East or in close contact with Berlin—stood nearer to the ideas which were voiced by Schumacher and other Socialist leaders. But the personality of the old Chancellor and his insistence that alliance with the West, security, freedom, and strength for the Federal Republic could in time force the hand of the Russians and compel them to give up their East German bastion, eventually silenced them. The Chancellor also seemed peculiarly favored by fortune; the most controversial item of the Paris Agreements of 1954, the international status of the Saar, was luckily replaced by retrocession to Germany. This outstanding event, together with the negative effect of the Hungarian tragedy of 1956, demonstrated that friendship with the West pays and that only a policy of strength could impress the Soviet Union.

But by 1958 open doubts arose, even within the ranks of the CDU/CSU, with regard to official policy on reunification. The second struggle for Berlin, the pat positions of the Geneva Conference of 1959, and the erosions of the one-state doctrine confused many of Adenauer's admirers. Only when in 1960 the erstwhile fervent critics of the Federal government's German policy (the Social Democrats) went over to the official view on reunification was the self-confidence of the CDU/CSU somewhat restored.

[34] For these and other semantic "blunders," see Schuster, *Deutschlands staatliche Existenz,* pp. 152–56.

Nevertheless, there was no return to "blind faith" in Adenauer's concept of "spontaneous" reunification. The necessity for giving up some of the earlier dogmatic rigidity developed various approaches which, at present, divide leaders and factions on the issue of reunification. The revolts against Adenauer, the travails of his succession, and, finally, the transfer of power to the tolerant Erhard increased divisive tendencies within the Union parties.

Divergent trends within the CDU/CSU are not restricted to the policy issues of reunification. Different views exist on the intensity of alignment with the United States or France, on matters of European integration, and on alternatives of defense strategy and nuclear preparedness. On the reunification issue proper, it is possible to distinguish between adherents of the old rigid, strictly legalistic attitudes and advocates of more flexible, mobile, or pragmatic views. Adherents of both opinions may envisage a long-term view (the "patient" ones) or urge immediate measures and pressures, both against the Western Allies for greater support and against the Eastern foe for concessions. All these trends and their representative groups intersect one another within the party, resulting in an even greater variety of views and shifting attitudes whenever a concrete problem emerges or a decision is to be taken on any particular point.

1) The *hard-liners* advocated a rigid maintenance of the Adenauer policy; that is, nonrecognition of the East German regime in all its aspects, no contacts whatsoever with East German leaders, insistence on four-power responsibility for German unity and Berlin, and no acknowledgment of the incorporation of eastern territories into Poland and the Soviet Union. They held the view that any loosening of the doctrinal-legal position must lead to an all-out erosion and collapse of their policy and, sooner or later, to a recognition of Germany's partition. They insisted that Soviet intransigence must be opposed by even greater intransigence in the West. Adenauer himself, since he has given up the reins of government, has returned to his original inflexibility and considered any United States policy of relaxation (even the wheat sales to Russia) a dangerous and ominous experiment doomed to failure or a confirmation of the division of Germany.[35] In March, 1966, at the Congress which elected Erhard chairman of the Party, the ex-Chancellor stated that "the Soviet Union wants peace" and later added that the Soviets wanted peace because they needed peace.[36]

[35] *New York Times,* October 13, 1963.
[36] *Ibid.,* March 24, 1966.

In this hard stand Adenauer was supported by a considerable number of Party leaders and Bundestag deputies. Former Foreign Minister Heinrich von Brentano, leader of the parliamentary group of the CDU/CSU who died in 1965, and Heinrich Krone, Minister without portfolio, were known to oppose any easing of tension without meaningful concessions by the Soviet Union; otherwise, they claimed it would be Germany that would have to pay the price.[37] This inflexible attitude is shared by many members of the Catholic group of the CDU leadership and, in particular, by the CSU branch led by former Defense Minister Franz Josef Strauss and the influential deputy, Karl-Theodor Freiherr zu Guttenberg.[38] Other geographical factors are significant: the Chairman of the CDU's Berlin organization, Franz Amrehn, has sternly opposed any "impatient abandonment" of positions—even the concept that an economic improvement or other humanization of conditions in the Democratic Republic would lead to a relaxation of tensions. He criticized the Socialist press chief of Berlin, Egon Bahr, for having suggested the omission of quotation marks around the words "German Democratic Republic," so as to suggest the real existence of such a state.[39]

2) The *flexible-liners* wished to emerge from frozen and merely negative attitudes. They were far from advocating the recognition of the East German state or from giving way on Berlin or on the Eastern Territories. But they favored contacts, negotiations, and a flexible diplomacy without abandoning the essence of earlier positions. Thus, they had no scruples against signing the Nuclear Test Ban Treaty even when the German Democratic Republic also became co-signatory. They had also favored the establishment of trade missions in countries which maintain diplomatic relations with East Germany.

The Foreign Minister, Gerhard Schröder, who succeeded Heinrich von Brentano in the post-1961 Adenauer cabinet, dared to adopt a "policy of movement" or a "change through rapprochement." This mobile and pragmatic view on reunification was then supported by only a few influential members of the CDU/CSU. Erhard, however, has rallied to Schröder's views and so, apparently,

---

[37] *Ibid.*, December 6, 1963, and April 23, 1964.
[38] Both have published books wherein their and their adherents' political apologia is set out. Karl-Theodor Freiherr zu Guttenberg, *Wenn der Westen will: Plädoyer für eine mutige Politik* (Stuttgart, 1964); Franz Josef Strauss, *The Grand Design—A European Solution to German Reunification* (New York, 1966).
[39] Franz Amrehn, "Gefährlicher Richtungswechsel," *Politisch-Soziale Korrespondenz* (Bonn), July 22, 1963.

has Eugen Gerstenmaier, the President of the Bundestag. Gerstenmaier himself has always shown a certain disposition toward flexible views; he once favored the linking of disengagement with the question of reunification and was ready to reverse the priorities on "free elections" versus "peace treaty."[40]

The flexible-liners favored co-operation with the United States and have seemed undisturbed by direct Soviet-American exchanges on Berlin and negotiations aiming at the easing of international tensions. Though Schröder and his supporters asserted that the Federal Republic cannot afford a harder policy line than that of the United States, they have come under the heavy fire of their opponents in the Party whenever they have tried to implement their "pragmatic" and "realistic" ideas.[41] Schröder's future depended on the support which he could obtain from the Chancellor and that segment of the Party which was ready to follow similar policies; on the vehemence of the attacks of his opponents, themselves divided; and, last but not least, on international developments and the possibilities for conformity with the official policy of Washington without appearing to infringe on vital German interests.

After the 1965 elections when Erhard was called to reorganize his cabinet, the post of the foreign minister, together with the policy to be followed, became the bones of contention between the warring factions of the CDU/CSU. Erhard had to protect Schröder against the onslaughts of the "hard" group led by Adenauer himself. The struggle developed into a three-cornered fight when the leaders of the FDP, the coalition partner, joined the battle. Although the FDP leader, Erich Mende, himself a candidate for the office of a foreign minister, did not see eye-to-eye with Schröder, he was even more opposed to Franz Josef Strauss, who would have been the favored son of the hard-liners for that ministerial post.[42]

The new cabinet continued to include Schröder as Foreign Minister; the struggle thus ended with a score in favor of the "policy of movement" and "gradualism" to create a "change through rapprochement." Mende, in addition to his post as Vice-Chancellor, obtained the Ministry of All-German Affairs. Johann Baptist Gradl,

[40] See *East-West Tensions*, conversations in Bad Godesberg, October 1–4, 1959 (Freiburg/Br., 1960), pp. 22–25.

[41] See "Schröder's Mission," *Sonntagsblatt* (Hamburg), September 22, 1963; *New York Times*, April 14, 1964. When Schröder's conciliatory policy toward East Europe was sharply attacked in the *Bayern-Kurir*, organ of the CSU, Chancellor Erhard called it "an unjustified and unqualified attack." *New York Times*, April 14, 1964.

[42] *New York Herald Tribune*, October 3, 1965.

the CDU deputy for Berlin, received another key post concerning reunification: he became the Minister for Refugee and Expellee Affairs. He had rallied to Schröder's views and shortly after his appointment even dared to express the view that West Germany would have to make concrete "sacrifices" if there was to be any hope for reunification of Germany. He particularly hinted that some changes in the 1937 frontier in favor of Poland could be recognized by a future all-German government.[43]

3) The *impatient ones* are to be found both among the flexible and inflexible leaders of the CDU/CSU. The flexible-impatients wish to speed up certain "dynamic" moves for the opening of meaningful negotiations on the reunification question. They are particularly anxious to alleviate the sufferings of the inhabitants of Berlin and of East Germany. But many more impatients are to be found among the ranks of the advocates of tougher policies. Their impatience presses them to demand sterner measures of retaliation and use of pressures against the Pankow government and its Soviet protector. Their discontent is often expressed against the Western Allies who, in their view, fail to show sufficient vigor and determination for German unity. They reproach the West for having missed good opportunities and predict that, failing the achievement of German unity within reasonable time, Germans "could lose their patience" and in their frustration would either turn toward Russia or turn their backs on "democracy." The erection of the Berlin Wall is advanced, partly as evidence of Western passivity, partly as a reason for urgent action and for a change.[44] Accordingly, impatience may work both ways: it is an inducement to rapprochement or to increased tension.

In the view of the impatient ones, consistent patience is, in fact, a policy of doing nothing. Schröder opposed such an attitude when he said: "I am of the opinion that a solution to the German Question cannot be attained in long-term, allegedly natural developments in Europe. This problem can be solved only if political tensions are removed and a formal agreement is reached."[45] The adherents of "automatic" or "spontaneous" reunification (the old Adenauer school) were opposed to the tactical moves suggested by the impatients which would reveal that the Germans had lost their nerve.

4) The *patient ones* are prepared and have tried to prepare the

[43] *New York Times,* January 18, 1966.
[44] See the article by Johann Baptist Gradl, *Die Welt,* June 15, 1963.
[45] Gerhard Schröder, *Die Zeit,* November 5, 1965.

German public for a long waiting period before German unity can be achieved. Patients are to be found both among the advocates of hard policies and among the flexible ones. The latter foresee a long process which will lead to a gradual relaxation in the Cold War and create an atmosphere that will render a favorable solution to the German question possible. Many adherents of flexible politics favor a Polish-German *rapprochement* which, in their opinion, will be conducive to the implementation of German unity; but they have to admit that the road toward a genuine understanding with the Poles will, inevitably, be a long one.

Patient-inflexibles are perhaps more numerous. They generally are those who remained faithful to the concept of an automatic or spontaneous reunification of Germany. In their view, the Russians will one day feel obliged to change their attitude toward the German nation and give up voluntarily their hold over East Germany. They are convinced that, in the course of time, the question of German unification is bound to become "negotiable," and then the price, if any, to be paid for it will not be excessive. The intensification of the Sino-Soviet conflict is invoked by them as one of the possible reasons which, in the long run, will force the Soviets to give up their advanced positions in Central Europe.

5) The so-called Gaullists (they would disclaim such an appellation) have been impressed by the French President's active and energetic foreign policy which made nationalism fashionable again in Europe. They are not necessarily pro-French; they are German Gaullists. Translated into the realm of pro-unification policy, German "Gaullism" denies or minimizes the significance of ideological conflicts but stresses the existence of national power struggles and, by definition, wishes to apply a combination of toughness and flexibility. In the opinion of the Gaullists, the German problem is closely allied with the companion problems of the East Central European satellite countries. Unification of Germany is likely to be achieved simultaneously with what they call "the unification of Europe"—that is, when all the area between Germany and Russia will be given up by the Soviets.[46] The Gaullists are often suspicious of American designs and consider American policy "soft," especially when toughness seems more profitable. Together with De Gaulle, they doubt the likelihood of an all-out American

---

[46] See Karl Theodor Freiherr von und zu Guttenberg, "Ostpolitik und Status quo," *Sonntagsblatt* (Hamburg), September 22, 1963. The German "Gaullist" concept is expanded in Strauss, *The Grand Design*.

engagement in case of a Soviet attack against West Germany or Berlin.

6) The *"Atlanticists"* in the CDU/CSU support European integration and Atlantic partnership. They are definitely pro-American but not necessarily anti-French, though they distrust Gaullism. They are ready to favor a genuine European political federation. In their view, Adenauer's original concept was correct: it was indispensable, for the sake of German unity, first to establish security and prosperity in the Federal Republic and close alliance and co-operation with the Western powers, especially with the United States. It was, furthermore, this line of policy that enabled the Federal Republic to gain the Western powers' full endorsement for the German cause and protection against the East for the Federal Republic and Berlin. In their opinion, a neutral or uncommitted Germany would have become a no-man's-land exposed to a Communist take-over. They believe that a fully integrated Europe in close alliance with the United States will persuade Poles, Czechs, and even the Russians that they have nothing to fear from German nationalism should Germany regain her unity. But they are doubtful that the German problem could ever be solved without an all-out East-West settlement contributing to a solution of the status of the East Central European countries now under Soviet control.[47]

The Atlanticists agree that theirs is a long-term policy. Accordingly, they generally belong to the "patient" category of politicians. They may be adherents of a hard or of a flexible policy toward East Germany, but they try to adjust their views to the course set by Washington.

The divergences of approach to the reunification issue resulted in a paradox in German politics: the politician who favored an active, mobile attitude is often considered "soft" on German unity because flexibility and impatience might lead to concessions; on the other hand, the passive, patient politician preaching "immobolisme" is considered "hard." Thus, Adenauer is still thought of by many as the "strong" leader, and Erhard was suspected of being "soft." [48]

The Social Democratic Party and Reunification

In the years following the Geneva Conferences of 1956, the SPD never ceased to draw attention to failures and omissions of

---

[47] See Kurt Birrenbach, *Die Zukunft der Atlantischen Gemeinschaft* (Freiburg/Br., 1962), pp. 67–71; same author, "Integration und Wiedervereinigung?" *Die Welt*, August 11, 1962.

[48] Flach, *Erhards schwerer Weg*, p. 89.

Chancellor Adenauer and his Party that were said to have prevented the achievement of German unity. The Chairman of the Party, Erich Ollenhauer, at the Party Congress in July, 1956, derided the government for its stolidity in failing to pursue an "active policy for re-unification of Germany by the Germans themselves." He suggested full use of diplomatic relations with the Soviet Union for the sake of unification, the "normalization" of relations with Poland and Czechoslovakia (implying the abandonment of the Hallstein Doctrine), and establishment of a "maximum of relations" with the population of the "Soviet Zone" through agreements with the "competent agencies of the Soviet Occupied Zone of Germany."[49] The ambivalent position of the SPD was characterized by such contradictory theses as dropping, on the one hand, the claim to "one German state" and, on the other hand, refusing to recognize East Germany as a state. In the same speech Ollenhauer stated that the question of German unity could not be solved by direct negotiations between "Bonn and Pankow," but through four-power agreements. He did not, however, exclude the possibility of talks between the West and East German governments "should they become later indispensable and if they can be carried out in internationally unobjectionable forms."[50]

Such statements must have sounded extremely suspect to adherents of the official reunification concepts. It should be remembered that, while many exponents of political views in West Germany were critical of the Adenauer line on reunification, these critics very seldom objected to the doctrinal position held by the government. Even the state theory adopted by the SPD did not, in its ultimate conclusions, differ from the government concept. The SPD's rather diffuse and ambiguous views on the methods of achieving reunification voiced prior to the 1957 elections did not advance its popularity with the voters.

The Berlin crisis of late 1958 and the subsequent Foreign Ministers' Conference induced the SPD leadership to prepare, early in 1959, a comprehensive plan for the solution of the German question. The inconsistencies of earlier declarations were thus to be eliminated and proposals formulated which were not in direct opposition to solutions earlier advocated by the Soviet Union itself. On January 10, 1959, Soviet notes were handed to the three Western

[49] From Ollenhauer's Report addressed to the SPD Congress at Munich, July 10–14, 1956; *An der Wende der deutschen Politik*, pp. 9–10.
[50] *Ibid.*, pp. 11–12.

powers and to the Federal Republic proposing the convocation of a peace conference on Germany and enclosing a draft text of a peace treaty to be signed by Germany's adversaries in World War II and the "two German governments."[51] The reunification plan of the SPD was designed to persuade the German public that its terms, if adopted, would forestall the danger of a peace settlement with two Germanys, instead of one, or a separate treaty with only the German Democratic Republic—measures which in either case would perpetuate the division of Germany.

The SPD reunification program, known as the Deutschlandplan (Germany Plan)[52] was tailored to conform to some disengagement projects, such as those submitted by the British labor leader, Hugh Gaitskell; by George Kennan; by the former Belgian Foreign Minister, Van Zeeland; and by the Polish Foreign Minister, Rapacki.[53] It, therefore, proposed as a first stage the establishment of a "zone of relaxation" in Central Europe, including both parts of Germany, Poland, Czechoslovakia, and Hungary. This "zone of relaxation" would gradually be evacuated by all foreign forces and denuclearized; the four great powers and other participants in these agreements were to enter into a collective security convention.

The reunification process, according to the Deutschlandplan, was to be accomplished in three consecutive steps. First, an all-German conference was to be set up with representatives of both German governments on a parity basis. The conference was to pave the way toward unification by introducing provisions, common to all parts of Germany, in the field of human rights and economics. The second step was to be the convocation of an all-German parliamentary council, consisting of equal numbers of members elected in West and East Germany. This parliamentary council was to prepare the complete realignment of the legal, financial, and social systems of the two Germanys and to decide, by a two-thirds majority, on the date and circumstances of general elections for a constituent national assembly which was to frame and adopt the all-German constitution. All of these all-German

---

[51] For the text of the Soviet note and the draft of the peace treaty, see George D. Embree (ed.), *The Soviet Union and the German Question* (The Hague, 1963), pp. 81–100.

[52] The *Deutschlandplan* was published by the SPD in April, 1959, in Bonn. The Plan also contains an historic introduction and explanatory comments in question-and-answer form.

[53] For these disengagement projects, see Eugène Hinterhoff, *Disengagement* (London, 1959), *passim.*

bodies were to sit in Berlin; during the three gradual steps the status of this city was to remain unchanged.

The SPD's reunification plan clearly proposed the recognition, as an equal partner, of the German Democratic Republic. In allowing for equal representation of seventeen million Germans with the fifty-four million of the Federal Republic, it even conceded superior weight to a minority. But the weakest point of this scheme was the fact that the East German representatives could surely be expected to speak and vote according to the instructions of the Communist party, while the freely elected members from the Federal Republic would have represented different shades of opinion and one dissenting vote could have turned the balance in favor of the East. The two-thirds majority, required for the setting of general elections, could easily have been sabotaged by the Communist members, leading the whole procedure into an inevitable deadlock. In the meantime, however, the German Democratic Republic would have achieved its primary objective: its recognition as an independent German state. The Deutschlandplan argued that the opening of the border between East and West Germany—the free flow of people and goods from one part of the country to the other—as a result of the agreements would benefit unification and that the higher living standards and greater economic power of West Germany would compel the East to acquiesce in German unity; but these arguments were all based on speculations of a hazardous nature. After all, for many years after 1945 there had been free circulation between the two parts of Berlin; this had not led the East German Communists to change their economic and political system in their portion of the city. The Deutschlandplan evidently underestimated the techniques and potentialities of totalitarian regimentation. It offered the West Germans something they were anxious to avoid: an experiment which might jeopardize their hard-won security and political equilibrium.

The Deutschlandplan exposed the SPD to the criticism of the two other major parties, of intellectuals all over the country, and of many of their own Party members. The abandonment of the Plan, almost as soon as it was published, exposed its impracticality through hard experience.

In March, 1959, a German Social Democratic delegation, consisting of Carlo Schmid, Vice-President of the Bundestag, and Fritz Erler, Vice-Chairman of the Party, visited Moscow, met members of the Soviet Central Committee, high officials of the Soviet Foreign Ministry, and Khrushchev himself. The German Socialist leaders became fully acquainted with the Soviet views regarding Germany. Khrushchev claimed to have no further interest in whether the Federal Republic severed its ties with the North Atlantic Alliance: in neither case would the balance of power be altered. They were told that the Soviet government was interested only in the conclusion of a peace treaty with the two German states. Such a treaty would render the occupation status of Berlin superfluous. As for the unification of Germany, it was a matter for the Germans to decide; the Federal government should discuss this question with the East German government. The Soviet government could offer only its good offices for facilitating the conclusion of an agreement to this effect.[54]

The conversations in Moscow persuaded the Social Democratic leaders that, under the prevailing circumstances, the Russians would not consider any form of disengagement or neutralization of Germany as adequate compensation for the potential loss of their East German satellite. As Erler expressed it, they were intent on consolidating the status quo and, for that reason, were pressing for a treaty of peace based on the status quo. With regard to Berlin, on the other hand, they wished to change the status quo because the present situation of West Berlin was disturbing.[55]

It now became evident that the Deutschlandplan was as poor a tool for furthering the reunification of Germany as it was unpopular in the country. The inconclusive ending of the Foreign Ministers' Conference in Geneva during the summer of 1959 finally convinced Socialist leaders that their much-heralded Plan would, at the next general elections, be a burden on their Party rather than a launching pad to victory. It was easy to say that the bluff of the East German Communists should be called. But it was an accepted tenet of West German public opinion and a view largely held by Socialist voters, too, that the position of the Federal Republic should not be risked. The Deutschlandplan would clearly have opened West Germany to Communist infiltration, cajolery, and

[54] The Moscow conversations of Carlo Schmid and Fritz Erler are described by them in the following articles: *Frankfurter Allgemeine Zeitung*, March 19, 1959; *Frankfurter Rundschau*, March 21, 1959; and *Düsseldorfer Zeitung*, March 21–22, 1959.

[55] Radio broadcast by Fritz Erler over the South-West-German Station on March 21, 1959.

pressure. And to deal with the leaders of the SED, the persecutors of workers and students, was not to the taste of Social Democrats. They concluded that their estimate of Soviet intentions had been overoptimistic and, therefore, erroneous. The Deutschlandplan was dropped as quietly as possible, and a new reunification policy was turned over.

The SPD's abandonment of neutralistic or "third force" policies was not altogether easy. The policy change was decided by an extraordinary Party meeting in Bad Godesberg (known as the "Godesberg Plan") on November 15, 1959. The practical implementation of this *volte face* took place on March 18, 1960, when SPD Deputy Chairman, Herbert Wehner declared in the name of his Party that the Deutschlandplan had become "outdated by developments." And on March 24, 1960, he submitted to the Bundestag a new, four-point program which contained proposals for relaxation in Central Europe "with the view of promoting the rapprochement of Germany's two parts"; for demonstrations by the people of Germany to induce the four powers to open the road toward reunification; for the strengthening of economic, social, and cultural ties between the divided parts of Germany; and for a combination of moves which would lead toward German unity or would, at least, relieve Berlin from Soviet pressures and prevent any final international recognition of Germany's partition.[56]

During the Bundestag debates on international politics on June 30, 1960, the SPD undertook to align itself with the governmental views on foreign policy and, in particular, the reunification issue. Invited by Franz Josef Strauss, the Minister of Defense, to accept four basic policy theses of the Federal government, Herbert Wehner gave positive replies. He declared that the SPD was ready to accept the Western European and Atlantic alliance systems as the basis and frame for all efforts of the German foreign and reunification policies. Furthermore, Wehner declared, the SPD did not demand the withdrawal of the Federal Republic from the Western alliance and was ready to consider German participation in the alliance as a contribution toward the policy for reunification. The SPD, he said, endorsed the necessity of a powerful national defense and did not, in principle, favor any form of disengagement. On the other hand, it wished self-determination and free elections in East Germany.

[56] Siegler (ed.), *Wiedervereinigung und Sicherheit Deutschlands,* p. 307.

Questioned by CDU Minister Krone as to whether the Deutsch-landplan could, in all its details, be considered "past history," Wehner replied, "Certainly."[57]

It was now the turn of Herbert Wehner to ask the CDU/CSU whether it would not be preferable to recognize the moral and national integrity of the SPD opposition party in its desire to promote German unity. He pointed out that an irreconcilable enmity between the Christian Democrats and the Social Democrats would be too heavy a burden for a partitioned Germany.[58]

The SPD thus not only reversed itself on its attitude toward the ways and means of reunification but also suggested active collaboration on this national issue. It did not, however, acknowledge past errors or the propriety of Adenauer's policy. On the contrary, its reproach was that the government had missed opportunities to negotiate with the Soviet Union when it might have proved profitable.[59] The Socialists reached the conclusion that, for the time being, no more could be done for reunification than to rely on the possibilities inherent in the Western alliance and the diplomatic support of the West.

This change of fronts was no tactical move to attract voters but a policy change believed in and abided by. Simultaneously, their attitude toward the Federal Republic also changed. Earlier the Social Democrats had been inclined to regard the Bonn Republic as even more provisional than was warranted under the terms of the Basic Law. The West German state was frequently compared with the "Confederation of the Rhine," that puppet construction of Napoleonic domination.[60] Such attacks now came to an end and the SPD has, in every respect, become a loyal opposition, more loyal than in the past.

Subsequent to Ollenhauer's death, the SPD elected Willy Brandt Chairman of the Party. Brandt, the governing Mayor of West Berlin, could be considered a symbol of the resistance of Berlin and, at the same time, the embodiment of German desire for reunification. Willy Brandt was known as the initiator of the policy of "small steps," another way to express a gradual approach to the

[57] Ibid.
[58] Ibid.
[59] See, for instance, Fritz Erler, *Ein Volk sucht seine Sicherheit* (Frankfurt/ M., 1961), pp. 30–31.
[60] See, for instance, Jens Daniel, *Deutschland—Ein Rheinbund?* (Darmstadt, 1953), *passim*.

East (including East Germany), thus paving the way for reunification. It would be difficult to point to any principal difference between Schröder's flexible policy and that supported by Willy Brandt, though they did differ on concrete issues.

Willy Brandt's chairmanship helped little to secure for the SPD the much-hoped-for majority or even plurality at the 1965 elections. As stated earlier, these election results could hardly be considered an answer to the reunification question: this question simply lacked topical appeal. It is wrong to state, as did the author Günter Grass, who campaigned for the Social Democrats, that by refusing to give a majority to the Party of Willy Brandt, the German electorate "had voted against re-unification."[61]

But if bipartisan policy, which developed since 1961, was a complicated matter because of the various trends prevailing within the CDU/CSU, it became even more entangled because of different shades of opinion within the SPD itself.

Bipartisan Reunification Policy

Bipartisanship in German unity policy was not reached by any formal agreement; it was achieved by the alignment of the Social Democratic party with the basic course followed by the Federal government and the CDU/CSU. This endorsement could never, however, be complete because, as we have seen, even the official doctrine on reunification allowed manifold interpretations and applications. Even while official SPD policy now adjusted itself to governmental views, no absolute unanimity existed within the Social Democratic party on many questions of detail. Differing nuances of opinion which, according to the significance attached to them in a given situation, could occasionally grow into formidable political conflicts, beset the SPD no less than the CDU/CSU. It has thus happened that specific views held by one faction in the Union parties may come close to or even be identical with views held by a group within the SPD. This is the manner in which bipartisanship prevails: for divergent opinions, too, acquire a bipartisan character when they are shared by members of both participating political parties.

The basic though tacit agreement which now appeared to exist between the major German parties included the following theses:

1) The primary task of German politics is the restoration of German unity in "freedom and peace." This policy objective is,

<hr/>

[61] *New York Times,* October 17, 1965.

thus, inseparable from another postulate: the preservation of peace (by which is also meant the security of the Federal Republic).[62]

2) Any form of a two German states doctrine is to be rejected; the Federal Republic is the only true representative of the German nation.[63] This principle, worded in the form of the one-state roof theory [64] as endorsed by the SPD, was expressed by Fritz Erler in the course of the debate on the declaration of policy by the new Erhard government in late October, 1963, in the following manner: "The German Federal Republic is the form of state organization in the free part of our native land, and it will one day be merged into a free united Germany. That in no way takes from its dignity. . . ."[65]

3) The reunification of Germany is to be achieved by peaceful means only; preferably by an application of the right of self-determination (free elections).

4) The improvement of the fate of Germans in East Germany is, for humanitarian reasons, to be considered an immediate and urgent objective.

5) The Federal Republic remains committed to the defense and international representation of Berlin (the SPD is more inclined to stress the view according to which West Berlin is part of the Federal Republic).[66]

6) According to international law, the boundaries of Germany are those as they existed on December 31, 1937; the Oder-Neisse Line can, therefore, not be recognized as a frontier until the border question is settled by a peace treaty.[67]

7) The bipartisan policy for reunification also relies on four-power responsibility for the restoration of German unity and on

[62] See *Political Program of the SPD* as adopted at the Party Congress at Bonn on April 28, 1961; Willy Brandt, *Das Regierungsprogram der SPD* (Bonn, 1961), p. 18.

[63] *Ibid.*, p. 19.

[64] See p. 54 above.

[65] SPD Executive Committee, *News from Germany—Special Issue* (Cologne, n.d.).

[66] See Resolutions of the SPD Party Congress in Cologne, May 26–30, 1962.

[67] "It is the duty of every German government, in peace treaty negotiations— to use the words of Mr. Kurt Schumacher—to wrestle toughly for every square meter of German soil. We must not fail to express the German legal point of view, because to remain silent on this point would render us unworthy of belief and would not make things easier for us either with our allies or with our eastern neighbors. . . . " Fritz Erler, *Bundestag* debate on the program of the Erhard government, October, 1963.

three-power responsibility for the maintenance of the Berlin status quo. The solution of the German question should be sought in association with the question of European security. A secession of united Germany from the Western alliance, is, however, not foreseen by the adherents of bipartisanship.

The informal bipartisan handling of the problems arising from Germany's partition, including the Berlin question, have undergone serious trials during the past few years. The difficulties which arose in the wake of the Berlin crisis and the attempts of the German Democratic Republic to improve its international status were mostly not interparty disputes but rather divergences within the Union parties and within the SPD.

The first formidable test for the fledgling bipartisanship was presented on August 13, 1961, when the Berlin Wall rose in the former German capital to divide its eastern and western halves. No initiative to take physical countermeasures was suggested by Chancellor Adenauer to the three protecting powers of West Berlin. It remains a matter for conjecture whether the absence of any such measures was the result of Bonn's passivity or of a lack of initiative by Washington—or both. Probably both Adenauer and President Kennedy (or Secretary of State Rusk, who discussed the matter over the telephone with the President in Hyannisport) decided independently to practice restraint in this matter.[68] The CDU/CSU leaders, with few exceptions, shared the Chancellor's reluctance to seek an Allied action which might have precipitated an even more serious crisis. This reluctance was tacitly approved by the SPD leadership.[69] But the SPD's Berlin organization, headed by Mayor Willy Brandt, urged active resistance of the rising Wall.[70] On August 16, Adenauer received Andrei A. Smirnov, the Soviet Ambassador, who conveyed Khrushchev's message to the Chancellor expressing hope that nothing would be done to aggravate the situation, an assurance gladly given.[71]

On August 18, Adenauer made a declaration before the Bundes-

[68] The story is told by Jean Edward Smith, *The Defense of Berlin* (Baltimore, 1963), pp. 265–66, 270–74; John W. Keller, *Germany: The Wall and Berlin* (New York, 1964), *passim*.
[69] Information given to this writer by an SPD leader.
[70] See Willy Brandt's letter to President Kennedy, dated August 16, 1961, which was to remain confidential but was, by some indiscretion, made public. Heinrich von Siegler, *Von der Gipfelkonferenz 1960 bis zur Berlinsperre 1961* (Bonn, 1961), pp. 103–4. The President's reply, handed personally by General Clay on September 19, 1961, was never published.
[71] *Ibid.*, p. 102.

tag which was in sharp contrast with a speech delivered by Willy Brandt on the same day before the same forum.[72] But the governing Mayor of Berlin received scant help from his Party colleagues. The situation was, nevertheless, believed to be critical in West Berlin. After the usual protest notes, it was realized, both in Washington and in Bonn, that certain limited (and belated) actions were needed to reassure the West's Berlin stronghold. Troop reinforcements, the lining up of American and British tanks along the Wall, and General Clay's and Vice-President Johnson's arrival in Berlin restored morale but could not affect the complete partition of the city. The bipartisan policy helped to bail out the Chancellor; and, during the election campaign prior to the September 17, 1961, elections, the SPD tactfully refrained from exploiting the governmental inaction in Berlin in its own favor. As noted earlier, the election results registered some public censure by reducing CDU/CSU parliamentary representation and increasing the votes for SPD candidates. The voters must have felt that the government had not been seriously concerned to prevent the erection of the Wall. Thanks to Willy Brandt's performance, the SPD was, undeservingly, credited with having proposed effective countermeasures. The Free Democrats (who had been rather critical of Adenauer's inaction) increased their voting strength considerably.

In April and May, 1962, during the delicate and often acrimonious exchanges between the United States and the Federal Republic on the "package deal" (an American plan for establishing an international authority to control the access routes to Berlin, augmented by a nonaggression commitment between East and West and bilateral East-West German committees), the SPD observed calm understanding. The American plan had caused a major dissension between the "hard" group of the CDU/CSU, led by former Foreign Minister von Brentano and the "flexibles" supporting Foreign Minister Schröder; the former were in strong opposition to the plan while Schröder was inclined to align himself with the United States in this matter. The Chancellor adopted a practical approach; he was confident anyhow that the Soviet government would reject the "package." He also relied on the French, who rejected it without much ado.

The "package deal" plan had become known through an "indiscretion" probably managed by Von Brentano [73] and had aroused

---

[72] *Ibid.*, pp. 107–10.
[73] J. E. Smith, *The Defense of Berlin*, p. 334.

indignation in the ruling SPD circles in Berlin. The treatment of the issue remained bipartisan, though, of course, there were adherents and opponents to be found in both the CDU/CSU and the SPD.

The Nuclear Test-Ban Treaty of August 5, 1963, gave rise to serious conflicts within the Union parties, coinciding with frictions that had emerged between the Berlin SPD organization and the CDU branch in that city.

The Treaty of Moscow provided for accession by any state signing it in one of the capitals of the three original signatory powers: the United States, Britain, and the Soviet Union. Under this accession clause the German Democratic Republic could enter this multilateral convention by signing it in Moscow. The draft treaty was known to the Federal Foreign Office but its attention had not been drawn, prior to the initialing of the Treaty, to the accession clause.

Both the governmental coalition parties and the SPD expressed discontent because of this precedent which, they thought, might be interpreted as an indirect or implicit recognition of the East German state. For a moment it seemed questionable that the Federal Republic would be willing to sign the Treaty. However, talks and exchanges between Washington and Bonn, and Bonn and London, led to official disclaimers on the part of the American and British governments that the accession in Moscow of the German Democratic Republic could be taken as recognition. The Bonn government also joined in this denial. But the action raised the prospect of other, more consequential, treaties, such as the suggested convention against surprise attack, which would provide for inspections on both sides of the Iron Curtain and would require adherence by the German Democratic Republic.

The interparty Berlin dispute arose as a result of speeches made by Willy Brandt and his press chief, Egon Bahr, before the Evangelical Academy in Tutzing (Bavaria) in July, 1963. The two addresses, especially Bahr's, contained hints for a limited rapprochement with the East German regime, suggesting an abandonment of the official nonrecognition policy.[74] The former Mayor and Chairman of the Berlin CDU, Franz Amrehn, published a scathing criticism of these speeches in the CDU's Party release,

[74] Brandt and Bahr relied on President Kennedy's "strategy of peace" motto and hinted that a more flexible policy could bring about a relaxed atmosphere conducive to eventual reunification. Bahr suggested the setting up of a special federal authority to handle the contacts between the two parts of Germany.

which was then taken up by the daily press. Amrehn wished to refute the argument that a material improvement of life in the German Democratic Republic would be conducive to relaxation; he wrote that the greatest suffering is not material but is caused by mental, moral, and political pressures. There was clearly a conflict between the humanitarian and the political approaches to reunification.

The gauntlet was then taken up by SPD Mayor Heinrich Albertz (after 1966 successor to Governing Mayor Brandt) in a memorial speech on the second anniversary of the Wall. Albertz reverted to the earlier SPD phraseology in calling the Federal Republic a "Confederation of the Rhine-State" and "a perfectionist state recently established between the Elbe and the Rhine." He asked for concrete German proposals to improve the "human situation" in the "Soviet Zone," unrestrained by the "provincial timidity" of Bonn in considering any contact with East Germany as an "upgrading" of the Democratic Republic.[75] This allocution elicited bitter polemics between CDU/CSU and SPD mouthpieces which almost heralded the end of bipartisanship on the question of German unity.[76]

The informal bipartisanship was, however, restored by the cooperative attitude of Schröder and by a conciliatory statement of SPD Vice-Chairman Herbert Wehner. The latter, in an interview which he gave to *Die Welt* on August 30, 1963, denied any intention of seeking an understanding with the East German regime. He brushed aside Bahr's suggestions as his (Bahr's) private opinions and admitted that Albertz' pronouncements were less than fortunate: "I would not have spoken of a Confederation of the Rhine-State, not even in the conditional mood." He said that the SPD had certain objections against the Berlin clause of the German-Polish Trade Agreement but that it did not wish to initiate a campaign on these grounds, especially because the Treaty had already been signed. He would not accuse the CDU/CSU of "softening tendencies" because of this event.[77]

It should be noted that earlier the Berlin SPD had held "harder" views than the Bonn Party Headquarters; after 1961, however, the attitude of the Berlin group had become significantly more "flexible" than that of the national Party leadership.

[75] Heinrich Albertz, *Frankfurter Allgemeine Zeitung*, August 14, 1963.
[76] See editorial ("Shortsighted Quarrels"), *ibid.*, August 31, 1963.
[77] *Die Welt*, August 31, 1963.

The violence of the reciprocal attacks abated and the accession of Ludwig Erhard to the office of Federal chancellor also contributed to the restoration of relative harmony between the two parties. Nevertheless, the opposition within the CDU/CSU of the "hard" and "Gaullist" factions against Schröder was occasionally channeled into attacks against SPD sympathy toward the ideas of the Foreign Minister. Thus, during the Bundestag debates on the ratification of the Test-Ban Treaty in January, 1964 (when the Treaty was called another "Munich" by some inflexibles), CSU Deputy Freiherr von Guttenberg reproached the SPD in words which could or should have been directed against Schröder.[78]

The Berlin border-pass question also threatened to divide both the CDU/CSU and the SPD internally. The division between adherents of a humanitarian-flexible approach to this question (e.g., the Berlin SPD) and the hard-line orthodox, who would refuse contacts with the representatives of East Germany, confronted Party leaders in both camps. The national SPD leadership disagreed in many respects with its Berlin organization, while the Berlin CDU supported the "hard" line represented by several factions in Bonn.[79] The Bavarian CSU, on the other hand, while being inflexible in many respects did not, generally, oppose "inofficial" contacts with the East for humanitarian reasons. Eventually, cooperation between Chancellor Erhard and Governing Mayor Willy Brandt rendered a bipartisan treatment of this question possible.

In order to secure the best results from bipartisan collaboration, Foreign Minister Schröder succeeded in establishing a system of consultation with the SPD leaders. He has regularly sought the opinion of the opposition Party's foreign policy experts, Herbert Wehner and Fritz Erler.[80] Furthermore, SPD specialists have fre-

---

[78] Already in September, 1963, it had been noticed that Schröder, in his approval of the Moscow Treaty, mustered heartier support from the SPD than from members of his own Party. See *Frankfurter Allgemeine Zeitung*, September 4, 1963.

[79] Willy Brandt's speech before the Foreign Policy Association in New York on May 15, 1964, almost gave rise to a suspicion that Brandt harbors "Gaullist" sympathies when he stated that De Gaulle, with audacity and resoluteness, "is thinking the unthinkable." "The balance of terror provides the opportunity to set rigid positions into motion. The French President takes advantage of this in his own way. Sometimes I ask myself as a German: why should he be the only one?" *New York Times*, May 20 and 25, 1964.

[80] The collaboration began when Foreign Minister Schröder consulted SPD leader Herbert Wehner on a diplomatic note sent to Moscow in February, 1962, suggesting that the Federal government would be prepared to discuss many questions if the Kremlin would not insist on a two-Germanys concept. *Christ und Welt*, January 21, 1966.

quently collaborated with members of the German Foreign Office. Such co-operation has become possible partly because of the change of the SPD's attitude, partly because of the more "mobile" policy of the Foreign Minister. But such a concurrence of views between the Foreign Minister and the opposition party has not facilitated Schröder's task of consultation with elements of his own Party.

The political chasm which almost since the beginning of the Federal Republic had divided the majority party from its main opposition was closed by the adherence of the SPD to the basic tenets of the government's reunification policy and definition of the role which the West German state should play in the restoration of German unity. Additionally, the participation of the Federal Republic in the Western defense system was also fully approved. Thereby, all major foreign policy differences were eliminated.

This loose co-operation, however, failed to satisfy the SPD. They suggested several forms of permanent consultation with the governing parties on questions of foreign policy, or the *Deutschlandpolitik*, in particular. The elimination of substantive policy differences opened the chance that even a coalition between the CDU/CSU and the SPD, with or without the FDP, might be contemplated.[81] When the question of "exchange of speakers" between the SPD and the SED, the Communist party of East Germany, came up in the spring of 1966, the need for joint decision prompted Chancellor Erhard to convoke the first "Germany discussion" on April 21, 1966, with the participation of the three parliamentary parties of the Federal Republic.

In March, 1966, the Central Committee of the SED sent an "Open Letter to the Delegates of the Dortmund Party Conference" of the SPD, signed by Walter Ulbricht, in his capacity as first secretary of the Communist party of East Germany, inviting the West German Social Democrats to join in a conference to promote better understanding and to prepare joint action against "the Bonn revanchists and imperialists."[82]

The SPD replied with another "Open Letter" in which it emphasized its loyalty to the text and principles of the Basic Law and questioned whether useful talks could be conducted with the ruling

[81] Talks concerning the inclusion of the SPD in the Government were conducted after the *Der Spiegel* crisis, which endangered the then-existing coalition between the CDU/CSU and the FDP, in December, 1962. The question of a Grand Coalition was again discussed after the 1965 elections. Federal President Heinrich Lübke is known to have favored such a cabinet; *Süddeutsche Zeitung*, January 17, 1966.

[82] See *East Europe*, May, 1966, p. 6.

party of East Germany as long as Germans were prevented by walls, minefields, and barbed wire from visiting each other and while those who tried to cross the border were being shot under the orders of the Communist government. The SPD was ready to discuss the problems of Germany but only under certain conditions. The correspondence, however, continued, and the suggestion that leaders of both parties should hold joint meetings on both sides of the demarcation line was accepted. The first public discussions were to be held in Karl-Marx Stadt in East Germany and, subsequently, in Hanover in the Federal Republic. SPD Chairman Brandt, together with the Vice-Chairmen, Erler and Wehner, were to participate in these meetings, which were to be given full publicity on both sides of the Iron Curtain.[83]

The SPD was acting in agreement with the government when it accepted the suggestion to embark on this venture; it did so partly in loyalty to the bipartisan policy and partly because it suspected that the real purpose of Ulbricht was to drive a wedge between the Social Democrats and the government of the Federal Republic. Erhard stipulated only that no high government official should take part in the discussions with the SED and that these contacts were not to affect the accepted basic position on the German question. The interparty conference also gave its blessing to the SPD's affair with the SED.[84] In the CDU/CSU some of the "hard-liners" criticized the project; others again wished to take further initiatives so as to prevent the SPD from reaping alone the fruits of their action: the ending of a deadlock in the *Deutschlandpolitik*.[85]

The exchange of speakers could not have been arranged without the consent of Bonn because the entry of SED leaders raised points of criminal law: these leaders were considered responsible for the shootings along the border and, as German nationals under the prevailing doctrine, could be arrested and sentenced according to the criminal code. Special amnesties were needed to secure their safety

[83] *New York Times*, April 16, 1966.

[84] *Ibid.*, April 22, 1966. The conference agreed on the following points: political meetings "with individuals or groups from the Soviet Zone" must be oriented by the aim of Germany's unification; they should not serve to enhance the established power system in East Germany; and humanitarian concessions must be demanded for the inhabitants of that part of Germany. *The Bulletin* (weekly survey issued by the Press Office of Bonn), April 26, 1966.

[85] Rainer Barzel, deputy charman of the CDU/CSU, made efforts to catch up with the SPD by submitting a number of concrete proposals during his visit to the United States in June, 1966. *New York Times*, June 16, 1966; see Chapter III, p. 121.

from prosecution.[86] The Temporary Immunity Act passed by the Bundestag subsequently served as a pretext for Ulbricht to call off the exchange of speakers.

Until mid-1966, the bipartisan line on the *Deutschlandpolitik*, despite intraparty cleavages, operated reasonably well. It was not even sorely tested in the election campaign preceding the 1965 Federal elections. However, the fissures within the CDU/CSU— centering mainly around the reunification policy issue, various initiatives taken by the SPD, and ensuing acrimonous polemics— created a political malaise which threatened, by the summer of 1966, to end all collaboration.

A series of humiliating reverses which Erhard sustained after leading his Party to victory in 1965 shook his coalition cabinet some ten months later. The partnership with the Free Democrats, always cumbersome for Adenauer, proved to be fateful for the second Federal Chancellor. The internal splits within the FDP on the reunification issue have often been embarrassing in the past to those who tried to collaborate with them.

The FDP and the Reunification

The Free Democratic party has always been a divided party—on practically all issues. It included so-called southern liberals, mainly from Baden-Württemberg, who had been inspired by the ideas of the Frankfurt Parliament of 1848; economic liberals of the Manchester school; and all shades of nationalists of the Weimar era. The question of German unity was probably the only theme on which all Party factions concurred in demanding a more active achievement policy. But the leaders of the FDP hardly ever saw eye-to-eye on how this unification policy was to be implemented, and many of them changed their opinions over time.

In 1949, at the first Bundestag elections, the FDP obtained fifty-two seats. The CDU/CSU, with a mere plurality of 139 seats, had to seek coalition partners. Adenauer invited the FDP into his cabinet, and the SPD with its 131 seats was forced into opposition. But the Free Democrats proved to be difficult partners. There were, especially, two areas in which the FDP opposed governmental policy: social legislation and the West European involvement. The latter was considered by the FDP, and by the SPD, as delaying or blocking reunification.

At the 1953 elections the CDU/CSU increased its Bundestag

[86] *Ibid.*, May 11, 1966.

representation to 243 (and the SPD, to 151), mainly to the detriment of smaller parties. But Adenauer was still compelled to rely on the 48 FDP deputies for a controlling majority in the assembly. But this time the Chancellor refused to recall to his cabinet the most recalcitrant FDP leader, former Minister of Justice Thomas Dehler. Thereafter, the FDP was already half way in opposition, though it had some ministers serving in the government. Dehler had been elected chairman of the Party. In February, 1956, the FDP overthrew the CDU-led state government of North Rhine-Westphalia by joining the SPD opposition. The Party then split; sixteen deputies joined the CDU/CSU while the rest went, also on the federal level, into opposition.

The FDP had always been critical of the Chancellor's Germany policy; it is to be remembered that one of the Party's deputies, Karl Georg Pfleiderer, had presented reunification projects of his own back in 1952.[87] In 1953 the election slogan of the Party had been "First Germany, then Europe."[88] Although this emphasis on nationalism and German unity strengthened the cohesion of the FDP, its views on internal politics were hopelessly split between a socially minded group (the so-called "Young Turks") and the irreconcilable bourgeois liberals who, for example, had announced that they would do away with the "social achievements" in East Germany when the day of unification arrived. The 1957 elections reduced the number of FDP deputies in the Bundestag to forty-one.

During the full third term of the legislature the FDP remained in opposition. Their main topic of criticism against the government was Adenauer's abortive reunification policy. The Soviet attempts to obtain control over West Berlin and, finally, the erection of the Berlin Wall, gave them ample material for chiding the Chancellor. Their suggested policies were, however, neither uniform nor consistent, nor even realistic. Thomas Dehler was succeeded in the chairmanship of the Party by Reinhold Maier in January, 1957; in 1960 he was replaced by Erich Mende, one of the "Young Turks." Mende, once a fervent supporter of "East-West talks" (in 1956 he participated in discussions with leaders of the East German bogus Liberal Democratic party in Weimar and was severely attacked for it at that time), in 1960 still advocated such contacts together with

[87] See above, p. 30.
[88] Alfred Grosser, *Die Bonner Demokratie* (Düsseldorf, 1960), p. 160.

the neutralization of a united Germany and the complete restoraion of the 1937 frontiers.[89]

The Free Democrats, possibly under the impact of the Berlin Wall, were able to increase their Bundestag representation to sixty-seven at the 1961 elections. The CDU/CSU was now compelled again to look for coalition partners. The FDP, after considerable hesitation and against the views of many of its influential members, agreed to participate again in the Adenauer government. The alternative could only have been an alliance between the SPD and the FDP; Mende had, in fact, pursued conversations to this effect with the Social Democratic leaders. But the influence of big industry, which had financed FDP's election campaign, led the Party to help Adenauer once again. Among the conditions which the FDP stipulated as a price for its collaboration were a more active reunification policy, including a plan to ask the three Western powers to open negotiations with the Russians, and even direct talks eventually between the Federal Republic and Moscow. Mende himself refrained from joining the new cabinet.

Shortly after the formation of the new Adenauer government, a Soviet memorandum of December 27, 1961, was presented to the Federal government. This long document, couched in carefully worded ambiguities, addressed flatteries to German talent and industry, alluded to the usefulness of past co-operation, and expressed hopes for similar collaboration in the future. It described in glittering colors the possibilities of Soviet-German reciprocal trade and, without giving up the Soviet theses on East Germany and Berlin, suggested direct talks on the Berlin issue between Bonn and Moscow.[90]

The Soviet memorandum caused a major shock in the coalition. The Free Democrats first suggested that the time had now come for Adenauer to live up to his commitment and agree to a bilateral talk with the Soviet Union. But the Chancellor refused; he was skeptical, as before, of Soviet sincerity. He had been trying hard, ever since the abortive outcome of the 1959 Geneva Conference, to

[89] See *Gibt es noch Wege zur Wiedervereinigung?* (Bonn, 1960), pp. 52–57, a symposium with such contributors as CDU Deputy Gradl, SPD Deputy Mommer, FDP Chairman Mende, and Herbert Schneider, leader of the German party (*Deutsche Partei*) a splinter party which supported the government.

[90] *Bulletin* of the Press and Information Office of the German Federal Government, January 10, 1962.

persuade the United States to restrict its "exploratory talks" (conducted alternatively in Moscow and in Washington) to the technical aspects of the Berlin question and not to undertake meaningful negotiations on the East-West German problem as long as the Soviets insisted on the participation of the German Democratic Republic. He foresaw that if the bilateral talks were not limited to the Berlin question on which, in his view, the Western Allies, and not the Federal government, were primarily competent to negotiate, they would lead to a discussion of the German question which, under the terms of the Soviet memorandum, could result only in an "upgrading" or even recognition of the East German regime. And even if these bilateral negotiations were conducted with close consultation, they would expose the Federal government to Soviet pressures or evoke sinister memories of Rapallo and the Hitler-Stalin Pact in the minds of Western leaders.[91]

Eventually, the Chancellor's arguments partly satisfied Erich Mende, though not the popular leader of the Party, Thomas Dehler. On February 21, 1962, the Federal government replied with another lengthy memorandum explaining the German point of view. It claimed to share the Soviet view that a genuine reconciliation of the two countries would banish the danger of war in Europe. But it also stated: "German-Soviet relations can only be normalized if the situation of the German people is normalized. What is abnormal is the division of the German people, what is especially abnormal are the conditions in the so-called German Democratic Republic and just as abnormal is the wall in Berlin. These are the problems that must be solved if we are to improve German-Soviet relations."[92]

Thus, the West German memorandum did not deny the usefulness of bilateral talks but suggested preliminary exchanges of view on the basis of the principles laid down in the text. This response to the Soviet initiative was, after some argument, accepted by Erich Mende, but not without "extensive soul-searching" in the FDP. Mende followed the Social Democratic example by admitting that many of his Party's earlier ideas on reunification had become "outdated."[93]

This event demonstrates the existing split within the ranks of the

[92] *Bulletin* of the Press and Information Office of the German Federal Government, February 23, 1962.
[91] *New York Times*, February 18, 1962.
[93] *New York Times*, March 13, 1962.

Free Democrats over the *Deutschlandpolitik*. After the dispatch of the German memorandum, Thomas Dehler, then Vice-President of the Bundestag, did not hesitate to accuse the CDU/CSU of having violated the coalition agreement. The bipartisanship between the Union parties and the SPD on the policy for reunification had not made the FDP's task easier: before the Social Democratic change-over they professed to stand on the reunification issue, as well as on other issues, midway between the views of the other two major parties. For instance, Reinhold Maier, then chairman of the FDP, stated on behalf of his Party in October, 1958, that they would never adhere to the CDU priority of the integration of "Little Europe" over Germany's reunification, nor would they adhere to the tendencies within the SPD to place the policy for reunification above the quest for the unity of Europe as a whole.[94] The FDP was always unable to convert the coalition and the government to the views held by its more nationalist and less pro-Western wing. With a basic understanding existing between the Union parties and the SPD, the FDP could hope even less to have its weight felt on the question of German unity.

The divergence of views on the *Deutschlandpolitik* between different factions of the FDP is considerably deeper than within either the CDU/CSU or the SPD. In fact, some of the FDP's internal conflicts are insurmountable. For instance, a member of the rightist wing of the Free Democrats, Bundestag Deputy Ernst Achenbach, who has a Nazi past and was involved in the Naumann Plot of 1953,[95] persuaded the Foreign Policy Preparatory Committee of his Party to submit a proposal to the Party Congress to be held in Munich in the summer of 1963 inviting the four former occupation powers to convoke, without delay, a new conference on Germany with the participation of "both parts of Germany," of Poland, and Czechoslovakia.[96]

Thomas Dehler, a Bavarian liberal with commendable record during the Nazi era, always opposed Adenauer's concept of an automatic reunification. He never credited the Chancellor with genuinely wanting reunification and considered integration of West Germany into the European Economic Community and the Atlan-

[94] Grosser, *Die Bonner Demokratie*, p. 364.
[95] About the Naumann Plot which involved the arrest of former Nazi leaders, headed by Werner Naumann, Secretary of State in Goebbels' Propaganda Ministry, see Horne, *Return to Power*, pp. 160–82.
[96] See *Christ und Welt* (Stuttgart), July 5, 1963, where Achenbach's conduct is strongly criticized.

tic alliance as measures blocking the path to German unity. He denied that Adenauer, or the Western powers acting on the Chancellor's advice, had ever seriously tried to come to grips with the Soviets in negotiating the German question. The policy of strength was an error; and the more the Federal Republic became entangled in European and Atlantic commitments, the more difficult it would be to satisfy Soviet demands in return for German unification. Dehler favored direct West German-Soviet talks which could discover the real Soviet price for reunification.[97] Thomas Dehler visited the Soviet Union in September, 1963, and had conversations with Khrushchev and Foreign Minister Gromyko. He was told that he had been right in considering the establishment of the Federal Republic as having prevented unification of his country. But since this mistake had been committed, the fact of two (or three, when including West Berlin) Germanys had to be recognized and reunification had to be negotiated between them. Germany's division was a result of the lost war and of Bonn's mistaken policy. Despite this frustrating insight into Soviet political thinking, Dehler continued to advocate direct German-Soviet conversations.[98]

When, after Adenauer's retirement, Ludwig Erhard formed his cabinet on October 17, 1963, the coalition between the CDU/CSU and the FDP was renewed. Five FDP members entered the new government, including this time Erich Mende, the Party chairman. He became not only the Vice-Chancellor but also Minister of All-German Affairs in recognition of the special interest of the junior coalition partner in matters of German unity.

The FDP's electoral success in 1961 proved to be temporary; when the Germans went to the polls in 1965, the FDP could muster only 9.5 per cent of the votes as against 12.8 per cent in 1961. Nevertheless, its participation in the coalition cabinet continued and so did the feud between Erich Mende and many of the CDU/CSU leaders, especially Franz Josef Strauss. On the whole, Mende and his faction within the Free Democrats wished to give a much more liberal interpretation to West Germany's principal position with regard to the reunification issue. Thus, the Vice-Chancellor would have preferred that the Bonn government negotiate the border pass agreement with East Germany, instead of leaving this matter, to save the principle of nonrecognition, to the Berlin Senate.[99] Mende

[97] See Dehler's statement in *Die Welt*, June 15, 1963.
[98] *The German Tribune*, September 21, 1963.
[99] *Süddeutsche Zeitung*, November 24, 1965.

and his group urged the opening of "contacts," "talks," or "colloquies" with the German Democratic government "on all levels," which they refused to consider "negotiations" for fear of implying recognition of the regime. Such moves were much against the taste of even the "soft" ones in the CDU/CSU. Strangely enough, Mende managed to combine his "flexibility" with certain rigid, highly conservative views, such as his insistence on the continued legal existence of the German Reich.[100] He saw no inconsistency in declaring, on the one hand, that the Hallstein Doctrine was obsolete, but demanding, on the other, the "sole right of representation" of Germany for the Federal Republic. He also pointed out that one day it might be possible for the Federal government "to confer"—if not negotiate—with the East German regime provided that such talks were conducted at the behest of the four former occupation powers of Germany.[101]

In the spring of 1966 the FDP was eager to take advantage of the possibilities of a "German dialogue." Even before the SPD was ready to accept a conference with the SED, the FDP Vice-Chairman, Wolfgang Mischnik, took part, for the first time since the division of Germany, in a televised discussion with the leaders of its splinter-branch in the German Democratic Republic, the so-called Liberal Democratic party.[102] The FDP has also sponsored, since 1959, the establishment of mixed commissions between East and West German officials—at all levels.[103]

Whether the initiatives of the FDP, as an opposition party, will result in a more active *Deutschlandpolitik*, including direct talks with the Soviets, and whether such talks will be more productive than Thomas Dehler's experience in Moscow must remain a matter of conjecture. Any movement along the congealed front of reunification may be fruitfully exploited by the Free Democrats because their members have submitted so many plans in the past: the authorship of any of these projects, if revived and adopted, could be claimed by the junior coalition party or one of its factions.

Probably to establish for itself greater maneuverability on the German issue, the Free Democratic party withdrew its ministers from the Erhard cabinet on October 27, 1966, and, once more, ended the coalition with the CDU/CSU. The official reason given

[100] See Mende's speech of March 12, 1966, over RIAS (Radio in the American sector of Berlin).
[101] *Frankfurter Allgemeine Zeitung*, April 5, 1966; *Die Welt*, April 5, 1966.
[102] *Süddeutsche Zeitung*, April 2, 1966.
[103] *New York Times*, June 16, 1966.

for this withdrawal was opposition to the Chancellor's fiscal policy measures; but, as in almost every political question of the Federal Republic, it was the German problem which loomed over the secession of the Free Democrats, a step which two weeks later led to the resignation of the Chancellor and his cabinet.

After Erhard—The Grand Coalition

Among the various factors and events which caused the eclipse of Chancellor Erhard, his reluctance or inability to launch meaningful initiatives for the promotion of German unity played an outstanding role. Adenauer, with his reputation as an architect of new Germany, was able to survive, at least for a number of years, without mustering any step forward toward the unification of his country. But Erhard, the contriver of West Germany's "economic miracle," whose prestige had already been undermined before his accession to the chancellorship, was unable to refute the long-standing doubts as to his political skills. Eventually, he proved unsuccessful even in the field of finance by running into difficulties about a budget deficit and about offset payments for the maintenance of United States and British forces in Germany. The elections in the *Land* of North Rhine-Westphalia in July and those in Hesse in November, 1966, favored the Social Democrats. These votes may also have reflected an increased popularity which the SPD has gained by their adroit exploitation of the cause of German unity.[104]

For the solution of the West German governmental crisis in November, 1966, different alternatives were available: the former partnership between the CDU/CSU and the FDP but under a new chancellor could be re-established; the much-heralded "Grand Coalition" between the CDU/CSU and the SPD could be set up; and, finally, for the first time in the eighteen years' existence of the Federal Republic, the CDU/CSU could be unseated from its governmental position if a coalition between the SPD and the FDP could be forged. Such a partnership would only dispose of a thin six-vote majority in the Bundestag which, in view of the lax disci-

---

[104] In October, 1966, Herbert Wehner, deputy chairman of the SPD, suggested in an interview the setting up of an "economic community" between West and East Germany, a project strongly repudiated by Erhard and most of the CDU/CSU deputies; *New York Times*, October 13 and 14, 1966. Earlier, Helmut Schmidt, another SPD leader, had proposed the establishment of diplomatic relations with Czechoslovakia and Rumania; *New York Times*, August 16, 1966. It is not known whether these two proposals were fully supported by the SPD leadership.

pline prevailing in the ranks of the Free Democrats, seemed insufficient. Of course, if the fifteen Social Democrat deputies from Berlin were able to vote, the majority of the SPD-FDP combination would be impressive. But under the reservations of the three Western military governors which saddled the Basic Law at the time of its acceptance by the Parliamentary Council the deputies from Berlin were not entitled to vote (except on procedural questions, as developed by practice). Thus, the status of Berlin impinged on the developments of West German internal politics.[105]

The cause of the governmental crisis was, partly, a personal one: the majority of the CDU/CSU leadership, beset by dissensions mostly relative to the handling of the reunification issue, decided to select another chancellor. Erhard was not again to head the new cabinet also because the FDP refused to accept his leadership. But as soon as Erhard declared his readiness to withdraw, the importance of a future political program, to be agreed upon by the parties which would form a new governmental coalition, came into prominence. In the course of the discussions over Erhard's heritage, the SPD and FDP were able to crystallize some of their basic positions. The Social Democrats made it clear that their participation in either the Grand Coalition with the CDU/CSU or in a "small coalition" with the FDP would be conditional on the acceptance of certain foreign policy positions such as a clarification of the Federal Republic's relations with both Washington and Paris, the renunciation of any West German nuclear sharing in NATO, "normalization" of West Germany's relations with her "East European neighbors," the promotion of some forms of "organized coexistence" with the German Democratic Republic, and a clear attitude on problems concerning Berlin.[106]

As far as the FDP was concerned, its Chairman, Erich Mende, already as Vice-Chancellor and Minister of All-German Affairs in the Erhard cabinet, had proposed the establishment of full diplomatic contacts with the East European countries, going beyond the respective plans of the Social Democrats. Now his Party advocated a policy "more in keeping with the sober facts of the East-West sit-

---

[105] Brandt asserted that the reservations on voting rights of the Berlin deputies had long since been eroded; *New York Times,* November 15, 1966. The stature of the Mayor of Berlin had grown since he was invited for a discussion by Pyotr A. Abrasimov, Soviet Ambassador to East Germany; *New York Times,* October 22 and 23, 1966.

[106] See the eight-point program of the SPD submitted on November 13, 1966, to both the CDU/CSU and the FDP; *The Bulletin,* November 15, 1966.

uation" making an end to "all dreams and illusions." Hans-Dietrich Genscher, chairman of the FDP parliamentary group, declared: "The German Problem cannot be solved without the cooperation of the German Communists."[107]

On all these issues the CDU/CSU continued to present a wide spectrum of opinions: while Erhard and Schröder appeared to be in favor of establishing diplomatic relations with Rumania, and later with other East European countries, Franz Josef Strauss, the leader of the CSU, opposed such moves. While Rainer Barzel deprecated "patent solutions and ideological prejudice," the "hard liners" of the Party rejected "hazardous" ideas suggested by the SPD and FDP, and by some "impatient soft liners" of their own Party.[108]

On November 10, the CDU/CSU parliamentary group elected Kurt Georg Kiesinger, Minister-President of the *Land* Baden-Wurttemberg to become Federal Chancellor provided that he proved able to form a government which would receive a majority vote in the Bundestag. Kiesinger was chosen in preference over Foreign Minister Schröder and Deputy Party-Chairman Barzel. It appeared that Franz Josef Strauss and the votes of his Bavarian group helped Kiesinger, another Catholic and South German, to defeat his rivals.[109] Kiesinger's first pronouncements showed him a middle-line politician who supported both Franco-German friendship and cordial ties with Washington, who advocated the avoidance of "labels that are divorced from reality"—meaning "Atlanticist, European or Gaullist" approaches to foreign policy—and of "sterile and artificial dilemmas" (whether relaxation or progress toward German unity should come first), and for the advancement to reunification suggested "fewer Sunday speeches and more work-day politics."[110]

The governmental crisis continued until after the elections in Bavaria on November 20, 1966. The Bavarian poll strengthened both the CSU and the SPD, and secured continued leadership to the former. The loser was the FDP whose vote was reduced below the statutory minimum which left this Party with no seats. On the other hand, the right-wing National Democratic party (see later) gained 7.4 percent of the votes and 15 seats of 204 in the Bavarian diet.[111]

[107] *The German Tribune*, November 12, 1966.
[108] *Ibid.*
[109] *New York Times*, November 11, 1966; see also C. L. Sulzberger, "The Kingmaker of Munich," in *New York Times*, November 13, 1966.
[110] *The German Tribune*, November 12, 1966.
[111] *The Bulletin*, November 28, 1966.

To end the interregnum, the SPD negotiated both with the FDP and the CDU/CSU. The Chancellor-elect negotiated but unsuccessfully with the Free Democrats for the re-establishment of the former coalition. The final decision rested with the SPD: it would have been easier for that party to reach an agreement with the FDP on questions of foreign policy and the reunification issue than with the other major party. But the Social Democrat leaders resisted the temptation of gaining the chancellorship with the support of a volatile coalition partner and a slim, uncertain majority in the Bundestag. They would have preferred new general elections, but these were opposed by the CDU/CSU. The negotiations, in view of the existing divergencies both between the two major parties, and within their own ranks, could not establish a common platform concerning the reunification issue except on most general and vague terms.

The Federal government announced on December 1, 1966, and approved by the Bundestag, included Kurt Georg Kiesinger as Federal Chancellor and Franz Josef Strauss as Minister of Finance. Schröder was moved to the post of a Minister of Defense; Kai-Uwe von Hassel, the former Defense Minister became Minister of Refugee Affairs. The SPD provided the Vice Chancellor in the person of Willy Brandt (he resigned as Governing Mayor of Berlin) who also became the Minister of Foreign Affairs. Herbert Wehner had become the Minister of All-German Affairs, and Gustav Heinemann returned to the cabinet as Minister of Justice. It was a cabinet of strong personalities and one of divergent views, particularly on the issue of German unity.[112]

The program of the Grand Coalition was submitted to parliament by Chancellor Kiesinger on December 13. He said nothing on the German question which would have conflicted with the Basic Law or the accepted doctrine; however, on certain points, he stretched the limits of the official doctrine as wide as compatible with the generally approved principles of Germany's international status. He pleaded reconciliation with Poland but stopped short of recognizing the Oder-Neisse Line and insisted that the boundaries of a reunified Germany can be laid down only in an agreement concluded freely with an all-German government. He offered the hand of friendship to the East European governments and hinted that

---

[112] *New York Times*, December 2, 1966. Heinrich Krone, a rigid "hard-liner" was dropped from the cabinet.

even diplomatic relations could be set up with them "whenever the circumstances allow" such a move. He rejected recognition of the East German regime but advocated expanded contacts across the zonal border.[113]

The new foreign policy lines of the Grand Coalition may thus be characterized: (1) General De Gaulle's priority of order, namely, "détente, entente, cooperation," seems to have been accepted; accordingly, relaxation may be sought even before reunification; (2) diplomatic relations, if no conditions are attached, may be established with East European states which, like the Soviet Union, gave recognition to the D.D.R. when West Germany became a sovereign state; their diplomatic ties with East Berlin will thus, "on a pragmatic basis," be overlooked while legal standpoints will mutually be upheld; (3) relations with East Germany in the fields of cultural, economic, and political life are to be improved but without abandoning the legal point of view; the Federal Republic is not to recognize, as either a foreign country or a legitimate state, the "other part of Germany."

The Grand Coalition was not intended by either of its participants to remain a permanent feature of West German politics; it is to end, if not earlier, before the next federal elections in 1969. The SPD, after a waiting period of eighteen years, was at last able to share in governmental responsibilities. It appears quite clear that without the adoption of the Godesberg Program such a participation would have been impossible. No Grand Coalition could have been forged with a Social Democratic party which was not in basic agreement with the official *Deutschlandpolitik*, even if its own interpretation differed in many respects from the former Adenauer-line, and even from the Erhard-Schröder line.

Although no detailed understanding could be reached between the two coalition partners of the Grand Coalition on how to promote reunification, an abandonment of all doctrinaire rigidity be-

---

[113] *New York Times*, December 14, 1966. Kiesinger's speech contained such important passages: "The present Federal government, too, considers itself the only German government to have been freely, lawfully and democratically elected and therefore entitled to speak for all Germans. . . . We wish to do our utmost to prevent the two parts of our nation from drifting apart. . . . That is why we wish to do all we can to encourage human, economic and cultural relations with our countrymen in the other part of Germany. Where this requires the establishment of contacts between authorities of the Federal Republic and of those in the other part of Germany it does not imply recognition of a second German state. We shall treat each case on its merits and in such a way that world public opinion cannot gain the impression that we are abandoning our legal standpoint." *The Bulletin*, December 20, 1966.

came part of the working-plan of the new cabinet. No Federal government had earlier enjoyed such a wide support, a quasi-unanimous support, in the Bundestag. Such a "strong" government, backed by the joint responsibility of the two major parties, appeared to be in the position of making "sacrifices" or agreeing to "concessions" on the reunification issue which either of the two major parties might not have dared to approve. But such a way of acting would presuppose a much greater homogeneity in outlook and intention than the Kiesinger-Brandt cabinet possesses. No doubt, this government could act with greater flexibility than its predecessor; even so, every measure which would appear as a deviation from accepted practices, would have to run the gauntlet between the opposing attitudes of Brandt and Strauss, of those of Wehner and Schröder, and the rest of the "hard-" and "soft-liners" both in the CDU/CSU and the SPD.

Furthermore, should a most liberal interpretation and application of accepted principles in the pursuance of the *Deutschlandpolitik* fail to accomplish at least some tangible gains toward German unity, a reaction on the part of "hard-liners" and "patient-ones" seems unavoidable. The demand for a return to the erstwhile rigid and inflexible policy lines is bound to follow. In any case, even a most imaginative and elastic *Deutschlandpolitik* cannot jettison certain essential ideas of Germany's status without betraying the very *raison d'être* of the Federal Republic. And a policy of unprincipled concessions, instead of promoting German unity, will find itself having sanctioned and hardened the division of Germany.

The Splinter Parties and Reunification

The FDP was the only smaller political party which, ground between the two major parties, was able to maintain itself and play a political role. Its relative resilience resulted from the popularity of the ideas it professed to represent and from the diverse personalities who stood for the Party. The other smaller or splinter parties did not present anything of persisting value to the electorate, nor did they possess strong leadership. After the experiences of nazism and communism, the radical extremism of some of the small parties was simply not to the taste of the masses. Even vociferous nationalism had, at least for the time being, ceased to attract a larger number of people.

Among the short-lived parties of the radical right, the Deutsche Rechtspartei (German Right party) was soon succeeded by the neo-Nazi Socialist Reich party. This party was declared unconstitutional by the Federal Constitutional Court in 1952. It was replaced by the Deutsche Reichspartei (German Reich party) which, however, proved unable to obtain sufficient votes to be represented in the Bundestag and later even failed to gain seats in *Land* parliaments. Even so, it continued to remain vocal by publishing newspapers and pamphlets which have limited circulation but still retain a number of obstinate devotees.[114]

The extreme right represents different shades of opinion on the question of German unity. The neo-Nazis insist that the re-establishment of the German Reich within her prewar boundaries is the only solution acceptable to the German people and the only one which can secure European peace. They are generally vague as to whether they include Austria or the Sudetenland in their schemes. For them, the reunification of East Germany with the Federal Republic would be only a partial solution, and they seem to be more interested in their highly unrealistic dreams for a "Greater Germany" than in "petty" questions of limited territorial scope. At least some of their leaders and organizations appear to have received financial support from the German Democratic Republic.[115]

A clearly neutralist policy is advocated by a group which, since 1956, has published the weekly *Neue Politik*. It refuses all co-operation with the West, supports a leaning toward the East and represents the nearest approach to national bolshevism.

The recently most successful rightist organization, successor to many small groups, including the German Reich party, is the National Democratic party which polled 2 per cent in the Federal elections of 1965. The partition of Germany is being propagandistically exploited by this party and used to inflame hatred against the former wartime enemies of Germany. The Party's reunification program, as announced by its leader, Adolf von Thadden, is not

---

[114] The weekly paper of the Deutsche Reichspartei is *Reichsruf* published in Hanover. Another rightist paper is the consolidated *Deutsche Nationalzeitung und Soldatenzeitung*. See Otto Büsch and Peter Furth, *Rechtsradikalismus im Nachkriegsdeutschland* (Berlin and Frankfurt/M., 1957).

[115] See Manfred Jenke, *Verschwörung von Rechts? Ein Bericht über den Rechtsradikalismus in Deutschland nach 1945* (Berlin, 1961), pp. 79-83, 94-95. The basic theory of the neo-Nazis is the denial of "legitimacy" of both the Federal Republic and the German Democratic Republic; according to them, none of these "satellite" states can be considered the successor of the Third Reich. See also Hans-Helmuth Knütter, *Ideologien des Rechtsradikalismus in Nachkriegsdeutschland* (Bonn, 1961), *passim*.

inhibited by doctrinal views; he said that he would negotiate with Moscow, with Walter Ulbricht, "without waiting for permission from the United States." Relying too heavily on the West was a mistake which should be corrected.[116]

The Refugee party, representing primarily the interests of expellees and refugees (some ten million people unevenly dispersed over the area of the Federal Republic), obtained a considerable number of seats in the *Land* parliaments where refugees were to be found in abundance (mainly Schleswig-Holstein, Lower Saxony, and Bavaria). In 1951 they formed a party on the federal level and gained twenty-seven seats at the 1953 Bundestag elections. They then entered into a coalition with the CDU/CSU and were, at one time, represented by two ministers in the cabinet.[117] In addition to concern for the welfare of the groups they represented, they professed enhanced interest in the reunification of Germany, including the Eastern Territories (where most of their constituents had come from). With the assimilation of most of the expellees and refugees into the main body of the West German population, the original success of the Party receded.[118] At the 1957 elections, the votes cast for the Refugee party could not even secure them one seat in the Bundestag. Refugees and expellees, nevertheless, individually or collectively through their various organizations, carry considerable weight within other political parties.

The Deutsche Partei (German party) stemmed from a particularistic Hanoverian background and had its roots almost exclusively in the Protestant Northwest. It is a conservative group advocating constitutional monarchism. The German party (DP) consistently maintained closed regional contacts with the CDU/CSU and supported Adenauer's European policy. Although strongly in favor of political reunification and German unity, it abhors any entangle-

---

[116] *The Bulletin*, March 15, 1966; *New York Times*, May 26, 1966; James Cameron, "A Shadow No Larger Than a Crooked Cross," *New York Times Magazine*, September 11, 1966. The National Democratic party attracted popular support in some regions and polled up to 6–7 per cent in state elections, notably in Hesse and Bavaria in November, 1966; *New York Times*, November 8 and 12, 1966.

[117] Hiscocks, *Democracy in Germany*, pp. 102–6.

[118] In 1950 they adopted the name Block der Heimatvertriebenen und Entrechteten (Union of Expellees and Dispossessed) wishing to represent also the interests of ex-Nazis who had been deprived of some of their rights. It was this circumstance which gave the Party a rightist tinge. In 1955 the words Gesamtdeutscher Block (All-German Union) were to precede the Party's name.

ments with East German politicians and wishes to avoid risks which would endanger the present status of West Germany.[119]

The Zentrum party which had played such an important role during the Weimar period was enormously reduced after its reorganization in 1945–46. Though in 1949 it still polled ten seats for the first Bundestag, by 1953 its number had been reduced to three and in 1957 it gained no seats at all. In its approach to the reunification question, it closely followed the SPD line.

Gustav Heinemann's Gesamtdeutsche Volkspartei (All-German People's party)[120] gave primary attention to reunification and, for this reason, opposed rearmament and Western ties which it considered an absolute obstacle to the essential national policy objective. The Party, founded in the heyday of the *Ohne mich* campaign, proved to be an utter failure. In 1953 it received insufficient votes to be represented in the Bundestag and, thereafter, dissolved itself, Heinemann joining the SPD.

The Bavarian party (Bayernpartei) pursued particularist policy aims and showed no interest in reunification; after 1952 it held no seats in the Federal Parliament.

The Communist party of Germany, operating in the Federal Republic, had always been a faithful mouthpiece of the East German Socialist Unity party (SED) and of the latter's Moscow-directed policies. In 1949 Communists held fifteen seats in the Bundestag. Events in East Germany soon made the Communist party more and more unpopular in the eyes of the German industrial workers. At the 1953 elections only 610,000 persons cast their votes for the Communist party (in 1949 the number had been 1,370,000), and it obtained no representation on the Federal Parliament.

The German Communist party always professed to be a fervent advocate of reunification; it endorsed all the resolutions and programs to this end of the so-called German Peace Council and the East German regime. Furthermore, the West German Communist movement was manifestly supported and financed by the East German Communists and, ultimately, by Soviet sources. In November, 1951, the Federal government petitioned the Federal Constitutional Court to declare the Communist party, under Article 21 of the Basic Law, unconstitutional.[121] After an extremely long and detailed pro-

[119] See, for this purpose, the declaration of Herbert Schneider, Chairman of the Parliamentary Group of the DP, in the volume, *Gibt es noch Wege zur Wiedervereinigung?* (Bonn, 1960), pp. 58–68.
[120] See above, p. 28.
[121] Article 21, paragraph 2, of the Basic Law provided: "Parties which, by

cedure, the Court ruled that the Communist party's objective—the establishment of a dictatorship of the proletariat—was incompatible with the liberal democratic principles prevailing in the Federal Republic. The objection that the Communist party had been admitted under the four-power control of Germany as a "democratic Party" was countered by the Court in this manner: in the interpretation, as understood under the four-power regime, "democracy" meant hostility against Nazism, but now the Court was called to assess this concept in the light of the provisions of the Basic Law. The Constitutional Court also ruled that present prohibition of the Communist party does not preclude that it might participate in future all-German elections.[122]

The prohibition of the Communist party in the Federal Republic was generally believed superfluous and, therefore, harmful. The Party's political role had become insignificant. The propaganda value of its poor performance at the polls fully equalled the dangers of its legal activity. The interdiction of Communism has been propagandistically exploited by the East German regime, which claims to allow "bourgeois parties" to operate. Public opinion in the Federal Republic was little impressed by the judgment of the Federal Constitutional Court; people did not need to be persuaded of the antidemocratic character of Communism as practiced, for instance, in the German Democratic Republic. Some observers felt that the prohibition of the Communist party was an added obstacle to the goal of reunification.[123]

reason of their aims or the behavior of their adherents, seek to impair or destroy the free democratic basic order or to endanger the existence of the Federal Republic of Germany are unconstitutional. The Federal Constitutional Court decides on the question of unconstitutionality."

[122] Communists and Communist fellow-travelers operate a political organization under the name of German Peace Union; it obtained 1.3 per cent of votes in 1965 (1.9 per cent in 1961). In West Berlin the local branch of the East German Socialist Unity party (SED) is permitted to function, but its role and membership are more than insignificant.

[123] Grosser, *Die Bonner Demokratie*, pp. 125–28; Hiscocks, *Democracy in Germany*, pp. 109–10. The judgment is published in *Entscheidungen des Bundesverfassungsgerichts* (Tübingen, 1956), Vol. V, pp. 85–393.

Amid the pressure of great events,
a general principle gives no help.

—Georg W. F. Hegel
Philosophy of History

Seek ye learning unto China.

—Mohammed
The Koran

CHAPTER III

WEST GERMANS AND THE REUNIFICATION QUESTION

The techniques and objectives of the Federal Republic's *Deutschlandpolitik* (the policy for German unity) were formulated by the fathers of the Basic Law and by the Federal government with the support of the coalition parties. They have received popular approval in a number of federal elections. With the adherence of the principal opposition party, the SPD, to government reunification policy, an even more integrated national consensus appeared to have emerged. But this apparent consensus is misleading: paradoxically, this official harmonizing of aims and means to achieve German unity coincided with the realization by some members of the elite that Adenauer's line had failed, that it was hopeless to wait for an "automatic" solution of the German problem. Even the bipartisanship of government and opposition failed to silence these dissident and critical voices which demanded mobility, flexibility, and, generally, a new strategy in West Germany's *Ostpolitik*.[1] Nor did the pragmatism and elasticity of the Grand Coalition fully satisfy all the critics of the official policy.

[1] A symposium with contributions by thirty-six German publicists and scholars on present-day West Germany, including much criticism of Adenauer's foreign policy, was published under the title of Hans Werner Richter, *Bestandsaufnahme* [stock-taking] (Munich, 1962).

Popular participation in the conduct of foreign policy is, even in traditional democracies, exceptional and reserved for events and decisions of outstanding significance. For the German public it was a new experience; earlier, except perhaps during the years of the Weimar Republic (1919–33), the voters were not asked to express opinions on foreign policy. Moreover, it may be correct to state that German proclivity for paternalistic government inhibited average Prussians—and later citizens of the Reich—from holding views beyond their average competence. There was, however, a "foreign policy elite" whose views carried weight in matters of foreign policy.

The relationship between internal and external politics took on a value in Prussia and Germany different from other countries. Because of Prussia's and Prussia-Germany's geographically exposed location, their bellicose history, and the expansionist ambitions of their leaders, the usual primacy of foreign policy over domestic was well recognized. This was just another reason to reserve foreign policy deliberation and decision-making to the rulers and specially qualified elites.[2]

However, the problem of German unity was a question of a very special nature: in the eyes of the average German it was essentially an internal German question, although, as was realized, it depended on foreign policy, especially regarding the Soviet Union. Unlike their direct participation in the Saar plebiscite, the West German voters were able to express opinions on German unification only in the most general terms: they expressed preferences for Adenauer's policy line (the opponents of the Chancellor derided it as "no foreign policy") which promised, first of all, security by integration into the Western system of alliances and a desire to abstain from "experiments," even for the sake of achieving German unity.

The influence of members of the elite groups on foreign policy has always been and remains of considerable importance in Germany. In the Federal Republic, elite influence on the reunification question is even more significant, partly because of the present free democratic structure of government and partly because of the vital national importance of the issue. Of course, as long as the reunification problem does not reach the stage of concrete decision, opinions of the members of the elite are bound to remain academic and without practical consequence. But if, in the future, any opportunity

[2] See Hans Rothfels, "Sinn und Grenzen des Primats der Aussenpolitik," *Aussenpolitik*, VI (1955), p. 277.

for meaningful decision should arise, the views represented by members of the cultural elites would become significant rallying centers.

Whatever the role of foreign powers in the achievement of German unity may be, this question is not and will not become "foreign" to German elites or people. It is, rather, a matter of personal experience or tragedy and almost always of personal interest. The apathy which a visitor to West Germany is likely to find when trying to elicit individual views on the reunification question is often the result of frustration ("nothing can be done, anyhow") or escapism from that deplorable subject ("I cannot help it, so I had better not think of it"). Naturally, there is also some genuine indifference. Others, again, indulge in empty verbosity on the subject without the will to act. Many Germans have reversed Gambetta's dictum on Alsace-Lorraine ("toujours y penser, jamais y parler") by speaking constantly of reunification without giving much thought to the problem. However, it cannot be denied that Germany's partition is a matter of personal drama for millions. Because of the division inflicted on families and friends, especially since the erection of the Berlin Wall, it is destined to remain a cause of personal unhappiness and irritation.

The divided state of Germany, despite seeming apathy, affects many leading West Germans. It produces strange psychological impacts on individuals—like the sudden visit of the Federal Minister of Finance, Fritz Schäffer, to East Berlin where he had a conversation with the East German Minister of Defense, Vinzenz Müller,[3] or the even more conspicuous cases of Otto John and Viktor Agartz.[4] The nightmare of the past, conscious and subliminal remorse for atrocities of the Nazi era, and memories of the apocalyptic destruction and upheaval of the postwar period are com-

[3] Prittie, *Germany Divided*, p. 246.

[4] Dr. Otto John participated in the anti-Hitler plot of July 20, 1944, but managed to escape to England. Upon his return to West Germany, he became head of the West German security services. On July 24, 1954, John escaped or was kidnapped and taken to East Germany; in 1955 he returned to West Germany and was sentenced to four years imprisonment for treason. He may have acted under a misconceived sense of duty to promote reunification. See Horne, *Return to Power*, pp. 360–70; Prittie, *Germany Divided*, pp. 223–47; Grosser, *Die Bonner Demokratie*, pp. 338–39.

Dr. Viktor Agartz, a leading trade-unionist and head of an economic research bureau, was accused of having betrayed secrets to the East German regime. In 1957 he was acquitted. He pleaded that he maintained contacts with the East for the purpose of promoting the cause of reunification. Prittie, *Germany Divided*, p. 246; Grosser, *Die Bonner Demokratie*, pp. 235–36, 339.

bining with partition to affect the minds of the German elite and of the people at large.[5] These reactions are not irrelevant to West Germany's present and future feelings about reunification.

The West German Elite and Reunification

In every nation, in addition to the official, an unofficial elite is likely to influence foreign policy; its members will vary from country to country.[6] With regard to reunification it must also be said that, because of its vital importance, the groups exerting pressure on government policy are necessarily larger than those who attempt to affect more distant questions of national interest.[7]

Policies are constantly influenced by individual refugees who occupy key positions in government or public life. In the Federal Republic it has been calculated that 26 per cent of its population in 1954 was born in East Germany, in the Eastern Territories, or in countries of East-Central Europe from which Germans were expelled after World War II.[8] Statistics also prove that 23 per cent of the West German elite who, officially or unofficially, are in a position to influence foreign policy were born in these areas. The percentage figure for diplomats in active service in 1954 was higher than this average, 36 per cent; that of SPD deputies was even higher, 41 per cent; whereas that of CDU/CSU deputies was only 4 per cent. Among journalists it was 33 per cent; among educators, 24 per cent.[9] It is only human that persons of East German origin would tend to be more interested in the question of reunification and to attribute greater importance to it than natives of other parts of Germany.

[5] Willy Brandt, *The Ordeal of Co-Existence* (Cambridge, Mass., 1963).

[6] The term "elite" is to include (1) political and governmental leaders (party leaders, top officials, and higher bureaucracy), and (2) "opinion leaders," who are "more important than others in the transmission of influence." See Elihu Katz's article in J. David Singer (ed.), *Human Behavior and International Politics* (Chicago, Ill., 1965), p. 295.

[7] Two important publications deal with the questions of foreign policy decision-making in the Federal Republic of Germany using various techniques of public-opinion testing. Hans Speier and W. Phillips Davison, *West German Leadership and Foreign Policy* (Evanston, Ill., 1957); Deutsch and Edinger, *Germany Rejoins the Powers.*

[8] At the end of 1965 the number of refugees and expellees born in East Germany, the Eastern Territories, or other parts of East-Central Europe shrank by natural mortality to 17.9 per cent (10.6 million), *Frankfurter Allgemeine Zeitung,* January 17, 1966.

[9] See Deutsch and Edinger, *Germany Rejoins the Powers,* p. 134.

Opinions of members of West German elites may thus be summarized:[10]

1) Among those who in general approved governmental policy on reunification (or the *Deutschlandpolitik* and *Ostpolitik* in a wider sense), we found many who represented the "patient" type. They refused to let their judgment or opinion be influenced by day-to-day events. They firmly and tenaciously clung to the thesis that in the long run reunification was inevitable. It was no longer upheld that it will come "automatically" or that West Germany as a "magnet" would attract East Germany. It was, however, maintained that opportunities were bound to arise making it possible "to have a serious talk" with the Soviet Union. They admitted that there was at present no *quid pro quo* to be offered to the Soviet Union against the abandonment of its East German "mortgage." But the fact alone that the "two Germanys" concept was unrealistic because of the political failure of the German Democratic Republic would sooner or later force the Russians to seek a solution which would both save face and give them needed security against a reunited Germany.

Among the developments which could make a favorable solution of the German problem attractive or imperative for the Russians, these factors were frequently referred to:

a) German unity remains a four-power responsibility; no permanent and fruitful East-West agreement can be reached without the solution of the German problem, that is, without the unity of Germany. Because the Soviet Union, for a great variety of reasons, will be compelled to seek a permanent settlement of the Cold War, the German question someday will have to be given a satisfactory answer.

b) The global balance of power will, in the future even more significantly than at present, shift in favor of the United States and against the Soviet Union. The Sino-Soviet conflict is adduced as the chief reason for the growing imbalance in disfavor of the Soviet Union. On the whole, the West German foreign-policy elite is

---

[10] It is realized that the summary presentation provided in the text does not amount to a detailed public-opinion analysis. Such an analysis would have required full statements on the character of the sample and, for such purpose, the writing of another book. The evaluation is based on personal impressions gained by this writer from interviews conducted in 1963 and 1965 with members of the official and unofficial elite in the Federal Republic, including West Berlin. It is believed that, despite its inevitable shortcomings, this presentation will be a necessary and useful contribution to this chapter.

strongly inclined to attribute outstanding importance to the "Chinese puzzle" for the furtherance of German reunification.[11]

c) A considerable number of interviewees believed that the solution to the German problem will coincide with the settlement of the East-Central European "satellite" problem. They consciously or unconsciously seemed to paraphrase Raymond Aron in saying that "Germany will be re-united when Europe is united," meaning that the Soviet-dominated countries are, at present, unnaturally separated from the rest of Europe where they belong, culturally and politically.[12] The same applies to East Germany, which is now controlled by the "non-European" Soviet Union. Holders of this view are mainly adherents of the European integration concept; they think that an integrated Europe must encompass East Germany together with Poland, Czechoslovakia, Hungary, Yugoslavia, and possibly also Rumania and Bulgaria. Advocates of the European federation movement who, simultaneously, are also supporters of German unity, stated that "the Common Market is, for Germany, no substitute for reunification." Some of the European federalists are, however, more absorbed in ideas of European integration than in the integration of the two Germanys.

A still smaller but growing number of interviewees appeared to be skeptical of a "wait and see" attitude. Often inspired by the precedent of the Berlin Wall, they emphasized that a more flexible and direct approach toward East Germany should be undertaken because the fate of the Germans beyond the Iron Curtain would not permit any procrastination. They reproached the government for lacking initiative. It is characteristic that even the patient ones welcomed the "policy of movement" though they failed to believe in it.

Both the patient and the impatient expressed periodic anxiety lest the United States should enter into some deal with the Soviet Union that would harm Germany. One or two of these interviewees, suspicious of United States motives, seemed to draw consolation from a belief that Ulbricht, similarly, might be anxious about a deal between the Soviet Union and the Federal Republic. Therefore, they advocated direct contacts with Moscow, favored the invitation of Khrushchev to Bonn and the loosening of the Hallstein Doctrine (without, however, abandoning it) by establishing direct links

[11] About the impact of the Sino-Soviet conflict on both elite and popular thinking in West Germany, see pp. 136–38 below.

[12] These ideas are developed in Raymond Aron, *Paix et Guerre entre les nations* (Paris, 1962), p. 677.

with Poland, Czechoslovakia, and other European Communist governments.

Almost all the members of the West German foreign-policy elite who were questioned reflected, in various degrees, a guilt complex toward Poland. Many of them emphasized that they wished to distinguish strictly between "the Soviet Zone of Occupation" and the territories beyond the Oder-Neisse Line. Although many showed reluctance to commit themselves to relinquishment of these territories in exchange for reunification, others suggested renunciation of claims to these areas as a price to be paid for reunification. But all of the respondents expressed readiness to compensate Poland for her suffering during the war and for the sake of making Polish-German friendship a working reality.

Most of the respondents, particularly the impatient ones, placed liberalization of the conditions in the German Democratic Republic and the elimination of the Berlin Wall among the most urgent aims of the government, but very few were ready to associate themselves with the ideas submitted by Professor Jaspers[13] of trading freedom in East Germany against consent to permanent severance of that territory.

While few respondents expressed themselves in the strict terms of the prevailing state doctrines or used legal arguments to support their views on reunification, their tendency did not suggest that these concepts should be abandoned or modified. A few remarked that these doctrines were difficult to understand or esoteric, but no active hostility against them was displayed.

A rather exiguous undercurrent of opinion, though refusing criticism of the government, admitted having no hope that German unity could be achieved. One or two of these respondents suggested that abundant lip-service to unification does not prove that it is being seriously considered.

The prevailing opinion, however, maintained that there was less talk on reunification than lucubration. "We do not speak of it as long as nothing practical can be done about it. But when the time comes, you will see: blood is not water."

2) A smaller group of the foreign-policy elite stated their disagreement with governmental policies on reunification. These respondents, with more or less emphasis, castigated Adenauer's "neglectful" attitude toward German unity or accused him plainly of not having wanted reunification at all.

[13] See pp. 113–18 below.

A considerable number of government opponents insisted that "facts and fictions" must be separated and "rigid, stupid principles" abandoned if the Federal Republic was to come to grips with the problem. However, on the assessment of the past and on what is to be done now there were widely divergent views:

a) Most of those who criticized Adenauer's *Ostpolitik* thought, nevertheless, that his Western policy was correct. They agreed with the basic concept that Germany's place is with the West; many even thought it had been good policy to secure West Germany's independence and strength by entering the Western alliance. But they still held that Germany's alliance with the West and her rearmament had either been "premature" or carried out in disregard for the *Deutschlandpolitik*.

Questioned as to whether they would have preferred reunification for the price of Germany's neutralization or the Federal Republic's adherence to the West without the Soviet zone, the majority of respondents answered that these alternatives never really presented themselves. In their opinion Adenauer's error consisted in the failure to explore certain possibilities which "might have" led to reunification with or without neutralization of Germany. As one interviewee said, "Adenauer has no alibi; he might have been right but he cannot prove it. And now it is too late."

The majority of Adenauer's critics agreed that, should the alternative of reunification or Western integration have presented itself, "some form of non-alignment" would have been preferable to the present division.

b) A small minority of the interviewees condemned Adenauer's foreign policy in all its aspects as disastrous to German unity. They suggested that Germany's rearmament and Western alignment should have been negotiated against reunification; as a result of such negotiations (which most likely would have been successful), united Germany should have become a neutralized or nonaligned power, even a "third force" between East and West. According to these views, Germany's 1952 conventional rearmament within the Western alliance constituted a serious threat; its abandonment in return for a unified Germany would have been a worthwhile bargain for the Soviets. After the Soviet Union achieved nuclear capability, Germany's conventional strength was no longer a matter of interest to the Soviet Union, and even a neutralized Germany could not be negotiated. The threat of West Germany's nuclear armament is mostly considered out of the question: "Nobody wants it, not even the Federal Government; in any case, it is too dangerous." But sharing in nuclear decision-making is generally thought of as "desirable."

According to some more negative and extremist views (which seem to ignore the part of the above argument which refers to the relative depreciation of conventional weapons), it has become evident that the "Cold War cannot be won" and, therefore, nothing remains to be done but to return to the 1952 status quo, the disengagement from all alliances and a new start "in the right direction." Holders of such radical (and generally anti-American) views went so far as to deny the sovereign statehood of the Federal Republic and to suggest that there was no longer a "German nation" because there was no German nation-state and because the former national capital, Berlin, had become a center of international competition and intrigue.

These opinions of the members of the elite interviewed may be typical of the various attitudes; they cannot, however, be taken as a quantitative guide. Their relative weight and importance depend on the momentary influence which given respondents can bring to bear on foreign policy. In their case *vota non numerantur sed ponderantur.*

Advocates of a Recognition of the Territorial Status Quo

Some dissident opinions of a few scholars will be registered here. Their opposition to the generally accepted postulate of Germany's unification has attracted much interest, though few converts, and has provoked violent criticism. These views of persons of highest renown in their fields of scholarship, motivated by theoretical rather than practical considerations, cannot be disregarded in the shaping of West German public opinion.

Ludwig Dehio, a patriarch of German historians, in an article published in 1953,[14] set forth historical-philosophical arguments against the need for or even the expediency of a restoration of German unity. The author thought that the traditional European balance of power was outdated and had been replaced by an integrated Western alliance. A demand ("more explosive than anything else") which West Germany could pose as a price for her

---

[14] The article was first published in the June, 1953, issue of the periodical *Aussenpolitik;* it was included in the volume *Deutschland und die Weltpolitik im 20. Jahrhundert* (Munich, 1955). An English translation of the book was published, Ludwig Dehio, *Germany and World Politics in the Twentieth Century* (New York, 1960).

participation in the Western alliance (the article was written in 1953) was the demand for reunification. But such a demand, if endorsed by other Western powers, would "weaken rather than strengthen the unity of the West" and would in any case be considered as stemming from "egocentric nationalism." In the eyes of Dehio, "liberty of the individual, not of the state" must now be the most precious aim. He continued:

> A hundred years ago the most pressing goal was national unity; for the preservation of freedom offered no problem in the sense in which it does today, whereas unity was the natural demand within that system of nation states which is lying in ruins today. Now, however, after the Third Reich has abused and thrown away our unity by denying freedom, *unity must be subordinated to the superior and wider aim of freedom*, for today a demand for unity surely has an anachronistic flavor about it. No political watchword can be transplanted into a new situation without carrying with it traces of the soil in which it grew previously.[15]

Dehio appears to consider that the freedom of Western Europe, including that of the Federal Republic of Germany, would be endangered if Germany, supported by the Western powers, should eventually achieve unification. It is not easy to follow an argument which predicates that a united Germany must become disloyal to her association with the West. The priority accorded to the principle of freedom, as against that of unity, does not secure freedom for the inhabitants of East Germany, and it appears that this lack of freedom is likely to create the demand for unification. Whether a desire for national unity—especially for the purpose of securing freedom for one's co-nationals—is, under present conditions, anachronistic is a philosophical view contradicted by historical facts. Dehio's opinion was not generally shared by German historians, but his thinking preceded similar ideas launched in the early sixties.

The well-known existentialist philosopher, Karl Jaspers, had earlier discussed the moral and philosophical-theological questions of Germany's guilt and the guilt of others for the tragedy of World War II. He had come to distinguish between criminal, political, moral, and metaphysical guilt, the last being the responsibility of persons and peoples for crimes committed in their presence or with their knowledge but without their complicity or consent.[16]

[15] Dehio, *Germany and World Politics*, pp. 136–38. Italics have been added.
[16] See Karl Jaspers, *The Question of German Guilt* (New York, 1947), *passim.*

In March, 1960, Karl Jaspers was interviewed on the German re-unification question and the interview was broadcast on August 10, 1960, on radio and television. He also wrote several articles in *Die Zeit* on the same subject. Both articles and the interview were subsequently published in book form.[17] He summarized his view in the following manner:

> I have been convinced for several years that the claim to re-unification is unrealistic . . . it is unrealistic both politically and philosophically. . . . The concept of reunification considers the Bismarckian state as its model. The Bismarckian state is to be restored. But this state had irrevo-cably—due to events—become past history. . . . Re-unification means the non-recognition of something that had happened . . . a legal claim based on a situation which had disappeared because of the guilt of Germany herself. . . .[18]

In Jaspers' view Germany had forfeited her right to national unity because of Hitler. What she retained was a right to freedom only,[19] as well as the right of demanding freedom for the population of East Germany. He recognized that the German people of the East must be freed "from slavery" but expressed doubt that the demand for reunification would not render liberation more difficult. His answer was that the price to be paid for this freedom should be the abandonment of the claim to reunification. The abandonment should not be "absolute" but should be made conditional to the grant of political freedom to East Germany.[20]

Jaspers denied the continuity of the German state and its right of self-determination (which must be dependent on the decision and consent of other powers); he also denied the factual independence of both the Federal Republic and the German Democratic Republic. He held the view that "facts cannot be changed by legal arguments."[21] He predicted the "end of the German national state but not that of the Germans" because "the unity of the West presup-poses a renunciation of the sovereignty of nation-states." He stated:

---

[17] Jaspers, *Freiheit und Wiedervereinigung*. In 1966, Jaspers published another book in which he essentially reiterated his thesis. He added, however, the proviso that the DDR should not be recognized by West Germany as long as the Berlin Wall exists; *Wohin treibt die Bundesrepublik?* (Munich, 1966), pp. 232–56.

[18] Jaspers, *Freiheit und Widervereinigung*, p. 110.

[19] *Ibid.*, p. 111.

[20] *Ibid.*, pp. 17–21.

[21] *Ibid.*, pp. 25–28.

"The task is not a return from nation-state to cosmopolitanism but the realization of freedom in the all-out life of confederate states."[22]

Jaspers refused to admit that the Federal Republic was only a *provisorium* (temporary arrangement); in his view "it is a new state." The founders of the Federal Republic did not see clearly, he explained, when they drafted the Basic Law. At this point he concluded: "The state becomes firmly established and does not remain temporary. To insist on the political concept of Germany which belongs to the past and is today an illusion appears to me, because of the political falsehood of such a thesis, a great tragedy for Germany herself and for the West."[23]

Jaspers seems to believe that an open renunciation of the demand for reunification would persuade the Russians to allow East Germany a status somewhat similar to that of Austria, provided that all claims for a union with West Germany were abandoned. After the creation of a free East Germany, Berlin should, according to Jaspers, be given the right to choose between becoming a small independent state, the capital of the East German state, or an exterior enclave of the Federal Republic of Germany. He also suggests that the name of the Federal Republic (which, in his view, implicitly raises a claim to East Germany) be changed to "German Federal Republic" or simply "West Germany."[24]

Jaspers' ideas were followed by a similar thesis of Alexander Rüstow, a sociologist and political scientist. Probably under the impact of the Jaspersian interviews, Rüstow developed his ideas in an address given to young officers of the German Air Force in the Evangelical Academy of Tutzing. Quotations of his speech were published in *Die Welt*, followed by articles in the same paper written by Professor Rüstow himself.[25] The key idea of Rüstow's concept was thus formulated: "The primary requirement is not Germany's re-unification but the liberation of the population of the Soviet Zone from totalitarian Bolshevik dictatorship. If we were asked to renounce re-unification we should agree. Austria received her freedom while she gave up re-unification with Germany. The Austrians hardly suffer now under the prohibition of re-unification. Freedom is more important to them."

In his articles Professor Rüstow also stressed the theoretical and practical necessity of giving priority to the demand for freedom

[22] *Ibid.*, pp. 53–55.
[23] *Ibid.*, p. 63.
[24] *Ibid.*, pp. 75–81.
[25] *Die Welt*, April 14, 1961, and May 6, 1961.

over that for reunification. In his original Tutzing address, Rüstow described the claim for reunification as "typically German"; this expression gave rise to misunderstandings and exposed the speaker to attacks. He later qualified his remarks by explaining that, while the demand for freedom for East Germany corresponds with the universal idea of freedom in the West, the demand for reunification is only a "special and specific German affair."

The Jaspers and Rüstow theses have been strongly assailed by politicians and academicians in Germany, especially by the publicist, Paul Sethe, by CDU Deputy Johann-Baptist Gradl, by FDP Party Chairman Erich Mende, and by the SPD Senator of Berlin, Adolf Arndt. Others, among them the historian, Golo Mann, paid tribute to Jaspers' courage in having said what hardly anybody dared to say; they, nevertheless, refused to share all his views. Golo Mann wrote in 1962:

It is Jaspers who has the courage to say aloud what many of his fellow-citizens nowadays think but do not wish to say: that the German demand for reunification as a sacred right is based on an illusion; that it is based on the mistaken assumption that the national state founded by Bismarck, crippled through the First World War and then wantonly risked again and destroyed, nevertheless still exists. It exists no more, Jaspers holds, and the Federal Republic is something new and therefore definite, not the mere *locumtenens* of a theoretically existing "Reich."
Personally, I am not quite as certain about this as Jaspers is. The victorious Allies themselves, in 1945, were operating with the idea of a continuing German unity and identity, first from Berlin, and then, when it did not work there, from Frankfurt, for the three Western Zones . . . they thought . . . that what had been achieved in the nineteenth century should not be entirely undone. . . . The drive toward unity is older than Bismarck, it began as early as the 1830's with the *Zollverein*. . . .[26]

Jaspers' abandonment thesis is a consequence of his theological-moralistic conception of German guilt, liability, and responsibility. The "metaphysical" guilt of all Germans as well as their liability, which Jaspers differentiates from individual guilt (he does not recognize collective guilt, only collective liability—a very subtle distinction), have, according to this view, led the Germans to forfeit their unity. Whether such an abstract philosophical-moralistic principle has validity in the process of international politics is highly questionable. Defeated nations have been compelled to pay a price for their defeat whether they were guilty of aggression or not.

[26] Mann, "Bismarck in Our Times," p. 13.

Whether Nazi Germany's aggression and unquestionable misdeeds, rightly condemned from the moral and legal points of view, could permanently justify partition is no longer a question of morality or right but of political facts of life. Though national policy-makers should be guided by considerations of justice and morality in their decisions, they will, obviously, where the fate of a collective entity, state, or nation is involved, be inclined to base their policy on expedience rather than abstract justice of morality. Besides, such principles are vague and open to divergent interpretations. And, as history demonstrates, many states and their leaders are ready to ignore obvious principles of morality and justice and base their policies on the Machiavellian policy of *sacro egoismo*.

Jaspers' thesis had earlier been suggested, but in a language devoid of philosophical-moralistic phraseology, by no less a person than Khrushchev when confronted by the arguments of Carlo Schmid and Fritz Erler at their meeting in Moscow. The Soviet leader told the Germans that they had to accept partition as an inevitable consequence of a lost war.[27]

Jaspers' historical argument concerning the discontinuance of the Bismarckian German state because of Germany's collapse and prostration at the end of World War II is far from conclusive. There are many historic precedents which demonstrate that defeated, subjugated, or divided nations strove successfully to re-establish their former territorial identities. Poland did so after more than 120 years of suppression. It is true that Bismarckian Germany had only existed for 75 years; but it was the smaller Reich in contrast to a former larger Reich which had existed through 900 years.

It is certainly correct to say that territorial claims based exclusively on history may be considered unjustified. This may apply to German claims to the Eastern Territories although here the Poles, apparently with success, made use of claims dating back six or seven hundred years. But it should be remembered that the demand for reunification is not only and not primarily territorial; it is also a demand for a union with German co-nationals and, simultaneously, for their liberation from a foreign-dominated regime, as is clearly recognized by Jaspers himself. Jaspers' refusal to admit the existence of the social force of national sentiment and the innate urge of members of the same nation to live within one political organization appears to ignore historical and political experiences.

Lastly, Jaspers' (and Rüstow's) Austrian analogy appears, as in-

[27] See pp. 72–73 above.

116

voked, to be highly unrealistic. Austria was never part of Bismarckian Germany and her will to be an independent state is nowadays
hardly questionable. Austria has not lost her "freedom" in the sense
that East Germany has; the Russian-controlled zone was only a
fraction of Austria, and it was not the Soviet Union, by withdraw-
ing its forces, that allowed Austria to live in freedom. The plan
suggested by Jaspers and Rüstow (freedom for East Germany
against prohibition of union with West Germany) would, no doubt,
be acceptable to many Germans and probably to the Federal government. But it is unlikely that it would be acceptable to the Soviet
Union. To abandon the claim to political reunification when there
is, at present, no chance for persuading the Soviets to agree to any
such transaction, could hardly be considered a realistic diplomatic
move. It would mean giving away "something" for "nothing."

The Jaspersian thesis of placing emphasis on the libertarian and
humanitarian aspects of reunification as opposed to political unification has certainly influenced West German statesmen and even the
public during the past few years. Even Adenauer expressed readiness to defer political reunification if it would insure greater liber-
ties and an improvement in living conditions for the people of East
Germany. On this point, West German practical politics and Jaspers'
point of view meet. The rest of Jaspers' thesis could, however, be
considered impractical, even utopian.

The atonement approach has inspired other intellectuals besides
Jaspers and Rüstow; but they have reached differing conclusions.
Theological and pacifist ideas have stimulated, in particular, Protestant theologians, such as Gustav Heinemann.[28] But while they
advocated the withdrawal of Germany from active international
politics into a self-imposed neutralism, they were unwilling to abandon political reunification.

The opposition of freedom against the demand for reunification
has led different people to diametrically opposed conclusions. For
some, security within an integrated Western alliance system was to
precede even the demand for German unity; but Jaspers and Rüstow used another set of priorities when they placed freedom for
East Germany above political unification of Germany as a whole.

Others, while not suggesting the outright renunciation of political
unity for Germany, consider unification impossible as long as Germany's guilt has not been atoned. Atonement requires time and patience. Such a view has been expressed by Eduard Heimann, an

[28] See p. 28 above.

economist and sociologist. In his opinion, only "reconciliation can bring about re-unification." And as he sees it, this is not a matter for diplomacy or politics but a "matter of the heart." He refers to the Franco-German reconciliation as a model of how reconciliation in the East might be implemented.[29] It seems, in Heimann's case, that the ideological and power conflicts which separate the Communist camp from the West are insufficiently appreciated.

Some years before the "opening up" of the East, the establishment of West German trade missions, later diplomatic missions, in some East European capitals began, or plans for an exchange of speakers between East and West Germany materialized, a number of publicists and political journalists—many of them writing for the periodical *Die Zeit*—suggested direct contacts with East Germany, including those with the government of the D.D.R. They revealed daring pragmatism, and irreverence toward established principles. West Germany's relationship to the D.D.R. should not be viewed legalistically but politically; legal rights were of no concern when interests were at stake. Recognition of the East German regimes should not be regarded as a moral issue but as one of expediency. Support for the material and spiritual well-being of East Germans should have priority over all other considerations.[30] Writers and other intellectuals—some of them sympathizing with leftist political movements—who had no reverence for accepted dogmas of Germany's status were scathingly denounced as the *"heimatlose Linke"* (the unpatriotic left).[31]

Not only academic scholars, writers, and journalists have undertaken to point out new ways of solving the question of German unity. Diplomats also, either unofficially, like Pfleiderer, or acting personally with the advantage of their official position, have endeavored to forward reunification. From this point of view, the story of Ambassador Kroll is of significant interest.

Ambassador Kroll's Individual Initiative

At the time when intensive talks between Washington and Moscow on Berlin were being conducted early in 1962, newspapers reported that Hans Kroll, the West German Ambassador in Moscow, was having conversations with Soviet officials, including

[29] See Eduard Heimann's article, "Kommunismus und Wiedervereinigung," *Die Zeit*, August 23, 1963.
[30] See Peter Bender, *Offensive Entspannung* (Cologne, 1964), pp. 163–64.
[31] For a good survey, see Melvin Croan, "The German Problem Once Again," *Survey*, April, 1965, pp. 171–76.

Khrushchev, on a settlement of the East-West German conflict. The exact theme of these conversations was never revealed, but it seems certain that Ambassador Kroll had acted without instructions from Bonn.[32]

Ever since Adenauer's near-fiasco in Moscow in 1955, the aged Chancellor had been reluctant to enter into direct negotiations with the Kremlin on the sensitive German problem. He either considered such conversations useless or did not wish to face Soviet pressure without the direct support of the United States. He preferred, in any case, to leave any such negotiations to the Western powers and to stay in the background while advising them. It is improbable that Adenauer wished to neglect the reunification issue, for he was not indifferent to the return of the Saar. After 1956 when, almost against his will, the question of the Saar was solved in favor of Germany, he may have developed a preference for relying on the "inevitable evolution" instead of talks with the Soviet Union.

With regard to the Saar, it should be remembered that the Chancellor had, in 1954, consented that the Saar area be given a "European status." With great difficulties and against the votes of the Free Democrats, the Paris Agreement on the Saar was ratified by the Bundestag. When it came to the referendum to have the agreement approved by the population of the Saar, the Chancellor strongly recommended its adoption. The refusal of the majority of the Saar voters to accept European status was a windfall; it came against the intent and expressed will of Adenauer and made the return of that territory possible.

Perhaps the Chancellor was thereafter hoping, though less realistically, for a windfall in the East. But luck in the West did not mean that such a *trouvaille* would be forthcoming from the East as well.

Adenauer may also have felt reluctant to undertake direct or confidential talks with the Soviet Union because of the suspicion that would have been aroused in Western capitals. Were not the Chancellor and many German leaders anxious lest Washington and Moscow come to an understanding on the issue of Berlin without the approval of Bonn? Secret German-Soviet negotiations had been particularly in disrepute since the time of Rapallo and especially since the confidential contacts leading to the Hitler-Stalin pact of 1939.

For all these reasons the German Foreign Office intervened.

[32] *Die Welt*, February 17, 1962; *New York Times*, March 3, 1962.

Ambassador Kroll was not only instructed to discontinue his conversations but was ordered to return to Bonn for consultations. Evidently these consultations did not satisfy Adenauer and his advisers, and Kroll's attitude gave them no other choice than to recall the Ambassador from Moscow.[33]

After his retirement from active service, Ambassador Kroll gave several interviews to radio and press. He was regarded as an advocate of flexibility who wished to improve relations with the Soviets so as to take one step on the tortuous road to reunification. What Kroll had in mind was a four-point plan which he had suggested to Khrushchev and which, he claimed, was submitted with the knowledge of the Federal Republic's Western Allies.[34] These four points, aimed at reaching a "small solution" to the German question, included: (1) an assurance for Berlin against Communist attack; (2) humanization of the conditions in East Germany; (3) a "piercing through" if not an elimination of the Berlin Wall; and (4) the recognition, on principle, of a right to self-determination and reunification for East Germany.

What the reader of this interview with Hans Kroll is missing is the price which would have had to be paid for this "small solution" to the German question. Kroll is strangely silent on this aspect of his talks which, he said, were having some prospects of success. In his report he also stated that Khrushchev thought of reunification as the possible result of a long drawn-out historic process after the "two German states" had achieved a *rapprochement* and a "reciprocal assimilation of their conditions." Kroll does not say it, but the reader may guess what kind of assimilation might have been in the Soviet leader's mind when he made this suggestion. Kroll's diplomatic sortie was just that sort of "gamble" which the Chancellor—and with him the majority of the West German population—was reluctant to take.

The Kroll incident is another example of how the deadlock on reunification affects some in responsible positions. However, impatience hardly pays, especially in relations with the Soviet leaders who, partly by their national temperament, partly conditioned by the long-term objectives of the "inevitable" Communist victory,

[33] For the narrative and analysis of the Kroll affair, see Studnitz, *Bismarck in Bonn*, pp. 152–53, 172–78.

[34] See the interview "Gespräch mit den Kreml, aber kein neues Rapallo" (Talk with the Kreml but no new Rapallo), *Rheinischer Merkur*, July 5, 1963; on July 25, 1963, Ambassador Kroll gave a talk on the West German radio which mostly reiterated the arguments presented in the press interview.

are steeped in perseverance and tenacity. It is likely that Khrushchev was just setting a trap by being excessively accommodating
to Kroll. It is also interesting to note that, according to the former
ambassador's statement, his conversations with Khrushchev, Miko-
yan, and Kosygin during the New Year's Eve celebrations in the
Kremlin initiated the Soviet memorandum of February 17, 1961,[35]
which was considered in Bonn a clumsy instrument of intimidation.
Evidently, co-ordination between the policies of the German
Foreign Office and its ambassador in Moscow must have been out
of gear; but, on the other hand, Moscow's understanding of the
reception of its propaganda in Bonn was not distinguished.

Impatience, caused by the sense of frustration, might induce
persons of high rank to express ideas for ending the deadlock
almost "at any price." Thus, Rainer Barzel's sudden "personal
suggestions," made in Washington on June 17, 1966, at a meeting
commemorating the Berlin uprising of 1953, may psychologically
be explained by the urge to do or say something "new" rather
than by his wish to raise his political stature or to compete with the
SPD or FDP in their advances toward the East German political
circles. His proposals, quickly disowned by Bonn, offered that, in
return for reunification, the Soviet Union should be allowed to
maintain troops on the soil of reunified Germany; the Communist
party should have the right to function freely; and the economic
arrangements imposed on East Germany should be continued with
added financial benefits for Moscow. The impulsive Vice-Chairman
of the CDU/CSU had to be warned from the American side that
the Federal Republic should not too precipitously rush into bilateral
negotiations; otherwise the price for reunification would be too
high, and future bargaining positions of the West could be weakened—without producing reunification.[36]

The Churches and Reunification

The catastrophic collapse and partition of Germany have thoroughly changed the numerical proportion and the territorial distribution of the members of her two dominant churches, the
Lutheran-Evangelical Protestant and the Roman Catholic, in East
and West Germany. The religious split of the Germans in the
sixteenth century proved to be one of the important factors of

[35] For the text, see George D. Embree (ed.), *The Soviet Union and the
German Question*, pp. 290–96; Siegler, *Von der Gipfelkonferenz bis zur
Berlinsperre*, pp. 37–41.
[36] See the reports in *New York Times*, June 16, 17, and 18, 1966.

German particularism. Bismarckian Germany still smarted under religious strife; Protestant Prussia contained a strong Catholic minority, especially in Westphalia and in the Rhineland; and some of the predominantly Catholic states of South Germany held large Protestant minorities. In Weimar Germany the ratio of Protestants to Catholics was 60 per cent to 39 per cent.

In the Federal Republic the proportion between Protestants and Catholics significantly shifted in favor of the latter: according to the 1961 census, 50.2 per cent of the population is Protestant and 45.5 per cent, Roman Catholic. In the German Democratic Republic (including East Berlin) there is an estimated 80 per cent Protestant population and 10 per cent Catholic.

Within the Federal Republic the internal distribution of the two denominations also changed: among the 9.3 million expellees from the Eastern Territories, the Sudetenland, and other East-Central European countries, 4.9 million (53 per cent) were Protestants and 4.2 million (45.2 per cent), Catholics; among the 3.14 million refugees from the Soviet zone until 1958, 1.3 million were Protestants and a half million were Catholics. The settlement of Protestants in heretofore homogeneous Catholic areas and vice versa often changed considerably the religious character of certain regions.[37]

The simple fact that 43 per cent of all German Protestants live in the German Democratic Republic alone explains the greater stake which Protestants have in reunification.[38] Furthermore, the unity of the German Protestant Church, which was re-established after World War II, has seriously been threatened by Germany's division and is likely to be entirely lost as a result of the deepening partition.

It has been asserted that the Catholic Church of West Germany shows little concern with reunification lest the present balance of denominations be upset in favor of the Protestants. No doubt, the demand for German unity is being given lesser emphasis by Catholics than by Protestants—a circumstance explained by the

[37] See Eugen Lemberg et al., Die Vertriebenen in Westdeutschland (Kiel, 1959), Vol. III, pp. 1–22; G. C. Paikert, The German Exodus (The Hague, 1962), pp. 40–41; Federal Press and Information Office, Zehn Jahre Bundesrepublik Deutschland (Wiesbaden, 1959), pp. 658–62.
[38] See Speier and Davison, West German Leadership, p. 89; Deutsch and Edinger, Germany Rejoins the Powers, pp. 109–10; Grosser, Die Bonner Demokratie, pp. 252–53.

smaller number of German Catholics behind the Iron Curtain and by the weaker ties which Catholics in West Germany maintain with the co-religionists in the East.

There is, however, no reason to believe that Catholics or the Catholic Church in West Germany do not strive for the unification of their country. Except perhaps for an insignificant number of old-fashioned Bavarian priests steeped in anti-Prussian particularism, the desire for reunification of the West German Catholic clergy cannot be doubted.[39] Observers, however, are inclined to compare Catholic enthusiasm for European integration, especially among the six powers of the Common Market (all of which, except the Netherlands, which is half Catholic, are predominantly Catholic countries) with the greater reserve shown toward reunification.[40] It should not be forgotten, however, that geographical distribution strengthens Catholic sympathy for collaboration with Germany's Western neighbors while Protestant concern is also explained by relative proximity to the borders of East Germany. In great majority the Catholics of the Federal Republic live in the western, southwestern, and southern parts of the country (in the *Länder* of North Rhine-Westphalia, Rhineland-Palatinate, Saarland, and Bavaria; Baden-Württemberg is about evenly divided between Protestants and Catholics); that is, it is generally more removed from the Iron Curtain than the predominantly Protestant states, such as Schleswig-Holstein, Lower-Saxony, Hamburg, and Hesse. West Berlin's population is also overwhelmingly Protestant (80 per cent); Catholics there represent only 13 per cent of the population.[41]

It is not without interest to compare the geographical origin and religious membership of CDU/CSU and SPD leaders with their respective emphasis on the question of reunification. In 1956 (when the SPD opposed governmental *Deutschlandpolitik*) 41 per cent of SPD leaders came from the Soviet zone or East German Territories, as opposed to 4 per cent of CDU/CSU leaders. At the same time, 74 per cent of CDU/CSU leaders were Catholics and only 26 per cent, Protestants, whereas thirty-three out of one hundred SPD leaders professed to be Protestants and none, Cath-

[39] Speier and Davidson, *West German Leadership*, p. 87.
[40] Deutsch and Edinger, *Germany Rejoins the Powers*, pp. 106–7, 156–57; Grosser, *Die Bonner Demokratie*, pp. 248–49.
[41] A good appraisal is to be found in Lowenthal, "The Germans Feel Like Germans Again," p. 42.

olic.[42] These factors may partly explain the parallel preoccupation of Protestants and Social Democrats with the cause of reunification without, however, suggesting any co-operation between them.

After the Nazi collapse in 1945, the Lutheran and Reformed churches in Germany undertook to establish a central organization to replace the German Evangelical Church created under Hitler. The "Evangelical Church in Germany" (Evangelische Kirche in Deutschland) was set up in 1945 and strengthened in 1948. This organization included all the Lutheran and Reformed churches of Germany, in both western and eastern parts of the country. In its Council and Synod the individual churches were represented according to the numerical strength of their members. Church rallies with mass participation were held for some years, alternately in West and East Germany. Thus, for a number of years the Evangelical Church was the most important instrument of German unity. It is understandable that the bishops and other Protestant leaders were particularly anxious not to cause any severance of their ties in the divided parts of Germany and to preserve, at all cost, the precious unity of their church.[43]

But under the pressures brought by the East German Communist regime, it became increasingly difficult to maintain the central organization of the Evangelical Church. The question of West Germany's rearmament, which already divided Protestant theologians in the Federal Republic, was exploited by stooges of the Pankow government, such as the CDU of the Soviet zone, to disrupt meetings of their church. The church rally planned in West Germany in 1957 could not be held because the East German government set unacceptable conditions for allowing residents of East Germany to attend.[44] The attendance of Synod and Council meetings became, as the years advanced, more and more difficult; West German representatives were often refused admission into the East, and bishops and other delegates did not receive their exit permits from the German Democratic government. The manifest aim of the East German regime was to create a separate Protestant church within the area under its control and to sever all ties between the Protestants of East and West Germany. As under Hitler, the members of the church were faced with the dilemma of how far

[42] Deutsch and Edinger, *Germany Rejoins the Powers*, pp. 134–35.
[43] Grosser, *Die Bonner Demokratie*, pp. 250–54; *Zehn Jahre Bundesrepublik Deutschland*, pp. 664–65.
[44] Grosser, *Die Bonner Demokratie*, pp. 254–55, 404–6.

to obey the authorities, when to question the legitimacy of those authorities, and when to obey God alone.[45]

The pressures on the East German Evangelical churches increased when, in March, 1957, the Chairman of the Evangelical Church Council, Otto Dibelius, Bishop of Berlin-Brandenburg (whose diocese extended to both West and East Berlin) agreed to the Chaplaincy Agreement with the Federal government providing field chaplains for the Bundeswehr. He and his collaborators were, thereafter, styled NATO-bishops in East Germany, and Dibelius himself was refused entry into his East Berlin and East German parishes.[46]

Henceforth, the government of the German Democratic Republic announced its intention to discuss and handle state-church relations with the bishops of individual *Land* churches rather than with the representatives of the Evangelical Church of Germany or its chief organ, the Church Council. Dibelius, who had courageously fought nazism, now found himself opposed to the totalitarian regime of East Germany; he considered Saint Paul's Epistle to the Romans 13, the theological source of Luther's thesis of obedience toward the "governing authorities," no longer applicable to the atheist East German state. In this stand he was supported by the influential Bishop of Hanover, Hanns Lilje.[47]

The reactions of East German Protestant church leaders differed greatly; some of them, like the ultraconservative Bishop of Thuringia, Moritz Mitzenheim, undertook to co-operate fully with the government of the Democratic Republic in strict obedience to Luther's thesis and were encouraged by the supporting letters of the famous Protestant theologian, Karl Barth of Basel. Others, however, under the leadership of Günter Jacob, the Episcopal Administrator of East Berlin, who considered himself operating in a "besieged city," accepted the "Ten Articles on the Freedom and Duty of the Church"; these articles acknowledged obedience toward the *Obrigkeit* (lay authority), but refused the absolute demands made on human personality by Communist ideology. In case of conflicts between governmental and divine demands, the faithful "must obey God rather than men."

After the erection of the Berlin Wall, movements of all Protestant

[45] *Die Welt*, April 14, 1964.
[46] Richard W. Solberg, *God and Caesar in East Germany* (New York, 1961), pp. 224–41.
[47] *Ibid.*, pp. 283–88; *Die Zeit*, July 26, 1963.

ecclesiastical personnel were barred; *Präses* Kurt Scharf, the deputy of Dibelius in East Berlin, was also refused re-entry into the D.D.R. After August 13, 1961, no more joint meetings could be held between representatives of the all-German Evangelical Church, not even in Berlin. All personal contacts except by letter became impossible. The Protestant Church of Germany, a most important link between Germans on both sides of the demarcation line, has thus been severed. For a while it appeared as though Pankow's policy was aimed at setting up a "National Church" in East Germany.[48]

The eighty-six-year-old Dibelius resigned early in 1966. The West and East German members of the Synod, convened separately in East and West Berlin and elected Kurt Scharf Bishop of Berlin and Brandenburg in defiance of the government of the D.D.R., thus refusing to accept the split of their church and of the diocese of Berlin-Brandenburg. The two sessions of the Synod exchanged greetings across the Wall, emphasizing the unity of the church.[49]

The East German regime tried in vain to obtain separate recognition for the Protestant Church in East Germany at the meetings of the World Council of Churches. On the other hand, the D.D.R. government refused permission to the World Lutheran League to hold its international congress in 1969 in Weimar (East Germany). Otherwise, it appears that all leaders of the German Evangelical Church, except perhaps Bishop Mitzenheim, are determined to preserve their unity.[50]

In October, 1965, the Council of the German Evangelical Church issued a memorandum asking for a reappraisal of German policy toward Poland. The memorandum asserted that the enforced mass deportation of Germans living in the Eastern Territories was not in accordance with international law, but acknowledged that "a complete reconstruction of the former situation" would not conform to justice and that the German people should respect the right of Poles to live in the area which they needed for their development and economy.[51] West German expellee organizations im-

[48] *Süddeutsche Zeitung*, February 16, 1966.
[49] *New York Times*, December 19, 1965, and February 16, 1966.
[50] *Die Welt*, May 16, 1966; *New York Times*, July 20, 1966. In July, 1966, Bishop Friedrich Krummacher of Pomerania was re-elected chairman of the East German Bishops' Conference; *New York Times*, July 18, 1966.
[51] *East Europe*, May, 1966, p. 4. See also Ludwig Raiser, "Die Deutsche Ostpolitik und das Memorandum der Protestantischen Kirche," *Europe-Archiv*, June, 1966.

mediately reacted sharply by declaring the Council incompetent to make such political announcements which, as they wrote, were "a misuse of ecclesiastical authority in hasty judgments passed on questions of international law."[52]

The post-World War II political developments caused important changes in the administration of the Catholic Church in Germany behind the Iron Curtain. In the territories east of the Oder-Neisse Line, the former Roman Catholic German bishops were replaced by members of the Polish clergy though no final reorganization was undertaken by the Vatican.[53] Small parts of the Archdiocese of Wroclaw (Breslau) are now within the territory of the German Democratic Republic,[54] while the diocese of Berlin has lost some of its area in Pomerania.

The demarcation line between the Soviet zone and West Germany also separated Catholic ecclesiastical jurisdictions. Because the direct administration of these separated parts of East Germany became more and more difficult (after 1958 no West German bishop or archbishop was allowed to enter East Germany), they were placed under the administration of resident episcopal commissioners or vicars-general. The Bishop of Meissen and the Bishop of Berlin are the two diocesan bishops in the eastern part of Germany; there are episcopal and archiepiscopal commissariats in Magdeburg (belonging to the archdiocese of Paderborn in West Germany), in Schwerin (belonging to the diocese of Osnabrück), in Meiningen (belonging to the diocese of Würzburg), and an episcopal vicariate-general in Erfurt (belonging to the diocese of Fulda). Since August 13, 1961, the bishops and administrators of East German ecclesiastical jurisdictions have not been allowed to participate in the German Roman Catholic Bishops' Conference held in Fulda, West Germany. Thus, the ties of the Catholic Church in East and West have also been severed.

Special difficulties have arisen in Berlin: the jurisdiction of the Bishop of Berlin extends over Greater Berlin and parts of the German Democratic Republic. After 1958 he was no longer allowed to enter his diocese outside Berlin (though he was still able to enter East Berlin). After August 13, 1961, he was prevented from

[52] *The German Tribune*, October 30, 1965.

[53] The former German bishoprics (and one archbishopric) are administered by apostolic administrators (consecrated bishops) who are considered by Poland as diocesan bishops. See M. Dziewanowski, "Communist Poland and the Catholic Church," *Problems of Communism*, September–October, 1954.

[54] This area is administered by the archiepiscopal office in Görlitz, headed by a vicar-capitular.

going to East Berlin, too. When Cardinal Döpfner was appointed Archbishop of Munich-Freising, his successor, Bishop Alfred Bengsch, took residence in East Berlin (whence he can proceed to parts of his diocese in the Democratic Republic) and is allowed to leave occasionally for West Berlin, where he is permanently represented by Vicar-General Walter Adolph.[55]

For the rulers of East Germany, Catholicism presents a lesser problem than Protestantism, not only because of the smaller number of Catholics but also because organizational and personal ties of Protestant leaders in both parts of Germany are closer. While East German Protestants look ardently over the demarcation line to their brethren in West Germany and thus strengthen the idea of unity, the leaders of the Catholic Church in the German Democratic Republic, as elsewhere, wish to maintain their contacts with Rome. For the East German regime, contacts with the Vatican are considered less dangerous and important than those which remind their people of German national unity.

Mass Opinion and Reunification

Expression of popular will generally influence foreign policy decisions only in an indirect manner. The electorate decides only when there is a clear positive or negative position to take. Usually, however, the process of foreign policy, depending on a great many things lying outside the power and competence of the national society and government, is too involved to admit "yes" or "no" responses in elections and referendums. Timing is the essence of the diplomatic process, and it can be directed only in a very general manner by the popular will.

The question of reunification has never been directly put before the electorate. This was, rightly, taken for granted; just as the questions of public education and the public use of the German language are not election issues, reunification was a value which every reasonable person was assumed to accept. The issues which in the past years have come up in connection with reunification were: whether the adherence to the alliances of the West and rearmanent were or were not conducive to reunification; whether the security, freedom, and welfare of West Germany would eventually promote German unity; and which question was to be given over-all priority. When the majority of the voters at several Federal

---

[55] *Die katholische Kirche in Berlin und Mitteldeutschland* (Berlin, 1962), pp. 5–10.

elections pronounced themselves in favor of security, freedom, and welfare for West Germany—either in the belief of promoting thereby reunification or in the belief that reunification was, at the time of voting, unrealizable—one could not conclude that "the Germans do not want re-unification."[56] The gratuitousness of this conclusion is evident since no unqualified answer could be made to this question. What a German could say was that he wanted re-unification at a certain price, at a certain risk, and in a certain manner, or that he did not want it under the same conditions. It is doubtful that he would want it at any price.

The importance of timely response had clearly been shown in the Saar referendum: the Saarlanders had also proved that, when national integration was really at stake, the electorate would respond in a different manner than in elections on marginal changes.[57]

At the height of Franco-German tension over the Saar question before the November 30, 1952, elections, the CDU, the SPD, and the FDP enjoined the Saarlanders to vote blank or refrain from voting in protest. The response was meager, indicating indifference.[58]

On October 23, 1955, the population of the Saar was called upon to approve by referendum the statue providing for a "European status" for the Saar which would have barred it indefinitely from uniting with Germany. Adenauer, personally, and his government, bound by the Paris Treaty of October 23, 1954, felt strongly obliged to recommend an affirmative vote. But, unexpectedly, the people of the Saar, by 67.2 per cent of the votes, refused to endorse European status and clearly expressed their will to rejoin Germany.[59] Once again, as in 1935, the national issue was at stake, and the

---

[56] Khrushchev told Carlo Schmid and Fritz Erler in March, 1959, that "no one really wants Germany re-unified." In June, 1959, he told West German Socialist editors that "even Adenauer does not want re-unification." See Gerald Freund, *Germany Between Two Worlds* (New York, 1961), pp. 219–20.

[57] In 1935 the population of the Saar, in an internationally supervised referendum, voted overwhelmingly for re-unification with the then-Nazi Germany, although the majority of the voters consisted of Catholics and Social Democrats for whom Nazism must have been detestable. But they voted on a "national" issue and had no opportunity to choose a "certain type" of Germany. They simply chose: Germany, instead of France or a continued international status.

[58] See Schmidt, *Saarpolitik*, Vol. II, pp. 461–80.

[59] Schmidt, *Saarpolitik*, Vol. III, pp. 164–371; Grosser, *Die Bonner Demokratie*, p. 317.

majority of the Saarlanders voted according to their deepest conviction when it appeared indispensable to do so.

Some ideas about West German sentiment on reunification may be gained by studying the results of public opinion polls. The analyst must, however, admit two reservations with regard to these polls taken at various times and under various circumstances. The replies are naturally conditioned by the formulation of the questions, and they may not reflect so much what the respondent believes as what he wants the poll-taker to think he believes. Thirdly, the impact of popular opinion on foreign policy is bound to be limited and exceptional—a fact which further reduces the weight of popular opinion polls on these issues.

On the question, "What would most please you in politics?" asked in a public opinion poll of 1965, 66 per cent (in 1962 only 64 per cent) of the replies indicated "reunification of Germany." Questioned on the prospects of reunification, in October, 1961, only 2 per cent of the respondents thought that it could be achieved within twelve months, and 46 per cent believed that reunification could be realized only within "a few years." No prospect for it was seen by 45 per cent, and 7 per cent remained undecided.[60] In March, 1964, 69 per cent of those questioned believed that "reunification will become possible," and only 16 per cent thought it no longer possible; 16 per cent were undecided.[61]

In July, 1962, 61 per cent of the respondents expressed the opinion that the division of Germany was "unbearable" (in September, 1956, only 52 per cent). The increase must have been related to the effect of the Berlin Wall. In July, 1963, the figure decreased to 53 per cent, and 32 per cent now thought that it would be possible to adjust to Germany's partition. In August, 1963, 48 per cent answered that they would never renounce German unity, 18 per cent expressed readiness to do so, and 34 per cent were undecided.[62]

Among the various age groups the higher ones generally showed a greater proportion of affirmative views:[63]

[60] See Erich Peter Neumann, "Wiedervereinigung in der öffentlichen Meinung," Die Politische Meinung, January, 1964, p. 22. These public opinion polls were taken by the Allensbacher Institut für Demoskopie. The 1964 and 1965 results, if available, were received directly from the Institute. See also Frederick H. Hartmann, Germany Between East and West: The Reunification Problem (Englewood Cliffs, N.J., 1965), pp. 8–11.

[61] Neumann, "Wiedervereinigung in der öffentlichen Meinung," pp. 23–24.

[62] Ibid., p. 26.

[63] Ibid., p. 25.

Age Groups	Unbearable (%)	Possible to Adjust (%)	Undecided (%)
16–29	44	40	16
30–44	52	34	14
45–59	56	28	16
60 and above	66	22	12

Party affiliations hardly affected replies, as shown by the following polls:

Party	Unbearable (%)	Possible to Adjust (%)	Undecided (%)
CDU/CSU	56	32	12
SPD	57	30	13
FDP	54	34	12

The public opinion institute asked its respondents whether they would be willing to pay part of their income (on progressive scale ranging from DM 12.50 to 425 yearly) as a price for reunification for a period of ten or three years:[64]

	Ten Years (%)	Three Years (%)
For the Plan	37	42
Against the Plan	59	54
Undecided	4	4

The "priority" or "urgency" aspect of reunification as compared with other national goals was also a topic of public opinion polling. Thus, in January, 1950, only 1 per cent of the respondents considered reunification "the most urgent task facing the Federal Government." But this figure has since risen constantly, and it reached 27 per cent in January, 1957.[65]

In January, 1963, when asked, "What would you consider the generally most important question for the people in West Germany?" 30 per cent mentioned the question of reunification as most important. The maintenance and improvement of the economic situation was second-best with 21 per cent; the preservation of peace, third with 15 per cent; the Berlin question, fourth with 12 per cent; and European integration, fifth with nearly 12 per cent. Responses to the same question have fluctuated as follows during the past fourteen years:[66]

---

[64] Ibid., p. 29.

[65] Deutsch and Edinger, Germany Rejoins the Powers, p. 178; this poll was taken by the Emnid Institute.

[66] Neumann, "Wiedervereinigung in der öffentlichen Meinung," pp. 20–21.

Year	Reunification (%)	Economy (%)	Peace (%)
1951 (October)	18	45	20
1952 (July)	23	33	24
1953 (January)	17	37	17
1955 (January)	34	28	16
1956 (January)	38	22	13
1957 (January)	43	18	17
1959 (January)	45	15	16
1960 (January)	46	15	16
1961 (February)	35	20	19
1962 (February)	30	20	26
1963 (February)	31	21	15
1964 (January)	41	27	11
1965 (January)	47	27	10

The poll results seem to indicate that, after the improvement of the West German economy from its postwar low, the reunification issue had, by 1955, emerged as the most important goal of German politics, a priority maintained ever since. Hopes for the achievement of German unity and the sense of urgency attached to it are reflected in the oscillating percentage figures. The Berlin Wall is probably the cause for the 1962 decrease; on the other hand, the decrease in concern for peace from the February, 1962, high of 26 per cent to 15 per cent in January, 1963, is presumably a result of reassuring outcome of the Cuban crisis of October, 1962.

The year 1965 witnessed a rise in popular West German commitment to reunification: a poll conducted in the spring of that year by the Bielefeld Emnid Institute of Political Opinion Research resulted in 69 per cent of the respondents placing the need for reunification of Germany above that of a united Europe, while only 24 per cent considered the latter more important or necessary. But only 35 per cent of those questioned were ready to conceive of reunification within the next twenty years.[67]

To contrast German and European unity, as in the above opinion poll, is somewhat misleading; in the past, and even in 1965, many respondents may have believed that these two choices were not self-exclusive. Many might have thought that European integration would eventually lead to German unification. On the other hand, De Gaulle's stand against federated Europe may have disillusioned many and thus increased votes in favor of the priority being given to German reunification.

[67] *Die Welt*, August 12, 1965.

Questioned as to whether they believed that the United States would one day recognize the division of Germany and come to an understanding with the Russians, the respondents replied:[68]

Answer	October, 1959 (%)	February, 1961 (%)	September, 1962 (%)
No	41	39	44
Yes	27	23	23
Undecided or no opinion	32	38	33

Early in 1964, 43 per cent of the respondents believed that the the SPD was more likely to solve the reunification problem than any other party, but an equal number believed that the CDU/CSU was more reliable.

The desire for reunification is not only the result of patriotism or loyalty to German *Volkstum* but is a consequence of innumerable personal ties, personal impressions, emotions, and other imponderables. The symbiosis of the German people within the borders of the Bismarckian Reich; decades of social, political, and personal exposures; the experiences of two world wars and their aftermaths; the ups and downs of national history; and, finally, the internal migrations of the post-World War II period caused a high quotient of national cohesion. This solidarity was certainly stronger than one might have expected from the formerly particularistic Germans.

Even after the catastrophic postbellum years, the painful experience of national division was kept alive by the influx of refugees from East Germany ranging from 10 to 50 thousand per month on the average. About 3.2 million arrived between 1950 and August 13, 1961, when the erection of the Berlin Wall drastically reduced the exodus. These refugees (officially "resettlers") are, naturally, more intensively integration-conscious than the average inhabitant of the Federal Republic. Their presence and the memories which they are eager to share with any and all stimulate the demand for reunification even among those who might otherwise be indifferent.[69]

The determination to achieve reunification is also constantly fomented by the ties of kinship and friendship between residents of both parts of Germany. These ties were kept alive by reciprocal visits until the Iron Curtain finally closed down; thereafter, the

[68] Neumann, "Wiedervereinigung in der öffentlichen Meinung," p. 30.
[69] Deutsch and Edinger, *Germany Rejoins the Powers*, pp. 179–80.

impossibility of seeing relatives and friends made reunification seem more imperative. It has been stated that in the Federal Republic sixteen million persons over the age of sixteen (40 per cent of all adults) have relatives or friends in East Germany and that one third of the inhabitants of West Germany regularly exchange personal correspondence with residents of the German Democratic Republic.[70] In 1965 fifty-one million parcels were sent from the Federal Republic to East Germany and twenty-two million parcels in the reverse direction. In the same year 1.8 million visits were made by West Germans to see relatives and friends (they are not prevented to the extent that West Berliners are from visiting East Berlin) in the German Democratic Republic. About 1.2 million old people from East Germany were permitted to travel to see West German relatives.[71]

The attitude of the younger generation of Germans toward the problem of reunification is of considerable importance for the future fate of German unity. Popular polls have shown a comparative indifference of young people on this question (see above). It has been observed, however, at least in the case of university students, that in recent years their interest in German unity has constantly and dramatically increased in striking contrast to earlier apathy.[72]

Although somewhat less than half of the young West Germans show significant interest in politics in general, four fifths of them regard Germany's reunification as an imperative and urgent duty. Three fourths of those questioned opposed the recognition of the Oder-Neisse Line.[73] In the terminology of German youth, the word "fatherland" invariably includes East Germany.[74]

The issue of reunification is significantly promoted by unofficial organizations which rally refugees from the East and serve as pressure groups to influence branches of the government. While expellee federations (Landsmannschaften) are interested in areas

[70] According to a report by the Institute of Applied Social Sciences, *Hannoversche Allgemeine Zeitung*, March 20, 1964.

[71] *The Bulletin*, May 24, 1966, pp. 1–2; *The German Tribune*, February 19, 1966.

[72] See the volume, *Die Jugend und die Wiedervereinigung Deutschlands* (Frankfurt/M, 1962). This publication has been made available by the *Stiftung die Welt* and contains highly interesting contributions by young university graduates and endeavors to refute contentions that youth is disinterested in the issue of German unity.

[73] From a report by the Federal government on youth, as reported by the *Frankfurter Allgemeine Zeitung*, June 22, 1965.

[74] See David Schoenbaum, "What German Boys Say About Hitler," *New York Times Magazine*, January 9, 1966, p. 76.

behind the Oder-Neisse Line (and, therefore, only indirectly serve the purposes of reunification), the Kuratorium Unteilbares Deutschland (Council on Reunification or Committee Indivisible Germany) is the most important nationwide organization for the promotion of reunification.[75]

Economic reasons also play a limited role in the hopes for reunification. This is probably why the people living closest to East Germany display greater interest and stronger desires for reunification than the population of more distant regions. Undoubtedly, reunification is almost a matter of life and death for the future of Berlin. It is also very essential for the city of Hamburg which has lost most of its commercial hinterland through the division of Germany. Even harder hit has been the Hanseatic city of Lübeck, just a few miles from the border, and also some border areas in Lower Saxony.[76]

But the economic and demographic arguments for reunification are, on the whole, secondary to emotional and psychological factors. Although the popularity of European integration among intellectuals occasionally seems to overbalance pressures for German unity, public opinion polls clearly suggest that the overwhelming majority of average West Germans do not share this sense of priorities.

After the economic recovery of West Germany had been achieved, the popular concern with restoration of national unity constantly increased. In 1956 it was predicted that the demand for reunification would continue on its upward trend. The rising popular trend was not to be deterred by the weakening chances that practical politics could bring about the desired result.[77] However, the negative energy directed toward the defense of West Berlin superseded the positive clamor for reunification. The government's passive acceptance of the Berlin Wall was only partly met by popular furor. But Soviet failure to achieve control over West Berlin, together with the dismal ending of Khrushchev's Cuban adventure, again raised popular interest in the reunification issue.

In all likelihood, public interest in German unity will fluctuate according to international and internal developments. Its importance, as mentioned earlier, should by no means be overestimated: the solution of the German problem of the mid-twentieth century depends considerably less on the ups and downs of popular inter-

---

[75] For detailed information on the Kuratorium Unteilbares Deutschland see *The Bulletin*, September 20, 1966, pp. 3–6.

[76] Speier and Davidson, *West German Leadership*, p. 87.

[77] See Fritz René Allemann, *Bonn ist nicht Weimar* (Cologne, 1956), pp. 438–39; Deutsch and Edinger, *Germany Rejoins the Powers*, pp. 177–78.

est than on the will and skill of governmental leadership, not to mention international developments, especially the foreign policy of the Soviet Union. The people and the government of the Federal Republic are closely following trends in the Soviet Union, searching for favorable signs that might herald a start on the road to reunification. It is also for this reason that the development of the Sino-Soviet controversy and the schism in the Communist camp are being watched with greater interest in Germany than anywhere else outside the Communist orbit.

Was Starlinger Right?

Long before the antagonism between the Soviet Union and the People's Republic of China had burst into the open, the attention of the German public and its leaders had been directed to the potentialities of such a struggle.[78]

As early as 1954 a study had been published by Dr. Wilhelm Starlinger, a former professor of internal medicine at the University of Königsberg, under the title, *The Limits of Soviet Power*.[79] This book stirred the imagination of its readers, including many in leading circles in Bonn. Chancellor Adenauer received Starlinger and, subsequently, made reference to Starlinger's thesis: that reunification would be in sight when the Soviet Union experienced the inevitable pressures of Chinese expansionism.

The author had been taken prisoner by the Russians and spent many years in Soviet captivity. He wrote his book after his return from Russia. He predicted the split between China and the Soviet Union on the basis of impressions he had gained from interviews with various types of people in the prison camps where he had practiced medicine.

Starlinger relied for support on his thesis of the "bio-geological" factors of China's population explosion which, in his view, was bound to inundate the empty spaces of Siberia. In the author's view, this would be the proper time for Germany to open negotiations with the Soviet Union for the settlement of the German problem. The author felt that the event was inevitable within a few years.[80]

Starlinger died in 1956. In a posthumous book,[81] he further enlarged on his subject and also predicted the schism in world com-

---

[78] See Speier and Davison, *West German Leadership*, pp. 179-80.
[79] Wilhelm Starlinger, *Die Grenzen der Sowjetmacht* (Kitzingen/M, 1954).
[80] *Ibid.*, pp. 118-25.
[81] Wilhelm Starlinger, *Hinter Russland China* [Behind Russia—China] (Würzburg, 1957).

munism, the abandonment of Communist East Germany by Moscow, and possibilities arising for Germany from the global triangular confrontation between the United States, the Soviet Union, and China.[82]

No doubt, Starlinger was much influenced by "geopolitics" and *lebensraum*-concepts; but his thesis did not fail to impress the West German public. His predictions were recalled again in 1963 when the first part of his prophecies proved to have been correct.[83]

The appeal of Adenauer's "automatic" reunification concept, so pleasing to the mentality of the postwar German public, combined the promise of German unity with that of a "spontaneous" realization of this national goal. The Germans had been told by Adenauer that reunification could be achieved without risks or any direct action as a result of outside pressures on the Soviet Union. The Starlinger thesis admirably fitted this picture.

For fifteen years the question of German unity elicited no interest among writers of fiction until Uwe Johnson published his two masterly portrayals of the nightmarish, inscrutable, and seemingly insoluble problem.[84] These books were also an apologia for the political escapism practiced by many Germans in the face of their tragic national predicament.

The popular hope that the Sino-Soviet animosity might create conditions for German unity is a notable example of how West German public opinion relied on "outward" forces that would involve no risks by the Germans themselves. The German propensity to think in terms of territorial power struggles also gave credence to Starlinger's thesis. "Behind Russia stands China," wrote Starlinger; so China will bring help.

Adenauer, even after his resignation as chancellor, has not given up his belief that the Sino-Soviet conflict will eventually force Moscow to disgorge its portion of Germany. He only expressed what is in the mind of many in Germany when he said: "In the long run, Soviet Russia will be confronted with a choice between subordination to Red China or keeping hands off Europe."[85]

A West German publicist, whose views are representative of wide influential circles, wrote that the policy to achieve reunification by *détour* was correct, only the *détour* made was wrong: it should

[62] *Ibid.*, pp. 127–41.
[83] See "Hatte Starlinger doch recht?" *Frankfurter Allgemeine Zeitung,* August 7, 1963, and August 16, 1963.
[84] Uwe Johnson, *Mutmassungen über Jakob* (Frankfurt/M, 1959), and his *Das dritte Buch über Achim* (Frankfurt/M, 1961).
[85] *New York Times,* March 24, 1966.

not have been undertaken via Warsaw or Bucarest, but via Peking.[86] And the SPD deputy, Wenzel Jaksch, an expellee leader, suggested that trade links with China were more likely to make Moscow ready for negotiations than similar contacts with East European Communist governments. In a similar vein, a CDU deputy, also an expellee, considered it irresponsible for the Federal Republic not to come to some trade agreement with such a large and important area.[87]

De Gaulle's recognition of Communist China, although an affront to United States policy, was not unpopular in the Federal Republic and was thought to be directed not only against the Soviet Union but also against the latter's most obedient satellite, the German Democratic Republic.[88] While Peking had earlier accused Moscow of being willing to abandon East Germany to the West German imperialists, a rumor of 1964 had it that China favored German reunification.[89] Walter Ulbricht's regime was no doubt beginning to feel the diplomatic pressures and strains caused by the Sino-Soviet conflict. The German Democratic Republic, the weakest member of the Communist bloc in popular support, was also clearly a military outpost for twenty-two divisions of the Soviet Union. Any seismic rumblings of the balance of power between the superstates will be increasingly felt in the D.D.R. But its greatest source of instability has been the natural desire of its people to rejoin the main body of Germans. This, an impulse which is probably stronger even than the antitotalitarianism found elsewhere in the satellite area, is a force against which the Ulbricht regime knows it must fight with all available means.

[86] Studnitz, *Bismarck in Bonn*, pp. 141–51.
[87] *Frankfurter Allgemeine Zeitung*, April 5, 1966.
[88] Trade between the German Democratic Republic and the People's Republic of China declined considerably after 1961 (to $53 million in 1962, a decline of 88 per cent), while the trade between the Federal Republic and China trebled in six years to $103 million in 1966. West Germany is the biggest single trading partner of China in Europe.
[89] See Chapter IV, pp. 164–65 below.

The West Germans will yet come to appreciate that it would not be so bad after all to have Walter Ulbricht as Federal Chancellor and Otto Grotewohl as President of a united German People's Republic of workers and peasants. . . . If the people in West Germany are not ready yet, there's no hurry. Let there be two states for the time being.

—Khrushchev at the
Leipzig Fair in 1959

CHAPTER IV

✻ ✻

EAST GERMANY AND REUNIFICATION

When the Soviet Union took control over East Germany, Moscow's intentions were not at first to establish a Communist state separated by watertight borders from the rest of the country. On the contrary, the principal Soviet objective was to maintain and increase its influence over the entire area of Potsdam Germany through the Control Council, the central German departments, and, eventually, an all-German government, which it wished to create. The Soviet zone was to be the Kremlin's stake in Germany, a base to secure its participation in Germany's affairs and, ultimately, universal control. A secondary but important purpose of the occupation regime was to extract reparations to help the ruined economy of the Soviet fatherland. During the first years of the postwar period, the political organization of the Soviet zone was a tertiary concern for the Soviet rulers.

Until 1948 the Soviet military and political administration showed marked restraint in Sovietizing East Germany. The German Communist leaders were permitted to pursue a *Sonderweg* (separate road), a kind of pseudodemocratic socialism by nationalizing big industry but supporting small business and artisanship and by dissolving large estates and distributing land among middle- and small-holders. Merger between the Social Democratic and Communist parties was preached under the banner of "national proletarian unity" throughout Germany. This *Sonderweg*, however, did not keep the rulers of East Germany from using political oppression, police terror, and intimidation of sorts. More than all the blandishments and coaxing with prospects of a united Germany under "German Socialism," this left its indelible imprint on the minds of the Germans.

The Soviet task in Germany differed from that performed in the small East European countries, because in Germany the Kremlin dominated only a fragment of the country and aspired to gain all of it. In Austria the Soviet position was somewhat analogous; but soon the central Austrian government, supported by nationwide free elections, was able to thwart Soviet aims. By 1948 it must have become evident to the Soviet leaders that they could not obtain a predominant influence over all of Germany either by an appeal to popular will or by obstructive tactics. By their withdrawal from the Control Council and their revelation of their true motives in the Berlin blockade, the Soviets had deprived themselves of the possibility of interfering in the affairs of West Germany. The alternative was to convert East Germany into a "People's Democracy" comparable to those of the other Soviet satellite countries. The *Sonderweg* was abandoned; the Socialist Unity party (SED) turned from a mass party into a cadre party.[1] Attempts were made to create a politically and economically viable state within the Soviet zone of occupation. Gradualism was practiced: the East German state was to emerge step-by-step, never in advance of the conversion of West Germany into independent statehood, but never much behind. While the Soviet bastion in Germany was to be strengthened, it was never forgotten that it might also be used as an advance base for the penetration and conquest of all of Germany.

The Soviet Union's use of its East German satrapy remained ambivalent. It tried to push the German Democratic Republic into the arena of German politics by insisting that reunification

---

[1] See Georges Castellan, *D.D.R., Allemagne de l'Est* (Paris, 1955), pp. 72–78. The the concept of *Sonderweg* was not entirely dropped as late as 1958 appears from an East German publication, evidently for West German consumption, by Wilhelm Koenen, *Das ganze Deutschland soll es sein—Zur Geschichte der patriotischen Volksbewegung in Deutschland* (Berlin [East], 1958).

could be sought only through agreement by the "two German states" in the form of a confederation or otherwise, but it also maintained that it had neither the interest nor the right to interfere in the affairs of the sovereign Germanys. However, when the Soviet Union recognized the "sovereignty" of the German Democratic Republic (Deutsche Demokratische Republik [D.D.R.]) in response to Western recognition of the Federal Republic, it was careful to retain "the functions connected with guaranteeing security and resulting from the obligations incumbent on the U.S.S.R. as a result of the Four-Power Agreement." This reservation covered not only Berlin but also "questions of an all-German character," as mentioned in the Soviet statement of March 25, 1954.[2] Similar reservations were made in the Treaty of Moscow of September 20, 1955, between the Soviet Union and the German Democratic Republic.[3]

Immediately after the Soviet bestowal of sovereignty on the D.D.R., the three Western powers, in a joint statement issued by the three High Commissioners of West Germany, refused to recognize the change in status and declared that they would continue to consider the Soviet Union the power internationally responsible for the "Soviet Zone of Germany." In the opinion of the Western powers, the East German regime did not rest on the freely expressed will of the population; they reaffirmed the Federal Republic as the freely elected and legitimate government in Germany.[4] Naturally, the Federal government also withheld recognition.

Recognition of the German Democratic Republic

Recognition of a new state or government is an action having both political and international legal significance. It implies acceptance of the new political unit into the family of states and bases relations with it on a level of formal equality. International lawyers disagree about whether there is or can be under certain

[2] Statement by the Soviet Government on the Relations between the Soviet Union and the German Democratic Republic, dated March 25, 1954; Beate Ruhm von Oppen (ed.), *Documents on Germany Under Occupation*, pp. 597–98.

[3] See Grewe, *Deutsche Aussenpolitik*, pp. 133–36. The Treaty reserves for the Soviet Union questions concerning international agreements relating to Germany "as a whole."

[4] On October 3, 1954, a similar declaration was addressed to the Federal Republic by the United States, Britain, and France in London. On October 23, 1954, when the Federal Republic joined NATO, all the other members of the North Atlantic Treaty Organization also signed such a statement.

circumstances an obligation to recognize a new state or government. The practice of most states over the past fifty years demonstrates, however, that the recognition of states or governments is not considered an obligation but a political decision guided by considerations of foreign policy.

The recognition of the independence of a state which had seceded from another or which has arisen as a result of a dismemberment of a state poses problems which, in many respects, differ from those cases where recognition means formal acknowledgment of the existence of a state and the resumption of diplomatic and other relations with it. For a truncated state to recognize the sovereign existence of its severed member implies, *inter alia*, the final and irrevocable acknowledgment of its own dismemberment. There are historical precedents in which states have refused, for many decades, to recognize the loss of former territories.[5]

As things stand, the West Germans not only refuse diplomatic communication with the German Democratic Republic, but also deny its natural existence as an independent political entity. German political theorists point out that, under the generally accepted criteria (territory, population, and governmental authority), the D.D.R. cannot qualify as a state. Though it has a territory, it possesses no population willing to support a "state" (evidence for this is the constant mass exodus until the erection of the Berlin Wall and the revolt of June 17, 1953, suppressed by the Russians); its government is "pseudo-autochthonous," in reality thrust upon the unwilling population by a foreign government; the government authority could not be maintained without the presence and support of the Soviet Army (from twenty to twenty-two divisions). It is thus, we are told, not the population which supports the regime but the Communist party, disguised as a government which controls the population by coercion.[6] From 1950 to August 13, 1961, 3.2 million people out of 18.4 million fled East Germany so that her population, despite natural growth, had decreased by 1961 to 17.07

[5] For instance, Spain refused recognition to the secessionist Seven Provinces (Netherlands) from 1572 to 1648. China, the United States, and other democratic powers refused to recognize the Japanese puppet-state of Manchukuo (Manchuria) after its establishment in 1931. The Arab states have refused the recognition of Israel since its foundation in 1948. Neither South and North Korea, nor South and North Vietnam, nor the People's Republic of China (Peking) and the Republic of China (Taiwan) recognize each other.

[6] See, for instance, Ekkehard Stein, "Ist die 'Deutsche Demokratische Republik' ein Staat?" *Archiv des öffentlichen Rechts*, Vol. 85, April, 1961 (4), pp. 363–91.

million (including East Berlin).[7] Since the closing of the Berlin escape hatch, the people of East Germany are literally imprisoned.

For the leaders of the Federal Republic, including major political parties, neither a full (so-called *de jure*) nor a limited (*de facto*) diplomatic recognition of the East German regime is conceivable; even the mental acknowledgment of the existence of the D.D.R. as a normal "state" is rejected.[8] That is why official circles in West Germany warn against "upgrading" the "Soviet Zone"—that is, acknowledging it, not diplomatically, but in its physical existence as a "state." This is a far cry from even *de facto* diplomatic recognition.

Any kind of recognition or near-recognition of East Germany would be, in the West German view, an abandonment of the claim to German unity. It would be a flagrant violation of the fundamental principles which the Federal Republic professes, a denial of the *raison d'être* of the West German state. To accept the legitimate existence of the D.D.R. would be an open breach of the West German constitutional system embodied in the Basic Law. Under its own constitutional rules, the Federal Republic considers itself the only legitimate spokesman in behalf of the German people.

Over and above doctrinal and political considerations, recognition of the East German regime would be interpreted as an abandonment of the German population of the Soviet zone to the terror and inhuman situation in which they are believed to live. Such a tacit approval of the D.D.R. regime is seen as treason against the German nation and against humanity. Any politician supporting recognition would at once be accused of wishing to perpetuate Soviet rule over a part of Germany. It should be remarked that no such strong feelings seem to exist in West Germany with regard to the Eastern Territories, though nobody in a responsible position would agree to their abandonment.

The recognition of the German Democratic Republic is thus a

---

[7] At the end of 1965, 3.4 million East German refugees lived in West Germany (5.8 per cent of the population). About a half million had returned to East Germany since 1950. *Frankfurter Allgemeine Zeitung*, January 17, 1966.

[8] ". . . the Soviet Union cannot force the West to accept the partition of Germany and recognize the colonial regime which exists in the Sovietized part of it. Nor can we Germans be forced to give up the political fight for the right of self-determination for our whole people . . . we [have to] maintain the belief of the Germans in the Soviet Zone that one day they will recover their freedom (which means we have to avoid upgrading the Communist regime internationally). . . ." Fritz Erler (SPD leader), *Foreign Affairs*, October, 1963, p. 95.

constitutional, political, and psychological *non-possumus* for West Germany. Even those who contemplate such ideas, like Jaspers, have made recognition conditional on liberalization and democratization of the East German regime. That would not only make it psychologically possible and palatable for the West Germans to consider some type of recognition but would also eliminate the doctrinal objections against such a move: if there were some free expression of a *Staatswille* (a will to run a state) by the East German people, the existence of a "state" in the East could no longer be denied. Even Adenauer conceded this point when he cautiously wrote: "The Berlin problem, just like the German problem, is in the last analysis a human one. This is why a starting point for a solution could be found in that sphere. If our countrymen in the Soviet-occupied zone are granted decent living conditions and *at least a certain amount of freedom and self-determination,* we shall be open to discussion on a good many points." [9]

The arguments which are generally advanced against the West German determination to concede no real existence to the German Democratic Republic may thus be summarized:

1) The German Democratic Republic is a "reality" that exists and cannot be done away with by nonrecognition. It cannot be made nonexistent as long as the Russians continue to support it. And the Soviet Union will never willingly abandon the protected state.

2) West Germany's nonrecognition policy is artificial, fictitious, and insincere because the Federal Republic maintains contacts with its eastern neighbor and does extended business with it.

3) Lastly, it is said that the West Germans, by extending recognition to the German Democratic Republic, would not thereby forego or even prejudice reunification, but would contribute toward the preservation of peace and the strengthening of West Berlin.[10]

Naturally, nobody can deny that the D.D.R. is a physical reality. Whether it is a normal "state" depends very much on the criteria

[9] Konrad Adenauer, "The German Problem," *Foreign Affairs,* October, 1962, pp. 63–64. Italics have been added.

[10] Among the more recent advocates of the recognition of the D.D.R. and their arguments, see Fred Warner Neal, *War and Peace and Germany* (New York, 1962), pp. 21–22, 24–25, 110–12; same author, "The Unsolved German Settlement," *The Annals,* January, 1964, pp. 148–56; Geoffrey McDermott, *Berlin—Success of a Mission* (New York, 1963), pp. 116–30; Carl Landauer, "The Case for Staying: Germany," *The Correspondent,* November-December, 1963, p. 39. See also Rudolf Augstein, "Wege zu einer neuen Politik," *Der Spiegel,* September 23, 1964.

we allow for the concept of statehood. If the East German regime had no physical existence, there would be no point in discussing its "upgrading" or recognition. The ominous "reality" of the D.D.R. is precisely what induces the West Germans to fight it. In international relations and diplomacy, one of the nonaggressive weapons is nonrecognition; the state whose existence or policies you utterly abhor is officially though not literally ignored, cold-shouldered, and isolated. This causes inconveniences to both parties. Whether one's own disadvantages outweigh those of the nonrecognized state will be an important standard of reference.

In the case of the Federal Republic, the reasons for nonrecognition are, as we have seen, much more profound than, for instance, those which the United States alleges against Communist China. For the Germans, recognition of their country's partition would be an abandonment of much of what their present West German state stands for. As former Chancellor Erhard has pointed out, these intangibles are, for them at any rate, a much stronger "reality" than the statelike manifestations of the East German regime.[11]

No doubt West Germany maintains manifold contacts with East German authorities. She is very careful to keep these contacts on a lower or technical level; they are restricted to exchanges between railroad, postal, and other technical administrations. For trade and other administrative contacts with East Germany, a special, officially nongovernmental agency is being maintained in Berlin (see ahead). One should not forget that, while the Federal Republic insists on the legal nonexistence of an East German state, it also insists on the continued existence of Germany as a whole. It is caught in a dilemma; on the one hand, it wishes to preserve unity for Germany; on the other, it desires to isolate the East German regime. If it is inconsistent, this is simply a result of the ambiguities of the situation and the unavoidable ambivalence of a doctrinal position which implies seemingly inconsistent courses of action.

The question is never whether a position taken is fictitious, but rather whether the assumption of a fiction is useful, necessary, or expedient. German unity, the continued existence of Germany, and the nonexistence of an East German political entity are fictions; but both the West Germans and the Allies have decided to operate with these fictions because they consider them useful, expedient, and necessary. Fictions may perform wholesome tasks in international politics; they may even help to support what is right and

[11] See quotation from Erhard's inaugural speech, p. 47 above.

just. The West Germans might submit that the pretense of running a proletarian and democratic state in the East is more mendacious and, therefore, fictitious than their assumption of the unity of Germany. In the West German view the German Democratic Republic is the real fiction: it is neither "German" nor "Democratic" nor even a "Republic."

The contention that official recognition would not obviate reunification, if realizable, is evidently erroneous. Bonn wishes to keep the German problem alive, to maintain a fluidity, and to prevent the freezing of the status quo. It does not intend to participate in any agreement which would contribute toward the solidification of the existing *de facto* partition of Germany. The recognition of a second German state would undoubtedly strengthen the German Democratic Republic and would persuade its inhabitants that they must give up hope of liberation from Soviet domination. Shortly, it would turn the *de facto* situation into a *de jure* division of the country. While the factual situation is not recognized, it is possible to oppose it and to do so by peaceful methods (nonrecognition being one of them). After an internationally binding recognition of Germany's partition, Germans would be more likely to resort to violent methods because other ways would be barred by convention. In any case, it is very unlikely that there could be a democratically elected West German government in the foreseeable future that would be willing to sign any document that sealed the fate of German unity.

The Western powers and all the signatories of the North Atlantic Treaty have endorsed the thesis that the government of the Federal Republic is the only legitimate government *in* Germany. There is, at present, no likelihood that the German Democratic Republic will transform itself into a genuine democratic state; should this happen, unification or some other solution of the German question would be around the corner, for neither the Western powers nor the Federal Republic could any longer object to recognizing a "freely elected" government.

The thesis of nonrecognition must remain the policy of the United States, Britain, and France. Any direct recognition of the D.D.R. by these powers would be a violation of the existing international agreements, and there can be no doubt that the Federal government would not concede the modification of these agreements. Of course, there are many "forms" of recognition: the Western powers or one or two of them might be tempted to open negotiations with the German Democratic Republic or to establish other limited contacts. Even the slightest degree of impairment of the thesis of nonrecognition would be sorely resented by West Germany. It would render West Germany an utterly discontented partner even if it would not directly destroy the Western alliance or induce the Federal Republic to seek *rapprochement* with the East. It would, however, foster internal strife in West Germany, provoke nationalistic reactions, and perhaps upset the present two-party system.

The determination of the threshold of permissible contacts with East Germany already created serious controversies between the major political parties of the Federal Republic in 1966. While none of these proposed an outright abandonment of basic principles and constitutional-legal positions, the SPD and the FDP were ready for a more daring and risky "policy of movement" than some leaders of the CDU/CSU or Foreign Minister Schröder himself.[12] Nonrecognition should not exclude all kinds of contacts, including negotiations and agreements, on any, even the ministerial, level. Recognition should receive a strict and narrow interpretation, as generally practiced in international relations: it should mean official and formal recognition only. Talks, meetings, and arrangements between political parties, officials, and even ministers of West and East Germany should not be considered a legitimization of the East German regime. Should the Federal government be willing to adopt such a dynamic and flexible interpretation of recognition, it would still insist on the strict continuance of the official non-recognition policy.

The nonrecognition of East Germany has time and again been reiterated by Germany's Western Allies. When the accession of the D.D.R. to the Moscow Treaty on the Limited Cessation of Nuclear Testing raised doubts in some minds on this issue, President Kennedy declared: "The treaty in no way changes the status of the authorities of East Germany. As the Secretary of State has made clear 'we do not recognize, and we do not intend to recognize, the Soviet occupation zone of East Germany as a state or an an entity possessing national sovereignty, or to recognize the local authorities as a government. These authorities cannot alter these facts by the act of subscribing to the test ban treaty.' "[13]

---

[12] See pp. 66–93 above.
[13] Letter from President Kennedy to Senate Democratic and Republican leaders, dated September 11, 1963; *New York Times*, September 12, 1963.

The partners of the North Atlantic Treaty have also given frequent assurances that they will abide by their Declaration made upon West Germany's accession. On May 14, 1964, the NATO Council sitting at The Hague issued the following statement: "The Council also reaffirmed that the Government of the Federal Republic of Germany is the only German government freely and legitimately constituted and therefore entitled to speak for Germany as the representative of the German people in international affairs."[14]

The nonrecognition of East Germany is, however, not only a question between the Federal government and other Western powers, on the one hand, and the German Democratic Republic, on the other. It is a problem which affects relations between all the states which maintain or wish to maintain normal relations with the Federal Republic of Germany. The attempt made by West Germany to prevent the recognition or upgrading of the German Democratic Republic has involved diplomatic complications that bear heavily on the problem of German unity.

The Hallstein Doctrine

Foreign policy guidelines, often known as "doctrines," have steered nations in the past and continue to do so. The Monroe Doctrine, the Stimson Doctrine, and more recently the Truman Doctrine have been lodestars for the United States. The German doctrine named, probably not quite accurately, after the then State Secretary in the Federal Ministry of Foreign Affairs, Professor Walter Hallstein (he himself denies the fatherhood of the Doctrine),[15] stems from the principle of nonrecognition of the East German state; in fact, it is an extended application of this negative attitude. Under the Hallstein Doctrine, the Federal Republic of Germany refuses to maintain normal diplomatic relations with any state which has recognized the German Democratic Republic and maintains diplomatic relations with it. This principle was made public in a declaration made by the Federal Minister of Foreign Affairs to a conference of ambassadors on December 9, 1955.[16] At

[14] *New York Times,* May 15, 1964.

[15] Professor Hallstein, who later became President of the Commission of the European Economic Community, was a jurist by profession, and the doctrine named after him is often erroneously considered to be an application of an international legal principle. See Grewe, *Deutsche Aussenpolitik,* pp. 160–61.

[16] *Frankfurter Allgemeine Zeitung,* December 10, 1955.

that time a number of uncommitted countries, including India, were preparing to recognize the D.D.R. The declaration was to make clear to them that, with the one exception of Moscow, there would be no "two German ambassadors" in any capital.

At the time of the announcement of the Hallstein Doctrine the Federal government had already breached the very same principle by agreeing to establish diplomatic relations with the Soviet Union. This "exception," the only exception until 1967, has been explained by the peculiar status of the Soviet Union vis-à-vis Germany, that is, its participation in the four-power responsibility. According to the West German view, since the Soviet Union is the government in control of the Soviet zone of Germany, Soviet recognition of the "sovereignty" of the East German state is overlooked. It should also be remembered that Soviet recognition of the German Democratic Republic preceded the setting up of West German-Soviet diplomatic relations.[17]

The Hallstein Doctrine is considered a political weapon against the two-state concept. By insisting on being the only representative of Germany abroad, the Federal government also seeks to be accepted as the only spokesman of the German people. The Hallstein Doctrine has clearly prevented a more general recognition of the German Democratic Republic though the price paid by the Federal Republic has, occasionally, been high, both in economic sacrifices and in loss of valuable official contacts.

Member states of the North Atlantic Treaty Organization and of other pro-Western alliances have refrained from recognizing the East German state. Most of these states, however, maintain contacts with the D.D.R. for purposes of trade and technical matters.

All the Communist states entertain full diplomatic relations with the German Democratic Republic; therefore, the Federal Republic has, until 1967, refrained from entering into similar relations with those countries, except for the Soviet Union. Yugoslavia is another exception; she resumed diplomatic relations with Bonn in late 1951. During the improvement of Soviet-Yugoslav relations in 1956–57, the government of Belgrade opened formal diplomatic relations with the German Democratic Republic, thus recognizing it as a sovereign "second" German state. Thereupon, the Federal govern-

[17] Rudolf Schuster, "Die 'Hallstein-Doktrin.' Ihre rechtliche und politische Bedeutung und die Grenzen ihrer Wirksamkeit," *Europe-Archiv*, 1963, p. 675; Schuster, *Deutschlands staatliche Existenz*, pp. 205–6.

ment severed diplomatic relations with Yugoslavia, though both countries continued to maintain consular and trade contacts.[18]

The rupture of diplomatic relations with Yugoslavia stimulated criticism of the rigorous application of the Hallstein Doctrine by, among others, the Ambassador of the Federal Republic in Belgrade, Karl Georg Pfleiderer.[19] The decision made by Bonn in the case of Yugoslavia was, nevertheless, carefully weighed. Yugoslavia, though Communist, was considered to be a "neutralist" power whose voice possessed influence among other uncommitted countries. Yugoslavia had recognized the Federal Republic of Germany many years before she decided to recognize the East German state as well. There can be no doubt that, had the Yugoslav precedent been accepted passively by Bonn, a chain reaction of recognizing the D.D.R. would have set in among the neutralist states. Since the real testing area of the Hallstein Doctrine is the camp of uncommitted states (the anti-Communist camp is formally or informally bound not to recognize the East German state; the Communist states are duty bound to recognize it), the principle for which Bonn feels obliged to fight would simply have been swept away. The question was not West German-Yugoslav relations, but whether the Hallstein Doctrine should be fully upheld or abandoned.

The Federal Republic had maintained diplomatic relations with Cuba since July, 1953. After Fidel Castro's takeover, Cuba established diplomatic contacts with the German Democratic Republic. In return, the Federal Republic broke off its relations with that country.[20]

Finland, on her part, has refrained from recognizing either the Federal Republic or East Germany. She maintains only trade missions in both parts of Germany. This reticence by the Helsinki government is based on its special relations with the Soviet Union: not wishing to offend either her powerful neighbor or West Germany, she decided to avoid the alternatives.

[18] The Federal government maintained a consulate in Zagreb, and Yugoslavia maintained consulates in Hamburg and Munich. West Germany, even after the rupture of diplomatic relations, remained one of the three best trade partners of Yugoslavia (with Italy and the United States). But the Federal Republic refused to discuss indemnification to Yugoslav war victims; in Bonn's view the Yugoslav government had "forfeited" its right to ask for damages because of the recognition of East Germany; *New York Times*, April 12, 1964.

[19] Grewe, *Deutsche Aussenpolitik*, pp. 149–60; *The German Tribune*, January 4, 1964; Schuster, *Deutschlands staatliche Existenz*, pp. 198–99. About Pfleiderer, see Chapter I, p. 30 above.

[20] Schuster, *Deutschlands staatliche Existenz*, pp. 194–95.

All the other uncommitted states have recognized only the Federal Republic of Germany, but almost all of them maintain more or less intensive nondiplomatic trade contacts with the German Democratic Republic. The great majority of these states refrain from entering into normal diplomatic relations with East Germany only because they fear West German retaliatory measures—rupture of diplomatic relations and sanctions of an economic nature, especially the latter. Is is, therefore, no exaggeration to say that the Hallstein Doctrine has operated successfully because of the greater economic power of the Federal Republic and the development aid ("bribes," as some like to put it) which it can afford and East Germany cannot. Still the operation of the Doctrine is constantly threatened by changing relations between some neutralist countries and the D.D.R.

The case of Israel is *sui generis*. The Federal Republic has concluded formal treaties with Israel which, in international practice, amount to a reciprocal recognition of both states. No normal diplomatic relations were established, however, before 1965. At first, because of Germany's tainted past, Israel did not stress an exchange of ambassadors; later, when Israel showed willingness, the Federal government preferred to have no formal diplomatic relations with her because this relationship would have induced the Arab states to extend recognition to East Germany.

The United Arab Republic approved the establishment of an East German consulate-general in Cairo without the right to hoist the flag of the D.D.R. In February, 1965, President Nasser, probably vexed because of West German arm deliveries to Israel, received Walter Ulbricht, Head of the East German state, on an official state visit. In retaliation, Bonn resolved to establish full diplomatic relations with Israel. In return, the United Arab Republic and nine other Arab countries severed their diplomatic ties with the Federal Republic without, however, giving formal recognition to the D.D.R.[21]

In March, 1960, Pankow announced the resumption of diplomatic relations with the Republic of Guinea. Upon pressures by Bonn, Sekou Touré, the Head of State, refused to accept the credentials of the East German ambassador, who was compelled to return home.[22] In February, 1964, the government of Ceylon an-

[21] *Frankfurter Allgemeine Zeitung*, March 11, 1965; *Der Tagesspiegel*, May 1, 1965.

[22] See Schuster, *Deutschlands staatliche Existenz*, pp. 196–98.

nounced the transformation of the East German trade mission into a consulate-general; simultaneously, the Ceylonese Prime Minister, Mrs. Bandaranaike, endorsed the concept of two German states. The Federal government protested and threatened reprisals.[23] The extreme leftist government of Zanzibar had entered into diplomatic relations with the German Democratic Republic; upon the merger of Zanzibar with Tanganyika (which entertains diplomatic and economic contacts with Bonn), the question of the new union's relationship with either of the German states raised a particularly delicate problem.[24]

The Vatican has never ceased to maintain a nunciature in Germany. The present nuncio is accredited to the Federal Republic (which, in turn, maintains an ambassador at the Holy See) but, officially, he is still heading the "Apostolic Nunciature for Germany." He is debarred from having official contacts with the German Democratic Republic though, in the view of the Vatican, the Concordat of September 12, 1933, concluded with the Reich, continues to be in force.[25]

In the last two decades one of the most important criteria of international recognition for newly established states was membership in the United Nations. Neither the Federal Republic of Germany nor the German Democratic Republic is a member. The former has never applied because its admission would either have been vetoed by the Soviet Union or have been made conditional on a simultaneous admission of East Germany. The admission of the D.D.R. to the United Nations would be regarded as a complete defeat for the one-state thesis and an endorsement, on a worldwide scale, of Germany's permanent partition—a situation even worse than Pankow's limited recognition.[26]

On March 1, 1966, the East German government submitted a formal request for admission into the United Nations. Simultaneously, Otto Winzer, East German Foreign Minister, declared that his government would prefer to see both "existing German states" as members in the World Organization.[27] The East German note

[23] *The Bulletin*, issued by the Press and Information Office of the Federal government, February 25, 1964.

[24] Eventually, the government of Tanzania reduced the East German representation in Zanzibar to a consulate-general. *New York Times*, May 4, June 3, and July 30, 1964; *Frankfurter Allgemeine Zeitung*, February 15, 1965.

[25] Schuster, *Deutschlands staatliche Existenz*, pp. 200–3.

[26] See the article by Hans Steinitz, "Deutschland und die Vereinten Nationen," in Jacobsen and Stenzl (eds.), *Deutschland und die Welt*, pp. 77–85.

[27] *New York Times*, March 3, 1966; *East Europe*, April, 1966, pp. 39–40.

was unofficially circulated among the members of the Security Council. The United States, Britain, and France immediately stated "that only the Government of the Federal Republic of Germany is entitled to speak on behalf of Germany as the representative of the German people in international affairs." They further declared: "Since it is not a state, the so-called German Democratic Republic has no right whatever to be admitted to the United Nations organization."[28]

The Security Council refrained from taking action in this matter. The East German move can be considered as an attempt to break out of the isolation in which it found itself.

The Federal Republic prefers to remain outside the United Nations but to participate in a peripheral manner in all activities which are not strictly limited to members of the organization. Thus, it finds itself in a favorable position to fight all attempts by the German Democratic Republic to gain a similar advisory or associate role.

Bonn maintains an official observer accredited to the Secretary General of the United Nations, whereas East Germany's similar request has been rejected because she is recognized by only a few member states. The Federal Republic is a member of all international organizations, dependent on the United Nations, such as UNESCO, the World Bank, the International Labor Organization, UNICEF, the International Civil Aviation Organization, and the Food and Agricultural Organization. The Federal Republic also participates in the technical commissions of the United Nations, such as the Economic Commission for Europe. The German Democratic Republic has not, so far, succeeded in obtaining admission to these organizations.[29] The Federal Republic contributes toward the budget of the United Nations as if it were a member (paying 5.7 per cent of total expenditure, the seventh highest contribution). On the other hand, payments by East Germany, even for such technical programs as the antimalaria campaign, have so far been rejected.[30]

Whereas the accession of the Federal Republic to so-called open international conventions which any state may join by unilateral declaration has not met with any difficulty, the German Democratic Republic has been generally unsuccessful in adhering to such treaties. Even its accession to the Universal Postal Convention was

[28] *New York Times*, March 4 and 22, 1966.
[29] Schuster, *Deutschlands staatliche Existenz*, pp. 203–5.
[30] *Rhein-Neckar-Zeitung*, April 19, 1964.

only accepted under the proviso that acceptance does not signify recognition of the depository.[31] The accession of East Germany to the Nuclear Test Ban Treaty of July 25, 1963, which could be done in Moscow, roused protests in West Germany; it was the first quasi-universal international convention of political character of which the D.D.R. had become a signatory.[32]

The Hallstein Doctrine has been subjected to painstaking criticism, outside and within West Germany. Most of the critics rely on the arguments against the West German refusal to accept the legal existence of the East German state. The "reality" of the German Democratic Republic should not be attacked uselessly all over the world; insistence on "fictitious" positions should no longer be maintained. Critics also point out that the success of the Doctrine simply results from the economic superiority of West over East Germany and, therefore, does not represent a sincere attitude by those governments who let themselves be "persuaded" by opportunistic and economic considerations. It is also submitted that the Hallstein Doctrine did more harm to the Federal Republic than it did to the East German regime because it barred diplomatic relations with the important area of East-Central Europe. Also, Bonn was reproached for inconsistency: if Moscow has been exempted, why should such countries as Poland, Yugoslavia, or Czechoslovakia be penalized?[33]

The Hallstein Doctrine, although resting on a theoretical basis (the one-Germany concept), is part and parcel of the West German policy for reunification. It is an adaptation of the nonrecognition thesis to the international scene but not an indispensable ingredient of it. Naturally, the Federal government could still resist recognition of the German Democratic Republic and maintain its claim to German unity while having normal diplomatic relations with states which have, at the same time, similar relations with East Germany. But, certainly then, the attitude of Bonn would be less

[31] See Joachim Peck, *Die Völkerrechtssubjektivität der Deutschen Demokratischen Republik* (Berlin, 1960), p. 159.

[32] See p. 80 above. Whenever the D.D.R. attempts to join a multilateral international convention, Bonn lodges a protest, claiming the right to speak for Germany. See, for West German protests against East Germany's accession to the International Civil Aviation Convention, *New York Times*, March 24, 1964.

[33] See, for instance, Walter Lippmann's articles, "Today and Tomorrow," *New York Herald Tribune*, April 6, 7, 8, and 9, 1959; Golo Mann, "Der verlorene Krieg und die Folgen," in Hans Werner Richter, *Bestandsaufnahme*, pp. 29–54; F. R. Allemann, "Adenauer's Eastern Policy," *Survey*, October, 1962, pp. 29–36.

consistent and forceful by failing to oppose diplomatic moves by other states toward which its hostility was a matter of central concern. Ultimately, the Hallstein Doctrine depends on its usefulness as a weapon in promoting the achievement of German unity.

As the above survey has demonstrated, the Hallstein Doctrine has been instrumental in preventing East Germany's recognition as a sovereign state and in excluding its presence from many areas of international life. The Federal Republic maintains full diplomatic relations with ninety-seven countries, the D.D.R. with only twelve. To maintain this diplomatic quarantine on the German Democratic Republic requires constant vigilance, material sacrifices, and even unsavory maneuvers; often this struggle has the character of a rearguard action, and seldom is lost territory recovered. The fact that the government of East Germany and her Communist allies, headed by the Soviet Union, are striving hard to break the Hallstein Doctrine demonstrates the importance of the issue.

The only area where the Hallstein Doctrine frankly harmed West Germany was in the East-Central European Communist countries. To be able to entertain direct contacts with these governments is important for the Federal Republic. Bonn was especially handicapped by its absence in Warsaw and Prague, two governments vitally interested, on their part, in the question of German reunification.

The Federal government, conscious of this disadvantageous effect of the Hallstein Doctrine, has undertaken since 1964 to set up permanent trade missions in the capitals of its eastern neighbors (except, of course, the D.D.R.), a process similar to that practiced by the German Democratic Republic in states where the establishment of diplomatic relations had been impossible. Such trade missions had been exchanged with Warsaw, Budapest, Bucarest, and Sofia. Whether these representations and their heads (who had reciprocally been given a personal diplomatic status) would be able to carry out, vicariously, the functions of official diplomacy will remain a matter of conjecture; thus far, their activities have proved to be modest and their success rather doubtful.[34]

[34] Even the establishment of trade missions in East European countries has elicited sharp criticism by opponents of Schröder's more flexible application of the Hallstein Doctrine. Thus, Federal Minister Krone stated:

It was very advisable that Federal Minister Schröder at the Party Congress in Hanover should have unmistakably clarified that the Federal Government does not intend giving up the Hallstein Doctrine, because it cannot be given up. It has often been misunderstood and sometimes overlooked that the Hallstein Doctrine is no arbitrary rule of German policy, but the consequential

The slow and frustrating results of the "policy of movement" have convinced Party leaders in the Federal Republic that, at least in the relations toward East-Central Europe, the Hallstein Doctrine must undergo a thorough modification or be dropped altogether. Thus, it has been suggested that the Doctrine should be waived for the Communist countries of eastern Europe for the same reason that it had never been applied to the Soviet Union: the countries should be considered as being under Soviet influence; they could not help recognizing another Communist regime; and, lastly, they already maintained official relations with the D.D.R. when the Federal Republic was given the status of a sovereign state.[35] Foreign Minister Schröder was said to be in favor of such a policy whose aim could also be to reduce the fear and mistrust of Germany in the countries concerned.[36] Opposition to such a drastic revision of the Hallstein Doctrine was, however, very strong, both in Bonn's official circles and among the foreign-policy elite.[37] It was being pointed out that the lack of response on the part of East European Communist countries to the feelers of friendship held out by the Federal Republic is not because of a lack of communication. Should these countries really be ready and free to find areas of understanding with West Germany, an understanding conducive to the reunification policy, they would do so under the existing arrangements. In other words, relaxation of the Hallstein Doctrine should follow, not precede, better relations.

result of the basic German decision that the Pankow regime cannot be recognized and that its legality must be denied. In the long run it would certainly be unreasonable and politically impossible to expect that the "D.D.R." would continue to be denied the character of a sovereign state, if the Federal Republic of Germany were to have suffered one state after the other to exchange ambassadors with the Pankow regime. We cannot tell other countries most urgently not to have relations with Pankow, while we ourselves take up such associations. Our policy would become dubious, and this discredibility in the long run would mean that the barrier of non-recognition that still hampers Pankow, and the conviction of the world that German division must never be accepted, would be destroyed.

Handelsblatt (Düsseldorf), May 1, 1964. For the frustrating experiences of the Heads of Trade Missions, see *Die Zeit*, November 5, 1965.

[35] See Strauss, *The Grand Design*, p. 28.

[36] *New York Times*, September 16, 1965. Schröder's own account, in this respect, was self-contradictory: "Under the statement of the Federal Republic of June 28, 1956, we could establish diplomatic relations with the East European countries in the same way we did with the Soviet Union. We must, however, constantly see to it that our right to be the sole representative of Germany in international affairs is neither impaired nor even endangered." "Germany Looks at Eastern Europe," *Foreign Affairs*, October, 1965, p. 24.

[37] Studnitz, *Bismarck in Bonn*, pp. 192-94.

The government of the Grand Coalition under Chancellor Kiesinger resolved in early 1967 to discontinue the application of the Hallstein Doctrine vis-à-vis the East-Central Communist countries. While the right of sole representation of Germany was officially to be reserved for the Federal Republic, full diplomatic relations were to be established with these states provided that this action was not made conditional on any demand (such as the recognition of the Oder-Neisse Line or the recognition of "two German states").

In a dramatic move, Bonn agreed on January 31, 1967, to set up full diplomatic relations first with Rumania. On the following day, Chancellor Kiesinger stated that this exchange of ambassadors did not alter the Federal government's position that it "alone has the right and duty to speak for all the German people."

The view that the Doctrine should be applied individually to each country concerned—that is, less rigidly than it has been applied so far—seems reasonable and likely to be followed. In essence, however, the Hallstein formula is and will remain an appendage of the struggle for German reunification; its future depends on the intensity, success, and failure of the campaign which is fought on many diplomatic fronts, along the Iron Curtain, and also in Africa and Asia.

The SED and Reunification

While West Germany's territorial configuration somewhat resembles that of the ninth- and tenth-century German Kingdom, the East German state is coterminous with no earlier country. In its center lies the province of Brandenburg, the historic core of Prussia; and all its other territories, except Saxony, have had close associations with Prussia.

If it was true that it was not Prussia that owned an army but the Prussian Army that owned a country, it would be even more correct to say now that the German Democratic Republic is not a country having a party but it is a party which possesses a country and uses it as its experimental field. The Socialist Unity party (SED), as the Communist party of East Germany is called since it forcibly incorporated the Social Democratic party of the Soviet zone, exercises a monopoly of control and direction which is the usual prerogative of other ruling Communist parties. The Party runs the government (as far as it is not identical with it), the judiciary, the economy, the armed forces, and all other organized life of the country. Other formal political parties are façades, remnants of former all-German parties (the CDU and the Liberal Democratic party) or direct creations of the SED (the National Democratic party and Democratic Peasant party). The various "mass organizations" like the FDJ (youth organization), the FDGB (Free Trade Union Federation), and others are all run by the SED. Elections are "administered," the official single-list receiving around 99 per cent of the votes. The SED's activities and control are generally carried out with Prussian thoroughness and heavy German bureaucratism.

We described earlier how the SED, in implementation of Soviet policy, cultivated agitation and propaganda for "German unity" against alleged Western attempts "to split Germany," against the "militarism, revanchism and Fascism" of the Federal Republic. Because of communism's bad reputation in the West where ill repute could not be effaced by the threatening presence of the Soviet Army, the Communist Security Police, or the omnipotent Party, anti-Western slogans had to be supplemented by arguments which still had an appeal for the average German.

The East German Communist campaign was carried out in a twofold manner: by attempts to promote the establishment of a proletarian regime in West Germany, addressed to workers, and by an "all-German" appeal to nationalism and democratic-liberal sentiment, minced with antimilitarist and pacifist catchwords, addressed to average Germans.[38] But the West German public proved to be, by and large, immune to these transparent tactics.

The leadership of the SED did not remain unaffected by the *Sonderweg* policy initiated early after 1945.[39] Two kinds of influence were peculiar to the German Communist movement and its leadership in the D.D.R. The first was of a national character: the uniqueness of the East German Party, consisting in the fact that, ruling over the truncated part of a country, it has not ceased to consider itself a territorially split party.[40] The second influence was ideological and historical. The *Sonderweg* had deeper roots than being a tactical device to attract non-Communists; it was rooted in the German Communists' consciousness of being the oldest and,

[38] See Carola Stern, *Porträt einer bolschevistischen Partei* (Cologne, 1957), pp. 98–104.
[39] See above, p. 140.
[40] "Unquestionably this division remains the single most decisive factor in East German political life. However useful to the Ulbricht regime, the Wall has by no means entirely eliminated the 'specially complicated circumstances' attending the building of socialism in the GDR—to use the outrageous jargon by which the SED denotes the problem of nationalism. . . ." Melvin Croan, "East Germany: Lesson in Survival," *Problems of Communism*, Vol. XI, No. 3 (May-June, 1962), p. 12.

for many years, the best organized and most influential Marxist party. Were not Marx and Engels, the fathers of the movement, of German origin? It was only by accident, so to speak, that Lenin had managed to gain control over Russia; even so, for years he had expected Germany to take the lead in the international revolutionary movement.[41]

These two factors—a subliminal feeling of national sentiment which spurred many Communists to seek, primarily, unification of their country and a feeling of ideological superiority over the Russians—contributed to factionalism in the Party. A third contributory reason was the person and power of Party leader Walter Ulbricht.

The emergence of the East German state, the organization of the SED, and the internal and external policies of the D.D.R. are closely linked with the person of Ulbricht, First Secretary of the Party and, since Wilhelm Pieck's death (1960), Chairman of the State Council. A close-mouthed, cautious *apparatchik* who survived the purge of German Party leaders in Russia under Stalin as well as the post-World War II Stalin era, he managed to maintain himself under Stalin's successors as the nonexpendable, irremovable leader of East Germany. While he and his Party are closely dependent on the help and good will of Moscow, he has been able to impress the Soviet leadership with his indispensability and thus to exercise leverage on the Kremlin. Disliked but maintained by Moscow, hated by the Germans, unpopular but obeyed in his Party, he is known to be ruthless but extremely shrewd and, while single-minded in purpose, adaptable to the requirements of Soviet policy. He traveled the *Sonderweg*, traced his steps through Stalinist monocratic dictatorship, and wound his way through the "thaw," the revolt of June 17, 1953, anti-Stalinism, and the Berlin Wall.[42]

[41] Before Stalinist uniformity descended on the East German Communists, efforts were made to rationalize the German way to socialism by drawing directly from the teachings of Marx, Engels, and Lassalle; many of these earlier theorists of Marxist application to Germany's socialization, like Fritz Selbmann, Anton Ackermann, Albert Norden, and Paul Merker, were subsequently subjected to self-criticism, censure, and even imprisonment. See Castellan, *D.D.R., Allemagne de l'Est*, pp. 72–86.

[42] See Carola Stern, *Ulbricht—A Political Biography* (New York, 1965); Ernst Richter, *Macht ohne Mandat—Der Staatsaparat in der sowjetischen Besatzungszone Deutschlands* (Cologne and Opladen, 1958); Franz von Nesselrode, *Germany's Other Half* (London, 1963); Fritz Schenk, *Im Vorzimmer der Diktatur—12 Jahre Pankow* (Cologne, 1962); Ernst Richert, *Das zweite Deutschland—Ein Staat der nicht sein darf* (Gütersloh, 1964); Carola Stern, "East Germany," in William E. Griffith (ed.), *Communism in Europe* (Cambridge, Mass., 1966), Vol. 2, pp. 41–154; Welles Hangen, *The Muted Revolution—East Germany's Challenge to Russia and the West* (New York, 1966).

Opponents of Adenauer like to draw parallels between the West German Chancellor and Ulbricht. As the first was said to depend on the Western powers, the East German dictator is a puppet of Moscow; both are said to pay lip-service to German unity, while giving priority in their actions to the solidification of the West and East German states.[43]

The grain of truth in the above analogy is the fact that both West and East Germany have had their respective problem of priorities. In the East the question was whether priority should be given to German unity or to the building of socialism.[44] Ulbricht definitely sided with the latter course; but the problem reverberated again and again through the leadership and rank-and-file of the Party and constituted a powerful incentive for faction-building.

Whether the expulsion from the Party and subsequent imprisonment of Politburo member Paul Merker and his associates was influenced by their attitude toward German unity cannot be proved. Similarly, the reason for the purge of another Politburo member, Franz Dahlem, remains obscure. These two leaders did not spend the wartime years in the Soviet Union; they may have opposed Ulbricht's tactics or even the official Soviet policy. They may have just arbitrarily been picked out by Ulbricht because they appeared potential rivals and because he needed scapegoats to offer for East German failures. These purges coincided with similar persecutions in Hungary, Czechoslovakia, and Bulgaria. The essential difference between East German and other Communist procedures was the absence of theatrical, rigged trials and also of executed death sentences. It may be that the "particular circumstances" of the SED and the caution against shocking West German public opinion with such atrocities account for the relative mildness of the East German purges.[45]

While accusations of pro-Western sympathy could be leveled against the members of the Merker group and against Dahlem, the official reasons for the expulsion of another group were of a diametrically different character. In this case the anti-Party group, led by Politburo member and Minister of State Security, Wilhelm Zais-

[43] Flora Lewis, "Why Ulbricht Keeps His Job?" *New York Times Magazine*, March 25, 1962; Charles Wighton, *Adenauer—Democratic Dictator* (London, 1963), pp. 233–34.

[44] The SED Party Statutes of 1954 included in their preamble the following sentence: "The Party is fighting for the re-unification of Germany on a democratic and peaceful basis." The new Party Statutes of January, 1963, made no reference to reunification. *East Europe*, December, 1962, p. 46.

[45] Stern, *Porträt einer bolschevistischen Partei*, pp. 119–30.

ser, and Rudolf Herrnstadt, editor-in-chief of the Party daily *Neues Deutschland*, was accused of conspiracy with Lavrenti P. Beria, the Soviet Security Chief, who was arrested and executed in 1953. Beria had been reproached by the Soviet leaders and Ulbricht as having "advocated a policy of retreat and capitulation" in Germany; in other words, he had suggested a relaxation of pressures in East Germany in order to promote reunification of a—we might presume —neutral Germany. Beria's arrest had been preceded by the uprising in East Germany on June 17, 1953. At that time, it appears, the majority of the Politburo had sided against Ulbricht in favor of a "new course" in the D.D.R.[46] Both the revolt and Beria's downfall prevented Ulbricht's defeat. The Soviet Presidium preferred to place the implementation of the "new course" in the reliable hands of Ulbricht, who then obtained a free hand to purge his opponents. Although the motivations and goals of the Zaisser-Herrnstadt group are not reliably known, it is believed that it considered Ulbricht's unpopular economic and political methods disastrous both for the "building of Socialism" in East Germany and for the achievement of reunification. Whether the intention of the "anti-Party" group was to reverse the priority communization versus reunification can only be assumed.[47] Zaisser and Herrnstadt were removed from their posts and expelled from the Party. The mildness of their punishment was again in sharp contrast with the fate of Beria and his associates.

While the Zaisser-Herrnstadt "plot" was motivated by the discontent that precipitated the uprising of June, 1953, the Polish upheaval and the Hungarian Revolution of 1956 can be considered as the main impetus of another opposition movement, this time undoubtedly inspired by some concept of national communism. The leader of this group was Wolfgang Harich, *Dozent* at the Humboldt University of East Berlin and editor of a journal of philosophy. His group was composed mostly of intellectuals belonging to the lower echelons of the Party hierarchy. His movement gained significance from the role which intellectuals had played in the events in Poland and Hungary.

[46] Hartmann, *Germany Between East and West*, pp. 69–71; Stern, *Porträt einer bolschevistischen Partei*, pp. 163–69; Stephan Thomas, "Beyond the Wall," *Survey*, October, 1962, pp. 58–59; for Ulbricht accusations against Beria, see *New York Times*, November 29, 1961.

[47] Ulbricht, in his report to the Central Committee of the SED, said in November, 1961: "As is known, Beria came out against the construction of Socialism in the German Democratic Republic. . . . Beria became incensed when in 1953 I spoke against his policy on the German question. . . ." Croan, "East Germany: Lesson in Survival."

Harich made his program public in November, 1956.[48] He proposed economic reform, abandonment of agricultural collectives, re-establishment of freedom of speech and legality, an approach to free elections, genuine independence and equality for the D.D.R., and alliance with the West German Social Democrats. A reunified Germany, according to his program, should become nonaligned, limit her armaments, and nationalize her key industries. Harich advocated free elections to bring about German unity. The program, though containing proposals for an internal transformation of the D.D.R., was clearly aimed at facilitating reunification; it may even be said that his entire program was tailored to meet the requirements for achieving German unity.[49]

On November 29, 1956, Harich and three of his associates were arrested. On March 9, 1957, the Supreme Court of the German Democratic Republic sentenced Wolfgang Harich to ten years' imprisonment and two of his co-accused to four and two years.

A year later Ulbricht had to defeat another, politically more dangerous and influential "faction." Politburo member Karl Schirdewan and Ernst Wollweber, successor to Zaisser as head of the Security Police, were the principals accused. It appears that this opposition group had advocated, after the Soviet Twentieth Party Congress, a slowing down of Socialist transformation with the intention of trying to solve the national question. This can be inferred, *inter alia*, from Ulbricht's subsequent disclosures: "The Schirdewan group did not understand that since the rejection of our proposal for re-unification in 1952 and West Germany's entrance into NATO, there had taken place a fundamental change in the situation. Sticking to outmoded positions led to opportunist errors. . . ."[50]

The "national question" or question of German unity thus has remained a disturbing element in the SED's policy-making and in the minds of East German Party leaders. Including Ulbricht, they must constantly be aware the the D.D.R.'s "special circumstances"

---

[48] Wolfgang Harich's political platform is printed in English in Edmund Stillman (ed.), *Bitter Harvest: The Intellectual Revolt Behind the Iron Curtain* (New York, 1959), pp. 293–94. See also Richert, *Das zweite Deutschland*, pp. 206–7.

[49] Stern, *Porträt einer bolschevistischen Partei*, pp. 214–23; Heinz Zöger, "Die politischen Hintergrunde des Harich-Prozesses," *SBZ Archiv* (Cologne), special issue, November, 1960, pp. 18–20; Carola Stern, "East Germany," in Griffith (ed.), *Communism in Europe*, p. 77.

[50] Ulbricht's report to the 14th Central Committee plenum in November, 1961, as quoted by Croan, "East Germany: Lesson in Survival."

require greater vigilance, caution, and resilience than is needed for the maintenance and development of Communist rule in other people's democracies. Any concession which Moscow might make on the problem of Germany could seriously endanger the existence of the German Democratic Republic and that of the SED.[51] It is natural that some of the leading East German Communists should support greater accommodation to the demands of the people and, therefore, should oppose Ulbricht's unyielding severity and inflexibility. They believe that, in the long run, it will be impossible to govern both against the pressures of their Western co-nationals and against the discontent of their own people. Lesser insistence on the pursuit of the "class struggle" and greater regard to the "special circumstances" of East Germany are the alternative to Ulbricht's policy. That such an alternative is still considered by the Soviet leaders may be deduced from the mild treatment which Schirdewan and Wollweber were given: on February 6, 1958, both were removed from their posts, censured, but not even expelled from the Party. Another member of this faction, Fritz Selbmann, deputy planning chief, practiced self-criticism and retained his post.

Resistance within the SED to the Stalinist type of leadership practiced by Ulbricht and his associates, such as his heir-apparent Erich Honecker, was rampant throughout 1965 among intellectuals and members of the economic-managerial segment of the Party. An example for the first category of dissidents was offered by Robert Havemann, professor at the Humboldt University of East Berlin who, after having been expelled from the SED in March, 1964, published an article in a West German periodical calling for the establishment of opposition parties in East Germany; he also demanded the readmittance of a reformed Communist party in West Germany—all this to pave the way for reunification.[52] A case for the other type of disenchanted elements was furnished by Erich Apel, head of the State Planning Office, who committed suicide rather than subscribe to a trade agreement with the Soviet Union— one he considered disadvantageous for the D.D.R.[53]

Walter Ulbricht is the only Communist leader of the Soviet bloc who has governed a country continuously since the postwar period.

[51] It is admitted by Ulbricht that the acceptance by the Western powers of the Soviet Note of March, 1952, would have endangered the position of Party and state in East Germany. Thomas, "Beyond the Wall," p. 60.

[52] *Frankfurter Allgemeine Zeitung*, December 20, 1965; *New York Times*, December 25, 1965.

[53] *Die Welt*, December 15, 1965; Hangen, *The Muted Revolution*, pp. 3–10.

His replacement (only Moscow could replace him) has often been hinted at but has never materialized. It was suggested that an East German "Gomulka" (the name of Schirdewan was mentioned in West Germany for such a role) who would introduce a more liberal and humanitarian regime could promote the easing of tensions between the two Germanys and both satisfy the people of East Germany and quiet down more violent demands for reunification. For Moscow such a step would evidently be a risky undertaking which might endanger the Soviet position in Germany. Relaxation might whet the appetite of both East and West Germans to achieve political reunification. It might also result in demonstrations, strikes, and revolts which would jeopardize the stability and existence of the regime. The uprising of June 17, 1953, had almost toppled it. Rather than take this risk, Moscow preferred to maintain Ulbricht with all his deficiencies and unpopularity; the question of succession to this septuagenarian will certainly tax the foresight and perspicacity of the Soviet leadership.

The uneasiness of the East German regime is betrayed by its extreme sensitivity to developments within the Communist camp and other parts of the world. Thus, the Sino-Soviet rift created new—partly imaginary, partly real—problems for the SED leadership. Peking, in the primary phase of its altercations with Moscow, advocated the pursuit of a strong Berlin and German policy and even accused Moscow of impermissible leniency. When the Sino-Soviet rift widened, Peking changed its tactics and criticism: having obtained recognition and some support from De Gaulle's France, the Chinese hoped to extend informal co-operation to other members of the European "third force," which, in their view, included West Germany.

It appears that the Chinese Communist party undertook to exert pressure on the leadership of the SED to dissuade it from supporting the Soviet thesis in the ideological and political struggle between Moscow and Peking by threats of Chinese collaboration with Western Europe and, eventually, with Bonn. Politburo member Hermann Matern raised the spectre of Chinese-West German collaboration and, at a Soviet-East German rally, accused Peking of being willing to surrender East Germany to Bonn. He re-evoked Beria's alleged plot against the security of East Germany when he said that the Chinese contemplated "the complete abandonment of the D.D.R. as a Western vanguard of the Socialist system in Europe and a new edition of the Germany policy of the Beria clique."

Matern stated that the Chinese also demanded that "we [the East German Communists] abandon our co-operation with Comecon and that we accept the adventurist, anti-Marxist conception of the Chinese Party leaders."[54] According to Matern, the Chinese are seeking potential allies against the United States and Russia among the West European states, including the Federal Republic. *Neues Deutschland*, the Party daily, accused the Chinese of demoralizing the workers of East Germany and added: "If we followed the advice of the Chinese leaders, we should have to consider the struggle against German imperialism as a second-rate issue."[55]

The relative independence which the East European people's democracies have gained as a result of the Soviet conflict with China has rendered the foreign policy of the D.D.R. hopelessly difficult. Pankow loses its breath when Peking, occasionally, woos Bonn and expresses a desire for the reunification of "both parts (not "states") of Germany.

Peking, perhaps only to harrass the Russians, sometimes accuses Moscow of cowardice in its Berlin policy, while at other times it charges the Soviets with robbing Germany of territory.[56] Many of Ulbricht's reactions—surprising as they may have been—were caused by the uncertainties created for East Germany by the transmutation of the erstwhile Soviet-Communist Bloc. Ulbricht would have preferred closer dependence on Moscow to the risks which are the lot of East Germany's unwonted independence.

The D.D.R. and Reunification

The doctrinal interpretation of the German Democratic Republic by its own leaders and jurists is an image of the ambivalent attitude displayed by the Soviet Union in its German policy. In 1949, when the D.D.R. was formally established, it wished to consider itself as the "core" of an all-German state; in 1950 the official attitude held the thesis that two new states had emerged within the area of Germany and, therefore, that the German Democratic Republic was not a successor-state to the Reich; after 1955 the now "sovereign" East German state, together with the Federal Republic, claimed

[54] *New York Times*, April 24, 1964.
[55] *Ibid.*, May 15, 1964. See also Walter Osten, "Moscow-Peking und die S.E.D.," *Ost-Europa*, June, 1964; *New York Times*, September 9, 1964. Under the "intermediate zone" theory of Mao Tse-tung, the Federal Republic may have common interests with the socialist countries against the "U.S. imperialists"; see Stern, "East Germany," in Griffith (ed.), *Communism in Europe*, pp. 142–44.
[56] *Münchner Merkur*, August 4, 1965.

succession to the former all-German state. In the first phase, the D.D.R. recognized the continuity of Germany after her collapse in 1945; in the second phase, all continuity was rejected; in the third and present phase, domestic discontinuity but international continuity in the form of successorship is being claimed.[57] The thesis of discontinuity, if upheld, would have contradicted the Soviet demand for conclusion of a peace treaty (there being no need to conclude such a treaty with a "new" state) and would have barred the German Democratic Republic from any claim to properties or assets of the Reich abroad.[58]

The theoretical basis of the East German position (whichever position it may be) is anchored in the Marxist-Leninist doctrine of the state. The state being, by this view, a power-structure serving the purposes of the "ruling class," the state itself undergoes a change whenever another "ruling class" takes over. The German Democratic Republic, we are told, is a country wherein the proletariat has seized power and, therefore, is a "new" state. Nevertheless, internationally, it is a partner in the succession to the former German state and a member of the international community.

The text of the East German Constitution does not, in many essentials, harmonize with constitutional reality. According to its preamble, "the German People has given itself this Constitution"; Article 1, paragraph 1, announces that "Germany is an indivisible democratic Republic; she is formed by the German *Länder*." Article 1, paragraph 4, provides: "There is only one German citizenship." Article 118, paragraph 1, states that "Germany forms a unitary customs- and trade-area, surrounded by a common customs-frontier." Thus, the Constitution distinguishes between Germany (meaning all-Germany, without closer territorial definition), the Republic (meaning the German Democratic Republic), and the *Länder*.[59] This document was originally intended to become the constitutional instrument for a united Germany;[60] thus, it was tailored

---

[57] Schuster, *Deutschlands staatliche Existenz,* pp. 164–72; Váli, "Legal-Constitutional Doctrines," pp. 34–36.

[58] See Siegfried Mampel, *Die Verfassung der Sowjetischen Besatzungszone Deutschlands* (Frankfurt/M, 1962), pp. 17–18. The Federal Republic, unlike the D.D.R., not only claims to be the successor of the Reich but was ready to assume liabilities of prewar and Nazi Germany by paying debts and indemnities.

[59] Since 1952 there have been no more *Länder* in the D.D.R.; they were dissolved and East Germany partitioned into fourteen administrative districts (exclusive of East Berlin).

[60] See Chapter I, pp. 23–24 above.

to suit the legislative requirements of the entire country.

The paradox of the German situation is well revealed by the nature of the West and East German Constitutions: the former was intended to be a transitional, provisional, legal instrument in expectation of reunification; the latter was a definitive, constitutional document intended for Germany as a whole but serving a political entity which is officially committed to German separatism. The unreality of this constitutional enactment is so glaring that one wonders why it has not been exchanged for a constitution based on the realities of the Communist dictatorship—one copied after the Stalinist Constitution of 1936 (as were most of the constitutions in the people's democracies). Failure to do so may partly be explained by the ideological disdain of the Communists for constitutions and law, in general; but it may also have reflected a wish to leave the door open for reunification. An outright Communist constitution may discourage opportunities for establishing a Confederation of the two German states or any other organic collaboration between the severed parts of Germany, as had frequently been suggested by Moscow and Pankow. The German Democratic Republic, while advertising the two-state or, more recently, the three-state (with West Berlin) theory, has not given up its pretenses of becoming a partner or a constituent part of a united Germany.

Be it as it may, German unity is not the first priority of Ulbricht's government although he must at least pay lip-service to it, because a nationalistic or Communist-messianic impulse calls for an eventual realization of German unity. Even so, reunification is projected only under the flag of communism. In May, 1962, Ulbricht stated: "The reunification of Germany is possible only as a result of the victory of Socialism in the German Democratic Republic, on the one hand, and the overcoming of militarism and imperialism by the most progressive forces in Western Germany, on the other hand."[61]

In March, 1963, the East German leader enlarged on his interpretation of the German national issue:

What is the meaning of our national question? Is our national question synonymous with re-unification or, better, with the unification of the two German states? . . . We . . . understand unity of Germany to be the end-result of an understanding between the two German states and closer and closer collaboration, on a peaceful and democratic basis. . . .

[61] Ulbricht made this statement in an interview with the editor of *Pravda; New York Times,* May 8, 1962.

Our national question is, therefore, not quite synonymous with the unity of Germany. The national question is in Germany, in its essence, a question of classes. The question is who should possess in Germany the leading role, the power—the working people or the monopoly-capitalists—this is the crucial question. . . .[62]

The blueprint of East German foreign policy (always synchronized with Soviet foreign policy aims), in order of priorities, may be formulated thus:

1) Strengthening of the political, economic, and international status of the German Democratic Republic;

2) For this purpose, advocacy of neutralization and eventual absorption of West Berlin;

3) German unity (first in form of a confederation with West Germany) with safeguarding of the "social achievements" in East Germany and elimination of "forces of resistance to democracy" in the Federal Republic; and,

4) Ultimately, a Communist takeover and complete unification of all-Germany.[63]

The East German government's primary concern is the implementation of the first objective. With the erection of the Berlin Wall, it was able to strengthen significantly the D.D.R.'s political and economic potential: the exodus of valuable manpower was prevented; stabilization of political authority was advanced through the expression of strength. However, East Germany's limited international recognition and role remained the weakest aspect of the regime.

Ever since 1955 the East German government has conducted a constant struggle to obtain recognition as a sovereign state by the Federal Republic, the Western powers, and all other states and international organizations. The Federal Republic, in complete harmony with other Western powers, as we saw earlier, refused recognition to the D.D.R. The Pankow government's numerous endeavors to enter into official contacts with either Bonn or the government of West Berlin, or with any of the Western powers, have been

---

[62] From Walter Ulbricht's address to the XVIIth German Workers' Conference, Leipzig, March 9, 1963; *Politische Studien*, May-June, 1963, pp. 333–34.

[63] In a so-called National Document published in March, 1962, the "historic task" of the D.D.R. was thus summarized: (1) the advance of socialism in the D.D.R. cannot be stopped; the final victory of socialism in the Federal Republic is equally inevitable; (2) but, at first, one has to reckon with the two states existing next to each other for a longer period; (3) during all this time the two states, because of their differing systems, will oppose each other like enemies. *Süddeutsche Zeitung*, October 3, 1964.

undertaken primarily to pierce the consistent front of nonrecognition. On the other hand, the Federal government's constant attention is directed to the prevention of any "upgrading" of the German Democratic Republic.

To avoid the necessity for entertaining higher or medium level contacts with East Germany, all sorts of fictitious devices have been employed by the Federal government and the Western powers. The trade between the two parts of Germany (called interzonal trade in West Germany) is negotiated on behalf of West Germany by a Trustee Office for Interzonal Trade (Treuhandstelle für Interzonen Handel), which, officially, is an agency of West German exporters and importers. This agency, which is stationed in West Berlin, also conducts negotiations on questions of transportation and a great variety of other subjects.[64] There are direct contacts of a purely technical nature between West and East German postal and railway authorities. Some other low-level contacts are carried on between officials of the West Berlin magistrate and East German or East Berlin officials. John Foster Dulles declared in 1957 that he would have no hesitation in dealing with officials of the German Democratic Republic as long as these could be considered "agents" of the Soviet occupation authorities.

The various complaints of the East German regime regarding derogation of its sovereignty were aired by Walter Ulbricht in a speech made before the Volkskammer on July 31, 1963. The three airlanes which United States, British, and French military and commercial aircraft use over the territory of the D.D.R. for flights from the Federal Republic to West Berlin were described by Ulbricht as "remnants of the war" which were illegal and never intended for civilian air traffic. A few days earlier, the Volkskammer had passed an Act on Civilian Air-Traffic which reserved for the D.D.R. the "unrestricted sovereignty over its national territory." Paragraph 3 of the act provided, however, that international treaties concluded or recognized by the German Democratic Republic might contain rules differing from the above principle.[65]

Another of Ulbricht's grievances concerned travel by citizens of the D.D.R. Nonrecognition has, in many important respects, not only hindered the official representatives of East Germany from reaching most parts of the world but also disrupted travel by her

---

[64] The various activities of the *Treuhandstelle für Interzonenhandel* are described in an article published in *Süddeutsche Zeitung*, August 26, 1964.

[65] *Frankfurter Allgemeine Zeitung*, August 1, 1963. Despite the passing of this act, Western air traffic to Berlin remained essentially unhampered.

individual citizens unless the latter submit to rules established by the Western powers. Individual (nonofficial) East Germans may enter the Federal Republic identified by their personal documents. But in any of the NATO countries (and many other countries belonging to the Western system of alliances) they can travel only when equipped with a Temporary Travel Document issued by the Allied Travel Board in West Berlin. Passports of the German Democratic Republic are not recognized in any of these countries. Furthermore, nongovernmental East Germans may attend international meetings only when joining a group from the Federal Republic and thus forming an all-German team.[66] Of course, all residents of East Germany are required to apply for an exit-visa before they can leave the D.D.R., thus making their traveling even more cumbersome. Furthermore, in March, 1967, the East German Parliament passed a law establishing special citizenship for the inhabitants (and former inhabitants) of the D.D.R.

These and other consequences of the policy of nonrecognition are extremely vexing and detrimental to the East German regime. It, therefore, seeks every loophole presented by international developments or by the necessities of international life. The East German government welcomed the opportunity to participate in the Nuclear Test Ban Treaty of August 5, 1963, by eagerly depositing its declaration of accession in Moscow. It also welcomed the plan of a Non-Aggression Treaty between East and West and was even ready to accept Western inspectors within its borders provided that the Federal Republic would also be subject to inspection. Such an arrangement would, of course, be workable only under an international convention to which the German Democratic Republic would be admitted as an equal partner.

We have described the impact of the Hallstein Doctrine on East Germany's international relations with the noncommitted countries. Except for Yugoslavia, none of these states has extended full diplo-

[66] In 1956 an all-German Olympic team participated in the Olympic games at Melbourne; at that time West and East Germany had the same national flags. In 1959 the D.D.R. added to its flag a Communist symbol: the hammer and a pair of compasses. To hoist this flag was prohibited, even at sports events, in NATO countries. For all-German participation in Olympic games, the Olympic Committee suggested the German colors (black-red-gold) with the five Olympic rings. Under such a "compromise flag" an all-German team continued to attend Olympic arrangements. See Grosser, *Die Bonner Demokratie*, pp. 336, 405-7. After erection of the Berlin Wall in 1961, West and East German sports collaboration broke down because the East German Sportbund refused participation to West Berliners; *Frankfurter Allgemeine Zeitung*, September 29, 1964.

matic recognition to the D.D.R. This does not, however, prevent Pankow from keeping trade missions in and exchanging goods with many countries. Representatives of the German Democratic Republic frequently visit countries in which they do not maintain diplomatic missions and use a variety of methods to intensify their contacts. The considerably greater economic strength of the Federal Republic prevents the D.D.R. from successfully using the bait of development aid in countries of Africa and Asia which otherwise might not be reluctant to enter diplomatic relations with East Germany.

Largely as a result of the Hallstein Doctrine, the German Democratic Republic maintained normal diplomatic relations only with the Communist countries, while the Federal Republic maintained such contacts with practically all states except the Communist countries (with the exception of the Soviet Union) and Finland. And later, Ulbricht has had to endure the Federal Republic's foray into Poland, Bulgaria, Rumania, and Hungary, where permanent trade missions (enjoying diplomatic privileges) were established for the intensification of reciprocal trade, cultural relations, and (as Bonn hoped) for confidential diplomatic contacts. Furthermore, in 1967, when the Federal Republic declared its willingness to enter into diplomatic relations with the other East-Central Communist states, Ulbricht attempted to set up a kind of counter-Hallstein Doctrine: no Communist government should establish diplomatic contacts with Bonn unless the latter recognized the existence of two German states and abandoned its claim to sole representation of Germany. However, Rumania openly defied East Berlin, agreed unconditionally to an exchange of ambassadors with the Federal Republic, and the hurriedly convoked meeting of Warsaw Pact foreign ministers ended in a failure. Except for Poland and Czechoslovakia, none of the "fraternal Socialist countries" was ready to apply the Hallstein Doctrine "in reverse" by committing itself not to establish diplomatic ties with West Germany without preconditions. Bonn's inroad into Eastern Europe divided the governments of that area and, in a way, added to the isolation of the German Democratic Republic. For some countries of East-Central Europe, West Germany is such a valuable trade partner that reasons of ideological solidarity have not prevented them from accepting the hand offered by Bonn.[67]

[67] See *Christ und Welt*, January 6, 1967; *New York Times*, February 3, 11, and 14, 1967.

East Germany ranks eighth or ninth among the world's industrial powers and is an important industrial producer and customer of the Communist camp; three-quarters of her foreign trade is with those countries. But not much more than 15 per cent of her exports and imports are with capitalist countries, including the Federal Republic. The share of her trade with West Germany is around 10 per cent of the total, but it includes industrial products which the D.D.R. could obtain elsewhere only with considerable difficulty. For the Federal Republic, with its huge export-import figures, the interzonal trade is of little economic significance; less than 2 per cent of its total.

It is no doubt true that a discontinuation of Western exports to the German Democratic Republic would considerably affect the economy of East Germany. Before the setting up of the Berlin Wall, Ulbricht undoubtedly speculated that Bonn might retaliate with an embargo; and he beseeched the Soviet Union and East European people's democracies for economic support in this eventuality. But Bonn decided not to take the action, partly because it did not wish to sever the few unofficial contacts which it still had with East Germany and partly because the ultimate sufferers would have been the people of the D.D.R. It also feared that Ulbricht might completely seal off the border from West German travelers who (except for the West Berliners) may still enter East Germany with their personal identity cards.[68] The mutual fear of retaliation still permits a modicum of unofficial contact between the two parts of Germany.[69]

The physical power which holds the D.D.R. together consists of its armed forces supported by "Soviet Armed Forces temporarily stationed in the territory of the German Democratic Republic."[70] The Soviet Army in East Germany is estimated to contain from 350,-000 to 400,000 men—about twice the number of the National People's Army (Nationale Volksarmee). The armed forces of the German Democratic Republic are characteristically called "na-

[68] *New York Times*, December 28, 1961, and May 6, 1962.

[69] The D.D.R. often submits demands for credits and other economic concessions accompanied with subtle threats or enticing offers. These included interference in the commercial traffic on the approaches to West Berlin or the freeing of political prisoners. One event is known when the West German government bought the freedom of such prisoners by indirect payments of up to $4,000 each. *New York Times*, October 1, 1964.

[70] See the Soviet-D.D.R. Treaty of March 12, 1957, which, nearly two years after the attainment of full sovereignty by East Germany, provided for agreement on the status of the Soviet occupation forces. *American Journal of International Law*, January, 1958, pp. 210–15.

tional" (although they are far from being German national); they number about 190,000 and are supplemented by the Bereitschafts-polizei (internal security forces), by the SED militia, and other smaller armed contingents. Only after the erection of the Berlin Wall, which also served to prevent desertion from the army, did the D.D.R. on January 24, 1962, formally introduce compulsory military service.

The military education and training of the National People's Army is based partly on "Soviet experiences," partly on the traditions of the Prussian-German Army. Ideologically, the Army, like all the population, is to be inspired by the tenets of Marxism-Leninism and by carefully selected and sifted traditions of German nationalism. The division of Germany necessitated a greater emphasis on "patriotism" in the D.D.R. than in any other East-Central European Communist country. The ideological task is partly defensive (to repel the appeal for national reunification from West Germany), partly offensive (to prepare the way for the Communist conquest of Germany). The patriotism advocated is a state-oriented nationalism which should weld the East German people to the Party and its leadership, making the German Democratic Republic a rallying ground for a new type of German proletarian nationalism.[71]

Reunification and the East Germans

Pre-1945 Germany undoubtedly possessed the criteria of a nation-state. Its division, to have permanency, had to rely on some significant reason, some desire for independent statehood by a part of the nation capable of sustaining its autonomy. Such a desire had prompted the American colonies to seek their independence; similarly, an historically directed political consciousness had determined the separation of the Swiss and the Austrians from the common German ethnicum. The national consciousness of secessionist peoples has often developed as a consequence of struggles against a common foe (often the state from which they had seceded), their allegiance to an outstanding leader or a dynasty, or their consciousness of religious or linguistic differences. One may ask whether there is or may develop such a political will on the part of the people of East Germany which could justify the independent state-

---

[71] See F. P. Martin, *Know Your Enemy: Background and History of the German Communist Army* (Cologne, London, 1962); Thomas M. Forster, *NVA—Die Armee der Sowjetzone* (Cologne, 1966); *Welt am Sonntag*, January 23, 1966.

hood of that country and whether, in the course of time, a separate East German nation may evolve.

The East German regime, in order to strengthen its own internal status and prestige, has, in the past years, endeavored to develop the political and ideological identity of the German Democratic Republic. This effort has met almost insurmountable difficulties. Still, to strengthen the cohesion and loyalty of the population under its control, it resorted to ambivalent, often self-defeating methods and devices.

Until about 1952 the main emphasis of the regime rested on a Marxist-Leninist indoctrination of the elite; this ideological Weltanschauung, together with the socio-economic achievements of the Soviet zone, were believed to be the appropriate basis of differentiation from western Germany. With the Federal Republic's phenomenal economic and political upsurge, East Germany's development was soon left behind. The attraction exercised by the West had to be matched by some additional incentive: Marxism-Leninism and proletarian internationalism were no longer sufficient spiritual fodder to justify the German Democratic Republic to its subjects. The cultural and linguistic affinity and blood-relationship of millions could not be satisfactorily opposed by a threadbare ideology refuted by economic and political realities. The regime could not continue to pay only lip service to German unity as a matter of mere ritual.

Early in 1966 it appeared that the East German government was preparing a new major offensive aimed "at solving the German Question." In December, 1965, the State Secretariat for All-German Affairs had been formed; one month later the founding of the Council for All-German Affairs was announced. The press repeatedly suggested a "Tashkent solution for Germany."[72] The intensive propaganda barrage wished to persuade West Germans (and also East Germans) that the desired *rapprochement* between the two parts of Germany should be undertaken under the device of a confederation on the basis of complete equality of the two German states.

The reunification offensive culminated in an Open Letter addressed to the Social Democratic party, and correspondence ensued. A tentative agreement was reached which foresaw televised con-

[72] A reference to peace talks between India and Pakistan in Tashkent (Soviet Union), mediated by the Soviet Premier, in the fall of 1965. The Soviet Union had several times offered its good offices to bring about a settlement for unification between the "two German states."

ferences, both in East and West Germany, with the participation of SPD and SED leaders.[73] The correspondence between the SED and the SPD was also to be published in East Germany. After initial hesitations, the Party daily, *Neues Deutschland*, published the full text of the SPD's two letters. The copies containing these first uncensored messages from West Germany were immediately sold out and were later available in the D.D.R. at black market prices only.

This time Ulbricht was caught in his own snare: the exchange of speakers, on second thought, was too risky; it already raised too much enthusiasm on both sides of the Iron Curtain; it might rebound on those who had first proposed it. Also, Moscow issued warnings; should it totter, it would be once again for the Soviet forces to bale out the regime. Eventually, Pankow shrank back from the test and let the reunification campaign wither away.

It must be assumed that, with the unification offensive, the East German regime wished to redirect a rising national feeling that followed the internal stabilization of East Germany subsequent to the erection of the Berlin Wall. After 1961 the German Democratic Republic gradually consolidated its economy, improved the standard of living of its people, and with the help of its economic strength—second after the Soviet Union in the Communist orbit—managed to increase its influence. No doubt, East Germans had become less critical of their regime, and their obsession to produce more and better (a German national trait) increased their self-confidence and created an aura of relative calm and content.[74]

East Germans had suffered more and longer than did the people of West Germany; lacking a Marshall aid, burdened for years by Soviet reparation payments, hamstrung by the ideological fetters of a Marxist-Leninist economy, they still managed to keep themselves above water and now hoped to have reached dry land. All this they achieved without outside help, by their own energy and endurance. As a consequence, self-consciousness and self-reliance largely replaced their earlier despondency. But with prosperity around the corner, their need for spiritual values rose. Pankow must have discovered that its subjects were unwilling to live "on bread alone." The trend of nationalism, which in Communist East Europe returned in the wake of post-Stalinist relaxation, could not stop short

[73] See Chapter II, pp. 83–85 above.
[74] For a report on East Germany's changed picture, see the series of articles in the *New York Times*, April 18, 19, 20, and 21, 1966; Arthur J. Olson, "Since August 13, Everything's Different," *New York Times Magazine*, September 19, 1965. See also Hangen, *The Muted Revolution*, esp. pp. 84–100.

before the borders of the D.D.R. Nationalism, however, in East Germany carried implications different from those in countries like Poland, Hungary, or Rumania. The division of the German nation acquired, in this context, a more significant meaning than ever before.

The partitioned status of Germany and the magnetism exercised by a free, prosperous, and bigger West Germany always strengthened diversionary and centrifugal forces in the East German Communist state. There was no impact of such magnitude in the other Soviet-dominated states of East Europe. The natural national sentiment in East Germany, as in other satellite countries, was directed primarily against the oppressor, the occupying power. This animosity had to be diverted to a direction consistent with the political aims of the regime. In Poland and Czechoslovakia, anti-German feelings were quite spontaneous, but to divert German animosity from its natural (eastern) direction into a rather artificial western course was no small feat of historic acrobatics for the leaders of the D.D.R. The fundamental Marxist-Leninist ideology had to be supplemented with stimuli drawn from the German past and adroitly manipulated for the purposes of the cause:

1) East German historical teaching has drawn on the traditions of Prussianism, both in its military and disciplinarian aspects. Prussian traditions are most conveniently invoked because they are supported by the *genius loci* and by precedents of Russo-Prussian military co-operation, especially during the anti-Napoleonic war. Freiherr von Stein (who had formed a German Committee in St. Petersburg in 1812), the Prussian generals who fought side-by-side with Tsarist armies (Blücher, Gneisenau, and Scharnhorst) the "day of Tauroggen,"[75] and even Bismarck ("who did not believe any controversies between Russia and Germany would be possible")[76] are presented as national heroes to the youth of East Germany.[77]

2) In addition to the emphasis placed on Prussian and pro-Russian traditions in German history, anti-Western precedents are

[75] In December, 1812, Prussian and Russian military leaders concluded the Convention of Tauroggen, by which Prussian forces withdrew from fighting the Russians in alliance with Napoleon.

[76] See the speech by Johannes Dieckmann, President of the Volkskammer, on May 7, 1962, as quoted by Jerzy Hauptmann, "Self-Determination of Nations: Fact or Myth," *The Central European Federalist*, June, 1962, p. 17.

[77] See Hans Kohn (ed.), *German History: Some New German Views* (Boston, 1954), p. 25; Fritz Kopp, *Die Wendung zur "nationalen" Geschichtsbetrachtung in der Sowjetzone* (Munich, 1962), *passim*.

stressed. Such precedents range from the Varusschlacht (the battle fought in 9 A.D., when the Teutonic leader Arminius defeated the Roman General, Publius Quintilius Varus)[78] to Luther, who fought Rome, and to the German statesmen who, in defiance to the West, signed the Treaty of Rapallo. Thus, East German historiography and schoolbooks try to bring Teutonic, anti-Christian, and anti-Western undercurrent of German nationalism into harmony with the anticapitalistic and anti-Western motivations of Soviet-Russian messianism.

3) While Prussia is praised as the state which achieved German unity, popular forces and their leaders who had allegedly worked for the unification of Germany in the past are glorified. At the same time, the West German leaders are described as lackeys of the West —those who, in the service of Western capitalism, are trying to prevent German unity. The Anabaptist peasant leader, Thomas Münzer (1490–1525), the peasant revolts of the sixteenth century, the anti-French revolutionaries in the Napoleonic era, the extremists of the 1848–49 epoch—all are set forth as forerunners of the people and leaders of the German Democratic Republic in its struggle for the liberation of the German nation and of German soil. Bismarck is presented as having achieved an "objectively progressive act" by unifying Germany under Prussian leadership in three wars.[79]

The East German experiment of playing with the fire of German power-oriented nationalism and opposing it to the "cosmopolitan and traitorous" West Germany was hardly compatible with a class-conscious Marxist-Leninist internationalism. The desperate need to build up some modicum of political cohesion, to establish a state-concept (*Staatsgedanke*) for the people of East Germany has led the leaders of the D.D.R. to resort to precedents from the Teutonic and Prussian past. At the same time, the ardent desire for reunification has had to be channeled in an anti-Western and antibourgeois direction. The success of these artificial and self-contradictory theses is highly doubtful. Naturally, a certain percentage of those exposed to such indoctrination will succumb to the force of verbiage and accept the conclusions as presented to them. But it is more likely that the indoctrinees will pick out only those theses that are personally acceptable and will derive their own more plausible and

[78] Kopp, *Die Wendung zur "nationalen" Geschichtsbetrachtung in der Sowjetzone*, pp. 37–38.

[79] *Ibid.*, pp. 52–54. Conversely, Socialist-Communist leaders, like Engels, Liebknecht, and Thälmann, are described as persons having striven for German national unity and against foreign oppression.

common-sense conclusions from them. Crude nationalistic traditions may have the reverse effect of turning the recipients of these teachings against the natural target of national animosity and of focusing their attention on the goal of national unity without regard for the socio-economic differences existing between East and West Germany. It may be revealed someday that "national-historic" indoctrination has contributed more to rousing anti-Soviet feeling than memories of past atrocities and sufferings under Russian occupation. The resort to nationalism is also considered by East Germans as an admission of the failure of the Marxist-Leninist doctrine to attract the loyalty of the masses, thus undermining conviction in the Communist state ideology.

The national anthem, written and composed for the German Democratic Republic in 1949, contains a dedication to serve "Germany, the united Fatherland" and expresses a hope that "the sun will shine as never before on Germany."

Discontent with his fate and deeper national emotions distinguish the average resident of East Germany from that of the West. East German refugees often consider their fellow-countrymen in the Federal Republic indifferent, complacent, hedonistic, and cosmopolitan. Daily differences of life cannot fail to introduce different traits into the East and West German characters, even to the extent of alienating them from each other. Even linguistic differences have appeared in the respective ways of expression, though not to the extent of threatening the basic linguistic unity of the German tongue.[80] Linguistic aberrations of colloquial speech in East and West are mainly results of the ideological and international contacts which the two states entertain. The East has adopted many expressions of Communist jargon, whereas in the West, American-English has not failed to leave its impact on the everyday speech. The Third Reich had also developed expressions and linguistic mannerisms of its own, which disappeared in everyday parlance, only to be replaced in the East by the *lingua sovietica*.

We may ask whether, despite the psychological and political contradictions of the East German regime, the people of the D.D.R. are ever likely to develop into a separate nation. Jaspers believed this to be possible, but only if a free East Germany were established by expression of self-determination.[81] At the time of this writing, such an assumption is clearly hypothetical. Before the Wall, East

---

[80] See Hugo Moser, *Sprachliche Folgen der politischen Teilung Deutschlands* (Düsseldorf, 1962); O. B. Roegele, "Spaltung der Sprache—Das kommunistische Deutsch als Führungsmittel," *Die politische Meinung*, May, 1959.
[81] Jaspers, *Freiheit und Wiedervereinigung*, p. 47.

Germans were "voting with their feet." The exodus of millions,[82] the necessity for setting up the Berlin Wall to prevent the depopulation of the D.D.R., were irrefutable proofs that the overwhelming majority of the population detested their government and preferred unification with the Federal Republic.[83] The present "incarceration" of the East Germans has necessarily led to their "acquiescence with reservation."[84] It is not believed that such a situation could result in the hoped-for strengthening of East German "state-consciousness."[85]

History has produced instances where emigrant populations (like the Boers in South Africa) created national states; but an area whose population has continuously sought to escape to the mother-country is hardly apt to develop its own national consciousness. Jaspers may be right in assuming that an East Germany, under free government but internationally prevented from joining West Germany, might in the long run develop a national consciousness of its own. But, at this time, East Germany has no free government, nor is there any international consensus to guarantee the independent existence of such a state.[86]

[82] The story of the East German exodus and the manpower problem facing the D.D.R.—all before the Wall—are described by George Bailey, "The Disappearing Satellite," *The Reporter*, March 16, 1961, Vol. 24, No. 6, pp. 20–23, and reprinted in Frederick H. Hartmann (ed.), *World in Crisis: Readings in International Relations* (New York, 1962), pp. 306–13.

[83] Geoffrey McDermott, who is certainly not biased in favor of reunification and who may have data to support his assessment, estimated that 10 per cent of the population of East Germany are "real Communists" and that there are plenty of opportunists who co-operate, *Berlin—Success of a Mission*, p. 120. Experience in Hungary, where the number of official communists was also around 10 per cent, has shown that even among those the ratio of "unreliables" is great; the opportunists, at a given moment, may turn into the most violent antagonists of the regime.

[84] Richert, *Das zweite Deutschland*, p. 331. In 1965, a devout member of the Communist Youth Organization was asked: "If the frontier were opened tomorrow, how many would leave?" "Millions," was the answer. Olson, "Since August 13," p. 52.

[85] See Marion Gräfin Dönhoff, Rudolf Walter Leonhardt, and Theo Sommer, *Reise in ein fernes Land* (Hamburg, 1965), p. 104. These authors believe that at the time of their visit (March, 1964) no more than 5 to 10 per cent of the population of East Germany were genuinely pro-regime, while the same percentage were ardently anti-regime; the remaining 80–90 per cent varied from displaying resignation to practicing opportunism, *ibid.*, p. 108.

[86] It is, however, asserted that, in the long run, time works for the hardening of the status quo; in other words, the regime is slowly gaining in popularity; Richert, *Das zweite Deutschland*, pp. 333, 336; Nesselrode, *Germany's Other Half*, p. 201. On the other hand, the Hungarian precedent demonstrated that the time factor, after an initial gain in favor of the regime, ceased to be operative; and relaxation and liberalization, if limited in scope, only raised further expectations, demands, and discontent. Ferenc A. Váli, *Rift and Revolt in Hungary—Nationalism Versus Communism* (Cambridge, Mass., 1961), esp. pp. 503–8.

Only an East Germany which could freely develop her political and cultural forces and cease completely to be a satellite could hope to emerge as another German-speaking nation-state like Austria. Historically—and this had been discovered by the present Communist promoters of Prussianism—it would be predestined to be a "little Prussia" augmented by historic Saxony. The Prussian ethos might certainly become the cultural-spiritual core of a new nation if purged of the imperialistic and power-worshipping traits of Prussianism.[87]

But, at present, the consciousness of the East German population, if consciousness there is, is that of moderately happy prison inmates who, willy-nilly, had to acquiesce in their fate. If they have developed a certain feeling of solidarity among themselves, it does not extend to their jailors. And the SED and East German armed forces, backed by the Soviet forces of occupation, act like the jailors of a huge prison. The real "national day" of the East Germans is not, as decreed by the regime, the "Day of Liberation" (May 8) or the "Day of the Republic" (October 7), but the Day of the Berlin and East German revolt (June 17, 1953). It remains one of the most important propagandistic endeavors for the East German regime to extinguish from the memory and consciousness of its people the souvenir of this uprising which, failing the intervention of Soviet forces, would irresistibly have resulted in a downfall of the German Democratic Republic and, eventually, in the reunification of Germany.[88] The forcible separation of East and West Germany has been made palpable and noticeable by the Berlin Wall, the living symbol of a divided nation.

[87] Jaspers, *Freiheit und Wiedervereinigung*, pp. 47–48.
[88] See *Süddeutsche Zeitung*, June 15–17, 1963 ("Der Aufstand eine offene Wunder der SED"); *Die Welt*, June 17–18, 1963.

Before I built a wall I'd ask to know
What I was walling in or walling out
And to whom I was likely to give offense.

—Robert Frost
Mending Wall[1]

I have read that the President of the United States of America viewed the Wall with great discontent. It did not give him any pleasure at all. But I like it extremely well.

—Khrushchev to workers in Marzahn, June 29, 1963.
Neues Deutschland,
June 30, 1963

CHAPTER V

BERLIN AND THE REUNIFICATION PROBLEM

In the post-1945 world, Berlin, the former capital of Prussia and of the Reich, has become a microcosm of divided Germany. But it has fared even worse: it has become, with a special status, an isolated enclave in the center of East Germany. If Berlin were situated along the borderline of East and West Germany (as divided Jerusalem lies along the Israeli-Jordanian borderline), its problem would be comparatively simple. The continued existence of the remainder of four-power control, more so in the western part of the city than in the eastern but still in evidence, is another complication. If the over-all German problem is a mixture of constitutional-legal and political factors operating in the context of the Cold War, the problem of Berlin is even more tangled. The dual military and political

[1] Robert Frost recited this poem before a Moscow audience on September 5, 1962; *New York Times,* September 6, 1962.

confrontation lays Berlin open to the ever-threatening possibility of violent conflagration. After 1945 Berlin ceased to be the capital of Germany; the former Reich had been partitioned. Instead of being the political center of Germany, it has become the focus and symbol of the East-West conflict.[2]

For the Germans, Berlin remains the visible sign and epitome of their predicament of division. In the post-1945 era the image of the Reich's former capital has changed: Bavarians, Rhinelanders, and other Germans in distant provinces no longer regard Berlin with envy, hatred, or disgust but with admiration for the struggle it has sustained. For the West Germans, Berlin is the frontier post of liberty; for the East Germans, a symbol of Germany's inevitable unity and their redemption from alien rule. And West Berlin is conscious of its role as an outpost of Western freedom in the sea of Soviet totalitarianism, extremely sensitive of events within and beyond its perimeter. Its sensitivity to any change or threat of change is caused by its highly complicated legal and political status—a status determined both by international enactments and by *faits accomplis* and by the policies of its own leadership and of Bonn's. Berlin is of strategic value neither to the West nor to the East; but its political value is beyond estimation. Berlin is the Achilles tendon of the West: its loss would probably destroy the Western alliance and immensely strengthen the Soviet grip over East Europe. On the other hand, West Berlin's survival is a victory for the Western will, for the superiority of the Western way of life, and, last but not least, for German unity.

Status of Berlin in Theory and Practice

The controversial status of Berlin lends itself to conflicting doctrinal interpretations: one may distinguish between West German, Communist, and Allied positions.

1) Under Article 23 of the Basic Law, its provisions apply in "Greater Berlin." According to the official West German view, sanctioned by the courts, Berlin is a *Land* of the Federal Republic. It is admitted, however, in deference to actual practice, that the application of the Basic Law and of West German law in general, is

---

[2] Former decentralization had provided secondary political, economic, and cultural centers (like Hamburg, Frankfurt, Munich, Cologne, etc.) for West Germany; thus, the loss of Berlin as a capital proved to be more expendable than would have been the loss of Paris for a truncated France, or that of London for a partitioned Britain; see Pierre Gaxotte, *Histoire de l'Allemagne* (Paris, 1963), Vol. II, p. 535.

de jure restricted by the continued exercise of authority by the occupation powers in West Berlin. Territorially, these applications are also limited by the *de facto* division of Greater Berlin.

Just as the Federal government considers itself the only legitimate government of Germany, the Magistrate of (West) Berlin regards itself as the only legitimate municipal authority of Berlin. The Governing Mayor of Berlin claims to have jurisdiction over the entire Greater Berlin area, even if temporarily prevented from exercising such authority in the eastern sector of the city.[3]

2) Article 2, paragraph 2, of the East German Constitution of October 7, 1949, provides that: "The capital of the Republic is Berlin." The German Democratic Republic was formed on the territory of the Soviet zone of occupation; and Berlin was, under the agreement between the United States, Britain, and the Soviet Union of September 12, 1944 (to which, subsequently, France also adhered), an area to be administered jointly by the four occupation powers. The Communist doctrinal interpretation of Berlin's status is not entirely consistent. It was, however, maintained that Berlin, as a whole, belonged to the D.D.R. until the Soviet-East German friendship treaty of June 12, 1964, introduced a new view by declaring that West Berlin is an "independent political unit."

According to views set forth in East German publications, Greater Berlin originally belonged to the Soviet zone; the three Western powers were subsequently given a right of administration in their respective sectors but they failed to obtain "sovereignty." The Western powers, by their violation of the Potsdam Agreement (or other agreements pertinent to the four-power status of Germany) forfeited their rights to be in Berlin. When the Soviet Union transferred its sovereign rights over the Soviet zone to the German Democratic Republic, the entire area of Berlin became part of this state. Consequently, the Western powers remain in their sectors of Berlin only "by sufferance" or "toleration" of the German Democratic Republic.[4] Inconsistent with this opinion is Ulbricht's view that the border between East and West Berlin is a "state frontier."[5]

[3] See Elmer Plischke, *Government and Politics of Contemporary Berlin* (The Hague, 1963), esp. pp. 63–74; Schuster, *Deutschlands staatliche Existenz*, pp. 103–6; Váli, "Legal-Constitutional Doctrines," esp. pp. 36–44.

[4] See Herbert Kröger, "Zu einigen Fragen des staatsrechtlichen Status von Berlin," *Deutsche Aussenpolitik*, January, 1958; B. Wewjura and I. Lukashuk, "International Legal Aspects of the West Berlin Problem," *International Affairs* (Moscow), 1963, No. 4, pp. 37–42.

[5] See Walter Ulbricht's speech at the XVIIth German Workers' Conference, Leipzig, March 9, 1963; *Politische Studien*, May-June, 1963, p. 333.

The municipal authorities of East Berlin claim jurisdiction for the entire Berlin area, though their authority does not extend beyond the Wall. On the other hand, from 1955 on East Berlin has been integrated, though not completely, into the German Democratic Republic and considered as a special district (*Bezirk*).[6] In October, 1958, Ulbricht stated that the "democratic" section of Berlin was no longer subject to any military occupation.[7] On August 23, 1962, even the office of the Soviet Commandant in Berlin was abolished.

The second campaign for Berlin, initiated by Khrushchev in November, 1958, relied theoretically on the contention that all Greater Berlin is part of the D.D.R. The Soviet leader's address before the Polish state delegation inveighed against the violations of the "Potsdam Agreement" by the Western powers and insisted that the obligations derived from this agreement "had outlived themselves.":[8] "The time has obviously arrived for the signatories of the Potsdam Agreement to renounce the remnants of the occupation regime in Berlin and thereby make it possible *to create a normal situation in the capital of the German Democratic Republic.*"[9]

Khrushchev's error in referring to the wrong document with re-

---

[6] For the special status of East Berlin in the D.D.R., see Siegfried Mampel, *Der Sowjetsektor von Berlin* (Frankfurt/M, 1963), pp. 385–87; see also *Dokumente zur Berlin-Frage, 1944–1962* (Munich, 1962), pp. 251–96.

[7] *Dokumente zur Berlin-Frage*, p. 296. But Khrushchev in his speech of November 10, 1958, threatened to hand over to the D.D.R. "the functions in Berlin that are still exercised by Soviet agencies." Embree (ed.), *The Soviet Union and the German Question*, p. 19.

[8] In referring to the Potsdam Agreement, Khrushchev committed a *gaffe* which was exploited by Secretary of State Dulles in his news conference when the latter stated:

it seemed as though Mr. Khrushchev had spoken initially without the benefit of legal advice which is, of course, a very bad thing to do [laughter] that he has based his case upon alleged breaches of the Potsdam Agreement.

Now, the rights and status of the allies in Berlin and the responsibilities and obligations of the Soviet Union do not in any way whatsoever derive from the Potsdam Agreements. Indeed that subject is, I am told by my own legal adviser, not even mentioned in the Potsdam Agreements. . . .

. . . if the Soviet Union takes the position that the Potsdam Agreement is nonexistent, the consequences of that would be not to destroy our rights in Berlin, because they don't rest upon the Potsdam Agreement at all, but it might greatly compromise the territorial claims of Poland which do rest upon the Potsdam Agreement primarily.

U.S., Department of State and Staff of Senate Committee on Foreign Relations, 87th Cong., 1st Sess., *Documents on Germany, 1944–1961* (Washington, 1961), pp. 346–47.

[9] *Ibid.*, p. 342. Italics have been added.

gard to Berlin was corrected in the Soviet diplomatic note of November 27, 1958. Here the Soviet Union formally denounced the Agreement of September 12, 1944, concerning the zones of occupation and the administration of Greater Berlin and suggested that "the most correct and natural way to solve the problem would be for the Western part of Berlin, *now actually detached* from the German Democratic Republic, to be reunited with its eastern part and for Berlin to become a unified city within the state *in whose territory it is situated.*"[10]

But the Soviet note wished to acknowledge the development of West Berlin, so different from that of the eastern part of that city, and also the desire of the West Berliners to preserve their present way of life. Accordingly, the proposal of the Soviet government for West Berlin ran as follows:

> In view of all these considerations, the Soviet Government on its part would consider it possible to solve the West Berlin question at the present time by the conversion of West Berlin into an independent political unit—a free city, without any state, including both existing German states, interfering in its life. Specifically, it might be possible to agree that the territory of the free city be demilitarized and that no armed forces be contained therein. The free city, West Berlin, could have its own government and run its own economic, administrative, and other affairs.[11]

The Soviet note further expressed the view that "the German Democratic Republic's agreement to set up *on its territory* such an independent political organism as a free city of West Berlin would *be a concession, a definite sacrifice* on the part of the German Democratic Republic for the sake of strengthening peace in Europe, and for the sake of the national interest of the German people as a whole."[12]

The West German and the Communist views on the status of West Berlin and of Berlin as a whole, are in direct conflict. And opposed to the Communist position is the Western view, itself not totally consistent with the official doctrine of the Federal Republic.

3) Under the "Protocol on Zones of Occupation and Administration of the 'Greater Berlin' area" of September 12, 1944, the United States, Britain, and the Soviet Union (and, subsequently, France) agreed that Germany would, for the purposes of occupation, be divided into three (subsequently, four) zones, to be allotted

[10] *Ibid.*, p. 359. Italics have been added.
[11] *Ibid.*, p. 360.
[12] *Ibid.*, p. 361. Italics have been added.

to each of the three (four) powers, and "a special Berlin area, which will be under joint occupation by the three [four] Powers."[13] The four-power statement of June 5, 1945, on zones of occupation in Germany further clarified the situation of Berlin: "The area of 'Greater Berlin' will be occupied by forces of each of the four Powers. An Inter-Allied Governing Authority (in Russian, Komendatura) consisting of four Commandants, appointed by their respective Commanders-in-Chief, will be established to direct jointly its administration."[14]

On the basis of these unequivocal texts, the Western powers have denied that any part of Berlin was ever part of the Soviet zone of occupation. The Western powers gained occupancy of their sectors in Berlin in return for the withdrawal of their forces from the zone allotted to the Soviets in July, 1945.[15] In addition to their treaty rights, the Western powers also derive their status in Berlin from a right of conquest—that is, their right to participate in Germany's occupation with sovereign authority as a result of Germany's military defeat and unconditional surrender. This would imply that the Allied status in Berlin is not *derivative* (transmittted by either the Germans or the Russians) but, under international law, an *original* right of sovereign power. Such a right can neither be forfeited nor lapse, except by voluntary relinquishment or mutual agreement. The Western powers maintain that their right to stay in Berlin is independent of the survival or efficaciousness of the Potsdam Agreement or any other inter-Allied agreement. They also deny that any of their actions have given cause for the denunciation of these agreements.[16]

The Soviet–East German contention which attempts to differentiate between "exercise of supreme authority" and "administration," the first being vested in the Commanders-in-Chief of the zones of occupation, the latter carried out by the Berlin Kommandatura, is based on a one-sided reading of the relevant texts and rejected by the Western powers.[17]

---

[13] *Ibid.*, p. 1.
[14] *Ibid.*, p. 19.
[15] See Chapter I, p. 13 above.
[16] See the Hammarskjold Forums, *The Issues in the Berlin-German Crisis*, with contributions by Robert R. Bowie, James Bryant Conant, Eli Whitney Debevoise, John J. McCloy, George B. Munroe, and Frederick A. O. Schwarz (Dobbs Ferry, N.Y., 1963), pp. 24–39.
[17] The Allied statement on "Control Machinery in Germany," dated June 5, 1945, provided for the "administration of 'Greater Berlin'" whereas the Control Council, composed of the four Commanders-in-Chief, was designated,

In the view of the Western powers, the Soviet withdrawal from the Kommandatura in 1948 did not destroy the authority of this organ; according to this view, the administrative machinery under the quadripartite agreements cannot be abolished without the approval of the three Western powers. The Kommandatura, reduced to the representatives of the three Western Allies and *de facto* limited in its exercise of functions to the three Western sectors of Berlin, continues to act under the wartime and postwar arrangements. It considers the Soviet seat vacant and to be filled at the will of the Soviet Commandant of Berlin. When, on August 23, 1962, the Soviet government announced the abolition of the office of Soviet Commandant in Berlin (though certain "limited functions" were still to be continued by the Soviet Army), the three Western powers protested and declared that such a unilateral renunciation could not impair the rights of the Allies in the city. Furthermore, the Western statement emphasized that "the Soviet announcement can in no way affect *the unity of Berlin as a whole*. Despite the illegality of the wall and the brutality of the East German authorities in preventing the inhabitants of East Berlin from leaving that area, Berlin remains a *single city*. No unilateral action by the Soviet Government can change this."[18]

From the Western point of view, the administrative incorporation of East Berlin into the German Democratic Republic was illegal and a breach of the Berlin Agreements. Similarly, the entry of East German armed forces (which raised and protected the Berlin Wall) was a violation of these agreements.[19] Though a threat to allow the entry of West German forces into Berlin (they could have been transported by air without being subject to Soviet or East German control) might have prevented the stationing of the Volksarmee in East Berlin; the timidity of Western conduct can be explained by a desire to maintain the fiction of a Berlin controlled directly by the

---

by the same instrument, to exercise supreme authority. However, the Allied statement of the same day (see above) spoke of *occupation* by the Allied forces of Berlin, the same term used for the taking over of the zones by the Allies. The Soviet argument is also refuted by the text of the September 12, 1944, agreement on the occupation of Germany. See R. Legien, *The Four Power Agreements on Berlin* (Berlin, 1961), pp. 11–22.

[18] *New York Times*, August 24, 1962. Italics have been added.

[19] The Soviet government lodged protests against alleged recruitment of West Berliners into the West German Bundeswehr, protests rejected as unwarranted by the Allies. Similar protests were launched by the West against recruitment into the East German Volksarmee in Berlin and the entry of such forces into East Berlin. *Dokumente zur Berlin-Frage*, pp. 442–46.

187

Four-Power Inter-Allied Governing Authority (Kommandatura) and its armed forces.

At times the Soviet military authorities attempted to regain a foothold in the administration of West Berlin, but the Western Allies would agree only if the Soviet Union acknowledged that East Berlin, too, was subject to four-power control.[20]

The Allied persistence in holding strictly to the letter of occupation rights in Berlin has occasionally created friction between the Western Commandants and the Berlin and Bonn authorities. To safeguard their authority the Western powers refused to recognize Berlin as the twelfth *Land* of the Federal Republic of Germany. Thus, the Three-Partite Kommandatura refused on August 29, 1950, to approve paragraphs 2 and 3 of Article 1 of the Constitution of Berlin. The two paragraphs declared, respectively, that "Berlin is a *Land* of the Federal Republic of Germany" and that "the Basic Law and Laws of the Federal Republic of Germany are binding in Berlin."[21] Any act passed by the Berlin House of Representatives had required approval by the Kommandatura before becoming effective. Under the practice developed as a consequence of the Allied refusal to accept Berlin as part of the Federal Republic, the Berlin Parliament now formally endorses the laws passed by the legislature in Bonn, which thereafter obtain the approval of the Allied Kommandatura.

Before 1958 the Bundestag held sessions in Berlin once in each legislative term in order to demonstrate the city's symbolic significance as the historical capital of Germany. After the opening of Khrushchev's campaign against Berlin, Allied intervention temporarily prevented the holding of further parliamentary sessions in Berlin. But the "right" of the Bundestag to sit in Berlin was formally upheld,[22] and the Federal government undertook to reconstruct the Reichstag building, destroyed first by fire in 1933 and again during the siege of Berlin in 1945.[23]

West Berlin is represented by twenty-two deputies in the Bundestag of Bonn; they exercise a consultative function.[24] Strangely enough, despite the total integration of East Berlin into the German

[20] *New York Times*, December 12, 1964.
[21] Mampel, *Dokumente*, pp. 154–55.
[22] When in April, 1965, the Bundestag again met in Berlin in full session, the Communist side retaliated by interrupting land communications and by flying planes low over the parliamentary buildings. Bundestag committees regularly meet in West Berlin. *New York Times*, January 23, 1966.
[23] *New York Times*, November 12, 1963.
[24] Electoral Law of May 7, 1956; *Dokumente zur Berlin-Frage*, p. 137.

Democratic Republic, the thirteen deputies of Berlin have no voting rights in the Volkskammer which holds its sessions in East Berlin.[25]

Although the Soviet Union has at different times proposed to clear away "the residue of World War II" and has moved in this direction, the Russians have still been reluctant to eliminate certain remnants of the defunct quadripartite occupation regime. These are:

1) The Inter-Allied Air-Safety Center which regulates air traffic between West Berlin and the Federal Republic;

2) The International War Crimes Prison in Spandau (West Berlin) where soldiers of the four powers take turns guarding the remaining prisoners;[26]

3) The Soviet cenotaph in the British sector of West Berlin guarded by Soviet detachments;

4) The Allied Military Commission in Potsdam (East Germany) and the Soviet Military Commission in Frankfurt/M in the Federal Republic.

Other, more important souvenirs of the postwar military regime affect the field of transportation and travel. Besides the access rights to Berlin (see ahead), Allied military personnel still exercise their right of free circulation in East Berlin; conversely, the Russians have similar rights in West Berlin.

In a declaration of 1952, reiterated at the time of the Paris Agreements of 1954, the Federal Republic promised financial assistance and economic aid to Berlin. It pledged further "to ensure the representation of Berlin and of the Berlin population outside Berlin, and to facilitate the inclusion of Berlin in the international agreements concluded by the Federal Republic, provided that this is not precluded by the nature of the agreements concerned."[27]

By virtue of this agreement, the Federal government represents the interests of (West) Berlin internationally as well as those of its

---

[25] Law concerning the elections to the Volkskammer of August 9, 1950, Article 49; subsequent electoral laws did not reiterate expressly that Berlin representatives have consultative rights only, but they are still separately elected. Since there is in practice no voting in the Volkskammer, the voting rights play no role whatsoever; *Dokumente zur Berlin-Frage,* pp. 199, 291; Mampel, *Die Verfassung der sowjetischen Besatzungs-zone Deutschlands,* pp. 24–25. See also *Neue Zürcher Zeitung,* August 3, 1963.

[26] After October 1, 1966, when Baldur von Schirach and Albert Speer were released, Rudolf Hess, the Deputy Führer, remained the only prisoner.

[27] Oppen (ed.), *Documents on Germany Under Occupation, 1945–1954,* pp. 631–34.

residents. The Federal Republic's trade agreements invariably include a "Berlin clause" which, not surprisingly, has created difficulties with Bonn's Communist trade partners. However, upon the Federal government's insistence, Poland, Rumania, Hungary, and Bulgaria have agreed to a text which, instead of directly mentioning Berlin, recognizes Bonn's right to represent the *"Deutsche Mark (West) area."*[28] Since such a clause is a practical recognition of West Germany's rights over Berlin, the Soviet refusal to accept this formula has impeded Moscow's trade and cultural relations with Bonn.[29]

Inhabitants of West Berlin use passports of the Federal Republic when traveling abroad; but they cannot identify themselves with such passports when entering or passing through East Germany or East Berlin. Federal Republic passports of West Berliners have frequently been confiscated by agents of the German Democratic Republic. East Berliners use D.D.R. passports, but only outside West Germany or West Berlin where they need only to show their identification papers and require no special entry or exit permits.

It should also be remembered that West German trade pacts (concluded on behalf of West German trade interests by the "unofficial" Treuhandstelle für Interzonenhandel in West Berlin) with the German Democratic Republic also include West Berlin. East German negotiators have tried several times to exclude West Berlin from such agreements and conclude conventions directly with representatives of West Berlin. Occasionally, the Federal Republic has had to make sacrifices in the bargaining procedure for retaining the Berlin clause. The trade agreements also provide guarantees for the travel of West Germans to and from West Berlin; but thus far it has not been possible to extend similar general safeguards for the inhabitants of the western sections of Berlin.[30]

The theoretical and practical problems of Germany's partition are compounded by involved conflicts between theory and practice in Berlin. Both East and West Berlin pretend to be Greater

[28] In November, 1964, the Soviet government refused to accept the West German ratification documents of the Nuclear Test Ban Treaty because they provided for the inclusion of Berlin in the operational area of the treaty. *New York Times,* November 29, 1964.

[29] *New York Times,* June 6, 1964. Since 1961, in order to oppose Moscow's three-German-states theory, Bonn insisted that a cultural agreement must cover West Berlin. When in 1964 the Bolshoi Ballet was invited to the Federal Republic, it refused to play in West Berlin; thereupon, the visit to West Germany was cancelled. *Stuttgarter Zeitung,* January 30, 1965.

[30] *New York Times,* January 23, 1964.

Berlin; the Federal Republic claims to be the sovereign power of all Berlin, while the German Democratic Republic claims the same sovereignty for itself. And the Western Allies consider all of Berlin to be under the control of the Kommandatura a three-power agency in reality, a four-power agency in theory. These theoretical divisions and their fictional character were accentuated when the city became physically divided by the Wall in 1961.

The Second Battle for Berlin and the Wall

After the end of the blockade of 1948–49 there was a relative lull in Berlin until Khrushchev opened the second Soviet campaign against the city in November, 1958. By that date the Soviet leader, having defeated his internal opposition, restored order in the Soviet camp (Poland and Hungary) and thus consolidated his power, considered the time ripe to resume the offensive. Khrushchev's objectives were, essentially, the same as those of Stalin: to gain advantages over the city, over West Germany, and, eventually, to obtain control over both. Whatever the net gain of this operation might be, it would strengthen the D.D.R., demoralize West Germany, disrupt and possibly destroy NATO, and pave the way for a Soviet conquest of Germany by peaceful means. The Berlin position of the West was so vulnerable that it presented latitude for a great variety of Soviet pressures and the opportunity to charge the West with inflexibility. The Berlin situation demonstrated that meticulous infringement on even those concepts that were largely fictitious might reap real benefit in terms of literal power.

Khrushchev's opening gambit, the speech of November 10, 1958, appeared to be an extempore performance, followed up later by a more carefully worded note.[31] Improvisations, skillful and artless declarations, honey and vinegar, deadlines and postponements marked the second Berlin campaign. The Soviet leader had created this "crisis," and he wished to keep it under his control; while probing the opponent's will to resist, he was always careful to avoid escalating the conflict into physical acts of violence.

After the unilateral abrogation of the four-power agreements on Berlin, the Soviets intended to create a "free city of West Berlin," demilitarized but guaranteed by the four powers, perhaps also by the United Nations, and the "two German states." The occupation

---

[31] See Elisabeth Barker, "The Berlin Crisis, 1958–1962," *International Affairs*, January, 1963, pp. 60–61. For Khrushchev's erroneous reference to the Potsdam Agreement, see p. 184 above.

status would thus come to an end, together with other residue of the last war: this meant, first of all, handing over to the authorities of the German Democratic Republic the control of access routes to Berlin. The Soviet note of November 27, 1958, also intimated that, in return for West Berlin's commitment not to allow subversion or other hostile activities against the D.D.R., Ulbricht's government would guarantee freedom of traffic to and from the city. In January, 1959, the Soviet government submitted its draft peace treaty and again threatened to sign a separate peace treaty with East Germany should the Western powers be unwilling to discuss and, eventually, sign such a document.[32]

The developments of the Geneva Foreign Ministers Conference in May-August, 1959, have already been reviewed. The Western powers were sufficiently impressed by the Soviet threats that they were on the verge of compromising with the Soviets on the separate status of West Berlin (disregarding both the official "unity" of Berlin and the dependence of the Berlin issue on the wider problem of German unity). To the enormous relief of the West German government, the Russians declined the last compromise offer of the Allies, the so-called "interim proposals for Germany and Berlin."

The invitation of Khrushchev to the United States promised to remove the impasse of Geneva. Under the mellowing "spirit of Camp David," President Eisenhower agreed that negotiations "would be reopened" on the "specific Berlin question" (and not the German question); Khrushchev agreed that there should be no time limit for these negotiations but they "should not be prolonged indefinitely."[33] Some furor was aroused in West Germany by the President's admission that the situation of Berlin was "abnormal." It was felt that he should rather have said that divided Germany was abnormal and that the "abnormality" of Berlin was just a consequence of this even greater abnormality.[34]

Another result of the Camp David negotiations was the Summit Conference, coveted by Khrushchev, to be held in Paris in May, 1960. The Berlin question was to be one of the items of this conference. This time the Americans preferred to have an overt fiasco

[32] For the Soviet diplomatic offensive in 1958 and 1959, see also Chapter I, pp. 44–66 above.

[33] For the Joint Communiqué by the United States and the Soviet Union regarding Camp David conversations, the statements of President Eisenhower and of Premier Khrushchev, see U.S. Senate, *Documents on Germany*, pp. 584–86.

[34] Khrushchev in his letter to Adenauer dated January 28, 1960, referred to this admission that the "situation in West Berlin is abnormal." *Ibid.*, p. 591.

instead of a second Geneva, and Secretary of State Christian Herter and Under Secretary of State Douglas Dillon gave warnings to Khrushchev that he should not expect any agreement on his terms.[35] These warnings did not remain unnoticed in Moscow! Khrushchev in his speech delivered in Baku on April 25, 1960, not only castigated these statements as "out of tune with the tenor" of the Camp David conversations but returned to his erstwhile threats: the signing of a peace treaty with the German Democratic Republic, the forfeiture of the right of access of Western powers to West Berlin "by land, water and air."[36]

It appeared as though the Western heads of government might at last be ready to call Khrushchev's bluff. Evidently, he could sign his peace treaty with Ulbricht only once; if the Western powers' access rights to Berlin thereafter remained in vigor, the Soviets would lose much of their leverage in Berlin. Rather than face such a setback, Khrushchev exploded the U-2 incident into an *affaire* to cause the collapse of the Summit Conference. Internal pressures or pressures by the Chinese may also have been among his reasons. But there is no proof to show that any of these causes were decisive.[37]

After the violent outbursts of the Soviet Premier in Paris, the world might have expected a new flare-up of the Berlin crisis when he addressed a meeting in East Berlin three days later. However, Khrushchev merely advised his audience that the "existing situation will apparently be preserved till the Heads of Government meeting, which, it is to be hoped, will take place in six or eight months."[38]

For more than a year there was a diplomatic standstill on Berlin. Khrushchev gave the appearance of wishing to abstain from any interference in the American presidential elections and, after their outcome, to give sufficient respite to the new President. However, he reverted to this question when he met President Kennedy in Vienna on June 4, 1961.

At Vienna Khrushchev presented the American President with

[35] See the address by Secretary of State Herter at Chicago, April 4, 1960, and that of Under Secretary of State Dillon at New York, April 20, 1960. *Ibid.*, 594–98.

[36] *Ibid.*, pp. 598–603.

[37] For speculation on the causes of Khrushchev's behavior in Paris in May, 1960, see Hans Speier, *Divided Berlin—The Anatomy of Soviet Political Blackmail* (New York, 1961), pp. 99–112; John Mander, *Berlin—Hostage for the West* (Baltimore, 1962), pp. 83–84; Alfons Dalma, *Hintergründe der Berlin-Krise* (Karlsruhe, 1962), pp. 66–80.

[38] U.S. Senate, *Documents on Germany*, pp. 604–6.

193

an *aide mémoire* on the German and Berlin problems. The document stated that a peace treaty with Germany was long overdue and that a peace conference should be convoked "immediately, without delay." The Soviet proposal did not tie the conclusion of a peace treaty to the recognition of the German Democratic Republic (this was a new approach), and it stated that "a peaceful settlement could be achieved on the basis of two treaties." The important provisions of both treaties were, however, to be identical. The *aide mémoire* then reiterated the well-known Soviet project for West Berlin as a demilitarized and neutral free city. As a guarantee of the city's freedom "token contingents of the United States, the United Kingdom, France and the U.S.S.R. could be stationed in West Berlin." Also, contingents from neutral states under the aegis of the United Nations could participate. The four powers should invite the two German states to agree on reunification; in the Soviet view only six months would be needed for the completion of such talks. In case of a failure to agree, the two peace treaties were to be signed.[39]

The Soviet *aide mémoire*, supplemented by Khrushchev's intransigence at Vienna, was interpreted in the West as a renewed threat against the safety of West Berlin. It was particularly that part of the Soviet document which again claimed for the Russians a right to participate in the occupation of West Berlin which provoked alarm. In the eyes of the West, the whole of Berlin was under the special occupation regime, and it had been illegal for the Soviets to hand over their sector to the D.D.R. Now the Soviet government, after having excluded the West from any interference in the eastern sector, wished to participate in the stationing of forces within the three western sectors.[40] Secretary of State Dean Rusk gave a precise definition of Washington's appraisal of the situation: "Due to the *de facto* division of Germany, the entire situation in that country is abnormal. The Soviet position in regard to this matter is predicated on the belief that the division of Germany is normal, that the division of Berlin is normal, and that the sole abnormality that persists is West Berlin. This is not a formulation of the problem which is acceptable to the United States."[41]

The United States replied on July 17, 1961, to Khrushchev's *aide mémoire*. The note sought to restore the logical priorities of the

---

[39] *Ibid.*, pp. 642–45; for details on the Vienna talks, see Arthur M. Schlesinger, Jr., *A Thousand Days* (Boston, 1965), pp. 358–74.

[40] Speier, *Divided Berlin*, p. 133.

[41] From statements made by Dean Rusk at his news conference on June 22, 1961, U.S. Senate, *Documents on Germany*, p. 666.

Western approach to the problem by insisting that "there will be no real solution of the German problem, nor any real tranquility in Central Europe, until the German people are re-unified in peace and freedom on the basis of the universally recognized principle of self-determination."

The note undertook to refute, one by one, the arguments advanced in the *aide mémoire* by pointing out their inaccuracy or impracticability. It ended by stating that "there is no reason for a crisis over Berlin. If one develops it is because the Soviet Union is attempting to invade the basic rights of others."[42]

Two days later, on July 19, 1961, President Kennedy in a news conference emphasized the three vital interests of West Berlin which, even at the price of war, must be preserved: (1) Western military presence, (2) freedom and viability of West Berlin's population, and (3) security of the access routes to and from West Berlin.[43]

It thus became clear that the Western powers were unwilling to discuss anything beyond some provisional arrangements to improve the status of West Berlin and eliminate certain differences; no final or fundamental alteration of Berlin's political and military position could be undertaken without simultaneous steps for the solution of the problem of German unity. The speeches of the American leaders were accompanied by certain military moves, reinforcement of the garrison of Berlin and of the forces stationed in West Germany. All these gestures were intended to impress the Soviet leadership with the Western determination to defend the status of West Berlin against any aggression.[44]

The motives that led Khrushchev to permit Ulbricht to raise the Wall between East and West Berlin can only be assumed. We are not sure whether the initiative for this move came originally from Pankow or from Moscow. The Berlin crisis created by the Soviets had increased considerably the economic and political difficulties of the East German regime. The number of refugees from East Germany flowing through the Berlin exit had risen significantly after the new Soviet offensive. This exodus reached a peak of 4,000 persons on August 8. For Ulbricht the outflow of valuable manpower was a first-class catastrophe; had the exodus not been stopped, it might

[42] *Ibid.*, pp. 681–87.
[43] *Ibid.*, pp. 687–89; for the interpretation of this statement, see Dalma, *Hintergründe der Berlin-Krise*, pp. 17–24.
[44] Speier, *Divided Germany*, pp. 145–59; Philip Windsor, *City on Leave: A History of Berlin, 1945–1962* (London, 1963), pp. 233–40.

have led to the loss of several million more persons, disrupting the economic and cultural life of East Germany and leading to the downfall of the regime. This, of course, was a development which the Soviet Union could not tolerate.[45]

In West Germany there was less concern about the economic and social consequences of the refugees than about the demographic depletion of the D.D.R. It was feared that Germanism would lose additional "living space" to the Slavs, that Ulbricht might be compelled to engage Polish or Russian labor, and that the German element might be driven back even further than the Oder-Neisse Line.

In Washington and London the avalanche of refugees making use of the Berlin escape hatch strengthened those critics of Western intransigence toward Soviet demands over Berlin. Senator Fulbright, Chairman of the Senate Foreign Relations Committee, suggested that the German Democratic Republic close the yawning gap of Berlin to prevent the outflow of its population by maintaining that every state had the right to control the movement of its people.[46]

The East German regime had for years taken measures to check the flight of its population to West Germany. All along the demarcation line separating the D.D.R. from the Federal Republic, barbed wire, minefields, and watchtowers—the usual paraphernalia of the Iron Curtain—already presented formidable obstacles to would-be refugees. The periphery of West Berlin was equally well guarded; but the boundary between the western sectors and the Soviet sector of the city cut across streets, squares, gardens, or open areas. Residents from more distant parts of Berlin or from East Germany made use of the city's traffic network where the legitimate movement of passengers could not be distinguished from the flight of refugees. The S-Bahn (city railway), using the elevated tracks of the Reichsbahn, the East German state railroad system, and run by

[45] The impact on East Germany's economy of the refugee exodus can be measured by Ulbricht's admissions in an article written for *Pravda*. The East German leader said that the westward flight had cost to the economy of the D.D.R. thirty billion marks (40 per cent of the national income in 1961). He also said that the flight had been promoted by "wrong conceptions of the national question." The refugees had thought that they were going from one Germany into another Germany but, in fact, "they were escaping the Socialist camp and going to the imperialist camp." *New York Times*, December 31, 1961.

[46] Windsor, *City on Leave*, p. 238. Senator Fulbright was reproached by West German writers of having encouraged the East German regime to set up the Berlin Wall. Klaus-Peter Schulz, *Berlin zwischen Freiheit und Diktatur* (Berlin, 1962), pp. 536–37.

the East German railroad administration, maintained many lines and stations in West Berlin. The U-Bahn (subway), run by the municipality of (West) Berlin, had lines and stations in East Berlin. Escapees had merely to buy tickets to some station beyond West Berlin (which they could produce as evidence if suspected of being fugitives) and get off at any stop within West Berlin.[47] They would then be flown into West Germany.

During the night of August 12, the East German authorities placed barbed wire along the border of the western sectors of Greater Berlin and, within a few days, protected by armed forces of the D.D.R., erected a wall which allowed only a few gateways for traffic between East and West Berlin. On August 13, 1961, the government of the German Democratic Republic issued a decree which provided that: "To put an end to the hostile activities of the revanchist and militarist forces of Western Germany and West Berlin, such control is to be introduced on the borders of the German Democratic Republic, including the border with the Western sectors of Greater Berlin, which is usually introduced along the borders of every sovereign state."[48]

The decree, furthermore, forbade citizens of the German Democratic Republic (including the residents of East Berlin) from crossing into West Berlin without special permission. West Berlin civilians were to present their identity cards when crossing into East Berlin; in practice, however, they were turned back unless they had received special permits. The decree did not alter existing regulations concerning the movements of West Germans into or across East Germany, nor did it touch upon the rights of Allied military personnel (the decree speaks of "West Berlin civilians") to enter East Berlin or to travel along the access routes on land to and from West Berlin.

The construction of a wall physically dividing the city of Berlin had a double objective: first, to stop the human outflow and, secondly, to terrorize and browbeat the people of West Berlin into obedience. In order to give the Wall an aura of collective approval, a declaration of the Warsaw Pact Powers on August 13, 1961, endorsed the measures taken by the German Democratic Republic against the subversive activities of the Federal Republic.

[47] Fritz Schenk, a high-standing Party member, in order to escape, first traveled around West Berlin to Potsdam, then took a train from there back to East Berlin but left the train at a West Berlin station. Schenk, *Im Vorzimmer der Diktatur*, pp. 411–12.

[48] U.S. Senate, *Documents on Germany*, pp. 723–25.

It will probably remain a moot question whether the Western powers could have prevented the building of the Wall either by the threatening presence of their Berlin garrison or, as was suggested, by sending their tanks through the concrete slabs.[49] There were no Soviet tanks present; had Allied military actions provoked their appearance, the Soviet responsibility for erecting the Wall would have become blatantly apparent. Later, at the end of October, 1961, American and Russian tanks faced each other at one of the crossing points; this "game of chicken" ended with the withdrawal of the Soviet vehicles.[50]

Beyond protests (which were rejected outright by both the Soviet Commandant of Berlin and the Soviet Ministry of Foreign Affairs) the Western powers and the Federal government found no suitable form of retaliation. Although Willy Brandt, the Governing Mayor of Berlin, had made various suggestions to both the Allied powers and the Bonn government, including troop movements along the Autobahn, the taking over of the West Berlin section of the Reichsbahn and the S-Bahn, and a ban on West German exports to the German Democratic Republic,[51] the visit of Vice-President Johnson and the mission of General Clay, together with minor demonstrations by the Allied military in West Berlin were the only soothing gestures which the West could afford to make for the highly disturbed and demoralized West Berlin people.

The erection of the Wall had greater material effect on the inhabitants of East Berlin than on the people of the West. It closed before their eyes the possibility of escape; it deprived persons of even a hasty visit to the resplendent "West" Berlin, a stimulant so badly needed in the drab everyday drudgery of Communist East Germany. The exasperation felt in the East was manifested by the hazardous and often fatal attempts to defy the Wall. With the Berlin Wall, Khrushchev certainly put the lid on the boiling kettle of East Germany and successfully prevented the evaporation of her manpower. But once the door had been closed, it could hardly be opened again without causing an explosion disastrous to the regime.

For the West Germans the shock of August 13, 1961, resembled that of June 17, 1953. Helplessness and reluctance to take risks increased bitterness, and these feelings were expressed in the returns

---

[49] For the various plans considered in the White House, see Schlesinger, *A Thousand Days*, pp. 394–400.

[50] The story of the Wall and its aftermath is told by J. E. Smith, *The Defense of Berlin*, pp. 267–341. See also *New York Times*, December 10, 1961.

[51] J. E. Smith, *The Defense of Berlin*, pp. 282–83.

of the September, 1961, elections.[52] For the first time the Berlin issue had directly affected West German elections by turning the electorate against the party of the Chancellor.

The Wall has considerably increased the personal and individual hardships caused by the division of Germany. While the East German Revolt of 1953 shocked and grossly offended popular feeling in the Federal Republic, its memory has slowly faded over the years. But the humiliating and exasperating experience of the Wall has remained a constant source of repulsion in the political life of Germany and the thoughts of her people. Although the future impact of the Wall is not yet foreseeable, it promises to revive nationalistic sentiments and to foment latent hostility toward the Western powers, especially the United States, whose inaction dismayed the public.

The second, but by no means secondary, objective of the Wall— the demoralization and ensuing capitulation of West Berlin—failed. Like Stalin, Khrushchev and Ulbricht had under-rated the mettle of the battle-hardened people of West Berlin. Although their morale was low during the months following their severance from the East and many left the city for West Germany which caused economic relapse, they slowly recovered their sense of mission for the German cause. After the second Cuban crisis, their spirit for survival and ultimate victory gained strength. President Kennedy's visit to the city in June, 1963, gave greater impetus to their quest. West Berlin now realized that, despite the hardships of separation, it could survive despite the Wall if its communications with West Germany remained intact.

In the aftermath of the Wall the main concern of the Western powers was the security of the access routes to Berlin. After a partial success with the Wall, the Soviets now seemed to shift their offensive against these routes; the harassments and situations of risk that followed were designed to obtain wider recognition for the German Democratic Republic, whose "sovereignty"—as it was repeatedly said—was being impaired by the Western use of land, water, and air routes to Berlin. The Berlin question now became largely identified with this delicate problem.

The Question of Access Routes to Berlin

The problem of Berlin is a product of the larger German problem; the question of access routes to Berlin reflected Berlin's pecul-

[52] See Chapter I, p. 47 above.

iar status, its location 110 miles from the dividing line of East and West Germany. We recalled earlier how a separate Berlin area, to be jointly administered by the four powers, had been established within, but not as part of, the Soviet zone of occupation, and how the Western powers had failed to ask for definite access routes by rail and road.[53] But in order to ensure safety of flights, the Four-Power Control Council approved the establishment of three air corridors, each twenty miles wide, along the lines: Berlin-Hamburg, Berlin-Hanover (Buckeburg), and Berlin-Frankfurt/M, on November 30, 1945. Flights along these routes (corridors) were to be "conducted without previous notice being given, *by aircraft of the nations governing Germany.*"[54] These transit rights were not restricted to military aircraft, an important circumstance which was not true of the land routes.

Under these provisions all the movements of American, British, and French airliners, military and civilian alike, are completely outside Soviet and East German control. The Inter-Allied Air Safety Center, in which the Russians have continued to participate, serves only for co-ordinating flights in order to insure their safety and does not exercise any rights of control.

During the Berlin blockade of 1948–49, the Soviet authorities did not seriously interfere with the "air lift" of the Allies, except for a few harassments. These interferences have continued; the Soviet government has also endeavored to restrict the use of the air corridors, partly by limiting the heights of the flights, partly by trying to exclude civilian aircraft or certain types of passengers, but to no avail.[55]

When by the Treaty with the German Democratic Republic of

[53] Chapter I, pp. 12–13 above.

[54] U.S. Senate, *Documents on Germany,* pp. 41–49. Italics have been added.

[55] Some of these attempts were made by the Soviet personnel in the Berlin Air-Safety Center. On September 2, 1961, the Soviet government, in a note addressed to the three Western powers, protested against the use of the air corridors by commercial airlines and against transportation of West German "spies," "militarists," and "revanchists." The three Western powers replied on September 8, 1961, in identical notes refuting Soviet allegations and rejecting the protests. See U.S. Senate, *Documents on Germany,* pp. 784–91; *Dokumente zur Berlin-Frage,* pp. 525–30; *New York Times,* September 9, 1961. The right to use unrestricted heights in the corridors was maintained in an American note of protest on February 15, 1962; *Dokumente zur Berlin-Frage,* pp. 532–34.

In May, 1964, the Soviet government protested against direct flights between New York and West Berlin; its contention was that under existing agreements foreign airlines were allowed to fly to West Berlin from West German airfields only; *New York Times,* June 23, 1964.

September 20, 1955, the Soviet Union recognized the complete sovereignty of the latter, surrendering to them the control and surveillance of lines of communication between the Federal Republic and the D.D.R., the three air corridors were expressly exempted from the application of the Treaty.[56] The East German Law for Civilian Air Traffic of August 1, 1963, also excluded from its scope those flights which were subject to "conflicting international treaties."[57]

The three air corridors for American, British, and French (but no West German) military and civilian aircraft have thus been effectively used since 1945 as extraterritorial access routes. These airlanes are, therefore, the most reliable links between West Germany and West Berlin; in 1948–49 they had been the lifelines of West Berlin's freedom and survival. The Western powers constantly use these airlanes; as far as the definition runs, they actually control them. Any obstruction of their use would be construed as an aggression by the Soviet Union or the German Democratic Republic, involving the probability of legitimate self-defense. In this case the Western powers might have the civilian aircraft passing through the corridors accompanied by fighter planes and perhaps also with bombers to take out anti-aircraft batteries on the ground. Thus, the security of air communications has two bases: legal clarity and actual possession. Only overt violence could change the situation.

On land the problem is different. Only "oral" and "temporary" arrangements had been made between General Clay and Marshal Zhukov for the allocation of one main highway and rail line. No record was kept of this meeting which was held before the Western Allied forces moved into Berlin.[58] The significance of a formal agreement in dealings with the Soviet Union, let alone any foreign government, was completely overlooked.[59] The military leaders felt at that time that access to Berlin was a purely "military matter"

[56] U.S. Senate, *Documents on Germany*, pp. 187–89; *Dokumente zur Berlin-Frage*, pp. 239–41.

[57] *Die Welt*, August 2, 1963.

[58] Clay, *Decision in Germany*, pp. 25–27. See Chapter I, p. 13 above.

[59] General Clay writes: "I think now that I was mistaken in not at this time making free access to Berlin a condition to our withdrawal into our occupation zones. . . . However, I doubt very much if anything in writing would have done any more to prevent the events which took place than the verbal agreement which we made. The Soviet Government seems to be able to find technical reasons at will to justify the violation of understandings whether verbal or written." Clay, *Decision in Germany*, p. 26. See also by same author, "Berlin," *Foreign Affairs*, October, 1962, pp. 47–58.

and that *de facto* recognition was more important than any definite written understanding.[60] Under the Potsdam Agreement and subsequent understandings, zonal borders were not to be closed to civilian passenger and goods traffic.

The Western military forces were given the use of the Helmstedt-Berlin railroad track and the Marienborn-Berlin Autobahn highway across the Soviet zone. Barge traffic on rivers and canals was covered by various technical agreements. These rail, road, and water access routes were successively closed after March 30, 1948, by the Soviet forces of occupation. After the lifting of the blockade, the Soviet Commander of the Soviet zone enumerated in an order of May 9, 1949, all the access routes (including points of entry and exit) which might be used both for military and for civilian passenger and freight (including mail) traffic to and from Berlin.[61]

Under the Treaty and simultaneous exchange of letters between the Soviet and East German governments of September 20, 1955, the German Democratic Republic was to exercise general control of the lines of communication between the Federal Republic and West Berlin, including rail, road, and barge traffic. While civilian traffic thus became subject to East German supervision and control, the movement of American, British, and French forces and their supplies continued to be exempt from East German control "on the basis of existing Four Power decisions." The Treaty provided that the control of Western military traffic was, as before, to be exercised "temporarily" by the Command of Soviet troops in East Germany. The agreement lists the Autobahn Berlin-Marienborn and the railroad line Berlin-Helmstedt (with empty rolling stock to be routed back on the Berlin-Oebisfelde line) as the authorized routes of access.[62]

The subjection of civilian traffic to the control of the German Democratic Republic elicited protests and reservations by the three Western powers but, henceforth, D.D.R. officials undertook the tasks of civilian inspection while Western military transports continued to be checked by Soviet military personnel.

On August 23, 1962, the Soviet government abolished the office

[60] See the interesting discussion of this point in The Hammarskjold Forums, *The Issues in the Berlin-German Crisis*, pp. 34–37.

[61] See the several technical agreements and the Soviet Order of May 9, 1949; *Dokumente zur Berlin-Frage*, pp. 38–42, 64–65, 109–11.

[62] Treaty between the Soviet Union and the German Democratic Republic, and exchange of letters between Lothar Bolz, Foreign Minister of the D.D.R., and V. A. Zorin, Soviet Deputy Foreign Minister, of September 20, 1955, U. S. Senate, *Documents on Germany*, pp. 187–89.

202

of Soviet commandant of (East) Berlin, thereby demonstrating the final transfer of East Berlin to the German Democratic Republic and the end of the occupation status of Berlin.[63] But, *de facto*, nothing had changed: the Soviet Defense Ministry was eager to announce to representatives of the Allied military authorities in West Berlin that "matters relating to control over the movement of personnel and supplies of the garrisons of the United States, Britain and France into and out of West Berlin, the guarding of the prison of chief German war criminals in Spandau and sentry duty at the monument to Soviet troops in *Tiergarten* temporarily are within the jurisdiction of the Headquarters of the group of Soviet forces in Germany."[64]

While the Soviet government adjusted to the notion that East Berlin was part of the D.D.R. by abolishing its military command, it was careful to maintain all the remaining privileges of this office in West Berlin. The characteristic Western response was to declare that, irrespective of organization, the Soviet Union would be held responsible for carrying out its obligations in Berlin.

The Soviet-East German Treaty of Friendship, Mutual Assistance and Co-operation of June 12, 1964, also refrained from introducing any changes concerning the access routes to Berlin by stating that the treaty "does not affect the rights and commitments of the Parties under the bilateral and other international agreements which are in force, including the Potsdam Agreement."[65]

The absence of clear written agreement concerning the rights of transit on land are a matter of constant anxiety and irritation to the Western Allies and West Germans. This lack of detailed regulations has created the need for developing certain usages or "procedures." Because these procedures have not received official acceptancy by both parties and because (like all customary rules) they are somewhat vague themselves, they offer a fruitful field for "salami" tactics or "incidents" that whittle down Western privileges.

A good example of how the vagueness of working procedures provides opportunities for Soviet harassment was the detention for

[63] Until the erection of the Wall on August 13, 1961, the Western Allied Kommandatura maintained contacts with the Commandant of the Soviet forces in East Berlin, whom they considered a nonparticipating member of the original four-power Kommandatura. After the Wall, when members of Allied forces occasionally were barred from entering East Berlin, the West resorted to retaliations by refusing, temporarily, the entry of the Soviet Commandant into West Berlin.

[64] *New York Times*, August 23, 1962.

[65] *Ibid.*, June 13, 1964.

fifty-two hours of United States military convoy on October 10 and 11, 1963, at the Babelsberg checkpoint at the exit of the Autobahn from Berlin. By unwritten convention the personnel of American convoys dismounted to show their number to the Russian guards whenever they exceeded thirty—not counting the plainly visible drivers and their assistants. This was a convoy of less than thirty passengers, and, therefore, the officer in command refused the Soviet invitation to dismount. The convoy was obstructed by Soviet military vehicles. Finally, the Russians gave in and the convoy was able to proceed. Similar incidents have been created to remind the Western Allies of their dependence on Soviet goodwill for maintaining their overland links with West Berlin and also to recall that West Berlin "is a bone in the throat" of East German and Soviet power.[66]

There is little doubt that the Western powers also possess legal rights of access on land to Berlin. It may, however, be questioned whether such rights are based on customary international law concerning enclaves,[67] on the "verbal" agreement between the wartime military commanders later confirmed by various technical arrangements,[68] or, finally, on local custom observed and thus developed into compulsory rules during the past twenty years. Transit rights across the territories of foreign states are not an unusual feature of international life;[69] Germany, from 1919 to 1939, enjoyed a right of passage, originally conceded by the Treaty of Versailles, across the so-called Polish Corridor in order to maintain secure communications on land with the East Prussian area.

The legal aspect of the Western access rights to Berlin (except

[66] For the convoy incident of October 10 and 11, 1963, see *ibid.*, October 13, 20, 1963; for the text of the U.S. protest note, see *ibid.*, November 7, 1963. The procedural rules as conceived by the Americans were thereafter handed over to the Russians so as to prevent them in the future from pleading ignorance. However, they were not acknowledged.

[67] Under this principle, states having enclaves (portions of another state within their own territory) are obliged to grant rights of transit across their area which divide the enclaves from the mother state. See the *Right of Passage Over Indian Territory* case (*Portugal* v. *India*) before the International Court of Justice (Oral Proceedings [Merits], Vol. I, pp. 197–243) and the judgment of April 12, 1960.

[68] Such as the arrangements lifting the blockade of 1948–49 around Berlin. Verbal agreements between persons authorized to represent their respective governments are undoubtedly valid commitments under international law; their proof and the determination of their exact provisions are, however, somewhat difficult.

[69] Obligations to allow free passage are called "servitudes" by international lawyers, a name derived from a Roman law institution; see Ferenc A. Váli, *Servitudes of International Law—Rights in Foreign Territory* (London and New York, 1958), *passim.*

for the air corridors) is, however, obscured by the uncertainty of their origin, by the absence of detailed written agreements covering the exact nature and content of these rights, and also by the quasi-exclusiveness of control exercised by Soviet authorities, which has largely reduced the claimed "unrestrictedness" of the access rights. Many of the original rights (e.g., civilian traffic) have been eroded or subjected to the control of the legally uncommitted East German partner.

But the legal aspect of access rights, though by no means inconsequential, has had only a limited bearing on the continued durability of these rights; their survival for twenty years is rather a result of the existing balance of power and the fear of violent conflict.

Nevertheless, the somewhat threadbare character of Allied access rights on land to Berlin has exposed the Western powers and the Federal Republic to the "blackmail" of a separate peace treaty with East Germany whereby the control of communications with Berlin would be handed over to the mercy of the German Democratic Republic. This threat, as well as the view held by many in the West that a detailed and formal agreement would forestall frictions and contribute toward the easing of the tensions over Berlin, persuaded the United States and Britain to seek a limited arrangement of the Berlin issue by concentrating on the problem of access routes.

On land—unlike the air corridors—the Soviet and East German forces are in possession. When these forces obstruct rail or road routes, Western Allied traffic may proceed only by using force. In such a case, the West would be the attacker and could be stigmatized as an aggressor. Still, plans of breaking through the Berlin blockade were weighed in 1948, and such contingencies have never been ruled out entirely.[70]

The informal conversations on Berlin conducted in Moscow and Washington in 1962 and 1963 were undertaken by the United States mainly for the purpose of strengthening the Allied access rights. The American attempt to establish the access rights on a firm and regular basis had to be bargained against Soviet endeavors to remove the Western garrisons in Berlin or lower them to a token force and to "upgrade" the East German regime by giving her an opportunity to participate in the control of army traffic on the access routes.

In November, 1958, when Khrushchev first voiced his threats,

---

[70] The Ambassadors' Steering Committees, in Washington and Bonn, considered to be in permanent session to watch and advise on developments on Berlin, have worked out contingency plans with support by the military. Advocates of more militant reactions are said to be suffering from "Berlinitis," in the current phraseology of these committees.

Secretary of State Dulles suggested that the Western powers might deal with D.D.R. functionaries as "agents" of the Soviet Union.[71] This concept was, however, rejected by the Russians. In March, 1962, the Soviet Union launched the idea of an "arbitration authority" on disputes over access to West Berlin which would decide conflicts between East German authorities (who would be in charge of the control) and the Western powers. The price to be paid for the "normalization" of access rights was to be the limited or full recognition of the German Democratic Republic and its exercise of control over access routes together with the reduction of Western garrisons in West Berlin to a "symbolic" force and their replacement by "neutral" forces. Even if the United States had been ready to negotiate improved communications with Berlin on such a basis, the Federal government would have strongly opposed any such deal.[72]

It is not in the interest of the Soviet Union to change the present vague status of access routes on land unless a more valuable *quid pro quo* is given in exchange. In view of the potential tensions between communism and the Western world, a really satisfactory solution of land access to West Berlin could only be achieved if the control of movements by rail and road routes were ceded to the Western powers. Unless there is a guarantee of co-operation between the interested powers, transit rights on foreign territory cannot be reliably exercised when the users of these rights belong to states different from the organs of control.[73] The Western Allies would enjoy a really "unrestricted" right only if their movements along the indicated routes were not subject to Soviet or East German control.[74] But there is no likelihood that agreement could be reached along these lines.

In all probability, the Western rights of access to Berlin will remain a constant source of irritation and danger unless the Soviet Union abandons its campaign to convert West Berlin into a "free

[71] News conference by Secretary of State John Foster Dulles in Berlin on November 26, 1958, *Documents*, p. 344. See also Mander, *Berlin: Hostage for the West*, pp. 83, 102.

[72] See *New York Times*, March 25 and May 8, 1962.

[73] Váli, *Servitudes of International Law*, pp. 314–317.

[74] Senator Claiborne Pell of Rhode Island proposed that the Berlin-Helmstedt Autobahn be ceded to West Germany as an "unlimited corridor of access to West Berlin." In exchange, the United States was to recognize the D.D.R., as well as the Oder-Neisse frontier; *New York Times*, December 22, 1963. It is very unikely that either the Soviets should consent to such a territorial corridor across East Germany or that West Germany, even at that price, would agree to the recognition of the D.D.R.

city" and to "blackmail" the West into recognizing the East German state. The present access rights are by no means secure; nevertheless, they critically affect the status and destiny of Berlin. They cannot be strengthened, except for a price: recognition of the D.D.R. or a deterioration of the status of West Berlin. The main thing not to be lost sight of is that the access rights are a means—crucial, to be sure—but that the integrity of West Berlin is an end, both for the West and for the free Germans.

After the Wall—Future of the Berlin Problem

The Wall did not lead to the demoralization or capitulation of West Berlin; it probably saved East Germany from economic collapse, but it created human problems which, in their turn, grew into weighty political problems. The physical separation of two parts of Berlin caused bitterness on both sides of the Wall; it was an admission of the weakness by the German Democratic Republic before its own citizens. Not only those 50,000 East Berliners who daily commuted to work in West Berlin but workers, in general, called for a removal of the "Wall of Shame."[75]

But the Ulbricht regime seemed little concerned with public pressures in the West or in the East. It wished to exploit the Wall for recognition purposes. Before Christmas, 1963, Pankow announced its willingness to issue day passes to West Berliners to enable them to visit relatives in East Berlin at the Christmas season. The Federal government suggested that the plan should be negotiated by Dr. Kurt Leopold, then head of the Interzonal Trade Office (who negotiates East-West German trade agreements); the East German government, however, insisted that the arrangements should be made by the West Berlin municipality.[76] Bonn gave reluctant consent that the agreement should be made by the Governing Mayor of Berlin with the East German authorities. In order to "de-politicize" the issue, East German postal officials were to come to West Berlin to issue the border passes.[77]

From December 22 to January 5, 1964, 1.3 million West Berliners

[75] For reports about discontent in East Berlin factories because of the Wall, after the 1963 Christmas visits, see *New York Times*, January 3, 1964.
[76] The East German regime wished to convey the impression that West Berlin is a political entity, separate from the Federal Republic, thereby creating a precedent for the future. See the reports in *New York Times*, December 7, 8, and 14, 1963.
[77] East Germany's press, nevertheless, was jubilant in declaring that the arrangement was a political deal instead of a nonpolitical, humanitarian one. *Ibid.*, December 23, 1963.

out of a total population of 2.2 million visited the eastern section of the city to meet relatives.[78] This mass pilgrimage from one part of Berlin to the other was a significant demonstration of the sentiment of unity.

The 1963 Christmas pass agreement was concluded by the West Berlin city government with the approval of both Bonn and the Allied occupation powers. Nonetheless, it elicited violent criticism by supporters of the "hard" line in the Federal capital, who charged Berlin with helping to erode the Western position on German unity. The Berlin magistrate was reproached with trying to have the best of all worlds, "security from the Americans, money from Bonn and passes from Ulbricht."[79] On the other hand, members of the Free Democratic party and also some CDU leaders approved of the arrangements, which they considered merely technical and well substantiated on humanitarian grounds. Even Governing Mayor Willy Brandt agreed, however, that this agreement should not be taken as a model. The United States, in afterthought, felt some misgivings about the pass deal when "humanitarian haste overshadowed political policy." Official spokesmen also pointed out that in any case occupied West Berlin has no legal status to "recognize" any state.[80] And West German official circles made it clear that with the agreement in question the Federal Republic had reached its extreme of sacrifice in the face of Communist inhumanities; no further gestures could be made without political harm to the well-known Western position about Berlin.[81]

Soon both the Bonn government and the West Berlin Magistrate came to the conclusion that the East German design was to exploit the humanitarian need to bring relatives together; they agreed that no temporary agreement should be concluded and that negotiations should be held strictly at a technical level. No East German officials (not even postmen) should come to West Berlin to distribute entry permits, which could be handled just as easily by mail.[82]

In February, the East German government renewed its offer to permit the entry of West Berliners for the Easter and Pentecost

---

[78] Polls conducted before the border pass agreement revealed that 80 per cent of all West Berliners maintain personal ties with residents of East Germany and East Berlin, and 66 per cent have relatives in those areas. *Bulletin* of the Press and Information Office of the Federal Government, January 14, 1964.

[79] *New York Times*, December 21, 1963.

[80] *Ibid.*, January 3, 1964.

[81] *Frankfurter Allgemeine Zeitung*, December 18, 1963.

[82] *New York Times*, January 4, 8, and 9, 1964.

holidays. Previously, an invitation to Willy Brandt by Alexander Abusch, East German Deputy Prime Minister, to discuss the question of border passes and "related matters" had been rejected. It appeared at that time that Pankow was trying to push a wedge between West Berlin and Bonn. The aim of the new offer was evidently to raise the level of contact between East and West, and to establish permanent East German offices in West Berlin. One of the conditions set by Pankow was that henceforth East Berlin was to be referred to as "the capital of the German Democratic Republic." The rejection of this offer was announced in a joint statement by the Federal government and the West Berlin Magistrate.[83]

The contacts between West Berlin authorities and the officials of the D.D.R. were, however, not discontinued. After negotiations lasting almost nine months between Horst Korber, councillor of the (West) Berlin Senate, and Erich Wendt, East German state secretary, on September 24, 1964, another "pass" agreement was signed to apply for a period of one year. The Federal government, in agreement with West Berlin, consented to a formula which differed little from the earlier one. The D.D.R. insisted that (East) Berlin should receive the epithet: "Capital of the German Democratic Republic." Earlier, Bonn had suggested that the West Berlin negotiator should sign "on behalf of the responsible authorities," to avoid the implication that West Berlin was a political entity, entitled to sign an agreement. But the Western Commandants objected against such vague terminology because it might have been interpreted as having committed the occupation powers, ultimately responsible for West Berlin.[84] Eventually, Horst Korber signed, "on instructions by the Chief of the Senate's Chancellery, directed by the Governing Mayor of Berlin."[85] The only apparent concession by Pankow had been to agree that the entry permits were to be handled jointly by both East German postal clerks and West Berlin officials.

The Federal Chancellor, in order to counteract criticism against the form of the agreement, issued a declaration emphasizing that "the significance of the agreement is in the human sphere"; that it "in no way affects or changes the status of the German capital, Berlin"; that, despite the agreement, "the democratically not legit-

[83] *Ibid.*, February 14 and 15, 1964.
[84] *Ibid.*, September 7, 1964.
[85] *Ibid.*, September 24, 1964. The full text of the agreement of September 24, 1964, was made public by the Federal Press and Information Office on September 25 for the purpose of radio transmissions.

imized regime of the Soviet-occupied zone is not a subject of international law." Therefore, no importance should be attached to what name it gives itself.[86]

Bonn continued to be unhappy with the border pass agreement. In August, 1965, it refused to agree to an extension of the earlier agreement for another year because it considered the East German offer too narrow. Nevertheless, in November, 1965, a new agreement opened the gates of the Wall for visiting relatives during the Christmas season, and another renewal took place in the spring of 1966 for Easter and Whitsuntide visits.[87] No such agreement was, however, concluded for Christmas 1966.

As a result of these agreements, West Berliners were enabled to meet their relatives during holiday seasons in East Berlin, widely referred to as visits "to relatives in prison." The evident hesitations of the Bonn cabinet reflect the peculiar implications of these arrangements: humanitarian considerations compete with political viewpoints. While the SPD, the majority party in West Berlin, considered these arrangements as one of the "small steps" suggested by its leader, Willy Brandt, opponents of the "soft" approach objected for reasons of principle. Other political leaders, especially those of the FDP, while approving the contacts, would have preferred to have them between some Federal agency and the East German authorities rather than between the Social Democrats of West Berlin and Pankow.[88] Ultimately, however, the humanitarian principle won over political strife and punctilious legalism for the benefit of millions of West Berliners.

Like the Federal government, the Western occupation powers refused to acknowledge any change in the status of Berlin, as they conceived it, despite the Wall and the liquidation of the office of Soviet commandant in Berlin on August 23, 1962. The three occupation powers promptly issued a communiqué stating that the abolition of the post of Soviet commandant did not destroy the authority of the Kommandatura and asserting that:

the commandants in the Western sectors of Berlin will continue to exercise their rights and discharge their responsibilities both in their individual sectors and jointly in the Kommandatura in accordance with long established procedures and agreements. *They will continue to consider the Soviet officials as responsible for carrying out their obligations regarding the Soviet Sector of Berlin.*

[86] The declaration is published in *Bulletin,* September 29, 1964, pp. 1–2.
[87] *New York Times,* August 19, 1965, March 5 and May 24, 1966.
[88] *Süddeutsche Zeitung,* November 25, 1965.

Moreover, the Soviet announcement can in no way affect the *unity of Berlin* as a whole. Despite the illegality of the wall and the brutality of the East German authorities in preventing the inhabitants of East Berlin from leaving that area, *Berlin remains a single city*. No unilateral action by the Soviet Government can change this.[89]

The Soviet campaign against West Berlin abated by 1964. After the second Cuban crisis no major move took place, no new deadlines were set, and little was heard of the threat to conclude a separate peace treaty with the German Democratic Republic. The final anticlimax came in June, 1964, when the Soviet Union concluded a Treaty of Friendship, Mutual Assistance and Co-operation with East Germany. Before the signature of this instrument in Moscow, the Kremlin gave official notice to the Western powers that the treaty to be signed would not be the oft-threatened "Peace Treaty" abolishing Western rights in Berlin, including the access rights.[90]

The treaty signed by Khrushchev and Ulbricht on June 12, 1964, contained nothing of a revolutionary nature. The signatories promised to work "for the elimination of the remnants of World War II, for the conclusion of a German Peace Treaty and for the normalization of the situation in West Berlin on this basis."

The Treaty, once more, guaranteed the "inviolability" of the borders of the D.D.R. (which had already been guaranteed by the Warsaw Treaty of 1955) and confirmed the opinion that "the creation of a peace-loving democratic united German state can be achieved only through negotiations on an equal footing and agreement between both sovereign German states."

As for Berlin, the Treaty merely affirmed that "the High Contracting Parties will regard West Berlin as an independent political unit."

Thus, the Treaty in no way suggested that West Berlin was part of the German Democratic Republic. That Khrushchev had no intention of conferring further rights on the East German state and that no *de facto* change in existing arrangements was planned is made evident by this provision: "The present Treaty does not affect the rights and commitments of the Parties under the bilateral and other international agreements which are in force, including the Potsdam Agreement."[91]

It may be assumed that this text relates to the rights of control

[89] *New York Times*, August 24, 1962. Italics have been added.
[90] *Ibid.*, June 12, 1964.
[91] The Treaty is printed in *New York Times*, June 13, 1964.

211

which the Soviet Union had reserved for itself when the German Democratic Republic was granted sovereignty. Thus, the Treaty has implicitly given up the earlier thought of extending East German rights to the Western access routes to Berlin. It is not likely, after having concluded this rather anodyne diplomatic instrument, that the Kremlin will revert to its earlier menacing attitude in the near future.

With the conclusion of the Treaty of June 12, 1964, the second long and drawn-out battle for Berlin appeared to have ended. The net gain of this campaign was the Wall, the sealing off of East Germany's border to save her from bleeding to death. If we consider that Khrushchev's broader objective may have been not West Berlin alone but the disruption of the Western alliance and disorientation of Western Germany, his offensive failed both in the narrower and broader perspectives. Despite hardships and bitterness caused to the German people on both sides of the Wall, this arbitrary act did not change the essentials of the delicate balance in Berlin. Soviet provocations only hardened Western determination to defend the city and also stiffened the spirit of resistance among the Berliners. The Soviet Union was given to understand that any attack on Berlin or interference with Allied rights in Berlin would eventually be resisted by force.[92]

On the other hand, there seems little chance at present of doing away with the monstrosity of the Wall. Should this barrier be lifted suddenly, the ensuing mass exodus would certainly be a deadly blow to the German Democratic Republic. Only after a significant decompression of the East German regime's totalitarian and terroristic rule could the Wall be torn down without extreme risk. Of course, in view of popular sentiment in East Germany, decompression itself could be hazardous. And so, the people of West Berlin will have to live—however difficult it may be—with the Wall.

West Berlin will also continue to endure various kinds of harassment, attempts to whittle down Allied and West German rights and to create precedents that weaken the Western doctrinal and practical positions. In all likelihood, West Berlin will take all these dangers in stride. After a few months of frustration and dependency it appears that the city has regained its resilience; after some signs of economic decline, productivity has been recovered.[93] Naturally,

[92] See the joint communiqué issued on June 12, 1964 (on the day when the Soviet–East German Treaty was signed) on the meeting of President Johnson and Chancellor Erhard in Washington. *Ibid.*, June 13, 1964.

[93] For an appraisal of West Berlin's economy after the erection of the Wall,

the mood of the city is a very sensitive barometer of international and local tensions. Every event on the home or international front is related to its own situation and future.[94] However, Berliners can cultivate optimism by comparing their situation with that of their fellow-citizens on the other side of the Wall.

The Berliners are much encouraged by any sign manifesting the intention to restore this city as capital of a united Germany. All major government construction in Bonn is interpreted as a tacit admission of the permanency of Germany's division, while the restoration of the former Reichstag building was viewed with satisfaction.[95] Gestures to reassure Berlin are not infrequent; the Federal Convention (Bundesversammlung), which elects the Federal President, has, since 1954, met every fifth year in Berlin despite protests by East Germany and the Soviets and the misgivings of the occupation powers.[96]

As Berlin has to go on living with the Wall, so the world will have to live with the Berlin situation, dangerous and unsettled as it may be. This writer foresees no realistic possibility for solving the Berlin problem without a settlement of the total German question. The settlement of controversial points of the Berlin imbroglio would necessarily upset the delicate legal and political equation by which the city has lived during the past twenty years. While the Federal Republic may be reproached by its Allies for being too doctrinal and rigid, the occupation powers themselves are compelled to be scrupulously "legalistic" when defending their rights in Berlin against Soviet and East German "nibbles."

Internationalization of the Berlin area, placing it under United Nations protection with international garrisons, would not, as we have suggested, be considered equivalent to the present three-power

---

see Karl Schiller, "Berlin, Germany and Europe," *Europa-Archiv*, October, 1965. The author was Senator for Economic Affairs in the Berlin Senate.

[94] For instance, the statement by Richard Nixon on July 23, 1963, that he was going to show his passport to the East German guards at the Wall, as when he crossed the Hungarian or other Communist borders, was unfavorably commented upon. He should have emphasized that he was entering as a private citizen (in an official capacity he would not have had to show a passport), and his reference to other "real" state borders appeared to the Berliners to be misplaced. When, for reasons of finance, the American Ambassador gave up his special train (with which he could travel to West Berlin without passport and customs examination), anxiety was felt in Berlin that he was giving up some of his "rights."

[95] *New York Times*, June 14, 1964.

[96] Elmer Plischke, *Government and Politics of Contemporary Berlin*, pp. 70–71.

213

protection. The Soviet "Free City" concept would leave Berlin disarmed and defenseless. This proposal as well as other plans, like the project of McDermott[97] or of Senator Pell, would involve recognition of the German Democratic Republic, a move which would not be acceptable to West Germany. Any of these changes would be construed as a further perpetuation of Germany's division and would, therefore, be anathema to Bonn. Only the status quo, manifestly anomalous despite its twenty years' duration, is consistent with the political and sentimental demand of the Germans for an eventual reunification of their country. Berlin is not only a microcosm of partitioned Germany; it is also a symbol of its hopes for unity.

[97] Geoffrey McDermott's Plan is described in his book, *Berlin: Success of a Mission*, pp. 116–30.

> *. . . the Nation, which indulges towards
> another an habitual hatred or an habitual
> fondness, is in some degree a slave.*
>
> —from Washington's Farewell Address
> to the People of the United States,
> September 17, 1796

> *We have no perpetual allies and we have
> no perpetual enemies. Our interests are perpetual.*
>
> —*Lord Palmerston*
> British Foreign Secretary

CHAPTER VI

✳✳✳✳✳✳✳✳✳✳✳✳✳✳✳✳✳✳✳✳✳✳✳✳✳✳✳✳✳✳✳✳✳✳✳✳

THE REUNIFICATION PROBLEM AND INTERNATIONAL POLITICS

By aligning herself with the Western Allies and endorsing the idea of European and Atlantic co-operation, West Germany appeared to have divorced herself from the tradition of German foreign policy. Instead of pursuing ethnocentric interests through the ill-famed *Schaukelpolitik* or the even more abused *Weltpolitik*, the Federal Republic and the majority of Germans declared a readiness to embrace supranational integration.

But the foreign policy of a large power is scarcely ever this simple: its multiple interests may expose it to the charge of ambivalence or insincerity. Germany's political and military association with the West was not and could not be unconditional. And the Western powers, in return for the Federal Republic's commitment, pledged to protect West Germany and to support the cause of German unity.

215

The German claim for reunification was somewhat reminiscent of old-time nationalism. To impress the new allies with Germany's devotion to integration, Chancellor Adenauer preferred to tone down the national impulse for unity. However, this temporary priority was not entirely in harmony with the demanding goal of unification that had been grafted onto the West German constitutional and political structure.

The antithesis of West German foreign policy is clear: the Federal Republic is a leading champion of European integration and, simultaneously, a fervent promoter of German national unity. The attention of West German policy-makers is divided between these objectives. As long as the West is ready to support German reunification, the danger of contradiction is avoided. But if the West changed its view, a dilemma would clearly be posed for the West Germans. Then a choice would have to be made between Western association and the German national goal. Although territorially divided and dependent as never before since Bismarck, Germany again stands facing both the East and the West. Against the East she has a national territorial claim; from the West she insists upon support for her national cause. Should the Western anchor drag, the German ship of state would again swing more freely between the East and West.

Conditions of German dismemberment and integration had never been merely an internal problem. When one group of German states sided with protestantism against the Catholic princes, the local battle was only one scene in a continental struggle. Up to the time of Bismarck, external powers had constantly interfered with the political structure of the Reich. Thus, history has only repeated itself when the problem of German unification arose anew in the broader context of Europe.

Since the end of World War II, Germany's partition has been an essential component of the global struggle called the Cold War, probably its most sensitive and ominous issue. Any evolution may affect the European and global balance of power; escalation into an all-out nuclear exchange is more likely to begin in Germany than in any other part of the world. Therefore, the international ramifications of the German reunification question are multiple. West Germany, together with the three former occupation powers, confronts the Soviet Union on this issue, and also Poland on the related issue of the Oder-Neisse frontier. The Polish-German relationship in itself is of a particularly delicate nature. Moreover, the Federal

216

Republic of Germany wages an all-out diplomatic war against the recognition of East Germany; this conflict extends into East Europe and other areas of the globe, notably Africa and Asia. The problems of German partition closely affect West Germany's relations with those Western powers which are committed, under treaty agreements, to supporting her policy of reunification. They also affect the role of West Germany in NATO and her participation in the European integration movement.

When the Federal Republic joined the Western camp in the early fifties, the unity of NATO, under the uncontested leadership of the United States, was solidly established. At that time the Communist bloc was also impressively monolithic. Since those halcyon days of political and military cohesion on both sides of the Iron Curtain, fissures have appeared. France's separate strategy under De Gaulle created another problem of choice for the leaders of West Germany: that between close collaboration with France and continued intimacy with the United States. Despite the Gaullist blows against European integration, West Germany has been unable to derive any profit for her unification policy. But the split in the Communist camp, with regard both to China and the East European satellites, appears to have opened new avenues for diplomatic probing.

During the first decade of the Federal Republic's sovereign independence, it preferred to remain a rather docile member of the Western alliance and to play, by and large, a passive role in the diplomatic exchanges between East and West. This relative passivity is now likely to undergo a change with erosion of the guilt-complexes, new leadership, and transformations of the international scene. Whether attempted initiatives will bring much advance toward the desired goal will essentially depend on the development of Germano-Soviet relations; this vital evolution will decide whether the German problem will remain the potentially most dangerous issue in East-West contacts.

Soviet Foreign Policy and the German Question

The postbellum vagaries of the German policy of the U.S.S.R. have been described in earlier chapters. It cannot be doubted that what the Soviets, originally, desired most of all was the extension of Communist rule over Germany. Both the geographical location of Germany (Lenin is said to have remarked, "Who has Germany, has Europe.") and its industrial potential, together with the skill and diligence of its inhabitants, made it priceless booty for the Communist empire.[1]

Stalin had overplayed his hand by prematurely revealing his designs on Germany. The Western powers were persuaded to save what could be saved of the prostrate body of Germanism from engulfment in the Red tide. The creation of a West German state, immune to Soviet penetration, deprived the Russians of two thirds of the country and three fourths of its population. For the time being, Moscow had to be content with the establishment of a German satellite state within its zone of occupation.

While superior tactics, ruthlessness, and singleness of purpose gave advantages to the Soviets, an almost complete lack of popular support by the Germans thwarted many of their endeavors. The Soviet government was soon thrust on the defensive. The Communist capture of West Berlin remained foreclosed, both in 1948–49 and again in 1958–63, largely because of the anti-Soviet attitudes of the local population. On the other hand, the reunification policy of the Federal Republic and the Western powers bore no fruit.

Two ultimate objectives—unification of Germany "in peace and freedom," on the one hand, and Soviet control over entire Germany, on the other—clashed head-on, excluding any compromise. Short-term policies mostly sought to counter the moves of the opposite side.[2] Just as the consolidation of the East German state was not the final goal of the Kremlin,[3] the defense of West Berlin could for the Western powers and the Federal Republic be only a temporary measure in the quest for German unity.

The attempts to obtain recognition of the German Democratic Republic by the Western powers and the Federal Republic served the purpose of consolidating the position of the East German regime. The Soviet Union is well aware that even a *de facto* or limited recognition would significantly weaken the demand for

---

[1] Raymond Aron expressed a disbelief in intermediary solution of the German question, including Germany's neutralization, mainly because the messianic mission which drives the Soviets to convert all of Germany would contradict any such scheme. Aron, *Paix et Guerre entre les nations*, pp. 492–93. On the other hand, recently doubts have been expressed as to whether Moscow, in view of its Chinese experience, would genuinely desire a unified Communist Germany now; see, for instance, Strauss, *The Grand Design*, p. 35.

[2] In May, 1966, the Federal government published a White Book containing documents on its policy of reunification for the past ten years. In its foreword it is stated that the achievements of this policy were rather of a "defensive nature" because the Soviet Union did not succeed in getting all of Germany under Communist control.

[3] See Freund, *Germany Between Two Worlds*, p. 190.

German unification. Recognition of East Germany by the Western Allies, without the consent of the Federal Republic, would be interpreted by the latter as a violation of existing agreements and would probably shatter the Western alliance and promote a reorientation of West German policy. Recognition would also enhance the status of the German Democratic Republic by effacing its imprint of impermanency.

The Soviet government is closely interested in East Germany as a working concern, a trading partner, and a military bastion. Communist ideology and Soviet self-interest demand the preservation of this region. The Soviet Union is, however, less interested, if interested at all, in allowing East Germany to become an independent factor in European politics.[4]

Exploiting differences within the Western partnership, especially between the Federal Republic and other Western powers, has always been a gambit of Moscow, though, so far, hardly a successful one. In fact, Soviet aggressiveness caused the establishment of NATO and gave it much of its cohesion. Moreover, the dependence of the Federal Republic on the West for the pursuit of German unity and its hypersensitivity to the question make the Western alliance vulnerable to varieties of Soviet interference. These modes include Soviet *rapprochement* with France against Germany,[5] Soviet understanding with the United States to the detriment of German political goals,[6] and a policy of closer contacts and possible collaboration between the Soviet Union and the Federal Republic to the disadvantage of NATO ties.[7] A fourth variable, that of Soviet cooperation with Britain against other members of the Western alliance, including Germany, has not been attempted so far; British gestures for establishing closer contacts with the Soviet Union and

[4] For years the D.D.R. pressed Moscow for the conclusion of a peace treaty giving full control of the access routes to Berlin to East German officials. Disappointment was felt in the SED when, so as not to endanger peace, Khrushchev refrained from this act. For East German reactions to Khrushchev's speech at the Twenty-second Soviet Party Congress, announcing the postponement of the treaty of peace, see *New York Times,* October 18, 1961.

[5] Cf. Khrushchev's anti-German campaign during his visit in France in March, 1960; De Gaulle's visit to Moscow in June, 1966.

[6] West Germany had viewed with increasing suspicion such closer U.S.-U.S.S.R. contacts; e.g., Eisenhower-Khrushchev talks at Camp David in September, 1959, or the American-Soviet bilateral exchanges on Berlin in 1962.

[7] Various attempts were made by the Soviets to establish direct contacts of understanding with Bonn though without concrete offers; e.g., Adenauer's invitation to Moscow in 1955; the Bulganin-Adenauer correspondence in 1957–58; conversations with Ambassador Kroll and Soviet memoranda in 1961 and 1963.

for mediating in the global conflict early in 1959 did not receive a favorable response from Moscow.[8]

The Soviets have displayed remarkable adaptability in the choice of their tactics vis-à-vis Germany and the Germans. These sharply contrast, however, with the monotonous proposals they offered for the solution of the German question. Here, they have wearisomely reiterated the plan of the two German states reaching agreements to establish a confederation on a parity basis. Another item has been the conclusion of a peace treaty with Germany providing for the creation of a free city of West Berlin (the "three German states" concept) and a nonaggression pact to be signed by the NATO and Warsaw Treaty powers. All these plans have met with stern refusals on the part of West Germany and her Allies, though finding limited approval among some Western foreign policy elites.

There is every possible instrument in the Soviet orchestra: flattering and villifying language, threat and cajolery, employed in close succession or simultaneously. Soviet foreign policy undertook with much ingenuity but little success to exploit German nationalistic sentiment; such attempts ran into a stone wall of real nationalism and Russophobia and the West German doctrine of state-unity.

Moscow's concern with Germany is not only prompted by its expansionism, it is also motivated by apprehension of potential German might. Which element is uppermost is hard to ascertain; in reality, the Federal Republic's alleged "revanchism," "war-mongering," and "militarism" have little foundation in view of West German military inferiority. But at times psychic factors may over-rule the otherwise down-to-earth considerations of the Kremlin. Of course, the bogey of German aggressiveness is successfully used against some of Moscow's allies, especially Poland and Czechoslovakia, where it helps to stabilize the Communist regimes.

The *Deutschlandpolitik* of the Federal government was for years characterized by poor tactics and humdrum strategy. The aim was to prevent the acceptance of any formula or agreement that conflicted with the official one-German state concept or which failed to include progress toward reunification. For these reasons, the Federal government opposed suggested plans for arms control, disengagement, inspection of armed forces along the line of demarcation, and arrangements for Berlin which did not include positive steps for reunification. "Upgrading" of the East German regime

[8] Cf. Prime Minister Macmillan's visit to Moscow in March, 1959.

was also strenuously resisted. Bonn never missed an opportunity to emphasize the provisional character of the German situation which had evolved after 1945.

This lack of inventiveness and flexibility in the West German approach to the problem of German unity can be explained partly by reliance on the former occupation powers, partly because of dogmatic views on the question itself. After Adenauer's retirement, however, Bonn tentatively and cautiously began to search for more flexible methods, ones which, nevertheless, would not entail doctrinal revision. There was still only one legitimate German government, and reunification had to be achieved on the basis of self-determination "in peace and freedom."

In many ways Chancellor Erhard displayed greater adaptability than his predecessor; Bonn's initiatives appeared to have strengthened its independence and relaxed its conformism. The dramatic action program of the Grand Coalition under Chancellor Kiesinger and his Foreign Minister Willy Brandt did not fail to impress Bonn's allies. The West German government could now afford to be more critical of Washington's moves and contacts with Moscow and press for a more active Western reunification policy.

To show his interest in German unity, Erhard also abandoned Adenauer's proposal for a ten-year "truce" on the reunification issue and free elections thereafter throughout Germany, a suggestion practically ignored by the Soviet government.[9] He sought to demonstrate that "the Soviet attitude towards the German problem is based on an erroneous concept, namely the assumption that Soviet interests would be better served by the division of Germany rather than by the restoration of its unity."[10]

Bonn has undertaken several times to enter into a fruitful dialogue with the Soviet Union. A lengthy West German memorandum, dated February 21, 1962, on the possibilities of a *rapprochement* remained unanswered. On March 25, 1966, the Federal government delivered a diplomatic note to 115 governments throughout the world with a comprehensive peace proposal. The initiative was primarily directed to the Soviet Union and its allies. Bonn, for the first time, offered to exchange nonaggression declarations with the Soviet Union, Poland, Czechoslovakia, and "any other East European state." Since the D.D.R. is not a "state" in West German

[9] *New York Times*, December 4, 1963.
[10] Inaugural statement by Chancellor Erhard in the Bundestag on October 18, 1963. *Ibid.*, October 19, 1963.

official eyes, this offer was not addressed to East Germany. The note contained a variety of proposals for "a simultaneous step-by-step removal of the causes of tension in the world" and undertook to prove that the policy pursued by the Federal government "is neither revanchist nor restorative." While the note, again for the first time, officially stated that the German people "would be prepared to make sacrifices for the sake of their reunification," it maintained the basic West German positions on the method of solving the German problem and invoked the Potsdam Agreement to show that the settlement of the border toward Poland was postponed until the conclusion of a peace treaty with an all-German government.[11]

On May 17, 1966, the Soviet government in its reply reiterated its stand: the existing frontiers should be confirmed and the two German states and West Berlin, as an "independent political formation," must be recognized.[12]

It is thus the fundamental problem of German foreign policy to induce the Soviet Union to give up its hold over East Germany. How could the Soviets be shown that their interests would better be served by allowing Germany to be united than by insisting on Germany's present division? How could Germany improve her negotiating position; what interest or formulas could be invoked to bring about the long-expected "change of heart" in Russia? What might be an adequate price, if a price had to be paid, for a renunciation of East Germany? We have seen earlier that at no time was Moscow genuinely prepared to relinquish its booty in return for Germany's neutralization, a price which neither the West German government nor the Western powers were ever ready to pay.

It seems impossible that arguments could ever by themselves persuade the rulers of the Kremlin to give up real estate having strategic and ideological value. Only a radical change of the international situation could suffice. Something which could make Moscow change its heart.[13] What could be that "something," and what could be done to create it?

The following have been regarded as possibilities:

1) A major diplomatic campaign might be launched by the three

[11] The official English text of the note is published in *The Bulletin*, March 29, 1966.

[12] *New York Times*, May 19, 1966.

[13] George F. Kennan has written of the Soviet leaders: "They are men who can be directly influenced by situations, but not by words expressed in any terminology other than their own." Kennan, *Russia, the Atom and the West* (New York, 1957), pp. 23–24.

Western powers to keep alive the reunification issue, introducing the demand for German unity whenever contacts are made or negotiations are conducted with the Soviet Union on related or even extraneous problems. Plans would be prepared and submitted for the promotion of reunification; the presentation of a new version of the Herter Plan has been suggested by Bonn.[14] Another project would recommend the establishment of a permanent four-power ambassadorial group or committee, similar to the one which prepared the Austrian State Treaty, to carry on talks for solving the German problem. These direct pressures would not be expected to yield significant results by their own momentum. Depending, however, on other developments of the Cold War, and especially if other areas of contact were explored, some limited advance along the road to German reunification might be achieved. If, under the weight of these conditions, the Soviet Union expresses readiness to negotiate the question of German unity, these direct contacts among the four powers responsible under the Potsdam Agreement for Germany would be extremely helpful for the negotiation of a German settlement.

2) As was mentioned earlier, one of the immediate goals of the West German *Deutschlandpolitik* was to bring about at least a relative liberalization of the East German regime. Then, as Adenauer said, it would be possible to discuss other matters. Bonn also has hoped that internal conditions in the German Democratic Republic might compel the Russians to seek a "normalization" of the German area. For the time being, the erection of the Berlin Wall thwarted these expectations which were based on an economic and political collapse of the regime. Nonetheless, it appears that the Wall has only partially sustained Ulbricht's consolidation. Since the uprising of June 17, 1953, West German official circles have refrained from trying to incite the East Germans to rise against their oppressors; but the mood beyond the Wall is not necessarily passive.

Under these circumstances it is difficult to imagine how the Federal Republic could promote a relaxation of terror and economic oppression in East Germany. If the East German state, on its own, embarked on a venture of decompression, there might be fruitful possibilities. Such an evolution is not to be totally excluded although it is less likely to occur where irredentist or boundary problems intervene, as in East Germany. West German circles have hinted

---

[14] For the original Herter Plan, see Chapter I, p. 46 above; concerning the new version of the Plan, see *New York Times*, May 9, 1964.

that liberalization of the East German government might confer a legitimacy permitting the establishment of official contacts, thus leading eventually to the test of self-determination, which should then decide the reunification issue.

All this appears to be more or less Utopian at present; nevertheless, it would be unwise for the West German foreign policy-makers to disregard potentialities inherent to East Germany. After all, despite the Wall and other "technical impediments," innumerable ties still bind the inhabitants of the two Germanys, and there are ways to influence developments in the D.D.R., once a start had been made in the right direction.

3) Another avenue for easing tensions in central Europe for the purpose of promoting German unity has been the opening of diplomatic contacts with Poland, Czechoslovakia, Hungary, Rumania, and Bulgaria. The prospects and potentialities of this approach will be discussed later in this chapter.

4) A direct understanding with the Soviet Union on the issue of reunification would be the natural and normal way of solving a problem so important to both of these countries. However, for obvious reasons this is the most difficult and dubious approach. Ever since Chancellor Adenauer's ill-starred visit to Moscow, relations between the two countries have remained extremely cool. Significant contacts have not occurred, except for the period when Ambassador Hans Kroll endeavored to set events in motion and a few instances when Soviet ambassadors in the West German capital sought closer relations. Kroll was recalled, and Soviet innuendoes were received coldly in Bonn. Of course, most of these Soviet *démarches* coincided with East German vilifications of West Germany.

The Soviets have intimated to the Federal Republic that both Germany and Russia fared well in the past when they collaborated. Tauroggen and Rapallo are often cited, though the halcyon days of the Stalin-Hitler Pact are tactfully omitted. Although these references to the past occasionally find some resonance with a few elites, they hardly impress the official circles of Bonn. These historic precedents only underscore the changed environment of today.

In the instances of Russo-German (or Prussian) collaboration, Russia had been a direct or indirect supporter of German (Prussian) power interests and vice versa. In the Napoleonic wars, they fought together against a French imperialism which threatened both

224

nations; in the post-World War I period both countries were the "outcasts" of the Versailles system and were trying mutually to escape from an uncomfortable isolation. In Frederick the Great's time and during Bismarck's administration, both Germany-Prussia and Russia had possessed convergent interests in suppressing the Poles. Even between Hitler and Stalin a community of interest arose when both, for a short period, drew advantages from a fourth division of Poland.

At present, it is Germany that is partitioned, and the Soviet Union is one of the beneficiaries of this partition. Thus, Germany requires support not from but against Moscow. There is nothing significant which Germany would be willing to offer Russia; but there is much which she seeks from Russia. No community of interest seems to exist between the two countries except the elementary interest to avoid war, especially a nuclear war with the danger of annihilation. Since the Federal Republic is already pledged not to resort to force and is, anyhow, incapable of using force without the help of its Western Allies, the common interest in peace is unsuited to purposes of diplomatic pressure. Accordingly, historic analogies in this respect have no application whatsoever to the present situation.

Though vague ideas of Russo-German collaboration still linger in the minds of some Germans, there is no likelihood that this nostalgia can become a reality. Naturally, the Soviet Union would welcome the friendship of the Federal Republic, provided that the territorial status quo were accepted. But it is just this which is unacceptable to Bonn. Unification under the Red banner would be abhorrent, while neutralization would weaken the security of West Germany and leave her isolated without improving her power to achieve reunification. "Oceans of trade," another incentive offered by the Soviets, is neither attractive enough to supersede German unity nor is it considered realistic. The Soviet Union is not itself in the position to offer anything to the Federal Republic in place of reunification which would have the slightest chance of being acceptable. In fact, Moscow has, so far, offered nothing tangible at all.[15]

Relaxation of tension without tangible offerings can be no basis of negotiation, as the illusions of the "spirit of Geneva," "the spirit of Camp David," or the "spirit of Moscow" (at the time of signing

[15] The chances and prospects of Soviet-German understanding are discussed in Erfurt, *Die Sowjetrussische Deutschland-Politik;* Freund, *Germany Between Two Worlds,* pp. 189–237; Werner Feld, *Reunification and West German-Soviet Relations* (The Hague, 1963).

the Test Ban Treaty) have abundantly demonstrated. As President Kennedy explained: "A change of atmosphere and emphasis is not a reversal of purpose. Mr. Khrushchev himself has said that there can be no co-existence in the field of ideology."[16]

Something as unsubstantial as a change of atmosphere is unlikely to persuade leaders of West Germany to give up their political-legal position regarding the reunification of Germany. Such a state of relaxation might actually render matters more difficult for the Federal government if it wished to explore various initiatives; such moves might then be interpreted as disturbing the existing "tranquillity."[17]

After Erhard's promotion to the chancellorship, it was suggested that he accept an invitation to Moscow or invite Khrushchev to return Adenauer's visit to the Soviet capital. The chancellor first appeared reluctant, especially before the 1965 elections, to expose himself to another failure in Moscow or to give the Soviet leader an opportunity to lecture West Germans.[18] Eventually, Khrushchev was invited to Bonn, but his successors appear less eager to visit the Federal Republic.[19]

How the diplomatic stalemate between Moscow and Bonn could be brought to a meaningful end can hardly be foreseen. While Bonn waits for a change of Soviet attitude, Moscow is expecting a similar change in Bonn. Both sides are hopeful that the dispatch of new ambassadors is to herald a change in policy. Since early 1966, Gebhardt von Walther, an Eastern expert of the German Foreign Office, has been the West German Ambassador in the Soviet capital. The arrival of Semykon K. Tsarapkin, since June, 1966, the new Soviet Ambassador in Bonn, gave rise to some expectations that a more active Soviet policy toward the Federal Republic was in the offing.[20] His predecessor, Andrey A. Smirnov, who had few intimate con-

[16] Kennedy's address at the University of Maine on October 19, 1963, *New York Times*, October 20, 1963.

[17] See Mikolas Benckiser, "Die Frage an Deutschland," in *Frankfurter Allgemeine Zeitung*, July 30, 1963; Günter Geschke, "Chruschtschow eine Pause gönnen?" in *Sonntagsblatt* (Hamburg), September 22, 1963.

[18] See *Frankfurter Allgemeine Zeitung*, June 20, 1964.

[19] Chancellor Erhard declared that the invitation to come to Bonn had been extended to Prime Minister Kosygin. He favored open talks on all questions, "including borders," but opposed any previous commitment: "We cannot make a declaration of bankruptcy before entering into negotiations." *New York Times*, April 26, 1966. Willy Brandt, the Foreign Minister of the Kiesinger cabinet, planned, upon assumption of his office, to visit Moscow; *Rhein-Neckar Zeitung*, December 12, 1966.

[20] *New York Times*, May 4, 1966.

tacts with leading political persons, tried to reach understandings with dissident Party factions and interest groups that might have favored compromise solutions on East Germany or Berlin.[21] Such an evolution, some Germans believe, might ensue from the Sino-Soviet conflict.

5) How to exploit the Sino-Soviet rift to the advantage of the West is a question which affects Germany more significantly than any other nation of the Atlantic orbit. A menacing China (despite the present disparity of military power) along the Soviet Empire's exposed Asian flank would certainly weaken the Western-exposed position of Moscow. Ideological dissensions in the Soviet bloc might also further the cause of reunification. All these are possibilities but scarcely realities. A West German-Chinese collaboration against the Soviet Union seems more within the realm of realistic action. A certain limited *rapprochement* between Bonn and Peking has already taken place, but the establishment of permanent trade missions in both the Chinese and West German capitals was, however, prevented by American intervention.[22] On this point, more than in any other area, West German and American interests oppose each other. Bonn finds it hard to explain that, ultimately, it is in the interests of Washington that Communist China should support the policy of German reunification. Chinese statesmen seem to perceive that the German question, in which they are not directly interested at all, is one to which Moscow is exceptionally sensitive and vulnerable. A Bonn-Peking axis would alarm Moscow considerably more than the tie established between Paris and Peking. Suspicions of this danger have already been spelled out by Pankow.[23]

Whatever hopes Bonn entertains for the future of Sino-German contacts, their preparation requires the utmost prudence. We may readily assume that the Chinese support for Bonn is simply a gesture to vex the Kremlin and to punish unfortunate Ulbricht who is in no position to side with Peking.[24] The Chinese had, through their Albanian allies, first violently criticized Khrushchev for his braggadocio and cowardice regarding Berlin;[25] hardly a year later they seemed ready to recognize the attachment of West Berlin to the

[21] See Georg von Huebbenet, "Moskau überprüft seine Deutschland-Politik," *Aussenpolitik*, April 1963, pp. 237–41.
[22] See *The German Tribune*, July 4, 1964. President Johnson is said to have opposed this plan during his talk with Chancellor Erhard in June, 1964.
[23] See Chapter IV, pp. 164–65 above.
[24] Harry Hamm, "Maos Ost-Berliner Karte," in *Frankfurter Allgemeine Zeitung*, July 7, 1963.
[25] *New York Times*, May 17, 1963.

Federal Republic and to speak of the hope that "the two parts of Germany" (instead of "two Germanys") would soon be reunited, a semantic development which was quickly observed by West German commentators.[26]

It appears that German-Soviet relations can be shaken from their present rigidity only by changes outside Germany, developments affecting the global balance of power or within the Soviet orbit.[27] It is most improbable that the West Germans would be willing to give up their basic position and with it their claim for reunification. In this respect, they are the "have-nots" of international politics and the Soviets are the "haves." However important the East German glacis may be for the expansionist-ideological stance of Soviet foreign policy, the possession of East Germany itself is not absolutely vital to Soviet power. If the U.S.S.R., without doing damage to its ideological principles, could resign itself to giving up real estate, German unity "in peace and freedom" might have its first real chance. The fear of greater perils and of more vital losses might then persuade the Soviet leaders to withdraw from the German scene. Guarantees against German aggressiveness might then be another factor. This is well realized in Bonn. West German diplomacy is searching for arguments to demonstrate that the division of Germany harbors a danger to long-range Soviet interests; but it also expresses readiness to offer guarantees that no danger would arise for the Soviet Union or the East European countries through reunification.[28]

The outcome of the German unification issue will also be influenced by developments of the extremely sensitive and delicate Polono-German relationship. Reunification, if and when achieved, will make free Germany a neighbor of Poland; and at some point the question of Poland's western frontiers must be dealt with. Conversely, the question of these borders also has a bearing on the reunification issue itself.

Poland, the Oder-Neisse Border, and Reunification

The interdependence between the reunification issue and the

---

[26] *The German Tribune*, July 4, 1964.

[27] For future possibilities inherent in the new phase of world history, see Fritz Sternberg, "Die Deutschen in der Weltgeschichte," in Hans Werner Richter (ed.), *Bestandsaufnahme—Eine deutsche Bilanz, 1962* (Munich, 1962), pp. 79–81.

[28] See Chancellor Erhard's speech before the new Bundestag on November 10, 1965. *New York Times*, November 11, 1965.

problem of the Oder-Neisse border can be understood only in the light of over-all Polish-German relations. The antagonism at the root of this relationship is more than political; it is psychological and deeply felt by Poles and Germans alike. Although the guilt of Hitlerism has caused a meaningful change in the attitude of German intellectuals, emotions still encroach on realism when Germans and Poles consider their mutual relations.[29] Circumstances render the treatment and solution of Polish-German questions almost hopelessly difficult.

As a result of World War II, Poland lost 46 per cent of her prewar area to the Soviet Union; but her remaining territory was increased by approximately one third, under the Potsdam Protocol, which placed German territories and the area of the former Free City of Danzig "under the administration of the Polish State."[30]

Poland was the most victimized country of World War II; she lost 22 per cent of her population (including more than three million Jews) and an even greater percentage of her intellectuals. Not only Nazi aggression but also Soviet atrocities were responsible for these enormous losses; after the end of hostilities the losses were increased by internal migrations and repression of anti-Communist activities. Although the Russians surely share the guilt for Poland's crucifixion, German savagery made a stronger impression on the minds of the Poles: the Soviets wished to liquidate the Polish ruling class; but Nazis intended to exterminate the entire Polish nation.

Before the outbreak of the war in 1939 the population of the German territories acquired by Poland numbered 8.85 million. In 1945 about 1 million were recognized by Poland as being either of Polish nationality or "autochtonous" (mostly German-Polish bilinguals). Approximately 350,000 Germans were allowed to stay. The rest were expelled, over 6 million settling in Germany, most of them in the West; about 1.47 million must have died during or as a consequence of expulsion.[31]

In view of all these horrors it appears almost ludicrous to com-

---

[29] For an appraisal of attitudes of German intellectuals toward Poland, see Ellinor von Puttkamer, "Modifications of the German-Polish Relationship," in Kohn (ed.), *German History—Some New German Views*, pp. 175–86; Hansjakob Stehle, *Nachbar Polen* (Frankfurt/M, 1963); the article by Klaus-Peter Schulz, "Grenze von gestern—Brücke von morgen," *Der Monat*, August, 1963 (No. 179), is particularly illuminating.

[30] See Chapter I, pp. 13–14 above.

[31] See Paikert, *The German Exodus*, pp. 1–4; Georg Bluhm, *Die Oder-Neisse-Linie in der deutschen Aussenpolitik* (Freiburg/Br., 1963), pp. 19–21; Elizabeth Wiskemann, *Germany's Eastern Neighbours* (London, 1956), pp. 120–22.

pare the magnitude of inhumanities committed. While Germans like to juxtapose one horror against the other, more moderate Poles consider the German acts as an "abomination" crying to heaven but are ready to accept the expulsion of Germans as a "misdeed."[32] Furthermore, the Poles point out that the source of all the evil was the German attack on Poland, to which we may add: the Soviet complicity which paved the way for Hitler's war.

The acquisition of the German Eastern Territories is officially labelled the "recovery" of former Polish land. Since this threadbare historical argument is hardly convincing, more sophisticated Poles prefer to regard the territory as compensation for German aggression and brutalities. The formal legal basis of Polish acquisition is said to be the Potsdam Protocol which, however, only conferred the administration of these areas on Poland. From the Polish side it is maintained that, according to the "intentions" of the powers participating in the Potsdam Conference, these areas were to be given to Poland without condition and that only the "final delimitation" (demarcation on the spot) of Poland's western frontiers had to await the conclusion of the peace treaty with Germany.[33]

The Polish legal and historical arguments are equally weak: the two Western powers had certainly no intention to cede all the territories in question to Poland by the Potsdam Protocol. The expression used, "transfer of administration," stressed the provisional character of this transaction. Thus, the "final delimitation" of Poland's western borders, reserved to the Peace Conference, could have meant only the appropriate drawing of the frontier line, not just the *de jure* confirmation of the Oder-Neisse Line.

The strongest Polish argument derives from the possession and exercise of full authority over the territories in question during the past twenty years. The precariousness of the legal title explains

[32] These characterizations of misdeeds were originally made by Cardinal Döpfner, then Bishop of Berlin, and accepted by *Tygodnik Powszechny*, the Catholic weekly of ZNAK, the Polish Catholic Club (Party); Cardinal Döpfner's sermon of October 21, 1960, and the Polish reply are printed in Stehle, *Nachbar Polen*, pp. 384–89.

[33] For the relative text of the Potsdam Protocol, see Chapter I, p. 13 above; for the Polish argument, consult Alfons Klafkowski, *Podstawy prawne granicy Odra-Nysa Luzycka w swietle umów jaltanskiej i poczdamskiej* [Legal foundations of the Oder-Lusatian Neisse frontier in the light of the Yalta and Potsdam agreements] (Poznan, 1947); same author, *The Potsdam Agreement* (Warsaw, 1963). The official Polish legal argument was set out in the reply to the West German Note of March 23, 1966: the Potsdam Conference left only "the task of final confirmation" of the frontier to the future peace conference. *New York Times*, April 30, 1966.

the Polish insistence on obtaining recognition of sovereignty over the "recovered Western Territories" by the Western powers and the Federal Republic of Germany.

The western territories of Poland represent one third of the Polish national area; they were quickly resettled by Poles who now form somewhat less than one third of the population of Poland. The area is superior to the other parts of Poland in industrial productivity; since 1945 the Poles have made enormous efforts and spent much money and energy to develop these former German lands. It is certainly true that the possession of these territories is vital to Poland; without them she would be an unviable truncated state. Recovery of the former eastern provinces, now Soviet territory, is out of the question and, in any case, would require a new resettlement of Poles, unthinkable after the experiences of the past.

For Poland, therefore, her "recovered Western Territories" are simply nonnegotiable. Poles cling to these areas with the tenacity of a man clinging to his life. And they do so regardless of their political views. If there was ever anywhere a national question, this certainly is one: anti-Communists are collaborators with the regime, and Communists are fervent nationalists. This determination is strongly shared by the Catholic Church of Poland.

The territorial issue makes the country dependent on Soviet support—even in the eyes of Polish nationalists. This reliance on Poland's number two antagonist, Russia, is the primary source of strength for the present regime. Greater independence would necessarily weaken the Russian guarantee and strengthen the danger of German irredentism.[34]

Poles do not like East Germans any better than West Germans. The German Democratic Republic contains elements—Prussians and Saxons, mainly Protestants—who were formerly the most dangerous foes of Polish nationhood.[35] But the mere existence of the East German state as a buffer between Poland and West Germany (which is the real Germany, as the Poles well know) guarantees the western frontiers of Poland. Friendship with the German Democratic Republic is just a "marriage of convenience"; as Gomulka put it: "The security of the Polish border along the Oder and the Neisse rests today on the security of the frontier along the Elbe which divides the two German states."[36]

[34] See the well-informed article by Adam Bromke, "Nationalism and Communism in Poland," *Foreign Affairs*, July 1962, pp. 635–643.

[35] Stehle, *Nachbar Polen*, p. 307.

[36] Gomulka's speech of December 4, 1958; Stehle, *Nachbar Polen*, p. 348.

Almost as soon as it was formed, the East German government hurried to recognize the "inviolable frontier of peace and friendship" of the Oder-Neisse on June 6, 1950. A month later, on July 6, 1950, a formal agreement was concluded between the German Democratic Republic and Poland recognizing, once again, the "existing frontier" between Germany and Poland.[37] Notwithstanding, in 1946 East German Communists had expressly assured their adherents that the Oder-Neisse Line was only a provisional border.[38]

Although the German Democratic Republic is the "German state" which borders Poland, the Warsaw government has incessantly tried to obtain recognition from Bonn of the Polish western frontier. West Germany's commitment not to resort to force for the purpose of reuniting Germany is far from setting Warsaw at ease. For the Poles, even a formal renunciation by West Germany of the territories east of the Oder-Neisse would be an imperfect guarantee of the security of their western borders. The ideal solution would be a disarmed, neutralized, and, preferably, divided Germany. Hence, the Rapacki Plan, which sought to formalize this objective and surround it with international pledges. In no regard were Polish aims satisfied.

Under these conditions, the continued existence of the German Democratic Republic serves Polish national interests. Poland supports the D.D.R., less from feelings of Communist brotherhood than from self-interest. The tangible existence of a satellite Communist state is far preferable to an all-German guarantee or promise.

The German view of the Oder-Neisse border question is inseparable from positions that regard the entire German problem. Rationalism, as may be imagined, tends to stifle practicality. The German position may be summarized as follows:

1) The East German Territories were not legally acquired by Poland; the Potsdam Protocol only conferred the administration of these areas on Poland, pending the final decisions of a peace treaty with a united Germany.[39]

2) The expulsion of Germans from the Eastern Territories was carried out in contravention of international law. According to this view, the Potsdam Protocol authorized the removal of Germans

[37] See von Oppen (ed.), *Documents on Germany Under Occupation, 1945–1954*, pp. 497–500.

[38] On October 16, 1946, Chairman of the SED, Wilhelm Pieck, declared that his Party would undertake to have the Polish frontier reviewed and modified. *Berliner Zeitung*, October 17, 1946.

[39] The German view is presented, *inter alia*, by Zoltan M. Szaz, *Germany's Eastern Frontiers* (Chicago, 1960), *passim;* Jacobsen and Stenzl (eds.), *Deutschland und die Welt*, pp. 333–37.

from "Poland" only; that is, not from the German territories to be placed under Polish administration.[40]

3) Only a government of united Germany would have the legitimacy to negotiate a final settlement of the border with Poland. The agreement reached between Poland and the East German regime is legally and politically meaningless because the latter is no "state" and because it does not represent the German people.

4) To ask for the recognition by the Federal Republic of the Oder-Neisse frontier would be an "absurdity" because, at present, the Oder-Neisse Line is not the border of the Federal Republic either in fact or according to the view of the Polish government.[41] The frontier question would become negotiable only after East Germany had acquiesced in reunification.

The West German official view is, by and large, approved by the people, and there can be little doubt that the majority of East Germans, if consulted, would share this opinion. Nevertheless, there are divergences between the official pronouncements of the Federal government and resolutions passed by expellee organizations. Some times even Federal Ministers addressing rallies of *Landsmannschaften*, by a slip of the tongue or purposely, will express opinions which go beyond the governmental position. These statements are then taken by the Poles for official governmental declarations. Thus, expellee organizations and leaders often emphasize their *Heimatsrecht* (right to the homeland), which could be interpreted either as an individual right to return to the native region or as a right to have the Eastern Territories returned *en bloc*. But the Potsdam Agreement gave no promise for a return of these areas to Germany; it merely reserved the final decision to the Peace Conference. The Federal government, accordingly, has never demanded the complete retrocession of the territories east of the Oder-Neisse Line, but it has steadfastly refused to accept the present territorial status quo as final.

Just as the Polish government makes use of nationalist sentiment in order to strengthen its internal position, the political parties of West Germany cannot ignore the personal interest of millions of voters in the lost territories of the former German East.

[40] From the deliberations of the Allied leaders in Potsdam, the intention to agree to a removal of the "remaining Germans" from the East German Territories cannot be doubted. The ambiguity of the text is simply a result of the sloppiness of draftsmanship.

[41] See Helmut Allardt, "Deutschland und Polen," *Aussenpolitik*, No. 5 (May), 1963, pp. 295–300. Ambassador Allardt's views are of particular interest; he headed the West German delegation which negotiated the trade agreement with Poland of March 7, 1963.

The refusal of the Federal Republic to commit itself on the question of frontiers prior to reunification conveys the impression to the Poles that Germany is planning an insidious *pas de deux:* as a first step, to achieve unification with the "Soviet Zone," and, as a second step, to explode the question of the territories beyond the Oder-Neisse Line. However, the German stand rests on doctrinal grounds rather than on a preconceived scheme of deception.

The mutual lack of confidence and profound distrust of the Germans by the Poles has been magnified by the absence of official ties of communication between the two governments and the lack of contacts between elites of both countries. But the history of attempts to "normalize" the relations between Poland and the Federal Republic of Germany has been overshadowed by the rigor with which the Hallstein Doctrine has been applied and by the dilemma of the Oder-Neisse frontier.

When the Soviet Union established diplomatic contacts with the Federal Republic in 1955, Poland was desirous of doing the same, even without the demand of recognition of her borders.[42] Federal Foreign Minister von Brentano, however, rejected this overture on the grounds of the Hallstein Doctrine because Poland had opened diplomatic relations with the German Democratic government. In June, 1957, Gomulka stated that relations with West Germany could become "a positive factor" for German reunification.[43] But when West Germany broke off diplomatic relations with Belgrade because of the Yugoslav recognition of East Germany, it became evident that no *rapprochement* with Warsaw was possible.

After Khrushchev's diplomatic assault on Berlin in 1958, the Polish government was no longer willing to enter into formal relations with Bonn without a "clarification" of the frontier issue. The Warsaw regime was also offended by the rejection of the Rapacki Plan by West Germany. It now hoped for a solution of the German question on Soviet terms.

During the protracted Berlin crisis the Federal government came under the increased pressure of the SPD and the FDP and of the intellectual elite to take up direct contacts with Poland.[44]

[42] Polish Prime Minister Cyrankiewicz suggested twice (on March 13 and October 12, 1955) the establishment of "friendly relations."
[43] Stehle, *Nachbar Polen*, pp. 314–15.
[44] On June 14, 1961, the Committee for Foreign Affairs of the Bundestag unanimously voted a resolution urging the Federal government to normalize relations with East European states, especially Poland; the report of the Committee is printed in Wenzel Jaksch, *Germany and Eastern Europe* (Bonn, 1962), p. 35.

In January, 1961, Chancellor Adenauer sent Berthold Beitz, the General Manager of the Krupp Corporation, to Warsaw on an unofficial mission. Beitz was to offer a long-term trade and cultural agreement to Poland and the establishment of consulates or a trade mission with consular jurisdiction. The Polish government turned down the offer; Cyrankiewicz refused to accept any "substitute solution" for normal diplomatic relations and insisted on "clarity" in the frontier question.[45]

After Soviet failure at Berlin, the government of Poland again changed its attitude and was ready to accept, for the time being at least, an exchange of permanent trade missions in lieu of normal diplomatic relations with the Federal Republic. In March, 1963, the two governments agreed to set up permanent trade missions in Warsaw and in Cologne. In Bonn, and presumably also in Warsaw, it was hoped that the permanent exchange of missions would fulfill diplomatic functions.[46]

For the first time since the end of World War II, an independent German government had established direct contacts with Poland. What could be the prospects for the furtherance of the primary foreign policy objectives of the two countries?

With the initiation of the new German *Ostpolitik*, the abandonment of the Hallstein Doctrine in regard to East Europe, Bonn expressed its readiness to enter into full diplomatic relations with Poland. However, the inroad of West German diplomacy into that area was opposed by the resolve of Poland and Czechoslovakia (acting jointly with the German Democratic Republic), confirmed by formal agreement, to attach preconditions to the resumption of diplomatic ties. As far as Poland was concerned, it was not only the recognition of the Oder-Neisse border but also the recognition of the Elbe border, namely, that of a sovereign East Germany, which now stood in the way of normalization of relations. On the other hand, the leaders of the Grand Coalition could not be expected to accept any of these conditions.

The vital attention of West Germany is directed toward reunification with East Germany; Polish national interest strives for the optimum of security and guarantees for their western border. The Federal Republic asks: How can this relationship be utilized to pro-

[45] The full story of the Beitz mission is related in Stehle, *Nachbar Polen,* pp. 321–34.
[46] See Allardt, "Deutschland und Polen." For the prospects of the new contacts between West Germany and Poland, see Alexander Bregman, "Polish-German Relations: A New Phase," *East Europe,* November, 1963, pp. 2–7.

mote German unity? On the other hand, Poland's policy is governed by the thought: Will it lead to a recognition by Germany of the Oder-Neisse boundary and a genuine renunciation of former German areas?

No Federal German government or Federal Parliament is likely to feel free to make final a commitment with regard to the frontier issue before national unity has been achieved.[47] This is presently a dominant argument, whereas the excuse that the Federal Republic possesses no common frontier with Poland is hardly tenable: frontiers which exist between third states can be and are recognized in diplomatic practice.

Additionally, reasons of national sentiment militate against recognition of the Polish border. The renunciation by Germany of her ancestral Eastern Territories, though they have been gone for twenty years and are empty of Germans, would be an act of self-immolation, practically impossible without some tangible *contrepartie*.

What could be expected from Poland in return for a recognition of the Oder-Neisse frontier? It should be remembered that for Germans this is not a mere verbal acknowledgment of existing facts; it is an extremely painful sacrifice. Furthermore, the Germans know how valuable this recognition would be for the Poles, even though the latter would hesitate to place their entire confidence in it.

Advocates of recognition point out that such an act would strengthen "polycentrism"; that is, it would promote the emancipation and independence of East European countries, and primarily Poland. Relaxation of fears of German "revanchism" or "revisionism" would enable Poland to become less dependent on Russia. The centrifugal tendencies of the Soviet Empire would, according to this view, significantly weaken the Soviet posture in East Germany and eventually pave the way for reunification. Such a policy would also bring the Federal Republic more into step with the general diplomacy of its Western Allies.[48]

[47] Johann-Baptist Gradl, then Federal Minister for Refugee Affairs, in an interview published in *Der Spiegel* (January 17, 1966) recognized that Germany would have to make certain sacrifices for the sake of reunification; he hinted, in this respect, that the German-Polish border need not be "the frontier of 1937, unchanged down to the last comma and period, so to speak." *New York Times*, January 18, 1966; Alexander Bregman, "Germany's Search for an Eastern Policy," *East Europe*, March, 1966, pp. 2–13.

[48] Such is the view held by Bluhm, *Die Oder-Neisse-Linie*, pp. 139–44; Klaus-Peter Schulz, "Eine Chance zur Verständigung," in Jacobsen and Stenzl (eds.), *Deutschland und die Welt*, pp. 366–68. See also George F. Kennan, "Polycentrism and Western Policy," *Foreign Affairs*, January, 1964, pp. 171–83.

Poland's present precarious status undoubtedly results in part from her not unreasonable alarm over West Germany. The sudden surge of German wealth and power has added to the already existing sense of inferiority vis-à-vis Teutonic might. The present situation allows Poland—whether Communist or not—only one resolution for her security dilemma; namely, alignment to Russia. The other possible combination, an alignment with the West (as it existed in the interwar period but which, as events showed, provided no security), is excluded because of the geographical position of Poland.[49] It is, therefore, rather conjectural whether a simple border recognition would significantly contribute to the disintegration of the Soviet camp.

As stated earlier, Gomulka's "national" Communist rule is based on the support inspired by the fear of Germany and the necessity of Soviet alignment.[50] It is hardly profitable for Gomulka to allay this fear by any kind of *rapprochement* with Federal Germany. At present, nationalist and Catholic Poles may sincerely believe that his is the best possible regime they can have. Would they still continue to cherish such a belief when the fear of Germany had been dissipated? Gomulka's regime would try to play down the value of a German renunciation, which would be portrayed simply as a recognition of existing fact. And Germany would be giving "something" against "nothing." No German government would be willing to engage in such a risky operation involving one fourth of the Reich's 1937 territory, which might alarm and alienate public opinion.

It has been plausibly suggested that the solution lies in a com-

[49] See Adam Bromke, "Political Realism in Poland," *Survey*, April 1964, pp. 111–117. Alexander Bregman, *Jak Swiat Swiatem?* [For as Long as the World Remains the World?], *Polish-German Relations Yesterday, Today, and Tomorrow* (London, 1964), explains that Polish national interest demands the reunification of Germany because it brings the West closer to Poland.

[50] The memorandum of the German Evangelical Church (see Chapter III, p. 126 above), recognizing the importance of the Oder-Neisse border for Poland, made little impression on Warsaw. An exchange of letters between the Catholic Bishops of Poland and those of Germany aroused interest and sympathy in West Germany but elicited hostile reactions from the Polish government. The Polish Bishops, at the Vatican Council in the fall of 1965, invited their German colleagues to visit Poland in 1966 for the celebration of the millennium of Christianity in Poland; the letter asked for mutual forgiveness and mentioned that the Oder-Neisse frontier was for Poland "a question of existence." The German Bishops accepted the invitation, joined in a plea for mutual forgiveness without reference to the border question. The Polish government condemned the initiative of the Bishops, charging them with harmful interference in politics. Gomulka's speech of January 14, 1966, as reported by *Le Monde*, January 15, 1966; *The Bulletin*, December 14, 1965.

bined settlement of both the question of German unity and that of united Germany's eastern frontier.[51] This, of course, was the solution envisaged by the Western signatories of the Potsdam Agreement when they wished to reserve the final territorial arrangement for the Peace Conference. In the German view, the Oder-Neisse frontier question, as well as that of German reunification, are matters for which the former occupation powers are responsible. Therefore, the Germans are reluctant to broach the Polish frontier question alone, although, *in petto,* most responsible Germans are convinced that the Eastern Territories will have to be written off. But, even if they wanted, the Poles, under present conditions, would be unable to contribute meaningfully to German unity. Furthermore, no Polish government would be willing to "negotiate" the Oder-Neisse issue; it would at once be accused of preparing a "fourth partition" of Poland.

The only diplomatic action—necessarily protracted—that the Federal government can undertake is the creation of mutual understanding and a modicum of confidence between the two countries.[52] A permanent German representative in Warsaw might be able to explain to the Poles that the refusal to enter into full-fledged diplomatic relations was not a depreciatory attitude toward Poland but a necessity imposed by the claim for sole West German representation. He could also convey views of his government concerning the eventual recognition of the Oder-Neisse border and suggest methods whereby the Polish regime, if willing, could be helpful in promoting German unity. This is the modest but maximum hope for the present.

The greatest danger for Poland is that a united Germany might emerge on the Oder-Neisse without having renounced ex-German lands beyond those rivers. Such a contingency now appears remote; but if Russia should feel obliged, under future pressures, to retreat from her East German advance post, Poland would come up against a new peril.

Reunification and East-Central Europe

The Polish entanglement with the German reunification question has been unique. The other Communist successor states have also

---

[51] Grewe, *Deutsche Aussenpolitik,* pp. 420–21.

[52] Chancellor Kiesinger, in his inaugural address to the Bundestag, expressed understanding toward "the tragic history" of Poland and toward the Polish desire "to live in a state with secure frontiers" but, at the same time, insisted that "the boundaries of reunified Germany can be laid down only in an agreement with an all-German government." *New York Times,* December 14, 1966.

been affected by the split of Germany, but none of them has such a vital stake in the resolution of the question.

The members of the Soviet-dominated Warsaw Pact Organization—Poland, the German Democratic Republic, Czechoslovakia, Hungary, Rumania, Bulgaria, and Albania—have, together with the Soviet Union, at times issued declarations condemning West German "militarism," "revanchism," or "revisionism" and on their part recommended Moscow's projects for the solution of the German question. Nevertheless, the interest and concern of Hungary, Rumania, Bulgaria, and Albania for the problem of German unity are conspicuously less than those of Poland and the Soviet Union itself. The two nonaligned countries of that area, Austria and Yugoslavia, also possess only a secondary interest in those developments.

Czechoslovakia is the only non-German Communist state which has a common frontier with the Federal Republic. The ill-famed Munich Agreement of 1938, signed by Britain, France, Italy, and Nazi Germany, deprived Czechoslovakia of the so-called Sudetenland, the German-inhabited rim area of Bohemia and Moravia; five months later the Reich annexed the remainder of these two provinces, and Slovakia was made a German satellite. After World War II, the Czechs retaliated by expelling most of their Germans, about three million, and resettled the empty areas with their own people.[53] By the end of 1950, nearly two million German refugees from Czechoslovakia had settled in West Germany; many more moved west later from the Soviet Zone.[54]

The Potsdam Agreement and other postwar four-power pronouncements considered "Germany" to be that country within her boundaries of December 31, 1937. This territorial status has been officially accepted many times by the Federal Republic; reunification and nonrecognition of the Oder-Neisse frontier are concerns which affect the area of Potsdam Germany. The territories detached by the Munich Agreement have never officially been claimed by the Federal government; this government has several times denied territorial claims vis-à-vis Czechoslovakia.[55]

Leaders of Sudeten-German refugee organizations have, nonetheless, expressed views inconsistent with the official attitude taken by the Federal government, asking for "return of the Sudeten German homeland." Hans Christoph Seebohm, the then Minister of Transport, himself a refugee from Czechoslovakia, made similar demands,

[53] See Wiskemann, *Germany's Eastern Neighbours*, pp. 98–113; Wenzel Jaksch, *Europe's Road to Potsdam* (New York, 1963), pp. 420–39.
[54] Paikert, *The German Exodus*, p. 87.
[55] Grewe, *Deutsche Aussenpolitik*, pp. 411–12.

forcing Federal Chancellor Ludwig Erhard to reprimand his colleague.[56] Erhard, in an address made in New York on June 11, 1964, clarified West Germany's position:

> Today, the only direct neighbor of the Federal Republic among the East European countries is Czechoslovakia. Unfortunately, the policy of the Federal Republic of Germany toward Czechoslovakia has recently not been clear.
>
> I, therefore, state here explicitly and clearly: the Munich Agreement of 1938 was torn to pieces by Hitler. The German Government has no territorial claims whatsoever with regard to Czechoslovakia and separates itself expressly from any declarations which have given rise to a different interpretation.[57]

This unequivocal statement clearly places Czechoslovakia in a different category from Poland. Nevertheless, it is understandable that Czechs should feel some uneasiness about revived German power at their doorstep and, consequently, fear a reunification which would extend the common frontier. The Czechoslovak Government and people could possibly derive further assurance if the Munich Agreement were formally declared null and void by West Germany. Such action has been suggested from the West; official circles of the Federal Republic, however, prefer the postponement of such action until all outstanding questions can be settled with Czechoslovakia; questions of citizenship, the right of returning to their homeland for Sudeten Germans, questions of monetary compensation, the right of those Germans who still live in Czechoslovakia to opt for emigration. These matters might be amicably solved if there were a direct channel of communication between the two countries and an atmosphere of better understanding.[58]

After the advent of the Grand Coalition the Hallstein Doctrine no longer prevented the establishment of diplomatic relations between Prague and Bonn. Czechoslovakia, however, has joined Poland in insisting on the fulfillment of preconditions before diplomatic ties are established. A declaration that the Munich Agreement

---

[56] For Seebohm's earlier statements, see Wiskemann, *Germany's Eastern Neighbours*, pp. 198–200; for the latest incident, see *New York Times*, June 1, 1964.

[57] *The Bulletin* of the German Embassy, Washington, June 16, 1964. On December 13, 1966, Chancellor Kiesinger told the Bundestag: "The German people would also like to reach agreement with Czechoslovakia. . . . It agrees with the view that the Munich Agreement, which came into existence under the threat of force, is no longer valid." *New York Times*, December 14, 1966.

[58] See the article in *Die Zeit*, May 29, 1964.

was "initially invalid" and the recognition of "two German states" and the Oder-Neisse border are quoted by Prague as such preliminary conditions. Bonn has been unable even to exchange permanent trade delegations with Czechoslovakia, a move which might have improved contacts.[59]

The Czechoslovak apprehensions, like those of the Poles, are historically and psychologically motivated. Naturally, the millions of expellees from Czechoslovakia in Germany constitute a remote danger, but one which might eventually produce only a minimum of friction. To be sure, the balance of power around the Bohemian basin might, in case of German reunification, be tilted toward the West. But this is a contingency which is primarily feared by the Communist government of Prague, not by the people of Czechoslovakia. More artificially than in Poland, the fear of Germany is exploited by the Czechoslovak government and by Moscow.[60]

In Hungary, Rumania, and Bulgaria, the bogeys of West Germany and of united Germany are gambits played by the Communist governments in order to be in unison with the Kremlin. With the overwhelming majority of the politically conscious elements in these countries, reunification of Germany would carry the connotation of Soviet loss of power and prestige; it would be welcomed and not deplored. Wartime atrocities by the Germans have long been effaced by the more permanently brutal behavior of the Soviet forces, especially in Hungary where the memory of the forceful suppression of the 1956 revolution is bound to persist for a very long time.

The Federal government, prevented by the Hallstein Doctrine, until early 1967, from entering into direct diplomatic relations with these states, was usefully exploiting their growing need for trade with West Germany. As mentioned earlier,[61] permanent trade missions set up in 1963 in Budapest, Bucharest, and Sofia, and in West Germany, respectively, hardly compensated for the lack of normal diplomatic relations with these countries. The "Berlin clause" accepted by all these governments appeared to contradict the thesis of West Berlin as an "independent political unit," to which these

---

[59] A treaty of friendship and military assistance signed by Poland and Czechoslovakia on March 1, 1967, declared both nations' present frontiers inviolable and the Munich Agreement invalid as of the time of its conclusion. This treaty was signed in protest against West German overtures to exchange ambassadors with both countries. *New York Times*, March 2, 1967.

[60] Elizabeth Wiskemann, "Germany's Eastern Neighbours," *Survey*, October, 1962, p. 53.

[61] See Chapter IV, pp. 155–56 above.

governments, under the behest of Moscow, were supposed to be committed. Frictions with East Germany were inevitable because of the endorsement of the representation of West Berlin by Bonn. Already the trade agreements between Hungary, Rumania, and Bulgaria and the Federal Republic revealed the relative indifference with which even these governments viewed the question of German unity.

With the appointment of the Federal government under Kurt Georg Kiesinger, the road to normal diplomatic relations was opened. It was the government of Rumania, more independent-minded than other governments of the area, which, for reasons of prestige and also to impress Moscow, established full diplomatic contacts with Bonn, and without any condition whatsoever.[62] Moscow could hardly oppose that move; it had agreed to diplomatic contacts with West Germany, without conditions, as early as 1955. A split between the northern and southern members of the Warsaw Treaty bloc became apparent.

How the contacts at last established between the East-Central Communist regimes and West Germany are likely to facilitate a solution to the problems of German reunification is difficult to foresee. These regimes, even if they gained a more vigorous independence, could scarcely influence directly Moscow or East Germany to change their attitudes. Furthermore, it is unlikely that they would believe in gaining any special advantage from German unity. But, a disintegration of the Soviet East European empire might, as hoped for in some quarters, contribute to a change of the Russian position in Germany. While it seems farfetched to think that increased trade and political relations between these East-Central European countries and Bonn would alone significantly influence the desired result, the policy of isolating East Germany could demonstrate to the world, and even to Moscow, the anomalous nature of Germany's partition leading to a liberalization in the D.D.R. and, eventually, to reunification.[63]

[62] The agreement to this effect was reached on January 31, 1967, when Rumanian Foreign Minister Corneliu Manescu visited the West German capital. *New York Times*, February 1, 1967.

[63] For the suggested policy of "peaceful engagement" in the affairs of eastern Europe, see Zbigniew Brzezinski, *Alternative to Partition* (New York, 1965), esp. pp. 132–75; Zbigniew Brzezinski and William E. Griffith, "Peaceful Engagement in Eastern Europe," *Foreign Affairs*, July, 1961, pp. 642–54; see also the editorial, "Bonn's 'Opening to the East,' " in *New York Times*, November 14, 1963. In the Federal Republic Bundestag deputy Wenzel Jaksch advocated "economic partnership" with East Europe; see his study: *Westeuropa-Osteuropa-Sowjetunion* (Bonn, 1965).

Yugoslavia, the one uncommitted Communist country, traveled a circuitous path before arriving at her present attitude. In 1952 Yugoslavia, then engaged in a violent struggle for survival with Stalinist Russia, backed German reunification and even German re-armament, both of which she considered as legitimate interests of the German nation. In 1957, however, as described earlier,[64] she recognized the German Democratic Republic. This led to the rupture of diplomatic relations with Bonn. Although Belgrade only received diplomatic ministers and tactfully opened a legation in East Berlin only, reserving the higher rank of ambassador to the representative of West Germany, the consequences of the Hallstein Doctrine could not be avoided.[65]

Since then Yugoslavia has blown hot and cold toward West Germany. Trade exchanges have suffered little, but Belgrade has occasionally joined Moscow in defaming the Bonn republic. At one time Tito's government tried to cajole the Federal Republic into paying for war damages caused by the Nazi occupation of Yugoslavia. The Federal government, however, sternly refused to pay the debts of the former Reich to a country which recognized East Germany; there was, of course, no question of demanding indemnification from Pankow. Accordingly, while Bonn was willing to pay indemnities to Jewish victims, to Greece, Norway, and other countries which had suffered under Nazi aggression, Yugoslavia, despite sympathy expressed by Washington, was refused any such payments.[66] In fine, it may be said that Yugoslavia's recognition of the D.D.R. has not contributed to its strength, nor has it increased Tito's own influence within the Soviet bloc. Soon after her recognition of East Germany, Yugoslavia became, once again, the object of Soviet denunciations which lasted up to the revelation of the Sino-Soviet conflict. However, West German-Yugoslav full diplomatic relations could not be re-established before the partial abandonment of the Hallstein Doctrine under Chancellor Kiesinger.

Neutral Austria maintains cordial diplomatic, economic, and cultural relations with the Federal Republic of Germany. Her relations with the East German regime are restricted to trade and cultural exchange. The Austrian government neither can nor wants to influence the German question. The population of Austria does not entertain any fears of another annexation by Germany, whether it is

[64] Chapter IV, pp. 149–50 above.
[65] In 1966, Belgrade and East Berlin mutually raised their diplomatic representations to the rank of embassies.
[66] See *New York Times*, May 23, 1964.

united or not. The friendly political weight of Bonn is occasionally felt in Vienna; but the Austrian leadership is anxious to avoid any Russian accusations of partisanship.

When in the summer of 1963 the German Democratic Republic arranged to receive regular Austrian commercial aircraft on the Schönefeld airport near Berlin, a West German *démarche* frustrated this project. This would have been the first non-Communist airline to serve airfields in East Germany regularly. But the Viennese government was, eventually, unwilling to risk the displeasure of Bonn by breaking the cold blockade of East Germany by all non-Communist aircraft.

Thus, apart from Poland, Germany's partition is essentially an affair and concern of the Germans themselves, and of the four occupation powers, whose essential interests and political objectives are closely linked with the fate of Germany. Without the support of the West, not only would reunification be a forlorn hope, but also the security of West Germany would be seriously jeopardized.

The Western Powers and Reunification

The adherence of West Germany to the Atlantic alliance and her subsequent rearmament had been reciprocated by the Western powers with the conferral of sovereignty on the Federal Republic, the pledge to support reunification without a resort to violence, the recognition of the Federal Republic as the only spokesman for the German nation, and responsibility for the defense of West Germany and West Berlin. Thus, the implications of the German post-bellum state doctrines, if not the doctrines themselves, were endorsed by the United States, Britain, and France; and these concepts officially became the basis of their German policy.

In 1954–55, when the agreements restoring West German sovereignty were signed and came into force, the following premises seemed to apply: (1) The United States is and will remain the uncontested leader of the Western alliance; (2) American military aid is indispensable for the maintenance of the European political equilibrium; and (3) the assembling of NATO's strength, added to that of West Germany, would inevitably lead to the unification of Germany.

NATO, however, proved to be only a shield (as it was originally intended to be) and not a sword to conquer East Germany. And the Soviet Union soon built up its nuclear deterrents, organized its counter-NATO in the Warsaw Treaty Organization, and eventually launched another offensive against Berlin.

From 1954 on, the foreign policy of the three principal Western powers underwent significant changes with respect to the German problem. The slackening of Communist pressure in Europe, frictions among some members of the Western community, and a shift of focus to other areas led to a loosening of NATO ties.

In 1954 the attention of the Western powers was concentrated on Europe, especially Germany, and on Korea and Indochina. Ten years later this focus was globally diffuse. The centrality of the German question gradually received less stress, despite intermittent crises over Berlin. Differences even arose between the Federal Republic and the United States which would have been unthinkable a few years earlier. While America remained the single strongest power of the West, her leadership and authority were being challenged by France.

The emergence of the European Economic Community also contributed to the shaping of a new image of Europe and on a global scale added to the economic prestige of West Germany. The Franco-German *entente* did not fail to impress the chancellaries and public opinion of the world.

Naturally, in this evolving situation the interests and objectives of the Western powers regarding Germany could not remain static. It must have been clear at the time of West Germany's adherence to the West that the goal of German reunification could not remain as fundamental a policy objective to the Allies as it was for the Federal Republic. In fact, their own interest in German unity had at no time been identical.

In 1954–55 the ideal of German unification had been a weapon against the towering might of Russia, a weapon to prevent communism from making further inroads into Europe. Since NATO's *raison d'être* was the defense of the free world, and Germany was to become a part of that world, reunification seemed a natural consequence of the alliance.

But as soon as the Soviet zone was made into a quasi-independent state and its borders were sealed off from the rest of Germany, German unification changed from a defensive to an offensive goal. The official policy of "containment" was now no longer in harmony with the offensive aim of reunification. Containment now meant the defense of West Germany and West Berlin against encroach-

245

ments of the East, not a change of status quo for the purpose of assembling all Germans under one political roof. From that moment the vital interests of West Germany were out of step with essential policy goals of the other Western powers. What would happen when Western initiatives, such as arms control, disengagement, or prospective political and territorial settlements, were given priority over the goal of German unity?

The more "polycentric" the Western alliance became, the more evident became the conflict of views described above. It even seemed that German unity was no longer a question of national interest to some of the Western leaders.

Disruptions in the Communist camp also modified the quality of interest in the division of Germany felt by its members. While communism remained monolithic, Moscow's wishes had to be shared by all Communist powers. But as soon as this enforced unity broke down, the impact of individual national interests began to affect the diplomacy of Central Europe. The German problem ceased to be an exclusively ideological issue on both sides of the Iron Curtain. Also the danger of Soviet expansionism in Europe subsided.

It is essential for our purposes to trace the evolution of official thinking on the German question in the United States, Britain, and France:

1) The original German policy adopted by the United States soon after the outbreak of the Korean War was a complete *renversement des alliances*. It aimed at making West Germany the mainstay against Soviet imperialism in continental Europe. Germany was selected because of her exposed geographic location, the reliable anti-Communist sentiment of her people (in contrast to the French), and her past warlike disposition. This policy, it was thought, would also have the virtue of inhibiting German neutralist or pro-Soviet inclinations (as a price for reunification of their country). Former Secretary of State Dean Acheson, a strong advocate of the Germanocentric European policy, expressed the idea as follows:

Germany's division and its occupation [by Russia] threaten the stability and peace of Europe and the security of the United States.

Germany's geographical position and strength make that country indispensable to the existence of both a united Europe and a European defense.

. . . my thesis is that making political and military judgments affecting

Europe a major—often *the* major—consideration should be their effect on the German people and the German Government. It follows from this that the closest liaison and consultation with the German Government is an absolute necessity.[67]

Here, United States interests are completely identified with the paramount German interest of unification. This coalescence of policy objectives as well as the suggested commitment to consult Germany would, if fully implemented, confer a "right of veto" on West Germany concerning any decision on European or East-West questions.[68] It would also commit the United States to giving first priority to German unification.

In contrast to Acheson, many Americans, especially intellectuals, remain profoundly suspicious of Germany. Representatives of this view are scarce in the executive branch of the government, though there may be more in Congress.[69] They view with sympathy Germany's partition, which they consider indispensable for the maintenance of peace (holders of the opposite view consider German unification indispensable for peace). Some of them circulate the erroneous idea that the Germans themselves do not care about the unity of their country.[70]

The majority of the Washington decision-makers are by no means anti-German, though they are not pro-German to the extent that Acheson was. For them the question of German reunification is not *the* principal European issue but only one of many. Some think it is presently a dead issue. Therefore, they are willing to deal with the Soviet Union exclusive of the unity problem. Others are more concerned about German unity but little inclined to sacrifice possible diplomatic progress on its account.

American leaders have a bias against abstract and legalistic formulations. Thus, they are not appalled if their policy proposals clash with Bonn's doctrines of single statehood and monopoly rep-

[67] Dean Acheson, "Withdrawal From Europe? 'An Illusion,'" *New York Times Magazine*, December 15, 1963. This article is a publication of a speech delivered at the University of Connecticut. For the decision to make West Germany a principal ally, see Freund, *Germany Between Two Worlds*, pp. 138–39.
[68] See Zbigniew Brzezinski, "The Danger of a German Veto," *The New Leader*, January 20, 1964.
[69] *New York Times*, September 17, 1962.
[70] See Karl Loewenstein, "Unity for Germany?" *Current History*, January, 1960. For arguments against Germany's unification, see Jonas Lesser, *Germany: The Symbol and the Deed* (New York, 1965), pp. 7–17.

247

resentation.[71] For them progress in improving relations with Moscow is infinitely more important than small infringements on German doctrine. In this way, their diplomatic actions sometimes bring them into opposition with the political or diplomatic leader of West Germany.

The Federal Republic is still ready to consider the United States as the leader of the global anti-Communist struggle. Any communication between the United States and the Soviet Union is examined in Bonn from the point of view of its effect on reunification. Any deviation from the one-state doctrine is naturally considered harmful. Because Bonn accords first priority to German unity, it will oppose any arrangement which might contribute to the perpetuation of the status quo. For the Federal Republic the partition of Germany, the Berlin question, and the Wall are not just symptoms of the Cold War but a basic source of global conflict. The West German leaders cannot imagine any real relaxation of the Cold War without an advance toward the goal of reunification. Washington is far from sharing this view.

Bonn is inclined to interpret the Western commitment to support reunification in a very wide sense. Any statement or action conflicting—in West German eyes—with this common objective should strictly be avoided. For the opponents of an unlimited American commitment to promote German unity, this seems unreasonable and impractical. The result can be a reluctance to consult with Bonn meaningfully or at all.

Such are differences that cause friction between the United States and the Federal Republic. Bonn is today no longer entirely confident that Washington will represent its position in talks with the Soviets. The fact alone that reunification is no longer, if it ever was, a principal policy goal for the United States—whereas it is and is likely always to be one for the Germans—makes a wholly harmonious foreign policy impossible. Compromises are inevitable, but the legalistic German outlook poses considerable obstacles. While Bonn suggested four-power talks on German unity, Washington

---

[71] A lack of understanding toward the German official approach is thus revealed by President Kennedy's Special Assistant: "The German Ambassador to Washington, Wilhelm Grewe, so bored the White House with pedantic and long-winded recitals that word was finally passed to his government that his recall would improve communication." Schlesinger, *A Thousand Days*, p. 403. Grewe, a former professor of international law, former Head of the Political Section of the German Foreign Office, played an outstanding role in the negotiations of 1952–54 which determined West Germany's present status.

has made it known to the Germans that they should seek direct contacts with the Soviet Union and try to improve their relations with Moscow.[72]

Although the United States advocates greater flexibility, it would hardly welcome too much of it. The German doctrinal position is thus a guarantee against the sudden diplomatic somersaults which the Germans are accused of having undertaken in the past. Such a danger, Washington must know, could only be the result of utter despair and domestic upheaval in the Federal Republic. Desertion of the goal of German unity, by deed or word, might, however, cause a domestic crisis in West Germany and a radical change of foreign alignment.[73] The Federal Republic constantly needs assurances that nothing will be done to prejudice reunification.[74]

But Washington is less anxious at present about the potential perils of a German-Soviet understanding than about the "flirtations" going on between Paris and Bonn. Erhard resisted all the attempts made by General de Gaulle to throw overboard Bonn's intimate and special ties with Washington. Chancellor Kiesinger, upon his advent to office, undertook to improve relations with France without, however, imperiling the alliance with the United States. Still, West Germany's pro-American leaders feel that the Federal Republic will, for the foreseeable future, have most to gain from American support and friendship. "Reunification precedes European Union"—Erhard is supposed to have told De Gaulle.[75] As long as the United States is willing, even with a diminished emphasis, to support unification, the Federal Republic cannot neglect to play the American card.

As mentioned earlier,[76] Washington also objected to West Ger-

[72] Such advice must have been given during Erhard's visit to the Johnson ranch in December, 1963. A similar suggestion was made by President Johnson in an interview with the editor of the Munich magazine *Quick,* to which the West German press reacted rather sharply. *New York Times,* April 30 and May 8, 1964. After Erhard's visit to Washington in September 1966, President Johnson reaffirmed that German unity "in a restored Europe" remains a vital purpose of American policy. But it can only be achieved "through a growing reconciliation because there is no shortcut." Address to the National Conference of Editorial Writers, *New York Times,* October 8, 1966.
[73] United States and Soviet contacts always give rise to political unrest in Bonn. *Ibid.,* April 23, 1964.
[74] For a report on Germans asking for so-called "pleading sessions" with Secretary of State Rusk see Henry A. Kissinger, "Coalition Diplomacy in a Nuclear Age," *Foreign Affairs,* July 1964, p. 537; Schlesinger, *A Thousand Days.*
[75] *New York Times,* July 11, 1964.
[76] See p. 227 above.

many's closer trade relations with Communist China. Steps even less dramatic than those taken by De Gaulle in establishing diplomatic relations with Peking are considered prejudicial by Washington. In deference to President Johnson's wishes, Erhard refrained from establishing permanent trade missions with Peking, the same type of relationship which, following suggestions from Washington, he had set up in various East-Central European Communist capitals. Any estrangement between Bonn and Washington is likely to induce West Germany to follow somewhat France's example in handling the China "business." Diplomatic exchange would no longer be prohibited by the Hallstein Doctrine.

A clear recognition of the dangers of Germany's partition must remain an indispensable element of United States foreign policy even if priorities become more flexible. However, America's foreign policy has been accused of containing "dazzling improvisations and an absence of forethought."[77] These shifting global preoccupations are bound to confuse the sedate, doctrine-oriented German leadership. This pattern seems destined to continue. The more capricious oscillations should, however, be avoided.

If Washington wishes to abide by the spirit of its agreements with West Germany, it must accept the thesis that Europe cannot be stable in the presence of a divided Germany. This principle was repeated in the joint communiqué issued by President Johnson and Chancellor Erhard on June 13, 1964.[78] Whenever negotiations are conducted with the Soviet Union on obliquely related matters, such as arms control, it needs always to be made clear that such arrangements will not prejudice reunification. Washington should also show some understanding of the doctrinal bases of the German claim to unity. Disdain for these formulations and arguments causes unnecessary exasperation and misunderstanding. The United States should constantly indicate that *détente* is not intended to be the goal but only a means of reaching the goal, a goal which should not exclude the stated principle of German unity.

An improved political atmosphere, or the conclusion of a non-aggression pact, as was envisaged between the United States and the Soviet Union in the spring of 1963, will not necessarily promote internal liberalization in East Germany; on the contrary, it may contribute to a stabilization of the regime and strengthening of the dictatorship. Nonaggression treaties with Stalin and Soviet entry

[77] C. L. Sulzberger in *New York Times*, April 21, 1962.
[78] *Ibid.*, June 14, 1964.

into the League of Nations did not lead to internal relaxation in Russia. It would be a grievous mistake to try to settle the German question without or against the consent of the Germans. The credibility of American commitments should not be jeopardized by negotiating arrangements to which no West German government will give its consent.

2) One rarely encounters the Achesonian attitude in the United Kingdom. On the other hand, Vansittartite and other, less violent anti-German sentiment is still widespread within the circle of elites and policy-makers. Propensities to neutralism, denuclearization, and pacifism go hand-in-hand with anti-German sentiment in British politics and affect large segments of the British public. All these forces continue, in the words of Sir Lewis Namier, "to fight ghosts"; that is, nazism and aggressive German nationalism, which now have ceased to be a danger.[79]

Britain, together with the United States and France, signed and ratified the 1954 London-Paris Agreements, including the promise to support reunification of Germany, to recognize the government of the Federal Republic as the only representative of the German people, and to reserve the final determination of the boundaries of Germany for the peace conference.[80]

In the years following these agreements, the British government and the majority of the British public supported Adenauer's policy, but discouraged West Germany from any independent move which she might have undertaken to promote German unity. Similarly, they strongly opposed any idea of neutralization which might remove Germany from the Western alliance. Evidently, for the British policy-makers, the inclusion of the Federal Republic in the Western alliance structure was more important than German reunification. They opposed neutralization, not because they distrusted the Soviets but because they distrusted a neutral and powerful united Germany.[81]

[79] Sir Lewis Namier pointed out that in Britain, fear of Spain survived deep into the seventeenth century, and of France deep into the nineteenth, after neither was any longer dangerous; this misdirection of fears favored the rise of that nation which, in turn, became a menace. He indicates that a similar situation arose after World War II with regard to Germany, in neglect of the Russian menace; quoted in Fritz Stern (ed.), *The Varieties of History* (Cleveland, 1956), p. 373.

[80] See Chapter I, pp. 35–36 above.

[81] This reasoning emerged from the Anglo-German conversations held yearly in Königswinter between parliamentarians of the two countries; see Heinz Lehmann, "England und die deutsche Teilung," in Günther Franz (ed.), *Teilung und Wiedervereinigung* (Göttingen, 1963), pp. 201-3.

The Hungarian anti-Communist Revolution of 1956 alerted the leaders of the Labour party, then in opposition, to the dangers to peace of Germany's partition. Hugh Gaitskell and Denis Healey worked out a disengagement plan which combined the neutralization of the two Germanys (and of Poland, Czechoslovakia, and Hungary) with their demilitarization under international guarantee.[82] This plan would have created a united but demilitarized and internationally supervised Germany. In one stroke it would have united Germany and rendered her harmless.

The Eden Plan, submitted by the then Foreign Secretary to the Foreign Ministers Conference at Berlin in January, 1954, and in a somewhat revised form, as British Prime Minister, to the Geneva Summit Conference of 1955, did not foresee neutralization and demilitarization and was evidently predicated on the contingency that a united Germany would remain within the frame of the Western alliance.

After the failure of the 1955 Geneva negotiations, the British government tended to view the reunification issue as a laudable but, for the time being, Utopian ideal. Khrushchev's campaign against West Berlin persuaded London of the wisdom of concentrating on a compromise solution for that city. Important voices in Britain even advocated the abandonment of West Berlin (evacuation of its population and resettlement in West Germany). In official negotiations, however, Britain generally followed United States policy, as during the Geneva Conference on Berlin in 1959. In March, 1960, Prime Minister Macmillan undertook a probing *démarche* in Moscow but without success, except for the agreement on the later abortive Paris Summit Conference.

It seems that the British government, without spelling it out, was quite happy to have the question of German unity postponed *ad infinitum*. And the reason is not only the wish to put aside troublesome business but also the latent fear of a united, powerful, and perhaps unaligned Germany, playing off East and West against each other. This fear is also heightened by the possibility that Germany will acquire nuclear weapons. English public opinion is much less

---

[82] Hugh Gaitskell, leader of the opposition, submitted his plan on December 19, 1956, to the House of Commons. On January 11, 1957, he repeated his proposal in a lecture at Harvard University. On April 28, 1958, the British Labour party and the British Trade Union Congress, in a joint declaration, also approved the plan. Denis Healey, in an address at Chatham House on November 28, 1961, considered disengagement and neutralization of Germany the only solution for her unification. Healey, "The Crisis in Europe," *International Affairs*, April, 1962, pp. 145–55.

concerned by actual French bombs than by the slight chance that the Germans might have them—another application of Sir Lewis Namier's thesis.[83]

The relative coolness of Anglo-German relations results from the British suspicion of German motives and their tacit refusal of unconditional support for German unity. Both the West German government and people resent "the airs" of the British, and this anger sometimes bursts forth in the press.[84] Britain is accused more openly in the Federal Republic than anywhere else of flirting with neutralist concepts and of being generally "soft" on communism and the Soviet challenge. It is quite clear, however, that British public opinion is not yet ready to welcome Germany as a partner and a friend.[85]

The leader of the Labour party, Harold Wilson, has come out openly for the recognition of the German Democratic Republic. But, after he had become Prime Minister in the fall of 1964, his unofficial preference could not become official policy. He must have been reminded by his advisers of Britain's treaty commitments to promote German unity. Thus, when visiting Bonn in March, 1965, the British Prime Minister offered solid support for the Federal Republic on the vital questions of reunification, the defense of Berlin, and security.[86]

Failing to endorse the policy for German reunification, Britain could provoke a dangerous crisis in Anglo-German relations. Bonn would interpret such an attitude as another expression of "irrational anti-Germanism" promoting anti-Western jingoism.[87] And it is just this extreme German nationalism which the British wish to prevent. An open violation of the London-Paris Agreements might provoke a complete departure from the premises of present German foreign policy concepts and might make De Gaulle's maverick policies seem paltry by comparison.

3) France's German policy was dominated from 1944 to January, 1946, and again after 1958, by the towering figure of General de

[83] British views are perhaps best reproduced in the article by the Canadian, Lionel Gelber, "A Marriage of Inconvenience," *Foreign Affairs*, January, 1963, pp. 318–20.

[84] See, for instance, the leading article, "Die englische Krankheit," *Frankfurter Allgemeine Zeitung*, September 4, 1963.

[85] From this point of view, see the well-balanced "Germany" issue (April, 1964) of *Encounter*, listing views pro and con with regard to West Germany.

[86] *New York Times*, March 10, 1965.

[87] The dangers of British Germanophobia are ably described by an Englishman, Mander, *Berlin: Hostage for the West*, pp. 116–24.

Gaulle. After pressing for Germany's dismemberment and separation of the Rhineland and the Ruhr, the foreign policy of the Fourth Republic slowly fell in line with the Anglo-American approach: reconstitution of West Germany as a sovereign state, promotion of German unity in peace and freedom, and suspension of decisions concerning Germany's eastern border until the peace settlement. Cognizant of the dangers of Soviet threat to France, the French government completed the cycle by supporting the establishment of a vigorous Germany, allied with the West and integrated into European supranational institutions, serving as a glacis against the Soviet-Communist East and a source of Europe's economic prosperity. The federalist concepts of Robert Schuman and Jean Monnet were inspired both by the idealism of a united Europe and by the political expediency of tying Germany to the common endeavor. In a farsighted act of wisdom, France finally abandoned the Saar for the sake of friendship and co-operation with Germany.

Since the return of General de Gaulle to power, German policy has become more supple and artful. The French President always displayed a Bismarckian predilection for combinations of alliances and complex interlocking policies. As one writer has suggested, one has only to read De Gaulle's memoirs for an understanding of his aims and methods; he had intended "to assure France primacy in Western Europe by preventing the rise of a new *Reich* . . . to co-operate with East and West, and if need be, contract the necessary alliances, on one side or the other, without ever accepting any kind of dependency. . . ."[88]

Though before 1946 De Gaulle worked feverishly to prevent the re-establishment of a unified Germany and tried to be the arbiter between the Soviets and the Anglo-Americans, after 1958 he was ready to co-operate with West Germany on his own terms and in pursuit of his own objectives. His over-all aim was the emancipation of France and a French-led Europe from its dependence on America, on the one hand, and from the Soviet menace, on the other. He wished to secure French leadership, not within a federalized supranational European system, but within a "Europe of nations," a loose confederation of sovereign states accepting France's hegemony.[89] In such a tableau, the questions of German rank and German unity were critical.

[88] From De Gaulle's war memoirs, as quoted by Hans Kohn, "The Future of Political Unity in Western Europe," *The Annals*, July, 1963, p. 99.

[89] Robert R. Bowie, "Atlantic Policy: Tensions Within the Alliance," *Foreign Affairs*, October, 1963, pp. 55–57.

Just as De Gaulle undertook to use the European Economic Community for French advantage, he wished to utilize France's close relationship with the Federal Republic to the same end. He wanted to tie West Germany as closely as possible to France, and through France to Western Europe, partly to prevent her from taking an independent course, partly to exploit her resources, prestige, and geographical location for the implementation of his far-reaching program. West Germany's exposed situation, division, diplomatic passivity, and the pro-French feelings of her Chancellor were to be used to make her the "glorious second" in the "Europe of Fatherlands." To gain a margin of military superiority over Germany (deprived by treaty of nuclear capabilities) and most of the rest of the world, De Gaulle developed his nuclear programs, more for political than for military reasons.

In order to obtain a hold over the Federal Republic, France must constantly demonstrate that co-operation with her could be more useful than reliance on the United States. De Gaulle wishes to strengthen all existing relations with Bonn, while challenging the reliability of the United States in protecting German national interests.[90] While his policy appears *formally* to harmonize with that of West Germany, the idea of German unity is for him a tactical issue rather than a substantive goal. His reservations in this regard were expressed in his press conference of March 25, 1959: "The reunification of the two parts into a single Germany which would be entirely free seems to us the normal destiny of the German people, provided they do not reopen the question of their present frontiers to the West, the East, the North, and to the South, and that they move toward integrating themselves one day in a contractual organization of all Europe for co-operation, liberty and peace."

From this statement commentators conclude that De Gaulle has recognized, on behalf of France, the Oder-Neisse frontier as the legal border between Poland and united Germany.[91] On the other hand, he refused to recognize the "artificial creation" of East Germany. Nevertheless, doubts had been expressed whether De Gaulle is really willing to promote the reunification of East and West Germany.[92] It would appear that the resurrection of a Germany of

[90] C. L. Sulzberger in *New York Times*, July 4, 1962; Robert R. Bowie, "Atlantic Policy."

[91] Karl Epping, "Charles de Gaulle und die deutsche Wiedervereinigung," in Franz (ed.), *Teilung und Wiedervereinigung*, pp. 230–31; Zbigniew Brzezinski, "Russia and Europe," *Foreign Affairs*, April, 1964, pp. 439–40.

[92] See the well-informed article by André Fontaine, "What is French

over seventy million inhabitants would become an obstacle to De Gaulle's ambitious European scheme: would a much more powerful Germany permanently follow the French lead, and, in a Franco-German *entente* or confederate Europe, would she not set the tune?

De Gaulle undoubtedly has qualms in this respect. His stance on the concrete issue of reunification is extremely cautious as witnessed by the text of the Franco-German communiqué after the De Gaulle-Adenauer talks of July 5, 1962: "In the course of their examination of the international situation, both statesmen gave special attention to the question of Germany and Berlin. They noted their complete agreement on this subject. Only reunification of Germany under conditions of a relaxation of tension and observance of the right of self-determination would allow the problem of Berlin and Germany to be solved in a really satisfactory way. . . ."[93]

As to the defense of West Berlin, the official French attitude was much closer to that of Bonn than that of the Anglo-Saxon powers. De Gaulle's refusal to participate in Washington's and London's attempts to compromise the Berlin issue demonstrated a better understanding of the Soviet mentality than was shown by the other Western leaders.

France has genuine fears that the loss of Berlin might cause the whole of Germany "to tumble into neutrality" endangering the French frontier on the Rhine.[94] The bogey of Russo-German cooperation to the detriment of France is one of the compelling reasons that France seeks friendship and collaboration with West Germany.[95] Though De Gaulle is perhaps unprepared to expose the entire diplomatic and material strength of France to bring about the reunification of Germany, he certainly will avoid doing anything

---

Policy?" *Foreign Affairs*, October, 1966, especially pp. 75–76. See also Harold C. Deutsch, "The Impact of the Franco-German Entente," *The Annals*, July, 1963, pp. 89–90; Brzezinski, "Russia and Europe."

[93] *New York Times*, July 6, 1962. At a press conference on February 5, 1965, De Gaulle described thus the German problem, as it affected France: "To act so that Germany may become a sure element of peace and progress, within this condition to help her reunification, and to take the path and choose the framework that will permit its accomplishment." He also insisted that the problem is "essentially European." *Ibid.*, February 5, 1965.

[94] This fear of a Russo-German understanding, in case vital German interests are neglected, is given eloquent expression by Robert Schuman, "France and Germany in the New Europe," *Foreign Affairs*, October, 1962, pp. 68–73.

[95] When at Moscow in June, 1966, De Gaulle told the Soviet leaders that, just as Russia prevented an American hegemony in Europe, the United States prevented a Russian hegemony. *New York Times*, June 26, 1966. Of course, De Gaulle's nightmare would be a combination between Germany and the Soviet Union, supported by the United States.

to make the Germans feel that his support of this goal is faint-hearted.

Speaking of Europe "from the Urals to the Atlantic," De Gaulle has set his eye on the areas east of Germany which he would like to include in his continental scheme. It has been suggested that he wishes to counterbalance the might of a united Germany, not only by French nuclear power, but also by embracing the eastern European nations and Russia in the "Europe of nations" (the classical French alliance-system of pre- and post-World War I vintage).[96]

What De Gaulle meant by the "Europeanization" of the German problem is not entirely clear; he probably meant that the German question should be solved without active interference by the United States; he might also have meant that Bonn should not seek support, diplomatic and military, primarily from the transatlantic power but should rely rather on co-operation with France. And the solution of the German quest for reunification should be sought in direct contacts with Moscow, to be mediated by France.

In his speech before the French National Assembly on April 13, 1966, French Premier Georges Pompidou declared: ". . . there is no solution to the great problem, to the essential problem for Germany, and I mean reunification, except by affirming a resolutely peaceful policy and by improving relations with Russia. That is why the trip to Moscow should, far from disturbing the Federal Government, serve its interest at the same time as that of peace in Europe."[97]

Previous to the "trip to Moscow," mentioned by the French Premier, De Gaulle promised to advocate Germany's cause. Though seeking co-operation with the Soviets, he had no intention of concluding a formal alliance with France's "traditional ally." He even turned down the proposal of an early European security conference. He probably tried to persuade the Russians to collaborate with him to bring about the unification of Germany under the guarantee of a European security system.

The President of France, a convinced traditional nationalist, does not believe that the artificial division of the German nation could be maintained in perpetuity. If he could secure German unity of either a neutralized or de-nuclearized Germany tied by security guarantees, in co-operation with the Soviet Union and the East European countries, the European balance of power could be main-

[96] Brzezinski, "Russia and Europe," p. 439.
[97] The full text of the speech was published by the French Embassy's Press and Information Service, Nos. 243A and 245A, April, 1966, p. 6.

tained; and he would thereby have gained the lasting gratitude of the Germans and firmly established the leading position of France.

De Gaulle has shown himself to be much more flexible than his imitators, the "German Gaullists," who opposed Erhard and Schröder's plan of "opening the East." He is trying to strengthen French ties with the East-Central European Communist countries in the hope of dislodging them from the Soviet empire. The French even showed little reluctance, to the dismay of Bonn, to make contacts with the German Democratic Republic; this may also have been in response to the Federal Republic's reluctance to forsake its intimate ties with the United States for the sake of friendship with France.[98]

West Germany has abandoned neither the fear of Franco-Soviet co-operation nor uneasiness about De Gaulle's contacts beyond the Oder-Neisse Line. The policy of collaboration with France, authenticated in the Franco-German Treaty of Friendship of January, 1963, reflects Germany's sincere desire to end a futile antagonism, but it also betrays practical apprehension of a Franco-Soviet tie which would, once again, constitute an "encirclement" of Germany and deal a heavy blow at reunification.[99]

French pressures notwithstanding, Bonn refused to make a choice between its sympathies for Paris or Washington. Kiesinger told the Bundestag: "We refuse to be talked into making a false and dangerous choice."[100] The main consideration which had guided Erhard, who was less beguiled by the prospects of a Franco-German Grand Alliance than was his predecessor, was the support which he expected to receive for the benefit of German unity. From the German point of view, as Erhard said, "the treaty [i.e., the Franco-German Treaty of Friendship] is not an end in itself." And he is also quoted as saying: "De Gaulle does not have the German or Berlin problem with which we are burdened. We need all free nations to help us."[101]

If, ultimately, a real choice has to be made, the question of Germany's reunification will persuade Bonn of the greater usefulness

---

[98] As a typical gesture, strongly irritating West Germany, the French consent to allow an East German Communist delegation to come to Paris to the funeral of Maurice Thorez may be cited. This delegation entered France in disregard to the inter-Allied traffic regulation applied to residents of East Germany. New York Times, July 29, 1964.

[99] Adenauer warned his countrymen of this possibility but, simultaneously, encouraged them to "trust de Gaulle." Ibid., March 6, 1964.

[100] New York Times, December 14, 1966.

[101] Ibid., July 24, 1966. One of the primary foreign policy goals of Chancellor Kiesinger was the restoration of Franco-German intimacy. His attempts

of Washington's co-operation over that of Paris. However, De Gaulle's decision to establish direct diplomatic relations with China was greeted with concealed approval by the leaders of West Germany. Adenauer merely objected that France's allies should have been consulted. Should there open up a possibility of exerting pressure on the Soviet Union through the Chinese (and the Germans are convinced that such a day is inevitable), Bonn's close contacts with Paris might indirectly serve the German cause. But the Federal Republic's need to rely on Washington's support is likely to dissuade Bonn from following De Gaulle's China policy.

West Germany's inclusion in the Western alliance and complementary bodies was useful—in the minds of their projectors— because it harnessed German energies to the task of European integration and Atlantic co-operation. Supporters of this thesis seem to have believed that Germany's role in European integration would deflect her attention from the reunification question and dampen national sentiment.

It is, however, unlikely that this political surrogate can ever, in the long run, divert German attention from the fate of their brethren in the East and the cause of unity. The German leadership feels, on the contrary, that integration will provide the necessary dynamism and strength to achieve unification.[102] Of course, existing alliances and future integration may well exercise a restraining influence on the Germans. But the more Europe becomes a "Third Force" (which is De Gaulle's ultimate aim) through its rise in power and productivity, the more it will wish to extend its scope of action and its influence over those nations on its perimeter. In this situation, it will appear anomalous that the Swiss, Austrians, Scandinavians, and perhaps even the Yugoslavs and other eastern Europeans should be associating with the six of the European Economic Community but that, at the same time, the Germans of the D.D.R. should be prevented from joining. At such a point the political and material resources of integrated Europe might create pressure for a liberation of East Germany.

Even if these German hopes did not prove feasible, integrated Europe would never replace the ideal of an integrated Germany. The amputation of East Germany is so strongly felt that its forcible

---

to establish ties of friendship with East European countries can also be considered as an alignment of West German policy with the Gaulist policy of "uniting Europe."

[102] See C. L. Sulzberger's comments in *New York Times,* August 11, 1962.

normalization would be more likely to destroy European integration than cause the Germans to give up their desire for unity. For the Germans their integration into Western Europe does not presently appear incompatible with their desire for reunification. Should this situation change, it is no mystery which choice the Germans would make.

In the absence of an immediate Soviet peril, Germany's place in the Western alliance and the future of Western collaboration, in general, will depend on the amount of harmony that can be obtained for dealing with current practical issues. While some of the differing interests can be compromised, vital affairs of any member cannot be disregarded without endangering the system. Should the leading members of the Western alliance fail to support German aspirations to unity, a crisis in the West would be inevitable. The future of the reunification policy is likely to depend on (*a*) Soviet support of the German Democratic Republic, (*b*) Western support of the Federal Republic, and (*c*), last but not least, the disposition of the German people and German policy-makers in pursuit of their primary goal. The skill of Western diplomacy and the nature and strength of German national feeling will decide whether German unity is to be a quiescent or an active problem, and whether it will endanger the existing peace.

Though analogy is often misleading, it is the least misleading thing we have.

—Samuel Butler
Music, Picture, and Books

Healing is a matter of time, but it is sometimes also a matter of opportunity.

—Hippokrates
Precepts, Chapter I

CHAPTER VII

✳ ✳

THE GERMAN PROBLEM OF THE
MID-TWENTIETH CENTURY

Since the end of the Middle Ages, each century has produced problems related to the international implications of Germany's dismemberment. Though the present partition differs in many respects from earlier divisions of Germany, the potential consequences for the world at large are no less compelling than before.

As a result of World War II, Germany was deprived of the areas gained six to eight hundred years ago east of the Oder and Lusatian Neisse rivers; and, additionally, the territory between the Elbe and Werra rivers in the West and the Oder-Neisse rivers in the East, was politically severed from the main part of the German nation. Only the western portion of the former German capital continued to live as a precarious occidental enclave.

The French historian, Pierre Gaxotte, has characterized the Germans as an unfortunate people with an unbalanced history, discontinuous, replete with miraculous upsurges and catastrophic collapses, with extremes of order to chaos. He has reminded his readers that Bismarckian Germany in the course of her short history twice broke down and that as late as 1866 German states were fighting each other on the battlefield.[1]

[1] Gaxotte, *Histoire de l'Allemagne,* Vol. I, p. 9.

Indeed, history has turned full cycle in less than eighty years. Germany is again dismembered and is in quest of her unity. And, once again, this aspiration for unity constitutes an international problem which closely affects the stability and peace of the world and the balance of forces in Europe.

The problems of Germany's present division differ from earlier history in three important respects:

1) In the past, except for the short period of Napoleonic domination, German *Kleinstaaterei* meant the existence of members of autochtonous German units. These states of all sizes maintained themselves by the force of history, traditional *Staatsgedanke* (loyalty to a dynasty, civic pride in their separate statehood, etc.), and by the internal German balance-of-power system. Only during the period of French influence could some German states, especially the Kingdom of Westphalia, be considered outright satellites whose sole *raison d'être* was French military support and the Emperor's prestige.

Today, the East German state is not regarded by the majority of Germans (both in the West and the East) as an autochtonous German state structure. It is "German" only in form, not in substance. Its existence depends on foreign intervention. The first loyalty of its leaders is to a non-German political idea and the external power that embodies it. The East German government must rely on the support of the Soviet armed forces. It is, therefore, not a genuine "German" government in the accepted sense of the word. The area of the German Democratic Republic is considered by most Germans as a territory under foreign domination. From this point of view, Germany is really not divided into two (or three) state units but is semi-occupied.

2) Prior to the establishment of the Bismarckian Reich, Germany was essentially partitioned only politically. This did not prevent the expression of strong spiritual and cultural unity between the inhabitants of the different German states. While Germany was divided, German art, literature, and science were, following the end of the eighteenth century, basically uniform. Writers, poets, scientists, administrators, and students frequently emigrated from one German state to another; and their circulation prompted the development of a common German cultural and spiritual heritage.

While some of the German intellectuals, like Goethe, preferred to think of themselves as European rather than German, even they gave German culture self-confidence. Many Germans around the turn of the eighteenth century began believing that they possessed the profoundest culture and the most original and unadulterated language. The final development of cultural cohesion was the result of Napoleonic grand politics, long before political unification. Even the split between Protestants and Catholics was largely restricted to the field of politics and theology; otherwise, the unity of German language and culture did not significantly suffer from the religious cleavage.

At present, Germany is not only divided politically but also culturally and spiritually. The exchange of persons and ideas is artificially impeded by physical barriers. Thus, the division between the two parts of Germany is incomparably more radical and calamitous than any previous political separation.

3) In the past, the goal of German unity proceeded from the principle of German ethnic unity. To include all Germans and all the territories inhabited by them in one empire was the objective of traditional German imperialism. Hitler and a few other "extremists" wished to expand the German *Lebensraum* into other areas, but this was a relatively new trend.

The area of the former Reich east of the Oder-Neisse rivers no longer holds any significant number of Germans, having been resettled by Poles. West Germany refuses to recognize the annexation of these areas by Poland and the Soviet Union; she has thereby raised a claim to the territories because they had, in the past, belonged to Germany and been inhabited by Germans. This is another novel feature in the long history of the struggle for German unity.

The unique situation of Berlin is no less novel. And even the quest for reunification of the East German state with the Federal Republic can no longer be sought under the slogan of *Anschluss*. The D.D.R. is not only separated from the Federal Republic by a simple political frontier; it is separated by an ideological barrier, defended by the forces of a non-German superpower and its allies. What had seemed a relatively easy constitutional procedure in the late 1940's and early 1950's has now come to resemble a dead end. The meaning of German unity has undergone meaningful changes in the past few years; the problem does not merely affect territories but people as well. Thus, the corresponding matter of political goals requires a new clarification.

The Meaning of Self-Determination and Reunification

Before the establishment of the Federal Republic, German politicians, including Adenauer, expressed hope for a restoration of the "unity of the Reich." After the formation of the West German state and of the East German political unit, reunification was construed as the political merger of the two German entities. As envisioned by Bonn, only the West German state represented the continuity of the former Reich, and it alone could legitimately act on behalf of the German nation. Accordingly, most Germans foresaw reunification as an *Anschluss* of East to West Germany. The Basic Law, dedicated to "preserve the national and political unity" of the German people, even provided for an extension of its own application to "other parts of Germany . . . on their accession." (Art. 23)

The intra-German and international developments of the past fifteen years have greatly reduced if not ended prospects of an "accession" of East Germany or any of the *Länder* (which have now been dissolved) of the Soviet zone. The maximal demand for reunification is, therefore, no longer upheld by all segments of the West German leadership. Even the word "reunification" has often given way to the expression "self-determination," allowing for a much wider interpretation. Although negotiations between the "two German states" for the purpose of creating a "confederation" on a parity basis are considered unacceptable, solutions other than automatic "accession" are no longer excluded. Did not Konrad Adenauer himself admit that the German problem "is in the last analysis a human one?" And he added: "This is why a starting point for a solution could be found in that sphere. If our countrymen in the Soviet-occupied zone are granted decent living conditions and at least a certain amount of freedom and self-determination, we shall be open to discussion on a good many points."[2]

It appears, therefore, that "freedom" for the East Germans has, in the minds of some influential West Germans, gained priority over the demand for political integration of the two units. Self-

[2] Adenauer, "The German Problem—A World Problem," pp. 63–64. In May, 1958, the Chancellor had referred to the same idea: "I have in mind, and very much at heart, that at long last we should see to it that the seventeen million of our countrymen behind the Iron Curtain should be able to live as they like. For these reasons, I believe that the entire question should not be seen under national or nationalist aspects or even the aspects of the rule of force, but as the real fact that seventeen million Germans are compelled to live a kind of life under a kind of mentality they simply do not want. We would be much further in the restoration of peace in the world, in rapprochement, and in improving our relations with the Soviet Union, if at long last the Germans in the Soviet Zone were permitted to be really free." Quoted from Theodor Eschenburg, "A Definition of Self-Determination," *The German Tribune*, May 2, 1964, p. 4.

determination implies that a people undertakes a free decision regarding its destinies. It would precede reunification or, rather, reunification would be made dependent on the results of self-determination. But both self-determination and, later, reunification, would have to be preceded by democratic conditions, so that "free elections" could take place.[3]

Since "freedom" is a prerequisite for both self-determination and reunification, the question of the relation between democracy and the restoration of political union is posed. It concerns both doctrine and practical politics. Is the refusal to recognize the *soi-disant* East German state based on the fact of the Soviet domination which has secured one-party dictatorship over the country, or is independent statehood *per se* denied to the East Germans? Is the secession of a group of ethnic Germans from the main body of the Germans to be inadmissible?

The doctrinal argument against recognition of the East German state rests on the "lack of legitimation" of that government. The East German regime is said to be German only in form and not in substance; its source of power is foreign. Its source is not in the will and consensus of its own people. The leaders of the regime and their aids are "agents" of a foreign state or of a movement which is alien to the German *Staatsgedanke*.

We may ask whether the East German state could ever obtain "legitimation" from a progressive reduction of foreign domination, a trend which is perceptible in the East-Central European "satellite" area. What would happen if the East German regime were to win popular approval from its own people in the form of "free elections" or otherwise? Or would West Germany deny the existence or recognition of an East German state even in case of a liberalization of the Pankow regime and request political union *à tout prix?* In other words, could the German problem be solved by a transformation of the internal East German state structure?

These questions are, of course, at present highly hypothetical. The East German people, if granted self-determination, would undoubtedly favor union with the rest of Germany. But if the Soviet

[3] Herbert Wehner, Minister of All-German Affairs in the Kiesinger-Brandt cabinet stated in an interview: "We can neither recognize that the regime in the other part of Germany is democratically legitimate nor shall we consider it a foreign country." He added that Bonn would reconsider its policy of not recognizing the East German regime if the Communist government became "democratically legitimized by the people of the German Democratic Republic." *New York Times*, December 15, 1966.

Union became convinced that preservation of the internal status quo in the German Democratic Republic was no longer possible, it might possibly agree to a liberalized East Germany, provided that the territorial status quo would be preserved and an independent but democratic East Germany placed under an international guarantee.

We saw earlier[4] that a few scholars have argued against the official thesis of political reunification and have advocated "freedom" for East Germany in return for her political independence. When these suggestions were first made, the time was not ripe. Indeed these ideas are scarcely realistic at the time of this writing. But it should be noted that a certain evolution in West German thinking toward the possibility of an intermediate solution has taken place.

The greatest difficulty of such a plan might be its implementation in practice and the maintenance of East Germany's independence in the long run. Artificial separation of parts of the same nation is one of the most delicate and ungratifying tasks of diplomacy. When Bulgaria was given independence in 1878, Eastern Rumelia was set apart as an autonomous province of the Ottoman Empire. Seven years later, Eastern Rumelia, in defiance of the big powers, joined Bulgaria. The island of Crete could similarly not be prevented from joining Greece. It seems quite clear that this solution could have permanency only if the population of East Germany acquired a self-consciousness of its own identity.

The possibility is not excluded, however, that one day the solution of an independent non-Communist East Germany might be proposed as a compromise between outright unification or continued Soviet control. The "libertarian" thesis, insofar as circumstances oppose it to the idea of political unification, has certainly conditioned some West Germans to accept the "freedom" of East Germany as at least a temporary substitute for *Anschluss*. Adenauer's remark bears witness to this evolution. Others, however, feel that any compromise solution would create dangerous tensions; German national sentiment would never acquiesce in a partition imposed by foreign powers.[5]

If such a choice is ever squarely demanded, the reply will show

[4] See Chapter III, pp. 112–17 above.
[5] Karl Theodor Freiherr zu Guttenberg recognizes that "in the hierarchy of values freedom precedes unity." But he considers the freedom of East Germany without political unification unrealistic and replete with dangers. Guttenberg, *Wenn der Westen will–Plädoyer für eine mutige Politik* (Stuttgart-Degerloch, 1964), p. 173.

to what extent political nationalism, as opposed to humanitarianism, is involved in the relations of the two Germanys.

In this regard, the non-German powers are affected by motives of expediency rather than natural sympathy. Twenty years after the end of World War II, Germanophobia is still the *leitmotiv* for many. The reasons for the bias against a united Germany are partly political but also considerably moralistic.

The Moral Issue

After World War I, the humiliation of defeat, the enforced admission of war-guilt, territorial losses, and oppressive reparations were exploited by the German leaders to foment aggressive nationalism, which reached its zenith with the Hitlerite frenzy. Germany's grievances in the 1920's, not entirely groundless, became artificially exaggerated. Her sacrifices were then not altogether excessive for a country which had lost a long and bloody war, no matter who was responsible for its outbreak. On the other hand, at present, German grievances based on forcible partition and the subjugation of one third of the German people hardly appear to be morally justified unless one endorses the thesis of collective responsibility and punishment to be inflicted on later generations.

The division of Germany and the oppressive regime in East Germany are viewed with indifference or complacency by many sectors of Western public opinion, sectors which otherwise express vivid concern for inhuman and dictatorial treatment of peoples in East Europe, Africa, and Asia or elsewhere. This attitude is motivated by an implicit Germanophobia which has boiled up during the past fifty years as a result of aggressive traits attributed to the German national character and, especially, the berserk excesses of the Nazi regime. While it seems that in the pursuit of foreign policy, "excessive moralism"[6] is somewhat misplaced, in view of Germany's past sinister record, an ethical evaluation of Germany's predicament is surely relevant.

In sharp contrast to World War I, the majority of German leaders and intellectuals have admitted the responsibility of Germany for the outbreak of the last war. They have approved de-Nazification (though not all the methods used), the punishment of war criminals, and the indemnification of the victims of nazism, including the compensation paid to Israel. On the other hand, they have pleaded

[6] See J. W. Fulbright, *Old Myths and New Realities* (New York, 1964), p. 45.

267

against the collective condemnation of all Germans, referred to mitigating circumstances (such as foreign complacency and support for nazism and Soviet collusion in the outbreak of the war), and to the acts of resistance by the Germans themselves.[7] It is likely that the prosecution of Nazi criminals has not been pursued with entire vigor. But everybody who has investigated the details of de-Nazification will realize how difficult it has been to expiate the past without committing new injustices.

Moralistic Germanophobia is not unrelated to the political alarm that Germany's recovery has inspired. There is also much distrust for West Germany's democratic "experiment." Ethical condemnation, suspicion, and arguments of expediency combine to cast doubt on reunification. But even if German collective guilt were admissible (which this writer would deny),[8] there would seem no moral argument for trying to punish succeeding generations for the errors of their parents.[9]

Judgments on the "fledgling" German democracy should be neither more condescending nor more rigorous than standards applied to other countries. Democracy in the Federal Republic is not perfect. Adenauer may have correctly been called a "democratic dictator."[10] But where else is democracy without flaws? The Germans should be allowed to evolve their own type of democratic institutions so long as they are not in fundamental contradiction to the spirit and reality of popular government. Nobody can seriously pretend that the Federal Republic is not now governed in this way or that the few remaining admirers of nazism constitute a serious threat to democracy. On the contrary, the restoration of a stable and democratic *Rechtsstaat* in West Germany, after the discourag-

---

[7] Another admission of official German war guilt in 1939 and a refusal to admit sole responsibility for World War I were made by Eugen Gerstenmaier, the President of the Bundestag, on September 1, 1964, on the twenty-fifth anniversary of the outbreak of World War II. Gerstenmaier added: "Yet this established set of circumstances does not account for what has been termed the collective guilt of the German people. There is no such thing as this collective guilt. The war was begun against the will of the German people. Anyone who can remember the August days of 1914 and compare them with the beginning of September 1939 is well aware that fear and abhorrence of war predominated in 1939. . . ." *The Bulletin*, September 15, 1946.

[8] Prime Minister Churchill quoted Edmund Burke in the House of Commons in October, 1953: "I do not know the methods of drawing up an indictment against a whole people." *Parliamentary Debates*, Vol. 392, pp. 88–101.

[9] In the Federal Republic now more than 60 per cent of the population are under forty years of age; they could not have participated in Nazi excesses or crimes. This percentage is rapidly increasing.

[10] Wighton, *Adenauer—Democratic Dictator, passim.*

ing antecedents of the Nazi past, is no less a "miracle" than the economic one.

Moralistic attitudes toward the German question appear to be not only inexpedient but also ultimately incorrect and unjust. It should not be forgotten that *this time* the Germans have a good case, a well-justified grievance which, if not recognized, would only frustrate their confidence in the West. The victors of World War I themselves committed what proved to be "more than a crime" by making concessions to Hitler which they had previously withheld from Weimar Germany. Refusing the Germans sympathy and support for a righteous cause might result one day in German demands for a bad cause which could not be rejected.

In West Germany there is a growing antipathy against making "sacrifices" for the sake of global security and peace. It is considered in Bonn that Germany has already sufficiently paid for her past errors and crimes. The inferiority-superiority syndrome which in the past characterized German behavior is now expressing itself in growing impatience.[11] Chancellor Erhard, a patient man himself, evidently expressed the views of his countrymen when stating: "It is now Moscow's turn—not the free world's or Germany's—to state what contributions it is prepared to make towards peace. He who calls for German sacrifices ought first to ask himself how much room for negotiation the Soviet policy of accomplished facts has left open to the German people. Germany is a living organism, not a *reservoir of compensatory possibilities to be drawn upon at will.*"[12]

Opposition to the German desire to liberate their co-nationals

[11] In the Bundestag debate on the extension of the statute of limitation for the prosecution of Nazi criminals on March 10, 1965, Fritz Erler, the floor leader of the SPD, declared: "A feeling of shame cannot be a permanent condition for the rising generations of a people. We have a claim to understanding for our problem on the part of the world around us. To teach hatred against the German people is to succumb to racism in reverse. He who constantly treats a people as a black sheep runs the risk of invoking great dangers." *The Bulletin*, March 16, 1965, p. 6. See also Mander, *Berlin: Hostage for the West*, p. 119; Rudolf Walter Leonhardt, *This Germany: The Story Since the Third Reich* (Greenwich, Conn., 1964), "How long are the Germans to pay for the war? When is it to stop?" p. 251.

[12] Erhard's statement as published in *Washington Post*, May 25, 1964 (italics added). "If the world should ever force on the Germans the conviction that nothing they can do can ever gain them full acceptance—that there is no further use in their trying—then it will not be the Germans only who are the losers." From the address of George C. McGhee, United States Ambassador in Bonn, on May 30, 1965, at the graduation exercises of the University of Maryland, European Division, at Heidelberg; German News Service, Washington, D.C., June 13, 1965.

from a totalitarian regime or to unite their country "in peace and freedom" can hardly be sustained by invoking moral indignation. The quest for reunification "in peace" has the approval of the German people and is, therefore, a democratically based foreign policy. To require Germans to be democratic, on the one hand, and to condemn this democratically conceived policy, on the other, is contradictory. Another conflicting requirement had been the suggestion that the new German army should become strong enough to defend Western Europe against the Red Army but remain too weak to threaten Luxembourg.

The injunction to remain democratic, combined with expressions of approval for an antidemocratic solution of the German problem is felt by the Germans to be hypocritical. They also resent that their own war-guilt should be held against them at a time when for twenty years their fellow countrymen have been exposed to oppression by a power that has been blatantly guilty of comparable atrocities.

Even if the Germans stand rightly condemned for Nazi atrocities, it is felt that they have sincerely repented and been sufficiently punished. Germans also ask where the signs of expiation may be found for Stalin's crimes, such as the Soviet liquidation of kulaks, concentration camp brutalities, and the massacre of the Polish officers corps. Have the Russians not been as expansionist as Hitler? Whereas the Germans have purged their Nazi leaders, guilty Soviet leaders, including Khrushchev, who fully participated in Stalin's crimes, neither repented nor were reproved.[13] This double standard —which regrettably though perhaps unavoidably exists—has a disturbing effect on the German mind. Soviet participation in the judgment of the Nuremberg war-crime trials is especially felt by the Germans to have been an unparalleled example of iniquity.

Similarly, the unreflective and arbitrary condemnation of German nationalism is hardly soothing for German ears. While past aggressiveness is to be deplored, every nation must be allowed a national feeling of its own. Without national sentiment there could be no nation. What is important is that national feelings should not place other nations in jeopardy. West German leaders point to their excellent record of the past twenty years: West Germany, it is

---

[13] ". . . The Communists have the cynicism always begotten by the ruthless exercise of power; they are not in the least put out by the accusations made against them. They have committed stupendous crimes, but they have never behaved like guilty men. . . ." John Plamenatz, *On Alien Rule and Self-Government* (London, 1960), p. 28.

said, has given proof of restraint, even given priority to European integration over the cause of national unity. It seems, therefore, out of place to flail Germany for some hypothetical ultranationalism. In fact, West German policy-makers and their Western colleagues are often hindered by a certain lack of patriotic feeling in the Federal Republic.[14] On the other hand, rightist extremism is now restricted to a fringe of the electorate. References to the unique Hitler phenomenon are inappropriate. Only the severe frustration of legitimate goals, it is argued, could restore the aggressive nationalism that all agree in condemning.

Most Germans feel that reunification is not only dictated by political wisdom but also prescribed by principles of morality. Offended righteousness can become a political force in concert with national sentiment. This has, in fact, been the technique of most modern expansionist states. Hitler and his propagandists were well aware of this when they constantly invoked "moral right" and "justice" in support of their theses, whether it was the rejection of the Versailles Treaty, the Austrian *Anschluss*—or even anti-Semitism. The difference between Hitlerite "righteous" claims and today's claims concerning the freedom of East Germany are evident. While the former should have been denied, even by force, the present claims should be supported within the limits of nonviolence.

The Germans are not unaware of the complexity of the reunification problem. The Communist thesis that reunification must not endanger the "social and economic achievements" of East Germany is not rejected out-of-hand by many intellectuals. While it is denied that this is a sufficient pretext for rejecting reunification, it is often admitted that the East German developments must be taken into account and that no economic or social *gleichschaltung* should take place without the consent of the population concerned.

Some have argued that German unity can be realized only if it is based on "ideals"; that is, given a moral foundation. Immanuel Kant deplored that perpetual peace was handled as a political rather than a moral problem;[15] German unity is sometimes viewed in the same fashion. A moral consciousness, it is claimed, must accompany Ger-

---

[14] Erhard, in his address to the newly elected Bundestag on November 10, 1965, complained that critical public opinion "has often enough made it difficult for the Germans to identify themselves with their State and their achievements after the war." *The Bulletin*, November 16, 1965, p. 5.

[15] This reference to Kant's *Zum ewigen Frieden* is made by Hermann Bortfeldt, *Die deutsche Einheit als ethische Entscheidung* [German unity as an ethical decision] (Frankfurt/M., 1962).

man aspirations for reunification. It is not sufficient that the non-German world should recognize the ethical imperative of German unity; Germans themselves must become conditioned to an "ideal" value. National sentiment, democracy, and social welfare are moral values relevant to reunification; therefore, they should receive priority over other considerations.[16] Germans should be morally prepared to receive back their separated co-nationals. Ethical worthiness might achieve what politics and force have failed to do.

Neo-Kantianism aside, the man-in-the-street as well as the leaders of the Federal Republic rest their case for reunification primarily on traditional national sentiment. This feeling is so spontaneous that it often defies rationalization. Nevertheless, it remains the primary force which shapes the quest for German unity.

The National Issue

Love for and faith in one's own nation, without hostility against others—an emotional attachment which Plamenatz[17] prefers to call "patriotism"—is a natural and indispensable concomitant of nationhood. If we think in terms of nation-states, we are bound to think in terms of traditional nationalism, the cause and effect being inseparable.

No uniform standards for national feeling can be set: it is quite evident that British, French, American, or Japanese nationalism differ from one another and are different from the national feeling of the Germans, both in essential and in particular forms. National character, largely influenced by this factor, is an important determinant of state action, sometimes even more so than institutions or the physical environment.[18]

National character and national sentiment are subject to historical and environmental changes. Besides this fluctuation, however, there is a more permanent element that can be located and described.[19]

It is, therefore, often asked whether the earlier traits of German

[16] Bortfeldt, *Die deutsche Einheit*, pp. 18–19.
[17] Plamenatz, *On Alien Rule and Self-Government*, p. 13.
[18] See Washington Pratt, *National Character in Action* (New Brunswick, N.J., 1961), esp. pp. 69–95, 152–57.
[19] "I do not contend that nationalism is unchanging, eternal, but merely that it is extraordinarily persistent and slow to change." Crane Brinton, *From Many One* (Cambridge, Mass., 1948), p. 74. See also Sir Harold Nicolson's address to the University College of Nottingham, England, as quoted by Pratt, *National Character in Action*, p. 38. For further pertinent information, see Hans J. Morgenthau, "Another 'Great Debate': The National Interest of the United States," *American Political Science Review*, December, 1952, pp. 961–98.

nationalism have been meaningfully altered by the traumatic events of the recent past? Or are these changes of a merely transient character, leaving unaltered the basic core of German nationalism? Undoubtedly, nazism and its downfall have created a natural reaction of deepest disillusionment, inhibiting national sentiment and resulting in an increased indifference toward national politics. Although the analogy may not be fully pertinent, a somewhat similar loss of national *élan* was perceptible in France after the long experience of the revolutionary and Napoleonic wars that ended in defeat and restoration. Aggressive French nationalism never regained its prior intensity.

During the period of occupation the national consciousness of the Germans seemed to descend to a rather low ebb, and this state of mind continued after West Germany had regained her sovereignty. The Social Democratic party had counted on an upsurge of national feeling when it prominently raised the question of German unity in its platform. But the West German electorate failed to react in the manner expected by Schumacher and some of his colleagues. Caution over reunification had become the *leitmotiv* of German political thinking, and certain proclivities to cosmopolitanism (so characteristic of the eighteenth-century intelligentsia) came to the fore. A combination of the guilt complex caused by Nazi excesses and the exhaustion of nationalist dynamism is probably the basic explanation for this prudence.[20]

But France, after her defeat of 1814, received no further blows and was not exposed to comparable pressures in the aftermath of Waterloo. Even her traditional national area remained intact. It is not surprising that the West and East Germans seek their unity, but it may be remarkable that up to now this desire has not been expressed in more violent and dangerous forms, especially in the Federal Republic.

There is all likelihood that the aggressive pattern of German nationalism as displayed by the Nazis has been a unique experience. Indeed, the Hitlerite ascendancy itself was caused by a singularly tragic concatenation of events. The appearance of another Hitler and the crossing of intense frustration and hyperbolic messianic nationalism may be considered an event not to be duplicated. Under present international conditions, even a united Germany

[20] German enthusiasm for European federation is partly explained by the "spiritual void left by the collapse of the Nazi myth." And sometimes this enthusiasm "seemed to express a half-conscious wish to escape from being Germans." Lowenthal, "The Germans Feel Like Germans Again," p. 36.

would no longer be the superpower of 1939–45. Still, we must try to determine whether the militant nationalism that preceded the Hitlerian hysteria can have managed to survive the Third Reich's apocalypse.

Ordinarily, the involuntary territorial division of a nation will inspire an irredentist reaction in the form of militant national self-consciousness. Another symptom is apt to be the concentration of national antagonism against the state which is blamed by public opinion for the loss suffered. This was the case of France when, after the annexation of Alsace-Lorraine, French nationalism became directed primarily against Germany.[21]

The inescapable traumatic effect of Germany's division is bound, sooner or later, to produce stronger national feeling. There are already signs of this.[22] The loss of Alsace-Lorraine, a relatively small portion of France, was sufficient to create sustained hostility, revanchism, and an acute Germanophobe sentiment in Paris. But the magnitude of German losses may better be compared with the reduction of Hungary after World War I, involving the loss of two thirds of her territory and one third of the ethnically Magyar population. This amputation fostered nationalist passion and almost inescapably led Hungary into an alliance with revisionist powers.[23] Similarly, the Federal Republic may be led to make common cause with any power or powers that effectively support its policy of German unity.[24]

A nationalist reaction could hardly be blamed on the Germans. Any nation, however peace-loving, would react aggressively against a large-scale amputation or division of its national territory. Ameri-

---

[21] Before 1870 French nationalism was essentially anti-British as a result of Napoleon's defeat; see Hans Kohn, *The Age of Nationalism—The First Era of Global History* (New York, 1962), p. 23.

[22] The recrudescence of nationalism in West Germany can partly be interpreted as a natural by-product of Gaullism. It is not the first time that French example fostered German national feeling which in the past had, in return, menaced France. See *New York Times*, November 21, 1965, and April 12, 1966; Flora Lewis, "Large Query About the New Germany," *New York Times Magazine*, January 7, 1962, pp. 11, 65–66.

[23] See Váli, *Rift and Revolt in Hungary*, p. 26.

[24] "The German people will favor the side that does the utmost to restore their unity, not with words—words are cheap—but in action. This may involve exhibiting more activity, elasticity and willingness to take risks than at present. There is no such thing as a policy without risks; all we can do is choose the lesser of two risks. The German people must be made to feel certain that the problem of their unity is in better hands with the democracies than with the Communists. . . ." Fritz Erler, "The Struggle for German Reunification," *Foreign Affairs*, April, 1956, p. 382.

cans should try to visualize their reactions if Texas, California, Arizona, and New Mexico were annexed by a Mexican superpower, all Americans were expelled from these areas, and, furthermore, the remaining United States west of the Mississippi were forcefully severed from the rest of the Union by an Iron Curtain separating families and friends.[25]

Increased German national self-assertion would not necessarily weaken their dedication to the European idea as long as these goals seemed compatible. Adenauer's genius was to convince his people of the identity of these two objectives, or at least their causal relationship. Although the inaccuracy of his analysis has, by now, become fairly obvious to the Germans, they are yet far from schizoid on the subject. But European integration is no substitute for German unity. If it ever became manifest that participation in the affairs of a federalized Europe had a permanently retarding effect on the realization of the national goal, then "Europe" would suffer. Similarly, Western obtuseness toward the German dilemma might hasten the choice of national priorities.

Depending on future developments, the following speculative assessments of the trend of German nationalism may be attempted:

1) A rejuvenated German nationalism is likely to acquire the spirit of "frontier nations," approximately like that of West Berlin. The German national sentiment of the people of West Berlin is today more forceful and militant than in West Germany proper. However, in a less conspicuous manner than Berlin, West Germany is also a boundary state and is aware of being exposed to the first blows which might be administered from the East. It is almost axiomatic that nations thus exposed to external pressures should develop a higher degree of internal cohesion [26] and increased militancy and singleness of purpose.[27]

2) The German psyche has in the past shown its capacity to conceive of an extended national mission. The vision of universal

[25] "There can be no lasting peace in Europe with dismembered Germany, any more than there could be a lasting peace in North America if other nations tried to separate the states or to put parts of them under Mexico. In the light of historical experience, the sound course is to give the Germans an incentive for abandoning their old ways and becoming a peaceful nation." Herbert Hoover and Hugh Gibson, *The Problems of Lasting Peace* (Garden City, N.Y., 1942), p. 233.

[26] See Ralf Dahrendorf, "The New Germanies—Restoration, Revolution, Reconstruction," *Encounter*, April, 1964, p. 58.

[27] The "stimulus of blows and pressures" is examined in its historical significance by Arnold J. Toynbee in his *A Study of History* (New York, 1957), abridgement of Vols. I–VI, pp. 108–25.

THE QUEST FOR A UNITED GERMANY

empire and the identification of German and European culture contributed to the debased messianic tendencies of nazism. Bellicose
transgressions on the rights of others were sometimes justified by
the Germans in the name of culture, history, or humanity.[28] While
present doctrines regarding the unity and continuity of the "German state" do not seem to exceed the limits of reasonable nationalism, they could change into a metaphysical ideology of
anti-communism, a spirit of crusade against the nefarious forces of
the East. This impulsion would not necessarily reproduce the irrational climate of nazism but might simply be reflected in a much
more dynamic foreign policy. Should the present drive for European integration become frustrated, Germans might be led to
identify their national goals with the spiritual reconquest of East
Europe.

3) A new charismatic leader might arise then to act as the long-
sought "redeemer." He might be easily a refugee from the eastern
marches or an offspring of those who had suffered the descent of
tragedy on the fatherland. Refugee segments of a population often
take over leadership in a divided or amputated country. They may
develop a sense of solidarity among themselves, consciously or unconsciously helping one another to reach key posts or eventually
the key post of the country. In Germany such a tendency might
also develop as a reaction against the "Rhenish clique of Adenauer,"
thrusting a new East-Elbian leadership into power.[29]

4) Since the division of Germany is largely the result of Soviet
policy, the weight of German national animosity is directed against
the Soviet Union and the Communist camp, in general. Still, the
West German government would find it hard or impossible in the
future to refuse a "deal" for reunification even at a high price.
Though at present the Federal Republic would probably not turn
away from the West even in exchange for reunification,[30] a protracted period of frustration and suspicion might lead to this result.

[28] Gaxotte, *Histoire de l'Allemagne*, Vol. I, p. 136.
[29] Franz Josef Strauss, former West German Defense Minister, warned that
a "new Führer-type" who "would promise and probably also acquire nuclear
weapons" might emerge if Germany continues to be discriminated against,
especially in the field of nuclear sharing. *New York Times*, August 27, 1965.
However, at the time of this writing, there is no sentiment in the Federal
Republic for the manufacture (which is forbidden by treaty) or acquisition
of nuclear weapons.
[30] Henry L. Roberts, *Russia and America—Dangers and Prospects* (New
York, 1956), p. 199.

This is why the Russians dread moderate but consistently anti-Russian German nationalism and would prefer to see an extremist, irrational sentiment develop in West Germany, one that might demand reunification at any price.[31]

5) The resurgence of nationalism, coupled with the mission to free East Germany from communism and to carry the standard of anti-communism might create a willingness to sacrifice democracy for the sake of national unity. Should the aim of reunification become the obsessive national objective, then West German internal politics would again, just as under Bismarck, become the victim of foreign policy.[32] This single-mindedness could cut short democracy in the Federal Republic and help to bring about an autocratic and centralized regime. Such a government would find it easier to come to an understanding with Moscow, possibly to the detriment of Poland, and to achieve a reversal of alliances. It might even risk plunging the world into disaster for the sake of its policy objectives. It must be emphasized, however, that there are presently no convincing signs of this development.[33] This writer does not believe that such a course would become tempting to the Germans unless they felt genuinely betrayed by the West or came to associate democracy with impotence. Before this happened, West Germany might turn to neutralism if it seemed conducive to German unity.[34] One wonders, furthermore, whether the Soviet Union would be a willing partner in such an event. At the moment, West Germans continue to act like investors unwilling to risk their capital. The

---

[31] "Premier Khrushchev, knowing that he can offer German nationalists something the West cannot now give . . . reckons they will some day court him. Last year he told a visitor the time will come when the Germans would want another Rapallo, another pact with the U.S.S.R." C. L. Sulzberger in *New York Times*, May 27, 1964. See also Lowenthal, "Can We Make Common Cause with Russia?" pp. 34–35, 70–74. Author denies any such realistic possibility.

[32] Such fear is expressed by Fritz René Allemann, *Bonn ist nicht Weimar* (Cologne, 1956), pp. 439–40.

[33] "Narrow nationalism presents neither an option nor a temptation to Germany. *La Germania farà da sè?* The old slogan about Germany looking out for herself does not stand the test of sobriety. The spirit of Rapallo is dead; no one need fear that the Federal Republic will settle the German problem in a 'deal' with Russia, thus double-crossing her allies and sneaking out of the Western community again." Theo Sommer, "For an Atlantic Future," *Foreign Affairs*, October, 1964, p. 125.

[34] Guttenberg, *Wenn der Westen will*, p. 193. Author believes that extreme nationalism in partitioned Germany would assume the form of neutralism or even pacifism.

lunatic fringe of neo-nazism does not, at present, constitute any danger. Only a dose of Faustian activism combined with anti-Western sentiment might lead Germany to burn her bridges.

6) In the view of General de Gaulle and others, great-power status implies the possession and control of nuclear weapons. The Federal Republic renounced the manufacture of nuclear arms in 1954. Since then the French have developed nuclear capabilities (and Communist China has advanced on the road to becoming a nuclear power). Up to now, the Federal Republic has refrained from openly claiming "nuclear equality," but it may not always willingly accept this inferior status in the Western alliance.[35] Whether West German nuclear weapons could be used to obtain concessions from the Soviet Union seems to depend on the condition of the Western nuclear arsenal and the disposition of future West German governments. German possession of nuclear weapons would be regarded as an extreme provocation by the Soviet camp; coupled with an aggressive foreign policy, it might vastly increase the risk of global war in which Germany might easily perish. But the Germans might also be led to conclude that a conventional war for German unity could be fought under the protective umbrella of a deterrent if the German finger were on the trigger. A German leadership which called upon its people to risk such hazards would be desperately irrational. The hypothesis may be grossly exaggerated, but it reveals the dangers inherent in the division of Germany. Some years ago a German writer told his people that Hitler "only risked World War II" without wanting it and that a World War III appears to be for him the only way to solve the question of Germany's reunification.[36]

Any German demand for nuclear equality was to be satisfied by the American plan for a multilateral nuclear force to be set up by NATO powers. Implementation of such a scheme may have forestalled German claims for nuclear forces of their own. The Soviet-led Eastern bloc strongly opposed the M.L.F. plan, precisely because of West German participation. They failed to realize that internationalization of these nuclear forces would have precluded exclusive German ownership and the possibility that this weapon could be used to further the reunification of Germany. It has been suggested that Soviet opposition to West German nuclear "sharing" might eventually result in what Moscow wished to avoid; namely,

---

[35] Robert R. Bowie, *Shaping the Future* (New York, 1964), p. 68.
[36] Johannes F. Barwick, *Die deutschen Trümpfe* (Stuttgart-Degenfeld, 1958), pp. 26–27.

the acquisition of "national" nuclear arms by the Federal Republic (just as the collapse of the European Defense Community resulted in a national West German Army).[37]

The Kiesinger cabinet abandoned claims to nuclear sharing but insisted that when acceding to a general convention banning proliferation of nuclear weapons, West Germany's right to the peaceful use of nuclear power and her protection against nuclear threats should be secured.

7) German nationalism is unlikely to be diverted from its aim to reunite Germany, an aim shared even more vehemently by the people of East Germany. For many the union is highly relevant, for others irrelevant, to the political and economic system of the Bonn Republic. Self-determination for the East Germans is presently congruous with the demand for reunification of the two Germanys.[38] As long as the D.D.R. is ruled by a dictatorial and externally supported regime, there appears to be no possibility that East Germany could develop genuine national self-consciousness. This alone might conceivably dampen the West German ardor for unification. As long as both West and East Germans continue to regard themselves as "Germans," the principle of the "identity of indiscernibles" must logically apply to them.[39] The appearance of a special East (and, therefore, West) German nationality is today a remote possibility, even if it has caused some anxiety.[40]

The mutations of German national sentiment will bear heavily on Germany's future. They also decisively affect the Cold War, European integration, and Atlantic partnership. Conversely, the problems surrounding these wider issues weigh heavily on the evolution of the German question.

[37] "Moscow should realize that its disregard of these internal German pressures simply reinforces the suspicion that its policies toward the M.L.F. are in fact governed by purely Machiavellian calculations, and that in reality it does not mind Germany taking a 'Chinese' path. A temperate evocation of the Soviets' own experience with Peking may drive home the lesson—which Marx also taught—that frustrated nationalism becomes simply more nationalistic; that nationalism satisfied and controlled by multilateral arrangements becomes internationalism." Zbigniew Brzezinski, "Moscow and the M.L.F.: Hostility and Ambivalence," *Foreign Affairs,* October, 1964, pp. 132-33.

[38] ". . . self-determination carries within itself the seeds of reunification." Klaus Bolling, *Republic in Suspense* (New York, 1964), p. 264.

[39] This is the philosophical doctrine that things cannot exist together as separate entities unless they have different attributes.

[40] See Paul Sethe, *Deutsche Geschichte im letzten Jahrhundert* (Frankfurt/M., 1960), p. 442.

The International Issue

Undoubtedly, the problem of Germany is the most portentous single territorial issue in our deeply divided world. As Senator J. W. Fulbright expressed it: "The division of Germany is a most important issue in itself, but its global and historical significance, like that of the arms race, is that it has a critical bearing on whether we shall have war or peace."[41]

The nature of the issue is such that neither any satisfactory *détente* nor compromise solution appears to be in view. Meaningful concessions by either side would necessarily be perilous. Any partial abandonment of the one-Germany doctrine would sabotage the logic of the Western position. Relaxation of Soviet control over East Germany would erode the *raison d'être* of the separate East German state and precipitate reunification. A modification of the status quo of Berlin would either reopen the floodgates to East German exodus, or, conversely, jeopardize the freedom of West Berlin. Another assessment of great-power stakes in the German issue is needed.

For the Soviet Union, its *pied-à-terre* in Germany serves multifarious purposes. Militarily, it is a glacis against potential aggressions from the West, and a springboard for a possible Communization of West Germany. It is one arm of a pincer surrounding the always doubtful Polish ally. The D.D.R. is also an important supplier of industrial articles to the Soviet camp. Finally, East Germany is the linchpin of the Soviet hegemonial system in East-Central Europe. In the thinking of the Kremlin, a merger of East and West Germany would significantly tilt the European and global balances of power in favor of the West.[42]

These reasons make East Germany so highly valuable for the Soviet Union. And yet, the Soviet leaders cannot fail to realize that their control depends on military subordination of a hostile population. East Germany has come to serve rather as a deterrent against the spread of Soviet propaganda than as an instrument of its propagation. This negative aspect is well symbolized by the awful spectacle of the Berlin Wall.

How far the unification of Germany might affect the European and global balances of power depends largely on the strategic

---

[41] Fulbright, *Old Myths and New Realities*, p. 69.

[42] For a detailed evaluation of Soviet interests in East Germany, see James L. Richardson, *Germany and the Atlantic Alliance* (Cambridge, Mass., 1966), pp. 353–54, 373–74.

estimates of the interested powers, their military doctrine, and the status of their forces-in-being. As long as we think in terms of "conventional" strategy, a population of seventeen million and the economic and territorial value of East Germany must be considered. On the other hand, if we refer to the nuclear balance of terror (perhaps more meaningful), reunification would hardly affect the existing equilibrium. It appears that a withdrawal of Soviet forces from East Germany would, in any case, have to be matched by a pullout of non-German NATO forces from West Germany, and possibly also with some change in united Germany's system of alliances or a new European security system.[43] Seen in this light, Soviet fears of a resurgent Germany seem much less plausible.

The argument, so often lightly accepted in the West, that the Soviet Union is justified in claiming a protective buffer zone against potential aggression is hardly supported by history or precedent. Before the German onslaught of 1941, the Soviet Union was instrumental in destroying the tier of small states separating it from Germany. Hitler's aggression was rendered possible by Polish partition. Historical experience shows that the middle nations would require guarantees against both Russia and Germany. Realistically, a separate East German state is less a protection against possible West German aggressive designs than an incentive for German irredentism. Economic gains derived from the control of East Germany should be weighed against the efforts of maintaining the present fragile regime, the expenses for armaments required because of the unsettled status of Europe, and the American presence in Germany. A genuine easing of tensions could promote trade between the entire West and East.

Even in terms of the balance of power, one may doubt whether the control of a hostile population is an asset. Unfortunately, ideology blurs this type of analysis for the Soviets: they are committed to expanding their sociopolitical system or at least preserving its frontiers. The loss of East Germany is likely to precipitate a chain reaction within the Communist countries of East-Central Europe, as the Kremlin feared during the Hungarian secession of

[43] Even the neutralization of Germany might, in this case, be considered. See Denis Healey: "It is . . . obvious that, unless there is a completely unforeseeable shift in world power relations, the reunification of Germany will depend on the neutralization of a united Germany. Neither side will be prepared to see the assets at present available to the other in a divided Germany increased by German reunification. In other words, the only basis for German reunification is some form of disengagement. . . ." Healey, "The Crisis in Europe," p. 147.

1956. Thus, no reasonable price can probably be found in the diplomatic arsenal of the West to pay for a Soviet evacuation of East Germany. No Soviet leader would be willing to preside over the liquidation of the Soviet-Communist empire. But the successors of Churchill who employed these words with regard to the British Empire were compelled by circumstances to do what the great Prime Minister had refused to do. Under the impact of "polycentrism" the Soviet camp is already disintegrating. But in East Germany—more than elsewhere—the relinquishment of Soviet control would be a crushing blow to the movement.

American and West European attitudes toward the German quest for unity are, as we have seen, affected by a variety of political, legal, and moral arguments. Not all opinions, even official, favor reunification. Some writers and politicians have, at different times, suggested that the Federal Republic simply recognize the existence of the two German states.[44] Arguments against reunification are partly moralistic, partly political. George Kennan advanced a more specious argument in recommending that the Germans "*faire bonne mine au mauvais jeux*" because their demand for reunification would impede the disintegration of the Soviet satellite empire.[45]

This last argument might hold for Poland and, possibly, for Czechoslovakia, but hardly for Hungary, Rumania, or Bulgaria where opposition to reunification is merely a sign of conformity with Soviet policies. But even if Kennan's argument were more than an assumption, it would seem unreasonable to ask the Germans to make such a costly sacrifice. One cannot ask a nation to surrender the right of self-preservation.

This writer, consequently, concludes that a Western abandonment of the German thesis of reunification is neither expedient nor realistic nor legally and morally tenable for the following principal reasons:

1) The present territorial status of Germany, as well as that of East-Central Europe, is an artificial, unnatural Soviet *fait accompli*. This status quo is abhorrent to the local populations; it is ultimately maintained by Soviet military strength and is, therefore, precarious and politically inexpedient. Whether recognized by the Western powers or not, it will continue to be a source of dangerous friction. Germans could only be expected to accept their present partition

[44] For instance, Neal, *War and Peace and Germany*, esp. pp. 100–109.
[45] Kennan, "Polycentrism and Western Policy," p. 180.

under duress, with all possible mental reservations. Recognition of the status quo would be an *ex post facto* justification of Soviet acts of imperialism and violence; it would encourage Soviet leaders to pursue such policies in the future. It would, at the same time, enormously undermine Western prestige in Germany, East-Central Europe, and elsewhere.

2) The Brussels powers and the United States are committed by treaty to support the demand for German reunification by peaceful means. Abandonment of this commitment would be a most flagrant hypocrisy. It would, reciprocally, allow the Germans to denounce these agreements or consider them null and void. This might lead to their desertion of the Western camp and their return to the dangerous *Schaukelpolitik*. It would give them a free hand to manufacture nuclear weapons. Shortly, it would result in a disintegration of the Western alliance system, already shaken by De Gaulle's independence, and could open the road to all forms of adventure. This time the Germans could not even be blamed for actions resulting directly from a Western breach of faith.

3) The abandonment of the quest for German unity would also sharply conflict with the deepest Western principles: self-determination, the democratic form of government, and fidelity to international commitments. This renunciation would endanger the Western positions all over the world and create worse anarchy in international relations.

4) Compromise solutions are also fraught with danger. It is, at present, impossible to conceive of any solution which would not imply a Western surrender. As has been proved by past experience, the avoidance of increased tension in Berlin is best served by maintenance of the status quo. Attempts to break the present deadlock on the problem of Germany through negotiated arms control or disengagement are unlikely to succeed without granting recognition to the D.D.R.—a step which Bonn cannot accept.[46]

These arguments demonstrate that any authentication of Germany's division would involve far greater dangers than we know today. Meaningful *détente* with the Soviet Union cannot be sought as long as the primary source of conflict cannot be tackled. The

---

[46] "The German Government shall make energetic efforts to ensure that no system of disarmament, relaxation or security measures is established on the concept of a divided Germany thus aggravating the partition of our country." Chancellor Erhard on November 10, 1965, before the Bundestag; German News Service, Washington, D.C., November 15, 1965.

dilemma of choosing between the processes of *détente* to reunification (as hinted by Moscow and Pankow) or reunification to a *détente* (as suggested by Bonn) may possibly be relieved by a step-by-step procedure.[47] But this could come about only if there existed any willingness on the part of the Soviet Union to envisage some eventual German unity without the red banner.

Until the Soviets consider self-determination for East Germany (even if remote or dependent on certain conditions), the meaningful relaxation of tension has no hope of being achieved. Temporary arrangements, such as the Berlin passes, are no substitutes for the real issue. No new "Spirit"—of Geneva or of Camp David—will be effective unless its content is, for a change, realistic.

The solution of the German problem, as we see it now, depends primarily on the attitude of the Soviet Union.[48] It is, however, likely that German initiative will more and more influence developments. It may even happen that the official "four-power" responsibility for Germany will largely be replaced by dialogue between the Federal Republic and the Soviet Union. In any case, the wisdom, moderation, and foresight of German leadership will be greatly taxed by future events. German political behavior is bound to become an important factor in the quest for the unity of the German nation.

Whither Germany?

Some twenty years after the termination of World War II, the German problem remains unsolved. Not even Moscow can pretend that it is settled; it seeks the conclusion of a peace treaty with Germany two decades after hostilities have ended—a unique situation in modern history. The so-called reality of the two German states cannot be considered a solution: chronic illness is no substitute for health. And Moscow itself regards the Berlin issue (which, after all, is only part of the German problem) as abnormal. While the West has so far found no *quid pro quo* to offer the Soviet Union for an abandonment of East Germany, Moscow, on its part, is

---

[47] See Max Frankel's article in *New York Times*, June 22, 1966: whether "the egg of détente must come before the chicken of a German settlement and peace" or vice versa.

[48] "Only Moscow can negotiate on German unity. East Berlin cannot; it is hopeless to talk with a regime about the terms for liquidating it. Therefore the only hope lies in creating a Soviet interest in restoring German unity." Fritz Erler, "The Alliance and the Future of Germany," *Foreign Affairs*, April, 1965, p. 438.

unable to offer any inducement to forestall the quest for German unity. No "oceans of trade" with the Soviet Union, no guarantee for a free city of Berlin, no assurances of friendship could persuade the Federal Republic to give up its demand for the self-determination of the East.

Similarly, it is unlikely that ideological inoculation can dissuade the great majority of East Germans from aspiring to join their "brothers and sisters" beyond the Iron Curtain. Genuine liberalization could easily put an end to the Communist regime in the D.D.R. and be a prologue to reunification.

Not only is the Western policy on Germany deadlocked; Soviet policy has also reached a *cul-de-sac*. The difference between the two positions is that the Russians are *in possession* of the coveted object (except for West Berlin), a circumstance which they can exhibit as a "reality." But the strategic bulge which the East German area presents may just as well become a liability to the Soviets. The fragility of the Russian military position is not properly appreciated by the West.[49]

The German position is evidently unshakeable: no more sacrifices can be expected from any Federal government that wants to stay in power. All the major parties agree on this. Chancellor Erhard gave this attitude pertinent expression when he told the Bundestag: "To divide what inherently belongs together, what cannot be conceived save as one entity, cannot be conducive to peace. . . . While the Soviet Union concedes the right of self-determination to all the young nations, it continues—with the arbitrariness of the victor—to withhold this right from us, and expects us to accept the regime it has installed on German soil."[50]

And Willy Brandt, Chairman of the SPD and putative Federal Chancellor, should his Party take over the government, expressed himself in similar terms:

Peace in our part of the world cannot be stable . . . as long as German division, as long as the division of Europe continues. . . .

Peace cannot be made secure by perpetuating arbitrariness and injustice. Humaneness is a point in the program of peace, thus implying the undoing of an arbitrary division.

This claim of the German people has nothing to do with National So-

[49] See Terence Prittie, "Again the Issue of the Two Germanys," *New York Times Magazine*, August 16, 1964, p. 10.

[50] From the Federal Chancellor's budget speech on October 15, 1964, *The Bulletin*, October 20, 1964, p. 3.

cialism. This claim demands no privilege for Germany. By this we do not assert a claim to other nations. It is the same right which others demand as well.

The right of self-determination serves peace. . . .[51]

Arguing that the division of Germany is a threat to peace, the Federal government and the West German political parties attempt to convince both the Soviet Union and their Western Allies of the necessity of reunification. So far, the Soviet Union has appeared little impressed by this argument; they, on their part, argue that the demand for reunification, and even more so, its realization, are threats to peace. Thus, they try to interchange cause and effect —a hazardous gimmick in international politics. Soviet propaganda never ceases to attack West Germany for alleged chauvinism, militarism, and revanchism. However, the great majority of Germans in the Federal Republic are, at present, neither chauvinistic nor militaristic. They merely desire unification of Germany or, at least, freedom for their eastern compatriots. They have no desire to get involved in another war which could bring about only the destruction of what they have sedulously rebuilt since World War II.

By depicting Germans as would-be aggressors, incorrigible and irresponsible chauvinists, Soviet propaganda is not only inaccurate but self-defeating. After all the ups and downs of their stormy history, Germans are now eager to live the life of other European nations: to have legitimate national borders and remain at peace. Of course, the question of their borders must first be settled. They would, most probably, be ready even to accept the loss of their Eastern Territories, but they would never consent that one third of their people should live under foreign constraint.[52]

In the past, Germans have often been told by their leaders, by the Kaiser and by Hitler, that they are something "special," something different from and better than other nations. The poem by Hoffman von Fallersleben, "*Deutschland, Detuschland über Alles,*" became a cherished national anthem because of its connotation of Germany's superiority over other nations, although it was never

[51] Executive Committee of the Social Democratic party of Germany, *News from Germany* (Bonn, September/October, 1964), pp. 1–2.

[52] How unreasonable the present division of Germany appears to the Germans is well put by a German writer who considers it unbelievable that for so many years it has been easier to travel "from Kassel to Hawaii than to Weimar two hours distant." Michael Freund, "Das Deutschland von Morgen," *Die politische Meinung* (September, 1964), p. 36.

meant by its author to inspire German imperalism.[53] Sadly, many Germans came to believe that their nation and race were something "special" or "particular," exalted above other European nations.

Because of its territorial division, Germany, willy-nilly, has again become something "special": a nation partitioned, without legitimized boundaries and with a divided exclave capital city. In short, it has again become an international problem of magnitude. But not only is Germany, against her will, a center of controversies, she is accused, particularly by the Soviets and their allies, of being a pariah and a danger to peace.[54]

Those discriminated against are often ready to discriminate against others. The Germans have gone full circle from inferiority to superiority a number of times in their turbulent history. At present, they are evidently something "special" and have been told to regard themselves as such, and they are suffering from this singularity. Eventually, they may again choose to remain special but not to suffer.

While Adenauer was content to pursue reunification rather passively, Erhard favored greater flexibility but did very little. Kiesinger initiated a "policy of movement," a policy which might involve certain limited risks. The hazards may subsequently become greater. The very "special" situation of Germany might induce leaders and pressure groups, even mass political movements, to demand special favors and special treatment. Unwise handling by friend and foe might compound this natural impatience and encourage less rational behavior than that displayed during the era of "no experiments." [55]

[53] The author composed his poem on the island of Helgoland which, at that time, was a British possession. The Federal Republic adopted the third verse as its national anthem. Leonhardt, *This Germany*, pp. 1–4.

[54] At a Senate subcommittee hearing, John J. McCloy, former High Commissioner in Germany, declared that "discrimination" against Germany remains a Soviet policy objective. "Kept from any form of sharing nuclear potentials and denied an equal place at the table because of the claim that Germany is still not a sovereignty in the same sense as France, we have the seeds of ill-will, reminiscent to me of the discriminatory provisions of Versailles. . . . This attitude to me is like a fire bell in the night." *New York Times*, May 26, 1966.

[55] "The almost constant formula of other European nations in repression of Germany has been to divide the race into separate states. But the resultant agitation of this virile people for union has been one of the prime causes of European wars. . . .

"How just was the German complaint about its treatment is not the whole question. When a nation is humiliated by defeat and becomes indurated with such beliefs and resentments, she becomes hopeless of reasoned action—and

287

Germany's present status is so unusual that she may cultivate resentment if other governments add to her exasperation by harping on matters which bear no direct relationship to her predicament. The West German leaders have recognized Germany's responsibility for the outbreak of World War II; but they consider it unjust that this war-guilt should be used as a rejoinder to Germany's present division, the Berlin Wall, or other incidentals of the Cold War. Twenty years after the end of the war, this is a psychological and political error.[56] After all, nobody belabored France for Napoleon twenty years after Waterloo, nor is it thought expedient to flail the present Soviet leaders for Stalin's crimes.

The "miracle" of German reconstruction showed that the Germans had not lost their spirit of sacrifice, their vitality and energy, or a healthy egotism, which this time was put to a constructive purpose. But these are not qualities which it is wise to warp by humiliating treatment. The Federal Republic is no superpower, and it is territorially vulnerable; but it still, apart from the Soviet Union, has the largest population, the highest gross national product, the greatest industrial capacity, and the biggest conventional army in Europe. Such a country, even because of its exposed position, will not be impotent in world politics. If nothing else, it can make its nuisance value felt; like De Gaulle's France, it might embark on an independent foreign policy. It is, therefore, important that Germany should not be constantly vexed and wounded by the rigors of partition. By allowing the Germans their due, one may prevent them in the future from aspiring to more than their share.[57]

The demand for restitution of Germany's 1937 frontiers appears to be an unreasonable demand on Poland. But the settlement of the Oder-Neisse question is, at present, prevented by the division of East and West Germany. It seems most likely that reunification could permit the first problem to be settled. It is, therefore, in the ultimate interest of Poland and other eastern neighbors that the present partition should end. Should the Communist confraternity

this, regardless of real rights and wrongs." Hoover and Gibson, *The Problems of Lasting Peace*, pp. 146–47.

[56] "One way to create German nationalism, German revanchism, German neuroticism, is to push war guilt on them, though for a time it was an appropriate thing to do." Herman Kahn, "Multilateral Force or Farce," *New York Times Magazine*, December 11, 1964, p. 104.

[57] Willy Brandt said that the Federal Republic was "economically a giant and politically a dwarf." *Die Zeit*, October 1, 1965. Franz Josef Strauss used the simile when writing: "We cannot in the long run have a Germany which is an economic giant and a political dwarf." Strauss, *The Grand Design*, p. 81.

lose thereby one of its members, the result could not be considered unreasonable.

The West must pursue relaxation of tensions without, however, yielding on the principle of German self-determination. With regard to Berlin, it seems inevitable to insist on the status quo, however embarrassing, because the Berlin problem can only be solved through a settlement of the problem of two Germanys.[58] In the meantime, both the Federal government and the Western powers must strive to seek arguments and create pressures to show Moscow that it cannot have its own way in Germany. The Kremlin must be made to realize that its position in East Germany is impractical and ultimately hopeless. It should be offered the alternative of giving up its hold in Germany for a price that can be met and with all face-saving devices. Of course, much depends on what the West may be able or willing to offer.

The Soviet Union holds the key which can open the solution of the German problem. The Russians must feel convinced that the price to be paid for their withdrawal from the German theatre would be an adequate compensation, in security, political influence, and prestige. This transaction might forestall violent and dangerous crises in their German area, and might possibly save some Soviet influence in East-Central Europe which could otherwise be lost. Soviet obduracy might one day backfire in the form of renewed German aggressiveness.

It is, of course, understood that Soviet abandonment of East Germany would be exceedingly difficult because of prestige and ideological implications. Domestic and intra-Communist affairs might impede its realization. On the other hand, domestic and, to some extent, foreign Communist opinion has always been artificially shaped by the Soviet leaders; moderation (like the withdrawal of rockets from Cuba) might be made to look heroic.

We assume that the disintegration of the Soviet camp will continue. Thus, the ideological value of maintaining a Communist

---

[58] This appears to be the policy of the Johnson administration. Ambassador George C. McGhee declared in Berlin on November 11, 1964: "I am authorized to tell . . . that this Administration will continue to pursue reunification as a major goal." Among the aims of United States foreign policy, the Ambassador mentioned: "(1) In Berlin, to stay and maintain the West's vital interests, against the day when Berlin again will become the capital of a united Germany. (2) In the problem of German reunification, to search untiringly for an opportunity for progress in the conviction that, until this division in the heart of Europe is healed, there can be no stability or security in Europe." *The Bulletin*, November 17, 1964, p. 3.

East Germany may be considerably reduced. If the German Democratic Republic remained the last tightly controlled People's Democracy, this would seem anachronistic even in the Communist
world. Its transformation into a democratically ruled country might
usefully assuage tensions that benefited no one. The Polish people
are seeking increased access to the West; in this perspective they
might welcome true democracy in East Germany. Whatever the
developments in East-Central Europe are to be, the Soviet state
appears over-extended in Europe. One day, it will have to reduce its
commitments and withdraw its forces behind its ethnic frontiers. A
succinct Western strategy can hasten this day.

History has never spoken a "last word" and does not know the
meaning of "impossible." What is needed is "patience and time,"
the advice given to his countrymen by the Russian Field Marshal
Kutuzov with regard to Napoleon's inflated pretensions. Capitulation before the shaky "reality" of the present East German regime
cannot seriously be expected from the Germans. We are told that,
while one can do various things with bayonets, one "cannot sit
on them." The East German regime relies substantially on bayonets,
and the Russians must be more aware of this than any outsider.
Stalin foresaw the situation when he suggested at Teheran to
Roosevelt and Churchill that Germany must be divided and held
divided, "in the long run by force if necessary."[59] What lapse of
time he meant by "long run" we do not know. But John Maynard
Keynes's comment that "in the long run, we all will be dead" was
more apt because Stalin never lived to see the end of the German
problem. Stalin had also said, "Hitlers come and Hitlers go but the
German nation goes on forever." He could not then imagine but
one German nation, one far from being divided "by force."

[59] See Chapter I, p. 10.

BIBLIOGRAPHY

The literature on the German problem is overabundant. German concern, as can be expected, for their country's division is reflected by the gargantuan dimension of publications on this issue. While there is an abundance of books and articles, both within and outside Germany, dealing with particular aspects of this labyrinthian question, there hardly exists any fairly comprehensive study, not even in the German language, on the problem of German reunification.

The following list of publications is strictly selective. Limitations of space even forbade the listing of all articles consulted. Furthermore, many of the observations in this book rely on views expressed to this writer by persons in and outside Germany whose anonymity had to be safeguarded. In this respect, too, the source material hereafter submitted is necessarily incomplete.

In case both English and German renditions of publications were available, as a rule only the English language edition is listed. Among several editions of the same book, the one I have used has been included in this bibliography.

The division of published material into primary and secondary sources, as well as the separation of historical and background works from books and articles closely related to the topic, though often arbitrary, has been adopted for reasons of clarity and usefulness.

PRIMARY SOURCES

Documents and Official Publications

Berlin, Senat von. *Berlin—Ringen um Einheit und Wiederaufbau, 1948–1951.* Berlin: Spitzing, 1962.

Documents on International Affairs, 1951. London: Oxford University Press (for the Royal Institute of International Affairs), 1954.

Documents on International Affairs, 1952. London: Oxford University Press (for the Royal Institute of International Affairs), 1955.

Documents on International Affairs, 1953. London: Oxford University Press (for the Royal Institute of International Affairs), 1956.

Documents on International Affairs, 1954. London: Oxford University Press (for the Royal Institute of International Affairs), 1957.

Documents on International Affairs, 1955. London: Oxford University Press (for the Royal Institute of International Affairs), 1958.

Documents on International Affairs, 1958. London: Oxford University Press (for the Royal Institute of International Affairs), 1962.

Documents on International Affairs, 1959. London: Oxford University Press (for the Royal Institute of International Affairs), 1963.

Dokumente zur Berlin-Frage, 1944–1962, edited by the Forschungsinstitut der Deutschen Gesellschaft für Auswärtige Politik (Research Institute of the German Foreign Policy Association). Munich: Oldenbourg, 1962.

Embree, George D. (ed.). *The Soviet Union and the German Question, Sept. 1958–June 1961* (Documents). The Hague: Nijhoff, 1963.

Foreign Affairs Bulletin (published by the Press Department of the Ministry of Foreign Affairs of the German Democratic Republic).

Hillgruber, A. *Berlin—Dokumente, 1944–1961.* Darmstadt: Stephan, 1961.

Jaksch, Wenzel. *Germany and Eastern Europe—Two Documents of the Third German Bundestag.* Bonn: Atlantic-Forum, 1962.

Khrushchev, Nikita S. *The Soviet Stand on Germany—Nine Key Documents.* New York: Crosscurrents, 1961.

Mampel, Siegfried. *Die Verfassung der sowjetischen Besatzungszone Deutschlands.* Frankfurt/M.: Metzner, 1962.

———. *Der Sowjetsektor von Berlin.* Frankfurt/M.: Metzner, 1963.

Oppen, Beate Ruhm von (ed.). *Documents on Germany Under Occupation, 1945–1954.* London: Oxford University Press, 1955.

Pollock, James K., and John C. Lane (eds.). *Source Materials on the Government and Politics of Germany.* Ann Arbor, Michigan: Wahrs, 1964.

Secretary of State for Foreign Affairs. *Selected Documents on Germany and the Question of Berlin, 1944–1961.* London: Her Majesty's Printing Office, 1961.

Siegler, Heinrich von (ed.). *Wiedervereinigung und Sicherheit Deutschlands* (Documents). 5th ed. Bonn: Siegler & Co., 1964.

SPD Auslandsbrief (issued by the Information Service of the Social Democratic Party of Germany).

The Bulletin (issued by the Press and Information Office of the German Federal Government).

U.S. Department of State. *The Conferences at Malta and Yalta.* Washington, D.C.: Government Printing Office, 1955.

U.S. Department of State. *The Geneva Meeting of Foreign Ministers, October 27–November 16, 1955.* Washington, D.C.: Government Printing Office, 1955.

U.S. Department of State. *American Foreign Policy, 1950–1955.* (Basic Documents) Vols. I–II. Washington, D.C.: Government Printing Office, 1957.

U.S. Department of State. *Conferences at Cairo and Tehran, 1943.* Washington, D.C.: Government Printing Office, 1961.

U.S. Senate. *A Decade of American Foreign Policy.* (Basic Documents, 1941–1949) Washington, D.C.: Government Printing Office, 1950.

U.S. Senate. *Documents on Germany, 1944–1961.* Washington, D.C.: Government Printing Office, 1961.

Verhandlungen des Deutschen Bundestages. Vols. 22 and 23 (1955). Bonn: Deutscher Bundes-Verlag, 1955.

Memoirs, Diaries, and Reference Books

Adenauer, Konrad. *Memoirs, 1945–1953.* Chicago: Regnery, 1966.

Bundesministerium für gesamtdeutsche Fragen (Federal Ministry of All-German Affairs). *SBZ (Sowjetische Besatzungszone) von 1955 bis 1956.* Bonn: Deutscher Bundes-Verlag, 1958.

———. *SBZ von 1957 bis 1958*. Bonn-Berlin: 1960.
———. *SBZ von 1945 bis 1954*. Bonn-Berlin: 1961.
———. *SBZ-Biographie*. Bonn-Berlin: 1961.
———. *SBZ von A bis Z*. Bonn: 1966.
Byrnes, James F. *Speaking Frankly*. New York: Harper, 1947.
Churchill, Winston S. *The Second World War*. 6 vols. Boston: Houghton Mifflin, 1950, 1951, and 1953.
Clay, Lucius D. *Decision in Germany*. Garden City, N.Y.: Doubleday, 1950.
Eisenhower, Dwight D. *Crusade in Europe*. Garden City, N.Y.: Doubleday, 1948.
———. *Mandate for Change, 1953-1956: The White House Years*. Garden City, N.Y.: Doubleday, 1963.
———. *Waging Peace, 1956-1961: The White House Years*. Garden City, N.Y.: Doubleday, 1965.
Hull, Cordell. *Memoirs of*, Vol. II. New York: Macmillan, 1948.
Leahy, William D. *I Was There*. New York: Whittlesey, 1950.
Murphy, Robert. *Diplomat Among Warriors*. Garden City, N.Y.: Doubleday, 1964.
Schlüter, Hilmar Werner. *Die Wiedervereinigung Deutschlands—Ein zeitgeschichtlicher Leitfaden*. Bad Godesberg: Hohwacht, 1964.
Smith, Walter Bedell. *My Three Years in Moscow*. Philadelphia: Lippincott, 1950.
Stettinius, Edward R., Jr. *Roosevelt and the Russians—The Yalta Conference*. Garden City, N.Y.: Doubleday, 1949.
Survey of International Affairs, 1939-1946: Four Power Control in Germany and Austria. London: Oxford University Press (for the Royal Society of International Affairs), 1956.
Survey of International Affairs, 1947-1948. London: Oxford University Press, 1952.
Survey of International Affairs, 1949-1950. London: Oxford University Press, 1953.
Survey of International Affairs, 1951. London: Oxford University Press, 1954.
Survey of International Affairs, 1955-1956. London: Oxford University Press, 1960.
Truman, Harry S. *Memoirs*. 2 vols. Garden City, N.Y.: Doubleday, 1955, 1956.
Ulbricht, Walter. *Die Entwicklung des deutschen volksdemokratischen Staates, 1945-1958*. (Speeches) 2d ed. Berlin (East): Dietz, 1959.
Welles, Sumner. *The Time for Decision*. New York: Harper, 1944.

German Newspapers and Periodicals

Archiv des öffentlichen Rechts (Tübingen)
Aussenpolitik (Stuttgart)
Christ und Welt (Stuttgart)
Der Monat (Berlin)

Der Spiegel (Hamburg)
Deutsche Aussenpolitik (East Berlin)
Die Welt (Hamburg)
Die Zeit (Hamburg)
Düsseldorfer Zeitung (Düsseldorf)
Europe-Archiv (Bonn)
Frankfurter Allgemeine Zeitung (Frankfurt/M.)
Frankfurter Rundschau (Frankfurt/M.)
Hannoversche Allgemeine Zeitung (Hanover)
Münchner Merkur (Munich)
Neues Deutschland (East Berlin)
Rheinischer Merkur (Cologne)
Rhein-Neckar Zeitung (Mannheim)
Sonntagsblatt (Hamburg)
Stuttgarter Zeitung (Stuttgart)
Süddeutsche Zeitung (Munich)
Tagesspiegel (Berlin)
The German Tribune (Hamburg)
Vierteljahrshefte für Zeitgeschichte (Stuttgart)

SECONDARY SOURCES

Historical and Background Works

Aron, Raymond. *Paix et Guerre entre les Nations*. Paris: Calmann-Lévy, 1962.

Bossenbrook, William J. *The German Mind*. Detroit: Wayne State University Press, 1961.

Bossenbrook, William J. (ed.). *Mid-Twentieth Century Nationalism*. Detroit: Wayne State University Press, 1965 (with an article by the editor on "German Nationalism and Fragmentation," pp. 15–32).

Bracher, Karl Dietrich. *Die Auflösung der Weimarer Republik*. Stuttgart: Ring-Verlag, 1957.

Brinton, Clarence Crane. *From Many One*. Cambridge, Mass.: Harvard University Press, 1948.

Bühler, Johannes. *Deutsche Geschicte*. Vols. 1–6. Berlin: De Gruyter, 1960.

Burks, R. V. *The Dynamics of Communism in Eastern Europe*. Princeton, N.J.: Princeton University Press, 1961.

Carr, Edward Hallett. *Nationalism and After*. New York: Macmillan, 1945.

———. *German-Soviet Relations Between the Two World Wars*. Baltimore: The Johns Hopkins Press, 1951.

Craig, Gordon A. *From Bismarck to Adenauer: Aspects of German Statecraft*. Baltimore: The Johns Hopkins Press, 1958.

Dehio, Ludwig. *Germany and World Politics in the Twentieth Century*. New York: Knopf, 1960.

Deutsch, Karl W., and William J. Folts (eds.). *Nation-Building*. New York: Atherton, 1966.

Dill, Marshall, Jr. *Germany: A Modern History*. Ann Arbor, Mich.: University of Michigan Press, 1962.

Epstein, Klaus. *The Genesis of German Conservatism*. Princeton, N.J.: Princeton University Press, 1966.

Feis, Herbert. *Churchill, Roosevelt, Stalin—The War They Waged and the Peace They Sought*. Princeton, N.J.: Princeton University Press, 1957.

———. *Between War and Peace—The Potsdam Conference*. Princeton, N.J.: Princeton University Press, 1960.

Fischer, Ruth. *Stalin and German Communism*. Cambridge, Mass.: Harvard University Press, 1948.

Flenley, Ralph. *Modern German History*. Rev. ed. New York: Dutton, 1964.

Franz, Günther (ed.). *Teilung und Wiedervereinigung: Eine weltgeschichtliche Übersicht*. Göttingen: Musterschmidt, 1963.

Freund, Gerald. *Unholy Alliance: Russian-German Relations from the Treaty of Brest-Litovsk to the Treaty of Berlin*. London: Chatto & Windus, 1957.

Gaxotte, Pierre. *Histoire de l'Allemagne*. Vols. I and II. Paris: Flammarion, 1963.

Haffner, Sebastian. *Die sieben Todsünden des Deutschen Reiches— Grundfehler deutscher Politik nach Bismarck, damals und heute*. Hamburg: Nannen, 1965.

Hinrichs, Carl, and Wilhelm Berges (eds.). *Die Deutsche Einheit als Problem der europäischen Geschichte*. Stuttgart: Ernst Klett, 1959.

Hoover, Herbert, and Hugh Gibson. *The Problems of Lasting Peace*. Garden City, N.Y.: Doubleday, 1942.

Jaksch, Wenzel. *Europe's Road to Potsdam*. New York: Praeger, 1963.

Kertesz, Stephen D. *The Fate of East Central Europe*. Notre Dame: University of Notre Dame, 1956.

King, Jere Clemens. *Foch Versus Clemenceau—France and German Dismemberment, 1918–1919*. Cambridge, Mass.: Harvard University Press, 1960.

Klemperer, Klemens von. *Germany's New Conservatism—Its History and Dilemma in the Twentieth Century*. Princeton, N.J.: Princeton University Press, 1957.

Kochan, Lionel. *The Struggle for Germany, 1914–1945*. Edinburgh: Aldine, 1963.

Kohn, Hans (ed.). *German History—Some New German Views*. Boston: Beacon, 1954.

Kohn, Hans. *The Idea of Nationalism—A Study in Its Origins and Background*. New York: Macmillan, 1958.

———. *The Mind of Germany—Education of a Nation*. New York: Scribner, 1960.

Kraus, Herbert. *Die Oder-Neisse Linie*. Göttingen: Rudolf Müller, 1959.

Krieger, Leonard. *The German Idea of Freedom*. Boston: Beacon, 1957.

Laqueur, Walter. *Russia and Germany—A Century of Conflict*. Boston: Little, Brown, 1965.

Lauret, René. *France and Germany*. Chicago: Regnery, 1964.

Leonhardt, Walter. *This Germany: The Story Since the Third Reich.* Greenwich, Conn.: New York Graphic Society, 1964.

Lesser, Jonas. *Germany: The Symbol and the Deed.* New York: Yoseloff, 1965.

Mann, Golo. *Deutsche Geschichte des Neunzehnten and Zwanzigsten Jahrhunderts.* Frankfurt/M.: Fischer, 1961.

Meinecke, Friedrich. *The German Catastrophe.* Cambridge, Mass.: Harvard University Press, 1950.

Moras, Joachim, and Hans Paeschke (eds.). *Deutscher Geist zwischen Gestern und Morgen.* Stuttgart: Deutsche Verlags-Anstalt, 1954.

Morgenthau, Henry, Jr. *Germany Is Our Problem.* New York: Harper, 1945.

Niebuhr, Reinhold. *The Structure of Nations and Empires.* New York: Scribner, 1959.

Pieper, Hugo. *Preussentum westdeutscher Herkunft—Über Preussentum zum Reich.* Düsseldorf: Kämmerer, 1957.

Pinson, Koppel S. *Modern Germany—Its History and Civilization.* 2nd ed. New York: Macmillan, 1966.

Plamenatz, John Petrov. *On Alien Rule and Self-Government.* London: Longmans, 1960.

Platt, Washington. *National Character in Action—Intelligence Factors in Foreign Relations.* New Brunswick, N.J.: Rutgers University Press, 1961.

Plessner, Helmuth. *Die verspätete Nation—Über die Verführbarkeit bürgerlichen Geistes.* Stuttgart: Kohlhammer, 1962.

Pross, Harry. *Vor und nach Hitler—Zur deutschen Sozialpathologie.* Freiburg/Br.: Walter, 1962.

Rauschning, Hermann. *Deutschland zwischen West und Ost.* Berlin-Hamburg: Christian, 1950.

Schreiber, Hermann. *Teuton and Slav: The Struggle for Central Europe.* London: Constable, 1965.

Sethe, Paul. *Deutsche Geschichte im letzten Jahrhundert.* Frankfurt/M.: Scheffler, 1960.

Shafer, Boyd C. *Nationalism: Myth and Reality.* New York: Harcourt, Brace, 1955.

Sherwood, Robert E. *Roosevelt and Hopkins.* New York: Harper, 1948.

Snell, John L. (ed.). *The Meaning of Yalta—Big Three Diplomacy and the New Balance of Power.* Baton Rouge, La.: Louisiana State University Press, 1956.

———. *The Nazi Revolution—Germany's Guilt or Germany's Fate?* Boston: Heath, 1959.

Snell, John L. *Wartime Origins of the East-West Dilemma Over Germany.* New Orleans, La.: Hauser, 1959.

Snyder, Louis L. *From Bismarck to Hitler—The Background of Modern German Nationalism.* Williamsport, Penn.: Bayard, 1935.

Stern, Fritz. *The Politics of Cultural Despair—A Study in the Rise of the German Ideology.* Berkeley, Calif.: University of California Press, 1961.

Stimson, Henry L., and McGeorge Bundy. *On Active Service in Peace and War.* New York: Harper, 1948.

Strang, Lord. *Home and Abroad.* London: André Deutsch, 1956.

Strauss, Harold. *The Division and Dismemberment of Germany.* Geneva, 1951.

Váli, Ferenc A. *Rift and Revolt in Hungary—Nationalism Versus Communism.* Cambridge, Mass.: Harvard University Press, 1961.

Viereck, Peter. *Conservatism Revisited—The Revolt Against Revolt.* London: John Lehmann, 1950.

Vogt, Hannah. *The Burden of Guilt—A Short History of Germany, 1914–1945.* New York: Oxford, 1964.

Wagner, Wolfgang. *The Genesis of the Oder-Neisse Line.* Stuttgart: Brentano, 1957.

———. *Die Teilung Europas: Geschichte der sowjetischen Expansion, 1918–1941.* Stuttgart: Deutsche Verlagsanstalt, 1959.

Wheeler-Bennet, John. *The Nemesis of Power.* New York: Macmillan, 1953.

Wright, Gordon, and Arthur Mejia, Jr. (eds.). *An Age of Controversy: Discussion Problems in Twentieth-Century European History.* New York: Dodd, Mead, 1963.

Books

Allemann, Fritz René. *Bonn is nicht Weimar.* Cologne: Kiepenheuer, 1956.

———. *Zwischen Stabilität und Krise.* Munich: Piper, 1963.

Almond, Gabriel A. (ed.). *The Struggle for Democracy in Germany.* Chapel Hill, N.C.: University of North Carolina Press, 1949.

Altmann, Rüdiger. *Das Erbe Adenauers.* Stuttgart: Seewald, 1960.

———. *Das deutche Risiko: Aussenpolitische Perspektiven.* Stuttgart: Seewald, 1962.

Arndt, Adolf. *Der deutsche Staat als Rechtsproblem.* Berlin: de Gruyter, 1960.

Augstein, Rudolf. *Konrad Adenauer.* London: Secker & Warburg, 1964.

Baring, Arnulf. *Der 17. Juni 1953.* Bonn: Bundesmin. für Gesamtdeutsche Fragen, 1957.

Barwick, Johannes. *Die deutschen Trümpfe.* Stuttgart: Seewald, 1958.

Bathurst, M. E., and J. L. Simpson. *Germany and the North Atlantic Community.* London: Stevens, 1956.

Bender, Peter. *Offensive Entspannung—Möglichkeit für Deutschland.* Cologne-Berlin: Kiepenheuer, 1964.

Birrenbach, Kurt. *Die Zukunft der Atlantischen Gemeinschaft.* Freiburg/Br.: Rombach, 1962.

Black, Joseph E., and Kenneth W. Thompson (eds.). *Foreign Policies in a World of Change.* New York: Harper & Row, 1963 (with a contribution by Karl Dietrich Bracher on the "Foreign Policy of the Federal Republic of Germany").

Bluhm, Georg. *Die Oder-Neisse-Linie in der deutschen Aussenpolitik.* Freiburg/Br.: Rombach, 1963.

Bölling, Klaus. *Republic in Suspense: Politics, Parties, and Personalities in Postwar Germany.* New York: Praeger, 1956.

Bortfeldt, Hermann. *Die deutsche Einheit als ethische Entscheidung.* Frankfurt/M.: Europ. Verlaganstalt, 1962.

Bowie, Robert R. *Shaping the Future—Foreign Policy in the Age of Transition.* New York: Columbia University Press, 1964.

Brandt, Willy. *The Ordeal of Co-Existence.* Cambridge, Mass.: Harvard University Press, 1963.

Braunthal, Gerard, *The Federation of German Industry in Politics.* Ithaca, N.Y.: Cornell University Press, 1965.

Brecht, Arnold. *Wiedervereinigung—Drei Vorlesungen* (three lectures at the University of Heidelberg, July, 1957). Munich: Nymphenburger Verlag, 1957.

Bregman, Aleksander. *Jak Swiat Swiatem?* (For as Long as the World Remains the World?), *Polish, German Relations Yesterday, Today, and Tomorrow.* London: Polska Fundacja Kulturalna, 1964.

Brentano, Heinrich von. *Germany and Europe—Reflections on German Foreign Policy.* New York: Praeger, 1964.

Brzezinski, Zbigniew K. *Alternative to Partition—For a Broader Conception of America's Role in Europe.* New York: McGraw-Hill, 1965.

Bürger, G. A. *Die Legende von 1952.* Celle: Pohl, 1959.

Büsch, Otto, and Peter Furth. *Rechtsradikalismus im Nachkriegsdeutschland.* Berlin and Frankfurt/M.: Franz Vahlen, 1957.

Butz, Otto. *Germany: Dilemma for American Foreign Policy.* Garden City, N.Y.: Doubleday, 1954.

Castellan, Georges. *DDR: Allemagne de l'Est.* Paris: Seuil, 1955.

Chamberlin, William Henry. *The German Phoenix.* New York: Duell, Sloan & Pearce, 1963.

Collier, David S., and Kurt Glaser (eds.). *Berlin and the Future of Eastern Europe.* Chicago: Regnery, 1963.

Conant, James B. *Federal Republic of Germany—Our New Ally.* (Lecture) Minneapolis: University of Minnesota, 1957.

——. *Germany and Freedom—A Personal Appraisal.* Cambridge, Mass.: Harvard University Press, 1958.

Conlon, William H. *Berlin, Beset and Bedevilled: Tinderbox of the World.* New York: Fountainhead, 1963.

Cornides, Wilhelm. *Die Weltmächte und Deutschland—Geschichte der jüngsten Vergangenheit, 1945–1955.* Tübingen: Wunderlich, 1957.

Dalma, Alfons. *Hintergründe der Berlin-Krise.* Karlsruhe: Condor, 1962.

Daniel, Jens. *Deutschland—Ein Rheinbund?* Darmstadt: Leske, 1953.

Davidson, Basil. *Germany: What Now?* London: Muller, 1950.

Decker, Günter. *Das Selbstbestimmungsrecht der Nationen.* Göttingen: Otto Schwarz, 1955.

Deuerlein, Ernst. *Die Einheit Deutschlands.* Frankfurt/M.: Metzner, 1961.

Deutsch, Karl W., and Lewis J. Edinger. *Germany Rejoins the Powers.* Stanford, Calif.: Stanford University Press, 1959.

Dönhoff, Marion, Rudolf Walter Leonhardt, and Theo Sommer. *Reise in ein ferners Land—Bericht über Kultur, Wirtschaft and Politik der DDR.* Hamburg: Nannen, 1964.

Dornberg, John. *Schizophrenic Germany.* New York: Macmillan, 1961.

Edinger, Lewis J. *Kurt Schumacher: A Study in Personality and Political Behavior.* Stanford, Calif.: Stanford University Press, 1965.

Eich, Hermann. *The Unloved Germans.* New York: Stein & Day, 1965.

Epstein, Klaus. *Germany After Adenauer.* New York: Foreign Policy Association, 1964.

Erfurt, Werner. *Die sowjetrussische Deutschland-Politik.* Esslingen: Bechtle, 1956.

Erler, Fritz. *Ein Volk sucht seine Sicherheit.* Frankfurt/M.: Europ. Verlagsanstalt, 1961.

Ernst, Fritz. *Germans and Their Modern History.* New York: Columbia University Press, 1966.

Eschenburg, Theodor. *Die deutsche Frage—Verfassungsprobleme der Wiedervereinigung.* Munich: Oldenbourg, 1959.

Faust, Fritz. *Das Potsdamer Abkommen und seine völkerrechtliche Bedeutung.* 3d ed. Frankfurt/M.: Metzner, 1964.

Feld, Werner. *Reunification and West German-Soviet Relations.* The Hague: Nijhoff, 1963.

Fischer, Fritz. *Griff nach der Weltmacht.* Düsseldorf: Droste, 1962.

Fischer-Balling, E. *Besinnung auf uns Deutsche: eine Geschichte der nationalen Selbsterfahrung and Weltwirkung.* Düsseldorf: Verlag Pol. Bildung, 1957.

Flach, Karl-Hermann. *Erhards schwerer Weg.* Stuttgart: Seewald, 1963.

Forster, Thomas M. *NVA—Die Armee der Sowjetzone.* Cologne: Markus Verlag, 1966.

Freund, Gerald. *Germany Between Two Worlds.* New York: Harcourt, Brace, 1961.

Freymond, Jacques. *The Saar Conflict, 1945–1955.* London: Stevens, 1960.

Fulbright, J. W. *Old Myths and New Realities.* New York: Vintage, 1964.

Gablentz, O. M. von der. *Die Berlin-Frage in ihrer weltpolitischen Verflechtung, 1944–1963.* Munich: Oldenbourg, 1963.

———. *The Berlin Question in Its Relations to World Politics, 1944–1963.* Munich: Oldenbourg, 1964.

Golay, John F. *The Founding of the Federal Republic of Germany.* Chicago: University of Chicago Press, 1958.

Göttingen Research Committee, The. *Eastern Germany:* Vol. I, *Law* (1961); Vol. II, *History* (1963); Vol. III, *Economy* (1960). Würzburg: Holzner.

Gottlieb, Manuel. *The German Peace Settlement and the Berlin Crisis.* New York: Paine-Whitman, 1960.

Gradl, Johann Baptist, Karl Mommer, Erich Mende, and Herbert Schneider. *Gibt es noch Wege zur Wiedervereinigung?* Hamburg: Hermann, 1960.

Grewe, Wilhelm G. *Deutsche Aussenpolitik der Nachkriegszeit.* Stuttgart: Deutsche Verlagsanstalt, 1960.

Griffith, William E. *German Problems and American Policies.* (Mimeographed) Cambridge, Mass.: M.I.T., Center for International Studies, 1965.

Griffith, William E. (ed.). *Communism in Europe.* 2 vols. Cambridge, Mass.: M.I.T., 1966 (with a contribution by Carola Stern on "East Germany," in Vol. 2, pp. 41–145).

Grosser, Alfred. *Die Bonner Demokratie.* Düsseldorf: Rauch, 1960.

———. *The Federal Republic of Germany—A Concise History.* New York: Praeger, 1964.

Guttenberg, Karl-Theodor Freiherr von und zu. *Wenn der Westen will: Plädoyer für eine mutige Politik.* Stuttgart: Seewald, 1964.

Habe, Hans. *Our Love Affair with Germany.* New York: Putnam, 1953.

Hacker, Jens. *Die Rechtslage Berlins—Die Wandlungen in der sowjetischen Rechtsauffassung.* Bonn: Deutscher Bundesverlag, 1965.

Hammarskjold Forums (ed.). *The Issues in the Berlin-German Crisis.* Dobbs Ferry, N.Y.: Oceana, 1963.

Hangen, Welles. *The Muted Revolution.* New York: Knopf, 1966.

Harcourt, Robert d'. *L'Allemagne d'Adenauer à Erhard.* Paris: Flammarion, 1964.

Hartmann, Frederick H. *Germany Between East and West—The Reunification Problem.* Englewood Cliffs, N.J.: Prentice-Hall, 1965.

Hauck, Christian W. *Endlösung Deutschland.* Munich: Drömer, 1963.

Healey, Denis. *A Neutral Belt in Europe?* London: Fabian Society, 1958.

Heidenheimer, Arnold J. *The Governments of Germany.* New York: Crowell, 1961.

Hinterhoff, Eugène. *Disengagement.* London: Stevens, 1959.

Hiscocks, Richard. *Democracy in Western Germany.* London: Oxford University Press, 1957.

———. *The Adenauer Era.* Philadelphia: Lippincott, 1966.

Holbick, Karel, and Henry Myers. *Postwar Trade in Divided Germany—The Internal and International Issues.* Baltimore: The Johns Hopkins Press, 1964.

Hollos, F. T. *Zur Kontroverse über den gegenwärtigen Status Deutschlands.* Erlangen, 1948.

Horne, Alistair. *Return to Power.* New York: Praeger, 1956.

Hubatsch, Walther. *Deutsche Einheit geschichtlich betrachtet: Erinnerungen und Ausblicke.* Hanover: Heimatdienst, 1957.

———. *Die deutsche Frage.* Würzburg: Plötz, 1961.

Jaksch, Wenzel. *Westeuropa—Osteuropa—Sowjetunion: Perspektiven wirtschaftlicher Zusammenarbeit.* Bonn: Atlantic-Forum, 1965.

Jaspers, Karl. *Freiheit and Wiedervereinigung.* Munich: Piper, 1960.

———. *The Question of German Guilt.* New York: Capricorn Books, 1961.

———. *Wohin treibt die Bundesrepublik?* Munich: Piper, 1966.

Jenke, Manfred. *Verschwörung von Rechts? Ein Bericht über den Rechtsradikalismus nach 1945.* Berlin: Colloquium, 1961.

Johnson, Uwe. *Mutmassungen über Jakob.* Frankfurt/M.: Suhrkamp, 1959.

———. *Das dritte Buch über Achim.* Frankfurt/M.: Suhrkamp, 1961.

(*Die*) *Katholische Kirche in Berlin und Mitteldeutschland* (author unknown). Berlin: Morus-Verlag, 1962.

Kaufmann, Erich. *Deutschlands Rechtslage unter der Besatzung*. Stuttgart: Köhler, 1948.

Keller, John W. *Germany, The Wall and Berlin—Internal Politics During an International Crisis*. New York: Vantage, 1964.

Klafkowski, Alfons. *Podstawy prawne granicy Odra-Nysa-Luzycka w swietle unmow jałtanskiej i poczdamskiej* (Legal foundations of the Oder-Lusatian Neisse frontier in the light of the Yalta and Potsdam Agreements). Poznan: Instytut Zachodni, 1947.

————. *The Potsdam Agreement* (in English). Warsaw: Panstowe Wydawnictwo Naukowe, 1963.

Klefisch, Johannes W. *Schluss mit Deutschland?* Cologne: Verlag Wissenschaft und Politik, 1963.

Klemperer, Victor. *Die unbewältigte Sprache*. Darmstadt: Melzer, 1966.

Kluth, Hans. *Die KPD in der Bundesrepublik—Ihre politische Tätigkeit und Organisation, 1945–1956*. Cologne: Westdeutscher Verlag, 1959.

Knütter, Hans-Helmut. *Ideologien des Rechtsradikalismus im Nachkriegsdeutschland*. Bonn: Röhrscheid, 1961.

Koch, Thilo. *Wohin des Wegs Deutschland?—Ein Wiedersehen*. Munich: Kindler, 1965.

Koenen, Wilhelm. *Das ganze Deutschland soll es sein—Zur Geschichte der patriotischen Volksbewegung in Deutschland*. Berlin (East): Kongress-Verlag, 1958.

Kogon, Eugen. *Die unvollendete Erneuerung: Deutschland im Kräftefeld, 1945–1963*. Frankfurt/M.: Europ. Verlag, 1964.

Köhler, Hans. *Pseudo-Sakrale Staatsakte in Mitteldeutschland*. Witten/Ruhr: Luther-Verlag, 1962.

Kopp, Fritz. *Die Wendung zur "nationalen" Geschichtsbetrachtung in der Sowjetzone*. Munich: Olzog, 1955.

Kraus, Herbert. *Der völkerrechtliche Status der deutschen Ostgebiete innerhalb der Reichsgrenzen nach dem Stande vom 13. Dezember 1937*. Göttingen: Schwartz, 1964.

Kuby, Erich. *Das ist des Deutschen Vaterland: 70 Millionen in zwei Wartesälen*. Stuttgart: Scherz & Goverts, 1957.

Legien, R. *The Four Power Agreements on Berlin—Alternative Solutions to the Status Quo?* Berlin: Carl Heymanns, 1961.

Lemberg, Eugen (ed.). *Die Vertriebenen in Westdeutschland—Ihre Eingliederung and ihre Einfluss auf Gesellschaft, Wirtschaft, Politik und Geistesleben*. 3 vols. Kiel: Hirt, 1959.

Löwenstein, Hubertus Prinz zu, and Volkmar von Zühlsdorff. *Deutschlands Schicksal, 1945–1957*. Bonn: Athenäum, 1957.

Luza, Radomir. *The Transfer of the Sudeten Germans—A Study of Czech-German Relations, 1933–1962*. New York: New York University Press, 1964.

McClellan, Grant S. (ed.). *The Two Germanies*. New York: H. W. Wilson, 1959.

McDermott, Geoffrey. *Berlin: Success of a Mission*. New York: Harper & Row, 1963.

McInnis, Edgar, Richard Hiscocks, and Robert Spencer. *The Shaping of Postwar Germany*. New York: Praeger, 1960.

301

Macridis, Roy C. (ed.). *Foreign Policy in World Politics*. 2d ed. Englewood Cliffs, N.J.: Prentice-Hall, 1962 (with a contribution by Karl W. Deutsch and Lewis J. Edinger, "Foreign Policy of the German Federal Republic").

Majonica, Ernst. *Deutsche Aussenpolitik—Probleme und Entscheidungen*. Stuttgart: Kohlhammer, 1965.

Mander, John. *Berlin: Hostage for the West*. Baltimore: Penguin, 1962.

Marienfeld, Wolfgang. *Konferenzen über Deutschland—Die alliierte Deutschlandplanung und -politik, 1941–1948*. Hanover: Verlag Literatur u. Zeitgeschehen, 1962.

Martin, F. P. *Know Your Enemy—Background and History of the German Communist Army*. London: Ind. Inf. Centre, 1962.

Meissner, Boris. *Russland, die Weltmächte und Deutschland—Die sowjetische Deutschlandpolitik, 1943–1953*. Hamburg: Nolke, 1953.

Merkl, Peter H. *The Origin of the West German Republic*. New York: Oxford University Press, 1963.

———. *Germany: Yesterday and Tomorrow*. New York: Oxford University Press, 1965.

Milosz, Czeslaw. *Verführtes Denken*. Cologne: Kiepenheuer, 1959.

Morgenthau, Hans J. (ed.). *Germany and the Future of Europe*. Chicago: University of Chicago Press, 1951.

Moser, Hugo. *Sprachliche Folgen der politischen Teilung Deutschlands*. Düsseldorf: Schwann, 1962.

Neal, Fred Warner. *War and Peace and Germany*. New York: Norton, 1962.

Nesselrode, Franz von. *Germany's Other Half—A Journalist's Appraisal of East Germany*. London-New York: Abelard-Schuman, 1963.

Noack, Paul. *Deutschland von 1945 bis 1960—Ein Abriss der Innen- und Aussenpolitik*. 3d ed. Munich: Olzog, 1960.

Paikert, G. C. *The German Exodus—A Selective Study on the Post-World War II Expulsion of German Populations and Its Effects*. The Hague: Nijhoff, 1962.

Peck, Joachim. *Die Völkerrechtssubjektivität der Deutschen Demokratischen Republik*. (East) Berlin: Akademie Verlag, 1960.

Peckert, Joachim. *Die grossen und die kleinen Mächte: Möglichkeiten der Weltpolitik Heute*. Stuttgart: Deutsche Verlags Anstalt, 1961.

Plischke, Elmer. *Governments and Politics of Contemporary Berlin*. The Hague: Nijhoff, 1963.

Pounds, Norman J. G. *Divided Germany and Berlin*. Princeton, N.J.: Van Nostrand, 1962.

Prittie, Terence. *Germany Divided—The Legacy of the Nazi Era*. Boston: Little, Brown, 1960.

Pritzel, Konstantin. *Die wirtschaftliche Integration der sowjetischen Besatzungszone Deutschlands in den Ostblock und ihre politischen Aspekte*. Bonn: Ministry of All-German Affairs, 1962.

Rabl, Kurt (ed.). *Das Recht auf die Heimat*. 3 vols. Munich: Lerche, 1958, 1959.

Reuther, Hans. *Bundesrepublik Deutschland und Deutsches Reich*. Erlangen, 1951.

Reuther, Helmut (ed.). *Deutschlands Aussenpolitik seit 1955.* Stuttgart: Seewald, 1955.

Richardson, James L. *Germany and the Atlantic Alliance—The Interaction of Strategy and Politics.* Cambridge, Mass.: Harvard University Press, 1966.

Richert, Ernst. *Macht ohne Mandat—Der Staatsapparat in der sowjetischen Besatzungszone Deutschlands.* Cologne: Inst. Pol. Wiss., 1958.

Richter, Ernst. *Das zweite Deutschland—Ein Staat der nicht sein darf.* Gütersloh: Mohn, 1964.

Richter, Hans Werner (ed.). *Bestandaufnahme—Eine deutsche Bilanz 1962.* Munich: Kurt Desch, 1962.

Roberts, Henry L. *Russia and America—Dangers and Prospects.* New York: Harper, 1956.

Robson, Charles B. (ed.). *Berlin—Pivot of German Destiny.* Chapel Hill, N.C.: University of North Carolina Press, 1960.

Schenk, Fritz. *Im Vorzimmer der Diktatur: 12 Jahre Pankow.* Cologne: Kiepenheuer, 1962.

Scheuer, Gerhart. *Der deutsche Staat in rechtlicher Sicht.* Bonn: Ministry of All-German Affairs, 1964.

Schlamm, William S. *Germany and the East-West Crisis.* New York: McKay, 1959.

Schlesinger, Arthur M., Jr. *A Thousand Days.* Boston: Houghton Mifflin, 1965.

Schmidt, Helmut. *Defense or Retaliation—A German Contribution to the Consideration of NATO's Strategic Problem.* Edinburgh and London: Oliver & Boys, 1962.

Schmidt, Robert H. *Saarpolitik, 1945-1957.* 3 vols. Berlin: Duncker & Humblot, 1959, 1960, and 1962.

Schneider, Johannes. *KP im Untergrund—Kommunistische Untergrundarbeit in der Bundesrepublik Deutschland.* Munich: Kopernikus, 1963.

Schulz, Klaus-Peter. *Berlin zwischen Freiheit und Diktatur.* Berlin: Staneck, 1962.

Schuster, Rudolf. *Deutschlands staatliche Existenz im Widerstreit politischer und rechtlicher Gesichtspunkte, 1945-1963.* Munich: Oldenbourg, 1963.

Schütz, Wilhelm Wolfgang. *Die Stunde Deutschlands—Wie kann Deutschland wiedervereinigt werden?* Stuttgart: Deutsche-Verlags Anstalt, 1954.

———. *Das Gesetz des Handelns—Zerrissenheit und Einheit unserer Welt.* Frankfurt/M.: Scheffler, 1958.

———. *Schritte zur Wiedervereinigung.* Göttingen: Mutterschmidt, 1959.

———. *West-Ost-Politik.* Göttingen: Vandenhöck & Ruprecht, 1963.

Sethe, Paul. *Zwischen Bonn und Moskau.* Frankfurt/M.: Scheffler, 1956.

Shulman, Marshall D. *Stalin's Foreign Policy Reappraised.* Cambridge, Mass.: Harvard University Press, 1963.

Skriver, Ansgar (ed.). *Berlin und keine Illusion.* Hamburg: Rütten & Loening, 1962.

Smith, Jean Edward. *The Defense of Berlin.* Baltimore: The Johns Hopkins Press, 1963.

Solberg, Richard W. *God and Caesar in East Germany*. New York: Macmillan, 1961.

Sonnemann, Ulrich. *Das Land der unbegrenzten Zumutbarkeiten—Deutsche Reflexionen*. Hamburg: Rowohlt, 1963.

Speier, Hans, and W. Phillips Davison (eds.). *West German Leadership and Foreign Policy*. Evanston, Ill.: Row, Peterson, 1957.

Speier, Hans. *German Rearmament and Atomic War*. Evanston, Ill.: Row, Peterson, 1957.

———. *Divided Berlin: The Anatomy of Soviet Political Blackmail*. New York: Praeger, 1961.

Stahl, Walter (ed.). *Education for Democracy in West Germany—Achievements-Shortcomings-Prospects*. New York: Praeger, 1961.

Stahl, Walter. *The Politics of Postwar Germany*. New York: Praeger, 1963.

Starlinger, Wilhelm. *Die Grenzen der Sowjetmacht*. Kitzingen/M.: Holzner, 1954.

———. *Hinter Russland China*. Vols. I–III. Würzburg: Marienburg-Verlag, 1957.

Stehle, Hansjakob. *Nachbar Polen*. Frankfurt/M.: S. Fischer, 1963.

Stern, Carola. *Porträt einer bolschevistischen Partei*. Cologne: Kiepenheuer, 1957.

———. *Ulbricht—A Political Biography*. New York: Praeger, 1965.

Stiftung die Welt (ed.). *Die Jugend und die Wiedervereinigung*. Frankfurt/M.: Ullstein, 1963.

Stolper, Wolfgang F. *Germany Between East and West*. Washington, D.C.: National Planning Association, 1960.

Stolper, Wolfgang F., and Karl W. Roskamp. *The Structure of the East German Economy*. Cambridge, Mass.: Harvard University Press, 1960.

Strauss, Franz Josef. *The Grand Design—A European Solution to German Reunification*. New York: Praeger, 1966.

Studnitz, Hans-Georg von. *Bismarck in Bonn—Bemerkungen zur Aussenpolitik*. Stuttgart: Seewald, 1964.

Szaz, Zoltan Michael. *Germany's Eastern Frontiers*. Chicago: Regnery, 1960.

Tempel, Gudrun. *The Germans: Indictment of My People*. New York: Random House, 1963.

Tetens, T. H. *Germany Plots With the Kremlin*. New York: Schuman, 1953.

———. *The New Germany and the Old Nazis*. New York: Random House, 1961.

Thayer, Charles. *The Unquiet Germans*. New York: Harper, 1957.

Thilenius, Richard. *Die Teilung Deutschlands*. Hamburg: Rowohlt, 1957.

Virally, Michel. *L'administration internationale de l'Allemagne, du 8 mai 1945 au 24 avril 1947*. Paris: Pedone, 1948.

Waldman, Eric. *The Goose Step Is Verboten—The German Army Today*. New York: Glencoe, 1964.

Wallich, Henry C. *Mainsprings of the German Revival*. New Haven, Conn.: Yale University Press, 1955.

Warburg, James P. *Germany: Nation or No-Man's Land.* New York: Foreign Policy Association, 1946.

———. *Germany: Bridge or Battleground.* New York: Harcourt, Brace, 1947.

———. *Germany: Key to Peace.* Cambridge, Mass.: Harvard University Press, 1953.

Wenger, Paul Wilhelm. *Wer gewinnt Deutschland?—Kleinpreussische Selbstisolierung oder mitteleuropäische Föderation.* Stuttgart: Seewald, 1959.

Wighton, Charles. *Adenauer: Democratic Dictator—A Critical Biography.* London: Fred. Muller, 1963.

Wildenmann, Rudolf. *Macht und Konsens als Problem der Innen- und Aussenpolitik.* Frankfurt/M.: Athenäum, 1963.

Willis, F. Roy. *The French in Germany, 1945–1949.* Stanford, Calif.: Stanford University Press, 1962.

Windsor, Philip. *City on Leave—A History of Berlin, 1945–1962.* London: Chatto & Windus, 1963.

Wiskemann, Elizabeth. *Germany's Eastern Neighbours.* London: Oxford University Press, 1956.

Wolfe, James. *Indivisible Germany: Illusion or Reality.* The Hague: Nyhoff, 1963.

Wolfers, Arnold. *Germany: Protectorate or Ally.* New Haven, Conn.: Yale University Press, 1950.

Zink, Harold. *American Military Government in Germany.* New York: Macmillan, 1947.

———. *The United States in Germany, 1944–1955.* Princeton, N.J.: Van Nostrand, 1957.

Articles

Acheson, Dean. "Withdrawal From Europe? 'An Illusion,'" *New York Times Magazine,* December 15, 1963.

———. "Europe: Decision or Drift," *Foreign Affairs,* January, 1966, pp. 198–205.

Adenauer, Konrad. "The German Problem, A World Problem," *Foreign Affairs,* October, 1962, pp. 59–65.

Allardt, Helmut. "Deutschland und Polen," *Aussenpolitik,* May, 1963, pp. 295–300.

Allen, Diane Manchester. "Development of Postwar Policy in Germany," *Western Political Quarterly,* March, 1964, pp. 109–16.

Augstein, Rudolf. "Konrad Adenauer und seine Epoche," *Der Spiegel,* October 9, 1963.

———. "Wege zu einer neuen Politik," *Der Spiegel,* September 23, 1964.

Baade, Fritz. "Nur noch zwei Deutschlandkonzeptionen," *Aussenpolitik,* May, 1954, pp. 753–64.

Barker, Elisabeth. "The Berlin Crisis, 1958–1962," *International Affairs,* January, 1963, pp. 59–73.

Bowie, Robert R. "Tensions Within the Alliance," *Foreign Affairs*, October, 1963, pp. 49–69.

Braunthal, Gerard. "The Free Democratic Party in West Germany," *Western Political Quarterly*, June, 1960, pp. 332–48.

Bregman, Alexander. "Germany's Search for an Eastern Policy," *East Europe*, March, 1966, pp. 2–7.

Bromke, Adam. "Nationalism and Communism in Poland," *Foreign Affairs*, July, 1962, pp. 635–43.

———. "Political Realism in Poland," *Survey*, April, 1964, pp. 111–17.

Brzezinski, Zbigniew K. "The Danger of a German Veto," *The New Leader*, January 20, 1964.

———. "Russia and Europe," *Foreign Affairs*, April, 1964, pp. 428–44.

———. "Moscow and the M.L.F.: Hostility and Ambivalence," *Foreign Affairs*, October, 1964, pp. 126–34.

Brzezinski, Zbigniew, and William E. Griffith. "Peaceful Engagement in Eastern Europe," *Foreign Affairs*, July, 1961, pp. 642–54.

Cameron, James. "A Shadow No Larger Than a Crooked Cross," *New York Times Magazine*, September 11, 1966.

Campbell, John C. "East Europe, Germany, and the West," *The Annals*, May, 1958, pp. 153–63.

Clay, Lucius D. "Berlin," *Foreign Affairs*, October, 1962, pp. 47–58.

Croan, Melvin. "Reality and Illusion in Soviet-German Relations," *Survey*, October, 1962, pp. 12–28.

———. "The German Problem Once Again," *Survey*, April, 1965, pp. 171–76.

Cromwell, Richard S. "Rightist Extremism in Postwar West Germany," *Western Political Quarterly*, January, 1964, pp. 284–93.

Dahrendorf, Ralf. "The New Germanies—Restoration, Revolution, Reconstruction," *Encounter*, April, 1964, pp. 50–58.

Daniel, Jens. "Ein Lebewohl den Brüdern im Osten," *Der Spiegel*, January 2, 1952.

———. "Was tun?" *Der Spiegel*, October 15, 1958.

Deutsch, Harold C. "The Impact of the Franco-German Entente," *The Annals*, July, 1963, pp 82–94.

Deutsch, Karl W. "Continuity and Change: Some Data on the Social Background of German Decision Makers," *Western Political Quarterly*, March, 1961, pp. 17–36.

———. "Electoral Politics and Voting Behavior in Western Germany," *World Politics*, April, 1961, pp. 417–84.

Dönhoff, Marion. "Germany Puts Freedom Before Unity," *Foreign Affairs*, April, 1950, pp. 398–411.

Dulles, Allen W. "Alternatives for Germany," *Foreign Affairs*, April, 1947, pp. 421–32.

Erler, Fritz. "The Struggle for German Reunification," *Foreign Affairs*, April, 1956, pp. 380–93.

———. "Disengagement und die Wiedervereinigung Deutschlands," *Europa-Archiv*, September–October, 1959, pp. 291–300.

———. "The Basis of Partnership," *Foreign Affairs*, October, 1963, pp. 84–95.

————. "The Alliance and the Future of Germany," *Foreign Affairs*, April, 1965, pp. 436–46.

Eschenburg, Theodor. "A Definition of Self-Determination," *The German Tribune*, May 2, 1964.

Fontaine, André. "What Is French Policy?" *Foreign Affairs*, October, 1966, pp. 58–76.

Gaitskell, Hugh. "Disengagement: Why? How?" *Foreign Affairs*, July, 1958, pp. 539–56.

Gelber, Lionel. "A Marriage of Inconvenience," *Foreign Affairs*, January, 1963, pp. 310–22.

Gradl, Johann Baptist. "Die deutsche Frage als internationales Problem," *Aussenpolitik*, August, 1958, pp. 487–96.

Grewe, Wilhelm G. "The Unification of Germany," *The Annals*, July, 1959, pp. 8–15.

————. "Other Legal Aspects of the Berlin Crisis," *American Journal of International Law*, April, 1962, pp. 510–13.

Grosse, Karl Friedrich. "Sowjetische Deutschlandpolitik," *Aussenpolitik*, April, 1953, pp. 417–25.

Grosser, Alfred. "France and Germany: Divergent Outlooks," *Foreign Affairs*, October, 1965, pp. 26–36.

Haffner, Sebastian. "Germany, Russia, and the West," *Encounter*, October, 1961.

————. "The Berlin Crisis," *Survey*, October, 1962, pp. 37–44.

Halle, Louis J. "Our War Aims Were Wrong," *New York Times Magazine*, August 22, 1965.

Hangen, Welles. "New Perspectives Behind the Wall," *Foreign Affairs*, October, 1966, pp. 135–47.

Hassel, Kai-Uwe. "Detente Through Firmness," *Foreign Affairs*, January, 1964, pp. 184–94.

Healey, Denis. "The Case for Berlin Negotiations," *New Leader*, September 18, 1961.

————. "The Crisis in Europe," *International Affairs*, April, 1962, pp. 145–55.

Huebbenet, Georg von. "Moskau überprüft seine Deutschland-Politik," *Aussenpolitik*, April, 1963, pp. 237–41.

Jacobi, Claus. "German Paradoxes," *Foreign Affairs*, April, 1957, pp. 432–40.

Kaplan, Lawrence S. "NATO and Adenauer's Germany: Uneasy Partnership," *International Organization*, Vol. 15, No. 4 (Autumn, 1961), pp. 618–29.

Kellen, Konrad. "Adenauer at 90," *Foreign Affairs*, January, 1966, pp. 275–90.

Kelsen, Hans. "The Legal Status of Germany According to the Declaration of Berlin," *American Journal of International Law*, July, 1945, pp. 519–26.

Kennan, George F. "Polycentrism and Western Policy," *Foreign Affairs*, January, 1964, pp. 171–83.

Kissinger, Henry A. "Strains on the Alliance," *Foreign Affairs*, January, 1963, pp. 261–85.

———. "Coalition Diplomacy in a Nuclear Age," *Foreign Affairs*, July, 1964, pp. 525–45.

Kostanick, Huey Louis. "Poland: Geography for Disaster," *Current History*, April, 1959, pp. 205–10.

Kracke, Friedrich. "Die Elbe—Europa's Schicksalsstrom," *Politische Studien*, May/June, 1963, pp. 324–29.

Kröger, Herbert. "Zu einigen Fragen des staatsrechtlichen Status von Berlin," *Deutsche Aussenpolitik*, January, 1958.

Kyle, Keith. "Munich and Berlin," *New Republic*, February 5, 1962.

Lach, Donald F. "What They Would Do About Germany," *Journal of Modern History*, September, 1945, pp. 227–43.

Laqueur, Walter. "Russia and Germany," *Survey*, October, 1962, pp. 3–11.

Lewis, Flora. "The Unstable States of Germany," *Foreign Affairs*, July, 1960, pp. 588–97.

———. "Large Query About the New Germany," *New York Times Magazine*, January 7, 1962.

Loewenstein, Karl. "Unity for Germany?" *Current History*, January 1960, pp. 37–45.

Lowenthal, Richard. "Can We Make Common Cause With Russia?" *New York Times Magazine*, November 21, 1965.

———. "The Germans Feel Like Germans Again," *New York Times Magazine*, March 6, 1966.

Mann, Golo. "Germany and the West," *Encounter*, December, 1961, pp. 54–57.

———. "Bismarck in Our Times," *International Affairs*, January, 1962, pp. 3–14.

———. "Rapallo: The Vanishing Dream," *Survey*, October, 1962, pp. 74–88.

Mason, Edward S. "Has Our Policy in Germany Failed?" *Foreign Affairs*, July, 1946, pp. 579–90.

Morgenthau, Hans J. "The Problem of German Reunification," *The Annals*, July, 1960, pp. 124–31.

———. "Germany Gives Rise to Vast Uncertainties," *New York Times Magazine*, September 8, 1963.

Mosely, Philip E. "Dismemberment of Germany," *Foreign Affairs*, April, 1950, pp. 487–98.

———. "The Occupation of Germany: New Light on How the Zones Were Drawn," *Foreign Affairs*, July, 1950, pp. 580–604.

Neal, Fred Warner. "The Unsolved German Settlement," *The Annals*, January, 1964, pp. 148–56.

Organski, A. F. K. "Berlin and Two Germanies," *Current History*, April, 1959, pp. 200–205.

Prittie, Terence. "Again the Issue of the Two Germanys," *New York Times Magazine*, August 16, 1964.

Rothfels, Hans. "Sinn und Grenzen des Primats der Aussenpolitik," *Aussenpolitik*, June, 1955, p. 277.

———. "Geschichtliche Betrachtungen zum Problem der Wiedervereinigung," *Vierteljahrshefte für Zeitgeschichte*, April, 1958, pp. 327–39.

Rumpf, Helmut. "Aktuelle Rechtsfragen der Wiedervereinigung Deutschlands," *Europa-Archiv*, July, 1957, pp. 9723–32.

Schick, Jack M. "The Berlin Crisis of 1961 and United States Military Strategy," *Orbis*, Winter, 1958, pp. 816–31.

Schröder, Gerhard. "Germany Looks at Eastern Europe," *Foreign Affairs*, October, 1965, pp. 15–25.

Schumann, Maurice. "France and Germany in the New Europe," *Foreign Affairs*, October, 1962, pp. 66–77.

Sommer, Theo. "For an Atlantic Future," *Foreign Affairs*, October, 1964, pp. 112–25.

Stein, Ekkehart. "Ist die 'Deutsche Demokratische Republik' ein Staat?" *Archiv des öffentlichen Rechts*, April, 1961, pp. 363–91.

Strauss, Franz Josef. "Soviet Aims and German Unity," *Foreign Affairs*, April, 1959, pp. 366–76.

Tauber, Kurt P. "German Nationalists and the European Union," *Political Science Quarterly*, December, 1959, pp. 564–89.

——. "Nationalism and Social Restoration: Fraternities in Postwar Germany," *Political Science Quarterly*, March, 1963, pp. 66–85.

Thomas, Stefan. "Beyond the Wall," *Survey*, October, 1962, pp. 54–65.

Váli, Ferenc A. "Legal-Constitutional Doctrines on Germany's Post-World War II Status," *North Dakota Law Review*, November, 1965, pp. 20–45.

Vetter, Gottfried. "Passierscheine in Deutschland," *Europa-Archiv*, September, 1964, pp. 305–18.

Vocke, Klaus. "Politische Gefahren der Theorien über Deutschlands Rechtslage," *Europa-Archiv*, December, 1957, pp. 10199–10215.

Wewjura, B., and I. Lukashuk. "International Legal Aspects of the West Berlin Problem," *International Affairs* (Moscow), 1963, No. 4, pp. 37–42.

Willner, Ann Ruth, and Dorothy Willner. "The Rise and Role of Charismatic Leaders," *The Annals*, March, 1965, pp. 77–88.

Wiskemann, Elizabeth. "Germany's Eastern Neighbours," *Survey*, October, 1962, pp. 44–53.

Wright, Quincy. "Some Legal Aspects of the Berlin Crisis," *American Journal of International Law*, July, 1961, pp. 959–65.

Zaremba, J. "Poland's Population and Material Losses During the War," *Poland and Germany* (London), Vol. VI, No. 4 (October-December, 1962), pp. 19–25.

INDEX

311

German question. *See* German Democratic Republic; Germany; Germany, Federal Republic of
German refugees: from Poland, 229; from Czechoslovakia, 239
German Right party, 97
German unity. *See* German Democratic Republic; German nationalism; Germany; Germany, Federal Republic of
Germany: dismembered status in earlier history, 3–5, 261–63; Holy Roman Empire, 4; German Confederation, 5; belated nation, 6–8; geographical location, 8–9; planning her dismemberment, 9–11; zonal division of, 12; postwar situation of, 16–17; currency reform, 19–20; formation of governments in West and East, 21–24; the Weimar Republic, 103; primacy of foreign politics, 104, 277; neutralization of, 110–11, 225, 252, 277, 281; religious split, 121–22; linguistic division, 178; foreign intervention, 216; Polish-German antagonism, 228–30; cultural division, 262–63; war-guilt, 267–69; problem of the mid-twentieth century, 261–90; unification and balance of power, 281–82. *For period after 1947 see also* German Democratic Republic; Germany, Federal Republic of
Germany, Federal Republic of: creation of, 21–24; joins the West, 24–30, 35–38, 216–17, 244–45; elections of 1953, 33; contacts with U.S.S.R., 38–40, 43; elections of 1961, 47, 198–99; name of state, 52, 114; territorial status, 52–56; reunification policy under Adenauer, 56–60; elections of 1965, 59–60; under Erhard, 60–64, 103; alternatives of cabinet formation, 92–94; Grand Coalition, 93–97; diplomatic relations with Rumania, 94, 157, 242; China and, 137–38, 227, 249–50, 259; refuses recognition to D.D.R., 142–48; relations with Yugoslavia, 149–50, 243; relations with non-aligned states, 151–52; member of international organizations, 152–54; relations with East Europe, 155–57, 171; represents Berlin, 188–89, 208–9; quest for unity, 217–18,

220–22, 285; relations with U.S.S.R., 219–26, 279, 286; opening of the East, 224, 240–42, 258; relations with Poland, 228–38; relations with U.S., 248–49; relations with Britain, 253; relations with France, 253–59; against further sacrifices and discrimination, 269, 277–79. *See also* Basic Law; German nationalism
German youth: attitude toward reunification, 134
Gerstenmaier, Ernst, 66, 268n
Gneisenau, Field Marshal, 176
Goethe, Johann Wolfgang von, 262
Gomulka, Wladyslaw, 234, 237
Görlitz, 127n
Gradl, Johann Baptist, 66–67, 115, 236n
Grand Coalition. *See* Germany, Federal Republic of
Greece, 266
Grewe, Wilhelm G., 34, 60, 248n
Gromyko, A. A., 90
Grotewohl, Otto, 23–24, 41
Guinea, 151–52
Guttenberg, Karl-Theodor Freiherr zu: 65, 82; quoted, 266n, 277n

Hallstein, Walter, 60, 148n
Hallstein Doctrine: theoretical basis of, 32–33, 55n; partial abandonment of, 94–96, 234–35, 240–42; Soviet exception, 149; application to East Europe, 154–57, 171; China and, 250
Hamburg: 135
Hapsburg Empire. *See* Austria
Harich, Wolfgang, 161–62
Hassel, Kai-Uwe von, 58, 95
Havemann, Robert, 163
Healey, Denis, 252, 281n
Heimann, Eduard, 117–18
Heimatlose Linke (Unpatriotic left), 118
Heinemann, Gustav, 28, 95, 100, 117
Helgoland, 287n
Helmstedt, 202
Herder, Johann von, 6
Hermes, Andreas, 27n
Herrnstadt, Rudolf, 161
Herter, Christian, 46, 193
Herter Plan, 46, 223
Hess, Rudolf, 189n

The Quest for a United Germany
by Ferenc A. Váli

designer: Gerard A. Valerio
typesetter: Kingsport Press, Inc.
typefaces: Janson
printer: Kingsport Press, Inc.
paper: Mohawk Tosca
binder: Kingsport Press. Inc.
cover material: Columbia Lynnbrook